The Native Population of the Americas in 1492

The New World-European encounter: Montezuma welcoming the army of Cortés outside Tenochtitlán, Mexico. Theodor de Bry engraving (Las Casas, 1598).

The Native Population

of the Americas

in 1492 EDITED BY William M. Denevan

Second Edition

With a Foreword by
W. George Lovell

The University of Wisconsin Press

The University of Wisconsin Press
114 North Murray Street
Madison, Wisconsin 53715

3 Henrietta Street
London WC2E 8LU, England

First edition printings 1976, 1978
Second edition
5 4 3 2 1

Printed in the United States of America

The Native population of the Americas in 1492
   edited by William M. Denevan.—2nd ed.
   398 pp.   cm.
     Includes bibliographical references and index.
     ISBN 0-299-13430-X (cloth)   ISBN 0-299-13434-2 (paper)
       1. Indians—Population. 2. America—Population.
   I. Denevan, William M.
   E59.P75N37   1992
   304.6′097309′024—dc20   91-40042

To Carl O. Sauer, 1889–1975

Contents

List of Tables

List of Maps

r

List of Figures

Foreword

I remember distinctly the circumstances under which I was first shown, and influenced by, a copy of this book.

It was the summer of 1977. Life as a graduate student was fast losing all semblance of appeal, for I was barely half-way through my initial exposure to colonial Spanish documents housed in the Archivo General de Centroamérica in Guatemala City. For months I'd been toiling, page after page, through a labyrinth of imperial paperwork, among other things keeping my eyes peeled for sources that would enable me to reconstruct, however crudely, demographic trends in one region of Guatemala, the Sierra de los Cuchumatanes, during colonial times. Systematic searching had unearthed some interesting fragments, but fatigue had set in, and I was in low spirits. The terrifying thought intruded yet again: will this dissertation *ever* get written? One particularly slow day, someone showed up at the archive who, in conversation over lunch, mentioned having brought with him to Guatemala a recently published volume he thought I might find useful. He kindly offered it on loan, sensing far more than I could at the time my need to step back from detail and contemplate a broader panorama. So it was that *The Native Population of the Americas in 1492* came my way, accompanied by a welcome desire to read late into the night. For the next twenty-four hours possession of the book provided a temporary but crucial respite from worm-riddled censuses and illegible tribute lists. It allowed me to escape the solitary tunnel of doctoral research long enough to appreciate that the minute exercise I was involved in was in fact part of a great scholarly debate, that whatever bits and pieces I uncovered could afterwards be assembled and interpreted in the light of this book's arguments and viewpoints. There was no heavenly glare, but a spark of illumination sent me back to the archive less weary of heart, more optimistic that perhaps something useful might come of my labors after all.

My reaction, I feel confident in asserting, must have been repeated scores if not hundreds of times over the past fifteen years by a new generation of scholars, as well as previous ones, reexamining the strengths and weaknesses of the evidence at hand. Whether one asks the question "How many Indians were there?" in relation to Canada or to Chile, to Mexico or to Hispaniola, this book offers if not definitive answers then at least intriguing ideas about the size of New World populations at the time of European contact. To the original essays by William M. Denevan and his seven contributors, the former has added a new introduction in which recent research is discussed and, based on its findings, a new hemispheric estimate advanced. The reader will find heated debate and sharp differences of opinion throughout, and would do well to remember, at all times, that controversy is fueled not by the numbers themselves but by the divergent views of history and what happened in history that the numbers represent. Carl O. Sauer (1963: 146–47), the great mind to whom this book is dedicated, captured the essence of this divergence, and cut to the quick of the 1992 quincentennial fanfare, when he wrote:

> We know of scarcely any record of destructive exploitation in all the span of human existence until we enter the period of modern history, when transatlantic expansion of European commerce, peoples, and governments takes place. Then begins what may well be the tragic rather than the great age of man. We have glorified this period in terms of a romantic view of colonization and of the frontier. There is a dark obverse to the picture, which we have regarded scarcely at all.

If the editor of this landmark work is correct in his range of calculations, then approximately the same number of Native Americans inhabited the New World five hundred years ago as do today. The symmetry has all the enigma of a Borges fiction. Between then and now, however, Sauer's words call for us to think about those native peoples who have disappeared forever, those who suffer the burden of conquest still, and those who strive to convince us of the worth of their cultures, even in the face of our most arrogant displays of superiority.

South Woodstock, Vermont   W. George Lovell
October 1991

Native American Populations in 1492: Recent Research and a Revised Hemispheric Estimate

This year, 1992, is witnessing an international reexamination of the significance of the "discovery" of the New World in 1492. The size of the native population at the time of Columbus has a bearing on many of the themes of exploration, conquest, settlement, labor, food production, environmental modification, and demographic decline that are central to colonial history. The question of Native American numbers remains highly controversial, one of the great debates in history. Were there few or many? Did Europeans discover, occupy, and fill in relatively empty lands, or did they invade and destroy a world as Las Casas said, "full of people like a hive of bees"?

In 1976, in the first edition of *The Native Population of the Americas in 1492,* I presented some original essays on the topic by authorities, provided regional reviews of methodologies and estimates, and gave my own regional estimates and a hemispheric total of 57.3 million (p. 291 here).

Since publication, most of the individual chapters have been cited frequently, some favorably, some less so. There were at least 20 reviews, including several by historical demographers.[1] These reviews and subsequent

1. Reviews include Robert Blakely (*American Antiquity,* 1979); Noble David Cook (*Hispanic American Historical Review,* 1977); Alfred Crosby (*William and Mary Quarterly,* 1978); Henry Dobyns (*Annals of the Association of American Geographers,* 1978); Don Fowler (*Western Historical Quarterly,* 1978); Charles Hudson (*Journal of Southern History,* 1978); Wilbur Jacobs (*American Indian Quarterly,* 1979); John Lombardi (*American Historical Review,* 1977); Nancy Lurie (*Wisconsin Academy Review,* 1977); Magnus Mörner (*Latin American Indian Literatures,* 1979); Gene Paull (*Professional Geographer,* 1978); Nicolás Sánchez-Albornoz (*The Americas,* 1977); Robert Quirk (*American Hispanist,* 1977); Clifford Smith (*Journal of Historical Geography,* 1979); Michael Swann (*Human Ecology,* 1978); Norman Stewart (*Historical Geography Newsletter,* 1984); Robert West (*Geographical Review,* 1978); and Wilbur Zelinsky (*Progress in Human Geography,* 1978).

research are indicative of the continuing importance of the topic and the stimulus of the 1976 volume. The original regional introductions and the eight individual essays are reproduced intact in this second edition.

What has happened to the authors of these essays since 1976? Woodrow Borah, the dean of Indian demographic studies, has retired from Berkeley but remains actively involved (Borah, 1991a, 1991b; Cook and Borah, 1971–79).[2] Ángel Rosenblat, after a lifetime of researching the topic of Indian numbers and defending his low estimates, died recently in Caracas. In a letter in 1977 he expressed appreciation for the opportunity to present his case in English. David Radell and Jane Pyle have left academia, somewhat unaware of the impact of their contributions to the great debate. Douglas Ubelaker remains at the Smithsonian Institution, still very much involved with estimates of North American populations (Ubelaker, 1981, 1988, in press). William Sanders, Pennsylvania State University, is firmly established as one of the principal archaeologists of Mesoamerica; his demographic interests continue (Sanders and Murdy, 1982). Daniel Shea at Beloit College has been working on the archaeology of terracing in the Colca Valley of Peru (Shea, in press). And I have persisted with cultural-ecological research in the Peruvian Andes and Amazon (Denevan, 1987; Denevan and Padoch, 1988). We thank the University of Wisconsin Press for this opportunity to have our research and thinking from the 1970s reheard and reexamined.

Following is a brief review of the considerable amount of research and commentary published since 1976 on Native American populations at contact and on their subsequent decline. The matter of the rate and degree of decline, especially from disease, is significant for estimating original numbers, and this has received substantial attention. General discussions of epidemics include Cook and Lovell, 1991; Crosby, 1976, 1991; Guerra, 1986; Henige, 1986b, 1986c; Joralemon, 1982; Lovell, in press; and Verano and Ubelaker, in press. Crosby (in press) examines the well-documented Hawaiian depopulation from epidemics (from possibly 800,000 to only 48,000 in 100 years) as a model for a rapid Native American decline. He also notes the importance of considering a reduced birth rate as well as a high death rate.

NORTH AMERICA

Subsequent to the pioneer studies in the 1920s and 1930s by Sauer (Denevan, in press, a), Mooney, and Kroeber, there were few immediate attempts to provide regional and tribal estimates of Indian populations in North America. The one major exception was the research on California Indians by S. F. Cook, much of which was republished in a single volume after his death (S. F. Cook, 1976b).

2. References in this essay appear either in the Supplementary Bibliography which follows it or in the original Bibliography.

Since 1976 there has been a resurgence of interest in Indian numbers, with controversy particularly over the role of disease in the proto-historic period. There have been more recent publications on Indian demography for North America than for any other region of the New World. Besides numerous articles, reviews, and commentaries, several books have been published: Dobyns (1983), Ramenofsky (1987), Reff (1991), and Thornton (1987). Most of the articles forthcoming in Verano and Ubelaker (in press) are on North America. The stimulus for this activity likely includes Ubelaker's review of Mooney's figures in this volume and his separate estimate in 1976; the tribal estimates prepared for the *Handbook of North American Indians* (Sturtevant, 1978––; see Ubelaker, 1988); and a provocative argument by Dobyns (1983: 42, 300) that there were 722,000 Timucuan Indians in Florida in 1517 and 18 million in North America, based on evidence for early pandemic diseases.[3] A heated debate has thus ensued, mainly between Dobyns and several archaeologists and historians, as to whether epidemics spreading widely and rapidly decimated Indian tribes prior to initial counts and estimates of numbers. Maintaining that there is little or no evidence for such declines are Henige (1986a, 1986b, 1989). Snow and Lanphear (1988, 1989), and Snow and Starna (1989). Dobyns (1988, 1989a, 1989b) subsequently defended his position. Milner (1980) agrees that there were epidemics in the Southeast prior to 1700, with significant demographic and social impacts, but maintains that those diseases did not necessarily spread throughout North America. Smith (1987) presents archaeological evidence of massive depopulation in the Southeast in the sixteenth century. Ramenofsky (1987: 173–76), who calls for a greater contribution by archaeologists to the debate, agrees with Dobyns that population decline "tended to precede written documentation and was catastrophic in nature." Disease was definitely a sixteenth-century factor in the Southeast, but she believes that a broader impact elsewhere is "probable," and that there was a differential rate of survival regionally. Upham (1986, 1987) and Reff (1987, 1989) discuss the dating of the introduction of smallpox in the Southwest. In a superb treatment of the documents, Reff finds evidence of numerous early epidemics in the Southwest "prior to sustained contact with Europeans"; he believes that "native populations throughout the Greater Southwest were reduced by upwards of 90 percent prior to 1678" (Reff, 1991: 276–77). The controversy was discussed at the 1989 Smithsonian Institution Conference on "Disease and Demography in the Americas" (Verano and Ubelaker, in press; see also Roberts, 1989).

One of the main means of estimating Indian populations at contact for North America, as well as elsewhere, is working backwards on the basis of mortality rates from epidemic disease. Thornton et al. (1991) point out that this assumes no population recovery between epidemics *or* additional decline from

3. A listing of reviews of Dobyns' controversial 1983 book is provided by Henige (1986b: 307).

other factors between epidemics. "Most populations have a surprising ability to recover from severe high mortality" episodes (Thornton et al., 1991: 29). Thus earlier population size may be greatly overestimated. On the other hand, additional mortality factors and indirect effects of epidemics such as decreased fertility and food shortages could minimize recovery. Kay (1984) presents evidence for the Sauk, Fox, Menominee, and Winnebago in Wisconsin that population growth between 1700 and 1840 increased rather than decreased. Other tribes for which population apparently increased in the nineteenth century, at least temporarily, were the Navajo and Gila River Pima (Meister, 1976), and the northern plains tribes in Canada (Decker, 1991: 387).

Recent regional and tribal estimates of contact populations include, for New England, 72,000 (S. F. Cook, 1976b: 84), 105,200 (Snow, 1980: 35), and 126,000 to 144,000 (Salisbury, 1982: 26–27); for the Mohawk, 13,700 to 17,000 (Snow, 1980: 41); for the Virginia Algonquin, 14,300 to 22,300 (Feest, 1973: 74); for the Arikara, 30,000 and for the Pawnee, 100,000 (Holder, 1970: 30); and for the Iroquois, 20,000 (Trigger, 1976: 98; see also Engelbrecht, 1987). Clermont (1980), however, estimated a total Iroquoian population of 110,000. Trigger (1985: 234) recalculated the pre-epidemic Huron population to have been 23,500, but Dickinson (1980) gives 25,000 to 30,000 in 1600. For the Canadian Maritime provinces, Miller (1976, 1982) estimates the late prehistoric Micmac population at 50,000, but Snow (1980: 36) has only 12,000. Trigger (1985: 229–51) provides an overview of estimates for southeastern Canada and New England and the evidence for early epidemics. Riley (1987) provides a good review of the various estimates for tribes in the Southwest. Reff (1991: 229), on the basis of reported baptisms, estimates over 100,000 Pueblo Indians in 1598. Other new tribal estimates are appearing in the volumes of the *Handbook of North American Indians* (Sturtevant, 1978––). Ubelaker (1988: 291) provides regional estimates mainly based on these.

In 1976, Ubelaker, using available *Handbook* data, estimated a total Indian population for North America at contact of 2,171,125. In 1988, with more tribal information available, he revised this downward to 1,894,350 for the year 1500. The tribal estimates, however, are still primarily for the times of initial contact and often later and assume little or no prior decline from larger populations. This is a very conservative position, even granting that epidemics were localized in the sixteenth century. A doubling of Ubelaker's total to 3.79 million is a reasonable minimum estimate for 1500 A.D.; this is what I did to obtain my 1976 estimate of 4.40 million (p. 291 here). This doubling is modest, and is supported by Reff's (1991: 276) 90 percent decline prior to 1678. One other recent estimate for all of North America is 7 million plus by Thornton (1987: 32). Earlier he gave 1,845,183 for just the United States in 1492, assuming simple linear decline (Thornton and Thornton, 1981: 51).

Finally, Ubelaker (1981) provides a useful discussion of methodologies for estimating prehistoric demography, and Dobyns (1976) reviews some of the studies of North American Indian populations. Johansson (1982) provides a bibliographic essay and raises important issues such as the distinction between physical and cultural extinction.

MEXICO

Central Mexico was the focus of Indian demographic research from 1948 through the mid-1970s by Berkeley scholars Lesley Simpson, Sherburne Cook, and Woodrow Borah, as well as by William Sanders and others. Their estimates, ranging from 11 to 25 million, were instrumental in shifting New World population estimates from low to high figures. Subsequently, there has been little new research, but there have been several critiques and revisions of the Berkeley calculations.

Rudolph Zambardino (1980, 1981), a British mathematician, has done a systematic examination of the methodology and estimates of Borah and Cook. He finds their 2.65 million for 1568 reasonable, but reduces their figures for 1548 from 6.3 million to 3.6 million, and adjusts their figure for 1532 from 16.87 million to a meaningless 2.7 to 35 million, and for 1518 (based on Aztec tribute data) from 25.2 million to an also meaningless range of 2.2 to 28 million. Based on extrapolation from his own figures, Zambardino arrived at an estimate for 1518 of 6 million, or a range of from 5 to 10 million, which "matches the evidence gathered and presented by Borah and Cook far more accurately than their estimate of 25 million" (Zambardino, 1980: 22). He later suggests that 8 to 10 million is credible for Central Mexico (Zambardino, 1981: 240).

Whitmore (1991: 477), using computer simulation models, obtains a 1519 population for the Basin of Mexico of 1,590,000. This compares to 2,960,000 derived from Borah and Cook (Whitmore, 1991: 466), and 1,155,000 (averaged) by Sanders (p. 130 here). If Whitmore's total for the Basin is projected to Central Mexico, using Borah and Cook's ratio of their Basin (2.96 million; Whitmore, 1991: 466) to Central Mexico (25.2 million) figures, his total would be 13,536,000. For all of Mexico, "using a scaling procedure," Whitmore gives a figure of 16 million. For the Basin, he uses a nadir of 180,000 for 1607, a decline of about 90 percent from 1519 (Whitmore, 1991: 477, 483).

Another recalculation of the Indian population of Central Mexico based on the Borah and Cook data is by Slicher van Bath (1978). By adjusting the factor for converting tributary counts to total populations, he reduces the Borah and Cook total of 25.2 million for 1518 by 15 percent to obtain 21.42 million, a number still too high for some interested scholars.

Henige also criticizes Borah and Cook for their methodology for deriving a 1519 population from Aztec tribute data: "I find the methods adopted by Borah and Cook for Central Mexico even less acceptable than their results" (Henige, 1978b: 711). Another critique is that of Jacques Houdaille (1986), who refers to the "résultats sensationnels de l'école de Berkeley."

On the other hand, Dobyns continues to find Borah and Cook conservative. He recently increased his original (1966) estimate for Central Mexico from 30.0–37.5 million to 58,178,666 for 1516 and 51,600,000 for 1492, no method given (Dobyns, 1988: 9).

Elsewhere, Gerhard (1979: 160, 169) using archival documents and other sources, obtains contact populations for several regions of southern Mexico: for Soconusco, 80,000; for Chiapas, 275,000. Wasserstrom (1983: 11) gives 200,000 for Chiapas, and Gasco (1987) has 67,500 to 90,000 for Soconusco. Watson (1990: 243, 377) estimates 350,000 for Chiapas, but his evidence is not presented. Pollard and Gorenstein (1980: 276–77) calculate 60,000 to 100,000 in the Lake Patzcuaro Basin in Michoacán, compared to a projected 210,000 for Borah and Cook. Doolittle (1988: 55) has 15,000 for the Valley of Sonora. For Baja California Robert Jackson (1981) estimates 60,000 Indians in 1697, and then examines the evidence for rapid decline of mission Indians in Baja California. Finally, Reff's (1991) tribal totals for Northwest Mexico in 1500 come to over one million (Sinaloa, Durango, Chihuahua, Sonora, and Baja California), and Gerhard (1982:24) estimates 1,218,000 for Northwest Mexico and 340,000 for Northeast Mexico.

CENTRAL AMERICA

Since 1976 there has been more original research on the historical demography of Central America than on Mexico. Two historical geographers have been particularly active—George Lovell on Guatemala and Linda Newson on Honduras and Nicaragua. A collection of relevant papers for Guatemala is provided by Carmack, Early, and Lutz (1982).

Lovell examined the Cuchumatán Highlands of northwest Guatemala, and based on size of Indian armies and partial tribute counts he suggests a total of 260,000 in 1520 (Lovell, 1981a, 1981b, 1982, 1992). For other regions of Guatemala, Veblen (1977: 497), in a study derived from his 1974 dissertation, obtains 60,000 to 150,000 Indians for Totonicapán in 1520. Zamora (1983: 318) gives 210,000 for western Guatemala for 1524 and 315,000 for 1520. Fowler (1989: 151) gives 100,000 for the Pipil area. Madigan (1976: 176–206) and Orellana (1984: 142) give 48,000 for Atitlán.

For Guatemala south of the Petén lowlands Lovell and colleagues examined data and estimates for the various regions and estimated a total of 2 million, comparable to Denevan's (p. 291 here) 2 million for all of Guatemala, including the nearly empty north (Lovell and Swezey, 1982: 75; Lovell, Lutz, and Swezey, 1984; Lutz and Lovell, in press, a; Lovell and Lutz, in press). Lovell (1991) also examines disease and depopulation in Guatemala.

Other estimates for Guatemala include 500,000 to 800,000 by Sanders and Murdy (1982: 32) for the highlands only. This is for 1524 and does not take into account the earlier devastating epidemics (possibly smallpox) of 1519–1521

(Lovell, in press). Solano (1974: 70) gives 300,000, but the area included is unclear and his analysis is unreliable (Lutz and Lovell, in press, b).

For Honduras, Newson (1981, 1986: 90–91) obtains 800,000 Indians at contact; for Nicaragua she obtains 825,000 (Newson, 1982, 1987: 88); and Fowler (1988: 114) obtains 700,000 to 800,000 for El Salvador, all totals which are fairly close to Denevan's (p. 291 here) 750,000, 1,000,000 and 500,000 respectively. Radell (p. 74 here) estimated that 448,000 Nicaraguan Indians were shipped as slaves to Panama and Peru between 1527 and 1548. Newson (1987: 105) gives a range from 200,000 to 500,000, the high figure being for slaves shipped from all Central America. Sherman (1979: 82) estimated that only 50,000 Indian slaves were shipped from all of Central America, but MacLeod (1973: 52) earlier estimated at least 200,000. Fowler (1989: 151) has 100,000 to 140,000 for the Nicarao in western Nicaragua in 1519.

There has been several reexaminations of the population of all of Central America (minus Panama), for which Rosenblat obtained a total of only 800,000 (p. 3 here). There are general discussions by MacLeod (1985), Newson (1985), and Lutz and Lovell (in press, a). The latter obtain 5,105,000 including Chiapas and Soconusco (now in Mexico), which compares with Denevan's (p. 291 here) total which would be 5,450,000 for the same area. Sherman (1979: 5) suggests only 2,250,000. Lutz and Lovell (in press, b) provide a useful annotated bibliography of publications on the historical demography of Central America.

HISPANIOLA

The Caribbean Island of Hispaniola continues to be a focus of heated demographic controversy, in part because it involves Columbus himself and in part because of the great extremes in the estimates by modern scholars: 100,000–120,000 for 1492 by Rosenblat (p. 59 here) in contrast to 8 million by Borah and Cook (1971–79: 1:407). All are examining the same evidence: an apparent census or partial census of the island in 1496 by Bartholomew Columbus, reports by Las Casas and others of populations of up to 4 million in the period 1492–1496, and later counts taken between 1508 and 1517.

Henige examines the early reports and concludes "that it is futile to offer any numerical estimates at all on the basis of the evidence now before us" (Henige, 1978a: 237). Zambardino (1978: 707), on the other hand, concluded that a 1492 "population figure of around one million can well be justified." Henige (1978b) responded by attacking Borah and Cook's methodology for estimating contact populations for Central Mexico.

The issue in part revolves around whether or not there were any epidemics on Hispaniola sufficient to have reduced a population of a million or more in 1492 to about 15,000 by 1518. Henige presents convincing evidence that smallpox was not present on Hispaniola, or anywhere else in the New World, until 1518. He is apparently wrong, however, in asserting "that there had been no serious or epidemic incidence of infectious disease in Hispaniola before late 1518" (Henige, 1986c: 19). The one new contribution to the discussion is by the Spanish medical historian Francisco Guerra (1985, 1988). He finds good evidence for a major epidemic of swine flu[4] on Hispaniola in 1493, which devastated the Spaniards and Indians both there and on other islands. The Indians "perished almost completely," from a 1492 total accepted by Guerra (1988: 319-23) of 1.1 million.

There are other estimates. The Dominican Republic historian Frank Moya Pons (1977: 15), based on projections from censuses in 1514 and 1508, obtains 377,559 (4.8 per square kilometer) for 1494. Presumably the total was higher in 1493 or 1492 before the swine flu epidemic. Watts (1987: 71-75) in his historical geography of the West Indies, reviews Rosenblat, Borah and Cook, Sauer, Zambardino, and Henige and "broadly" accepts the estimate of Las Casas of 3 to 4 million, and double that for the total on the other islands ("the generally accepted hypothesis").

ANDES

The Indian population of Peru from 1520 to 1620 is examined by N. D. Cook (1981, 1982b) who presents several methods or models for estimating the 1520 numbers. The four best projections range from 5.5 to 9.4 million. However, he believes that the upper part of the range is more likely, and he proposes a total estimate of 9 million (Cook, 1981: 113-14). Without eastern (Amazonian) Peru, the total would be 8,520,000. Nine million, or a range of 4-14 million, mainly based on Cook, is accepted in the demographic history of Peru by Varillas and Mostajo (1990: 6, 35-36). Recently, Cook suggested a total of 14 million for the Central Andes (Inca Empire), primarily highland and coastal Peru, Ecuador, and Bolivia (N. D. Cook, pers. comm.; also Roberts, 1989). To be consistent, however, if a ratio is used based on the proportions in Shea (p. 174 here), Cook's Central Andes total, using 8,520,000 for Peru, would come to 12,852,000.

The best review of Cook's estimates is by Zambardino (1984). He finds most of the models of limited use, but apparently believes the census projection method, using the decline rate from 1570 to 1600, is the best (as does Denevan, 1983). This utilizes 1570 and 1600 data to project a total of 3.3 million for 1520. Cook (1981: 95) considers this to be an absolute minimum, which does not take into account a higher rate of population decline from 1520

---

4. The influenza "epidemics with excessive mortality . . . are due to animal viruses, particularly that of the swine, which incidentally infect human beings and against which persons have less resistance than they have against human influenza viruses . . . the influenza pandemic . . . that in 1918 killed over 10,000,000 was due to the virus of swine influenza" (Guerra, 1988: 319-20).

to 1570 than from 1570 to 1600. If extrapolated by ratio to all of the Central Andes the total is 5.13 million. Zambardino is critical of Cook for using "impressionistic" estimates not based on census data in his final averaging. On the other hand, Cook is the most knowledgeable scholar regarding the Peruvian data and context, and weight must be given to his judgment of the appropriate evaluation.

Another recent estimate, using depopulation ratios, is about 10 million for the Inca Empire in 1530 by Nathan Wachtel (1977: 90). This would be increased by 1,200,000 if projected back to 1520, using ratios based on Shea (p. 174 here).

One of the lowest estimates of the population of Peru and the Central Andes is that by Shea, whose study examines disease behavior and decline rates to derive a total of 1.34 to 1.94 million for Peru and 2.03 to 2.93 million for the Central Andes (p. 174 here). Cook (1977, 1981: 95) finds Shea's uses of documentary sources incorrect and hence argues his estimates "must be rejected." Cook (1981: 41–54) also criticizes the methods and estimates of Rowe, Dobyns, Smith, and Wachtel.

Thus, other than Dobyns, who had an unreasonable estimate of 30 to 37.5 million (p. 3 here), recent estimates for the Central Andes in 1520 range from Shea's 2.03 million to Cook's 14 million. By 1620 only about 670,000 Indians remained in Peru (Cook, 1981: 246).

Cook (1982a) has done a study of a regional population in Peru, that of the Colca Valley, for which there are *visitas* (censuses) for 1572, 1591, 1604, and 1616. Projecting backwards he obtains a 1530 total of 62,500 to 71,000, compared to only 32,826 in 1972 (Cook, 1982a: 83–85). The Colca is a densely terraced valley, with about 61 percent of the terraces now abandoned (Denevan, 1987: 31). A study of the carrying capacity of the terraces of the Colca Valley village of Coporaque by Treacy (1989: 230, 242–43) gives a potential population of either 5,889 or 6,452, compared to his estimated 1520 population of 5,957 and a 1985 population of only about 1,200.

Elsewhere in the Andes, the Villamarins have estimated a 1537 contact population of 120,000 to 160,000 for the Chibcha in the Sabana de Bogotá in Colombia. For Venezuela they give a contact population of 200,000 to 350,000, which seems much too low (Villamarin and Villamarin, 1975: 83, 113). Newson (1991) and Brown (1984) documented the frequency of early colonial epidemics in Ecuador, as has N. D. Cook (in press, a, b) for the Andes in general.

AMAZONIA

In 1976 (pp. 230, 234 here) I estimated the 1492 population of Greater Amazonia to have been 6.8 million, but then reduced it by 25 percent to 5.1 million to allow for buffer zones between tribes or villages. This was probably too large an adjustment (see Dobyns, 1978); 10 to 20 percent would have been more reasonable. In any event, I was criticized for being both conservative (Myers, 1988: 63, 69) and excessive (Mörner, 1979: 28), while others found my densities the most acceptable to date (Frank, 1987: 113). Certainly, these figures are problematic, but there is not much evidence to draw on.

My estimates are based on "reasonable" habitat densities. For the *várzea* (floodplains) I obtained 14.6 per square kilometer, averaging 28.0 for the large floodplains and 1.2 for the high selva (upland forest). The large floodplain density was based on counts of Omagua Indians in 1647–1649 by Laureano de la Cruz (1942: 43–46). Based on Sweet's (1969: 41–43) interpretation, the density was 8.0 per square kilomeer, which I multiplied by 3.5 to get 28.0 per square kilometer for 1540. However, a more thorough examination by Porro (1981) of the counts by Laureano de la Cruz gives a density of 5.2, or 91,000 total, for 1647, and with my multiplier of 3.5 the density for 1540 is 18.2. Applying this to the Amazon River várzea in Brazil and using half this density (9.1) for the main tributaries in Brazil and in Peru and Bolivia results in a reduction of 84,500 in my floodplain totals.

On the other hand, Myers (n.d.), based on an examination of Laureano de la Cruz by Grohs (1974), obtains only 5,500 Omagua for 1646. Myers, however, assumes disease impact prior to Orellana's 1540 voyage down the Amazon, and then assumes a 75 percent mortality rate during each epidemic and a 1 percent recovery rate per year between epidemics. This gives a total of 1,974,950 Omagua in 1524. He further suggests 10 million for the entire Upper Amazon, including 5 to 10 million for Mainas and nearly 1.28 million for the Cocama on the Río Ucayali (Myers, 1988: 68–70, 76–77). These figures seem unreasonable a they imply several tens of millions overall in Amazonia.

Meggers et al. (1988: 291), on the basis of archaeological analysis of numerous prehistoric Amazon settlements, believe that most sites with large surface areas represent "multiple reoccupations rather than large single villages." Given an apparent similar settlement size and mobility for prehistoric and present day *tierra firme* (interflueve, upland) tribes, which is questionable, Meggers (in press) concludes that the population density of the former is similar to the latter, ca. 0.3 per square kilometer. She assumes that the várzea density was the same, but provides no evidence other than to argue that while local densities were higher, these were offset by large uninhabited areas. Historical accounts of high floodplain densities are discounted as exaggerations. For Amazonia she projects the 0.3 density to a pre-Columbian population of 1.5 to 2.0 million (Meggers, in press). The same density would give a total of 2.9 million for Greater Amazonia (6.8 million square kilometers). For the várzea I believe that 0.3 per square kilometer is unreasonably low. Large empty lands have not been proven. Densities were locally much higher in the seventeenth century. Anna Roosevelt (1991 and pers. comm.) reports archaeological evidence for very large numbers on Marajó Island and for the Tapajos Indians in the fifteenth and sixteenth centuries. On the other hand, for the tierra firme forests, Meggers' 0.3 density exceeds my own 0.2. I think the latter, or even less, is justified given that prehistoric Indians were dependent on the very inefficient stone axe for clearing forest and hence probably practiced limited shifting cultivation (Denevan, in press, b).

Hemming (1978: 492–93) did a tribe-by-tribe count for all of Brazil, but mainly Amazonia, based on the earliest data, often not until the nineteenth century or early twentieth century, arriving at a total of 2.43 million.

Dean (1985) examined evidence for the Tupinamba on the central Brazilian coast. He obtained a density of 9.0 per square kilometer, compared to my 9.5 (p. 219 here). For just the coast of the State of Rio de Janeiro his total for 1501 is 103,000 (Dean, 1985: 42). For the full central Coast (105,000 square kilometers), his total would be 52,500 less than my 997,500 (p. 230 here).

My density of 1.3 to 2.0 for the lowland savannas of Amazonia is based on research on Mojos in northeastern Bolivia which indicates about 100,000 in the 1690s based on Jesuit reports, with a modest 3.5 multiplier giving a contact population of 350,000 in 1580 (pp. 211–13 here) prior to reported epidemics. Leandro Tormo Sanz (1972) also looked at the Jesuit estimates and suggested only 7,200 Mojos Indians in 1679. However, the area covered is only the main trunk of the Río Mamoré and does not include the large additional terrain in Mojos, which contained numerous other tribes.

For the Orinoco Llanos of Colombia and Venezuela, Morey (1979) believes that my estimate of 513,000 for 1492 is too low (p. 230 here). He examines population decline but does not give a regional estimate.

Elsewhere in lowland South America, a critical region is that of the Tupi-Guarani Indians of central and southern Brazil and Paraguay. A study by Clastres (1973: 32) for the region between the Río Paraguay and the Atlantic coast and 22° to 28° S. latitude (ca. 500,000 square kilometers) gives a density of 4.0 per square kilometer for the Guarani, for a total of 1,404,000 (or 1.5 million) in 1530 in an area of 350,000 square kilometers. In the other 150,000 square kilometers there were additional tribes, both farmers and hunter-gatherers, with, I believe, a probable density of well under 1.0 per square kilometer. The Villamarins (1975: 106) estimated only 200,000 Guarani in Paraguay at contact.

REVISED HEMISPHERIC ESTIMATE FOR 1492

Table 1 shows my revised regional populations for 1492, based on the various new estimates since 1976. The total of 53,904,000 is a reduction of 3,396,000 from my total of 57,300,000 in 1976 (p. 291 here). Fifty-four million is a significant increase over the early estimates by Rosenblat, Kroeber, and Steward

Table 1
Revised Estimates of Aboriginal American Populations, ca. 1492

Region	1976	1992	Change
North America	4,400,000	3,790,000[a]	−610,000
Mexico			
Central	18,300,000	13,839,000[b]	−4,461,000
Chiapas	800,000	275,000[c]	−525,000
Yucatan-Tabasco	1,600,000	1,600,000	no change
Soconusco	none	80,000[d]	+80,000
North	700,000	1,380,000[e]	+680,000
Central America			
Southern Guatemala	2,000,000	2,000,000[f]	no change
Honduras-Belize	750,000	850,000[g]	+100,000
El Salvador	500,000	750,000[h]	+250,000
Nicaragua	1,000,000	825,000[i]	−175,000
Costa Rica	400,000	400,000	no change
Panama	1,000,000	800,000[j]	−200,000
Caribbean			
Hispaniola	1,950,000	1,000,000[k]	−950,000
Other islands	3,900,000	2,000,000[l]	−1,900,000
Andes			
Central	7,500,000	11,696,000[m]	+4,196,000
Colombia	3,000,000	3,000,000	no change
Venezuela	1,000,000	1,000,000	no change
Lowland South America			
Amazonia	5,100,000	5,664,000[n]	+565,000
Argentina	900,000	900,000	no change
Chile	1,000,000	1,000,000	no change
Remainder	1,500,000	1,055,000[o]	−445,000
Totals	57,300,000	53,904,000	−3,396,000

[a] Double Ubelaker's (1988: 291) 1.894 million at contact.

[b] Average of Zambardino's (1981: 240) 8 to 10 million; Sander's (p. 81, here) 11.4 million; Slicher van Bath's (1978: 92) 21.42 million; and 13.536 million projected from Whitemore's (1991: 477) Basin of Mexico total of 1.59 million.

[c] Northwest Mexico, 1,040,000, based on Reff's tribal figures; Northeast Mexico, 340,000, from Gerhard (1982: 24).

[d] Gerhard (1979: 169).

[e] Northwest Mexico, 1,040,000, based on Reff's tribal figures; Northeast Mexico, 340,000, from Gerhard (1982: 24).

[f] No change; Lovell and Swezey (1982: 81).

[g] Newson (1986: 91).

[h] Fowler (1988: 114).

[i] Newson (1987: 88); 50,000 is added for Belize.

[j] Reduction based on comparison with the rest of Central America.

[k] Zambardino (1978: 707).

[l] Double the estimate for Hispaniola; Watts (1987: 74).

[m] Average of adjusted totals for the Central Andes based on ratios derived from Shea (p. 174 here): 12,852,464 from Cook's (1981: 114) 8,520,000 for Peru only (without eastern Peru); 10,592,723 from Cook's (1981: 113) four most "reasonable" model totals for Peru only (without eastern Peru), which average 7,022,448; 11,200,000 from Wachtel's (1977: 90) 10,000,000 for

(8.4 to 15.5 million). It is well below the estimates by Dobyns and Borah (90 to 113 million, but it is close to Sapper's 37.0 to 48.5 million and Spinden's 40 to 50 million (see pp. 3, 15 here).

For most regions, the adjustments have been relatively minor, up or down. The major reductions are for the Caribbean (2,850,000) and for Central Mexico (4,461,000). The estimates for Central Mexico and the Central Andes (Inca Empire) are both unsatisfactory because they are averages of several conflicting figures. For Central Mexico, 13.8 million may still be too high, especially if more weight is given to Sanders (11.4 million) and to Zambardino (8 to 10 million). The Central Andes have been increased by 4,196,000 to a total of 11,696,000, which still may be too low given Cook's confidence in his figure of 9 million for Peru alone.

I believe my 1976 margin of error of 25 percent can now be reduced to 20 percent. Given the total of 53,904,000, the new range is from 43,123,000 to 64,685,000, or, more roughly, 43 to 65 million.[5] Future regional revisions are likely to maintain the hemispheric total within this range.

If the total Indian population for the Hemisphere had dropped from about 53.9 million in 1492 to only about 5.6 million by 1650 (Dobyns, 1966: 415; Ubelaker, 1988: 292), then the decline amounted to 48.3 million, or 90 percent. This is a human toll of a magnitude comparable to that suffered during World War II (ca. 45–50 million), although the Native American demise was spread over a longer period of time and involved not only brutality, including genocide, but the inadvertent introduction of disease.

Madison, Wisconsin
January 1992

William M. Denevan
Carl O. Sauer Professor
of Geography

5. Recent hemispheric estimates, uncalculated, include 80 million by Schwerin (1984: 34), 40 million by Lord and Burke (1991), 40 to 50 million by Cowley (1991), and 43 million by Whitmore (1991: 483). Colonial historian McAlister (1984: 85) accepts my 1976 range of 43 to 72 million.

1535 adjusted to 1520; and 12,140,000 from Smith (1970: 459), unadjusted. Estimates by Rowe (1946), Dobyns (1966), Shea (here), and others have less basis for inclusion in this average.

[n] Reduction of várzea by 84,500 based on Porro (1981); see Amazon discussion above. Reduction of central Brazilian coast by 52,500 based on Dean's (1985: 42) 9.0 per square kilometer density instead of my 9.5; and an increase based on a buffer zone of 15 (10–20) percent instead of 25 percent (p. 234 here).

[o] Southern Brazil and Paraguay-Uruguay. Based on Clastres' (1973: 31–32) 4.0 per square kilometer density for the Tupi-Guarani region (350,000 square kilometer minus 105,000 for the central coast (included in Amazonia), and allowing a rough 0.5 per square kilometer for the other tribes in the region (150,000 square kilometers).

Supplementary Bibliography

Borah, Woodrow. 1991a. "Introduction," in *"Secret Judgments of God": Old World Disease in Colonial Spanish America,* edited by Noble David Cook and W. George Lovell, pp. 3–19. Univ. Oklahoma Press: Norman.

Borah, Woodrow, 1991b. "Epidemics in the Americas: Major Issues and Future Research," *Latin American Population History Bulletin,* 19:2–13.

Brown, Suzanne. 1984. "The Effects of Epidemic Disease in Colonial Ecuador," Ph.D. dissertation, Duke Univ.: Durham.

Carmack, Robert M., John Early, and Christopher Lutz, eds. 1982. *The Historical Demography of Highland Guatemala.* Institute for Mesoamerican Studies, No. 6. State Univ. New York: Albany.

Clermont, Norman. 1980. "L'agmentation de la population chez les Iroquoiens préhistoriques," *Recherches Amérindiennes au Québec,* 10:159–63.

Clastres, Pierre. 1973. "Eléments de Démographie Amérindienne," *L'Homme,* 13:23–36.

Cook, Noble David. 1977. Review of *The Native Population of the Americas in 1492,* edited by William M. Denevan (1976), *Hispanic American Historical Review,* 57:723–25.

Cook, Noble David. 1981. *Demographic Collapse: Indian Peru, 1520–1620.* Cambridge Univ. Press; Cambridge.

Cook, Noble David. 1982a. *The People of the Colca Valley: A Population Study.* Dellplain Latin American Studies, No. 9. Westview Press: Boulder.

Cook, Noble David. 1982b. "Population Data for Indian Peru: Sixteenth and Seventeenth Centuries," *Hispanic American Historical Review,* 62:73–120.

Cook, Noble David. In Press (a). "Epidémias y dinámica demográfica: 1492–1600," in *General History of Latin America,* Vol. 2. UNESCO.

Cook, Noble David. In press (b). "Impact of Disease in the Sixteenth-Century Andean World," in *Disease and Demography in the Americas,* edited by John W. Verano and Douglas H. Ubelaker. Smithsonian Institution: Washington, D.C.

Cook, Noble David, and W. George Lovell, eds. 1991. *"Secret Judgments of God": Old World Disease in Colonial Spanish America.* Univ. Oklahoma Press: Norman.

Cook, Sherburne F. 1976b. *The Indian Population of New England in the Seventeenth Century.* Univ. California Publications in Anthropology, Vol. 12. Berkeley.

Crosby, Alfred W., Jr. 1976. "Virgin Soil Epidemics as a Factor in the Aboriginal Depopulation of America," *William and Mary Quarterly,* 33:289-99.

Crosby, Alfred W., Jr. 1991. "Infectious Disease and the Demography of the Atlantic Peoples," *Journal of World History,* 2:5-16.

Crosby, Alfred W., Jr. In press. "Hawaiian Depopulation as Model for the Amerindian Experience," in *Epidemics and Ideas,* edited by Paul Slack. Cambridge Univ. Press: Cambridge.

Cowley, Geoffrey. 1991. "The Great Disease Migration," in *1492-1992, When Worlds Collide: How Columbus's Voyages Transformed both East and West,* pp. 54-56. *Newsweek,* special issue, Fall/Winter.

Dean, Warren. 1985. "Las poblaciones indígenas del litoral brasileño de São Paulo a Rio de Janeiro: Comercio, esclavitud, reducción y extinción, in *Población y mano de obra en América Latina,* edited by Nicolás Sánchez-Albornoz, pp. 25-51. Alianza Editorial: Madrid.

Decker, Jody F. 1991. "Depopulation of the Northern Plains Natives," *Social Science Medicine,* 33:381-93.

Denevan, William M. 1983. Review of *Demographic Collapse: Indian Peru, 1520-1620,* by Noble David Cook (1981), *The Americas,* 39:281-84.

Denevan, William M. 1987. "Terrace Abandonment in the Colca Valley, Peru," in *Pre-Hispanic Agricultural Fields in the Andean Region,* edited by W. M. Denevan, K. Mathewson, and G. Knapp, pp. 1-43. British Archaeological Reports (BAR), International Series 359. Oxford.

Denevan, William M. In press (a). "Carl Sauer and Native American Population Size," in *The Legacy of Intellect: Carl Sauer and the Berkeley School of Geography,* edited by Martin S. Kenzer. Kluwer Academic Publishers: Dordrecht.

Denevan, William M. In press (b). "Stone vs. Metal Axes: Was Shifting Cultivation a Post-European Adaptation in Amazonia?," *Journal of the Steward Anthropological Society.*

Denevan, William M., and Christine Padoch, eds. 1988. *Swidden-Fallow Agroforestry in the Peruvian Amazon. Advances in Economic Botany, Vol. 5. New York Botanical Garden: New York.*

Dickinson, J. A. 1980. "The Pre-Contact Huron Population: A Reappraisal," Ontario History, 72:173-79.

Dobyns, Henry F. 1976. "Brief Perspective on a Scholarly Transformation: Widowing the 'Virgin' Land," *Ethnohistory,* 23:95-104.

Dobyns, Henry F. 1978. Review of *The Native Population of the Americas in 1492,* edited by William M. Denevan (1976), *Annals of the Association of American Geographers,* 68:433-36.

Dobyns, Henry F. 1983. *Their Number Become Thinned: Native American Population Dynamics in Eastern North America.* Univ. Tennessee Press: Knoxville.

Dobyns, Henry F. 1988. "Reassessing New World Populations at the Time of Contact," *Encuentro,* 4(4):8-9.

Dobyns, Henry F. 1989a. "More Methodological Perspectives on Historical Demography," *Ethnohistory,* 36:285-99.

Dobyns, Henry F. 1989b. "Native Historic Epidemiology in the Greater Southwest," *American Anthropologist,* 91:171-74.

Doolittle, William E. 1988. *Pre-Hispanic Occupance in the Valley of Sonora, Mexico: Archaeological Confirmation of Early Spanish Reports.* Anthropological Papers of Univ. Arizona, No. 48. Tucson.

Engelbrecht, William. 1987. "Factors Maintaining Low Population Density among the Prehistoric New York Iroquois," *American Antiquity*, 52:13–27.

Feest, Christian F. 1973. "Seventeenth Century Virginia Algonquin Population Estimates," *Archaeological Society of Virginia*, 28:66–79.

Fowler, William R., Jr. 1988. "La población nativa de El Salvador al momento de la conquista española," *Mesoamérica*, 9(15):79–116.

Fowler, William R., Jr. 1989. *The Cultural Evolution of Ancient Nahua Civilizations: The Pipil-Nicarao of Central America.* Univ. Oklahoma Press: Norman.

Frank, Erwin. 1987. "Delimitaciones al aumento poblacional y desarrollo cultural en las culturas indígenas de la Amazonía antes de 1492," *Tübinger Geographische Studien*, 95:109–23.

Gasco, Janine. 1987. "Cacao and the Economic Integration of Native Society in Colonial Soconusco, New Spain," Ph.D. dissertation, Univ. California at Santa Barbara.

Gerhard, Peter. 1979. *The Southeast Frontier of New Spain.* Princeton Univ. Press: Princeton.

Gerhard, Peter. 1982. *The North Frontier of New Spain.* Princeton Univ. Press: Princeton.

Grohs, Waltraud. 1974. *Los indios del Alto Amazonas del siglo XVI al siglo XVIII: Poblaciones y migraciones en la antigua provincia de Maynas. Bonner Amerkanistische Studien 2.* Bonn.

Guerra, Francisco. 1985. "La epidemia americana de influenza en 1493," *Revista de Indias*, 45(176):325–47.

Guerra, Francisco. 1986. "El efecto demográfico de las epidemias tras el descubrimiento de América," *Revista de Indias*, 46(177):41–58.

Guerra, Francisco. 1988. "The Earliest American Epidemic: The Influenza of 1493," *Social Science History*, 12:305:25.

Hemming, John. 1978. *Red Gold: The Conquest of the Brazilian Indians.* Harvard Univ. Press: Cambridge.

Henige, David. 1978a. "On the Contact Population of Hispaniola: History as Higher Mathematics," *Hispanic American Historical Review*, 58:217–37.

Henige, David. 1978b. "David Henige's Reply," *Hispanic American Historical Review*, 58: 709–12.

Henige, David. 1986a. "If Pigs Could Fly: Timucuan Population and Native American Historical Demography," *Journal of Interdisciplinary History*, 16:701–20.

Henige, David. 1986b. "Primary Source by Primary Source? On the Role of Epidemics in New World Depopulation," *Ethnohistory*, 33:293–312.

Henige, David. 1986c. "When did Smallpox Reach the New World (and Why does it Matter)?," in *Africans in Bondage: Studies in Slavery and the Slave Trade*, edited by Paul E. Lovejoy, pp. 11–26. African Studies Program, Univ. Wisconsin: Madison.

Henige, David. 1989. "On the Current Devaluation of the Notion of Evidence: A Rejoinder to Dobyns," *Ethnohistory*, 36:304–7.

Holder, Preston. 1970. *The Hoe and the Horse on the Plains.* Univ. Nebraska Press: Lincoln.

Houdaille, Jacques. 1986. "La population de l'Amérique avant Christophe Colomb,"
Population, 41:586–90.

Jackson, Robert H. 1981. "Epidemic Disease and Population Decline in the Baja California Missions, 1697–1834," Southern California Quarterly, 48:308–46.

Johansson, S. Ryan. 1982. "The Demographic History of the Native Peoples of North America: A Selective Bibliography," Yearbook of Physical Anthropology, 25:133–52.

Joralemon, Donald. 1982. "New World Depopulation and the Case of Disease," Journal of Anthropological Research, 38:108–27.

Kay, Jeanne. 1984. "The Fur Trade and Native American Population Growth," Ethnohistory, 31:265–87.

Lord, Lewis, and Sarah Burke. 1991. "America Before Columbus," U.S. News and World Report. July 8, pp. 22–37.

Lovell, W. George. 1981a. "The Historical Demography of the Cuchumatán Highlands, Guatemala, 1500–1821," in Studies in Spanish American Population History, edited by David J. Robinson, pp. 195–216. Dellplain Latin American Studies, No. 8. Westview Press: Boulder.

Lovell, W. George. 1981b. "Population Change in the Cuchumatán Highlands of Guatemala," Bulletin of the Society for Latin American Studies, 33:8–44.

Lovell, W. George. 1982. "Collapse and Recovery: A Demographic Profile of the Cuchumatán Highlands of Guatemala (1520–1821)," in The Historical Demography of Highland Guatemala, edited by Robert M. Carmack, John Early, and Christopher Lutz, pp. 103–20. Institute for Mesoamerican Studies, No. 6. State Univ. New York: Albany.

Lovell, W. George. 1991. "Disease and Depopulation in Early Colonial Guatemala," in "Secret Judgments of God": Old World Disease in Colonial Spanish America, edited by Noble David Cook and W. George Lovell, pp. 49–83. Univ. Oklahoma Press: Norman.

Lovell, W. George. 1992 [1985]. Conquest and Survival in Colonial Guatemala: A Historical Geography of the Cuchumatán Highlands, 1500–1821. Revised edition. McGill-Queen's Univ. Press: Kingston and Montreal.

Lovell, W. George. In press. "Heavy Shadows and Black Night: Disease and Depopulation in Colonial Spanish America," Annals of the Association of American Geographers.

Lovell, W. George, and Christopher H. Lutz. In press. "The Historical Demography of Colonial Central America," Yearbook, Conference of Latin Americanist Geographers.

Lovell, W. George, Christopher H. Lutz, and William R. Swezey. 1984. "The Indian Population of Southern Guatemala, 1549–1551: An Analysis of López de Cerrato's Tasaciones de Tributos, The Americas, 40:459–77.

Lovell, W. George, and William R. Swezey. 1982. "The Population of Southern Guatemala at Spanish Contact" Canadian Journal of Anthropology, 3:71–84.

Lutz, Christopher H., and W. George Lovell. In press (a). "The Population History of Spanish Central America," in The Peopling of Latin America: Sources, Interpretations, and Commentary, edited by Robert McCaa.

Lutz, Christopher H., and W. George Lovell. In press (b). El demógrafo y la conquista: Bibliografiá crítica del poblamiento de la Audienciá de Guatemala.

MacLeod, Murdo J. 1985. "Los indígenas de Guatemala en los siglos XVI y XVII: Tamaño de la población, recursos y organización de la mano de obra," in *Población y mano de obra en América Latina*, edited by Nicolás Sánchez-Albornoz, pp. 53–67. Alianza Editorial: Madrid.

Madigan, Douglas G. 1976. "Santiago Atitlán, Guatemala: A Socioeconomic and Demographic History," Ph.D. dissertation, Univ. Pittsburgh.

McAlister, Lyle N. 1984. *Spain and Portugal in the New World, 1492–1700*. Univ. Minnesota Press: Minneapolis.

Meggers, Betty. In press. "Prehistoric Population Density in the Amazon Basin," in *Disease and Demography in the Americas: Changing Patterns before and after 1492*, edited by John W. Verano and Douglas H. Ubelaker. Smithsonian Institution Press: Washington, D.C.

Meggers, Betty J., O.F. Dias, E. T. Miller, and C. Perota. 1988. "Implications of Archeological Distributions in Amazonia," in *Proceedings of a Workshop on Neotropical Distribution Patterns*, edited by W. R. Heyer and P. E. Vanzolini, pp. 275–94. Academia Brasileira de Ciências: Rio de Janeiro.

Meister, Cary W. 1976. "Demographic Consequences of Euro-American Contact on Selected American Indian Populations and their Relationship to the Demographic Transition," *Ethnohistory*, 23:161–72.

Miller, Virginia P. 1976. "Aboriginal Micmac Population: A Review of the Evidence," *Ethnohistory*, 23:117–27.

Miller, Virginia P. 1982. "The Decline of Nova Scotia Micmac Population, A.D. 1600–1850," *Culture*, 2(3):107–20.

Milner, George R. 1980. "Epidemic Disease in the Postcontact Southeast: A Reappraisal," *Mid-Continental Journal of Archaeology*, 5:39–56.

Morey, Robert V. 1979. "A Joyful Harvest of Souls: Disease and the Destruction of the Llanos Indians," *Antropológica*, 52:77–108.

Mörner, Magnus. 1979. Review of *The Native Population of the Americas in 1492*, edited by William M. Denevan (1976), *Latin American Indian Literatures*, 3:27–28.

Moya Pons, Frank. 1977. "Datos para el estudio de la demografia aborigen en la Española," *Estudios sobre Politica Indigenista Española en América*, Vol. 3, pp. 9–18. Seminario de Historia de América, Universidad de Valladolid.

Myers, Thomas P. 1988. "El efecto de las pestes sobre las poblaciones de la Amazonia Alta." *Amazonía Peruana*, 8:61–81.

Myers, Thomas P. N.d. "The Expansion and Collapse of the Omagua," paper presented at the Symposium on Amazon Synthesis, 1989, Nova Friburgo (Brazil).

Newson, Linda. 1981. "Demographic Catastrophe in Sixteenth-Century Honduras," in *Studies in Spanish American Population History*, edited by David J. Robinson, pp. 217–41. Dellplain Latin American Studies, No. 8. Westview Press: Boulder.

Newson, Linda. 1982. "The Depopulation of Nicaragua in the Sixteenth Century," *Journal of Latin American Studies*, 14:253–86.

Newson, Linda A. 1985. "Indian Population Patterns in Colonial Spanish America," *Latin American Research Review*, 20:41–74.

Newson, Linda A. 1986. *The Cost of Conquest: Indian Decline in Honduras Under Spanish Rule*. Westview Press: Boulder.

Newson, Linda A. 1987. *Indian Survival in Colonial Nicaragua*. Univ. Oklahoma Press: Norman.

Newson, Linda A. 1991. "Old World Epidemics in Early Colonial Ecuador," in *"Secret Judgments of God": Old World Disease in Colonial Spanish America*, edited by Noble David Cook and W. George Lovell, pp. 84–112. Univ. Oklahoma Press: Norman.

Orellana, Sandra L. 1984. *The Tzutujil Mayas: Continuity and Change, 1250–1630*. Univ. Oklahoma Press: Norman.

Pollard, Helen P., and Shirley Gorenstein. 1980. "Agrarian Potential, Population, and the Tarascan State," *Science*, 209:274–77.

Porro, Antonio. 1981. "Os Omagua do Alto Amazonas: Demografia e padrões de povoamento no século XVII," *Coleção Museu Paulista, Série Ensaios*, 4:207–31.

Ramenofsky, Ann F. 1987. *Vectors of Death: The Archaeology of European Contact*. Univ. New Mexico Press: Albuquerque.

Reff, Daniel F. 1987. "The Introduction of Smallpox in the Greater Southwest," *American Anthropologist*, 89:704–8.

Reff, Daniel T. 1989. "Disease Episodes and the Historical Record: A Reply to Dobyns," *American Anthropologist*, 91:174–75.

Reff, Daniel T. 1991. *Disease, Depopulation, and Culture Change in Northwestern New Spain, 1518–1764*. Univ. Utah Press: Salt Lake City.

Riley, Carroll L. 1987. *The Frontier People: The Greater Southwest in the Protohistoric Period*. Univ. New Mexico Press: Albuquerque.

Roberts, Leslie. 1989. "Disease and Death in the New World," *Science*, 246:1245–47.

Roosevelt, Anna C. 1991. *Moundbuilders of the Amazon: Geophysical Archaeology on Marajó Island, Brazil*. Academic Press: San Diego.

Salisbury, Neal. 1982. *Manitou and Providence: Indians, Europeans, and the Making of New England, 1500–1643*. Oxford Univ. Press: New York.

Sanders, William T., and Carson Murdy. 1982. "Population and Agricultural Adaptation in the Humid Highlands of Guatemala," in *The Historical Demography of Highland Guatemala*, edited by Robert M. Carmack, John Early, and Christopher Lutz, pp. 23–34. Institute for Mesoamerican Studies, No. 6. State Univ. New York: Albany.

Sauer, Carl O. 1963. "Theme of Plant and Animal Destruction in Economic History," in *Land and Life: A Selection from the Writings of Carl Ortwin Sauer*, edited by John Leighly, pp. 145–54. Univ. California Press: Berkeley.

Schwerin, Karl H. 1984. "The Indian Populations of Latin America," in *Latin America, Its Problems and Its Promise: A Multidisciplinary Introduction*, edited by Jan K. Black, pp. 33–47. Westview Press: Boulder.

Shea, Daniel, ed. In press. *Achoma Archaeology: A Study of Terrace Irrigation in Peru*. Occasional Papers of the Beloit College Museums. Beloit.

Sherman, William L. 1979. *Forced Native Labor in Sixteenth-Century Central America*. Univ. Nebraska Press: Lincoln.

Slicher van Bath, B. H. 1978. "The Calculation of the Population of New Spain, Especially for the Period before 1570," *Boletín de Estudios Latinoamericanos y del Caribe*, 24:67–95.

Smith, Marvin T. 1987. *Archaeology of Aboriginal Culture Change in the Interior Southwest: Depopulation during the Early Historic Period*. Univ. Florida Press: Gainesville.

Snow, Dean R. 1980. *The Archaeology of New England*. Academic Press: New York.

Snow, Dean R., and Kim M. Lanphear. 1988. "European Contact and Indian Depopulation in the Northeast: The Timing of the First Epidemics," *Ethnohistory*, 35:15-33.

Snow, Dean R., and Kim M. Lanphear. 1989. "More Methodological Perspectives: A Rejoinder to Dobyns," *Ethnohistory*, 36:299-304.

Snow, Dean R., and W. A. Starna. 1989. "Sixteenth-Century Depopulation: A View from the Mohawk Valley," *American Anthropologist*, 91:142-49.

Solano, Francisco de. 1974. *Los mayas del siglo XVIII: Pervivencia y transformación de la sociedad indígena guatemalteca durante la administración borbónica.* Ediciones Cultura Hispánica: Madrid.

Sturtevant, William C. ed. 1978--. *Handbook of North American Indians* (20 vols. anticipated). Smithsonian Institution: Washington, D.C.

Thornton, Russell. 1987. *American Indian Holocaust and Survival: A Population History since 1492.* Univ. Oklahoma Press: Norman.

Thornton, Russell, Tim Miller, and Jonathan Warren. 1991. "American Indian Population Recovery following Smallpox Epidemics," *American Anthropologist*, 93:28-45.

Thornton, Russell, and Joan Marsh-Thornton. 1981. "Estimating Prehistoric American Indian Population Size for United States Area: Implications of the Nineteenth Century Population Decline and Nadir," *American Journal of Physical Anthropology*, 55:47-53.

Tormo Sanz, Leandro. 1972. "Situacíon y población de los Mojos en 1679," *Revista Española de Antropologia Americana*, 7:151-59.

Treacy, John. 1989. "The Fields of Coporaque: Agricultural Terracing and Water Management in the Colca Valley, Arequipa, Peru," Ph.D. dissertation, Univ. Wisconsin, Madison.

Trigger, Bruce G. 1976. *The Children of Aataentsic: A History of the Huron People to 1660,* 2 vols. McGill-Queen's Univ. Press: Kingston and Montreal.

Trigger, Bruce G. 1985. *Natives and Newcomers: Canada's "Heroic Age" Reconsidered.* McGill-Queen's Univ. Press: Kingston and Montreal.

Ubelaker, Douglas H. 1981. "Approaches to Demographic Problems in the Northeast," in *Foundations of Northeast Archaeology*, edited by Dean R. Snow, pp. 175-94. Academic Press: New York.

Ubelaker, Douglas H. 1988. "North American Indian Population Size, A.D. 1500 to 1985," *American Journal of Physical Anthropology*, 77:289-94.

Ubelaker, Douglas H. In press. "North American Indian Population Size: Changing Perspectives," in *Disease and Demography in the Americas: Changing Patterns before and after 1492*, edited by John W. Verano and Douglas H. Ubelaker. Smithsonian Institution Press: Washington, D.C.

Upham, Steadman. 1986. "Smallpox and Climate in the American Southwest," *American Anthropologist*, 88:115-28.

Upham, Steadman. 1987. "Understanding the Disease History of the Southwest: A Reply to Reff," *American Anthropologist*, 89:708-10.

Varillas Montenegro, Alberto, and Patricia Mostajo de Muente. 1990. *La situación poblacional peruana: Balance y perspectivas.* Instituto Andino de Estudios en Poblacion y Desarrollo: Lima.

Veblen, Thomas T. 1977. "Native Population Decline in Totonicapán, Guatemala," *Annals of the Association of American Geographers*, 67:484-99.

Verano, John W., and Douglas H. Ubelaker, eds. In press. *Disease and Demography in the Americas: Changing Patterns before and after 1492*. Smithsonian Institution Press: Washington, D.C.

Villamarin, Juan A., and Judith E. Villamarin. 1975. *Indian Labor in Mainland Colonial Spanish America*. Latin American Studies Program, Occasional Papers and Monographs No. 1. Univ. Delaware: Newark.

Wachtel, Nathan. 1977. *Vision of the Vanquished: The Spanish Conquest of Peru through Indian Eyes, 1530–1570*. Harvester Press: Sussex.

Wasserstrom, Robert. 1983. *Class and Society in Central Chiapas*. Univ. California Press: Berkeley.

Watson, Rodney. 1990. "Informal Settlement and Fugitive Migration amongst the Indians of Late-Colonial Chiapas, Mexico," in *Migration in Colonial Spanish America*, edited by David J. Robinson, pp. 238–78. Cambridge Univ. Press: Cambridge.

Watts, David. 1987. *The West Indies: Patterns of Development, Culture and Environmental Change since 1492*. Cambridge Univ. Press: Cambridge.

Whitmore, Thomas M. 1991. "A Simulation of the Sixteenth-Century Population Collapse in the Basin of Mexico," *Annals of the Association of American Geographers*, 81:464–87.

Zambardino, Rudolph. 1978. "Critique of David Henige's 'On the Contact Population of Hispaniola: History as Higher Mathematics,'" *Hispanic American Historical Review*, 58:700–708.

Zambardino, Rudolph A. 1980. "Mexico's Population in the Sixteenth Century: Demographic Anomaly or Mathematical Illusion?," *Journal of Interdisciplinary History*, 11:1–27.

Zambardino, Rudolph A. 1981. "Errors in Historical Demography," *The Institute of Mathematics and its Applications*, 17:238–40.

Zambardino, Rudolph A. 1984. Review of Noble David Cook, *Demographic Collapse: Indian Peru, 1520–1620* (1981), *Journal of Interdisciplinary History*, 14:719–22.

Zamora Acosta, Elías. 1983. "Conquista y crisis demográfica: La población indígena del occidente de Guatemala en el siglo XVI," *Mesoamérica*, 6:291–328.

Preface to the First Edition

How many people were there in the New World when the first Europeans arrived at the end of the fifteenth century? The question has been debated since Columbus attempted a partial census on Hispaniola in 1496, and it remains one of the great inquiries of history. This collection of essays presents contributions to that inquiry, along with reviews of the massive and controversial literature.

The problem of Indian numbers can never be satisfactorily resolved due to the inadequacy of the data available, but attempts to estimate regional populations more carefully through refined techniques of historical, archaeological, and ecological analysis continue. They continue for very good reasons. Interpretations of fundamental social and economic events of the colonial period must relate to the size and distribution of the aboriginal population and to the nature of depopulation. It is quite understandable that social historians such as Woodrow Borah were diverted into historical demography. Second, anthropologists more and more find a causal relationship between size of population and cultural change and evolution; this concern is reflected even in the conservative demographic studies of Alfred Kroeber and Julian Steward. Third, there is the question of the potential of New World habitats for human settlement. Carl Sauer and other geographers have demonstrated that aboriginal land-use technology was often sophisticated and productive, capable of supporting large populations even in tropical, mountain, and arid regions now considered to have low carrying capacities. If it can be substantiated that such regions actually were once densely populated, then prevailing views about population and food production in Latin America today may have to be revised. Thus, it does make a great difference whether in 1492 there were 3,000,000 Indians in the central Andes or 30,000,000, or whether there were only 8,000,000 Indians in the New World or as many as 100,000,000. And a larger figure would means a catastrophic destruction of the American Indian, as there were only a few million remaining by the mid-seventeenth century.

The eight essays presented here provide both conservative and liberal interpretations of population numbers, with varied methodologies represented. They are organized regionally, with the sequence roughly following that of European-Indian contact: the Caribbean and Central America, Mexico, South America, and North America. Each regional part is preceded by a brief introduction to the relevant literature for that region.

Part I includes a summary by the editor of the methods that have been used to calculate or estimate aboriginal numbers. The first essay is by Woodrow Borah, whose research on central Mexico with his Berkeley colleague, the late Sherburne F. Cook, has forced a reconsideration upward of Indian populations throughout the hemisphere. Here he summarizes the history of scholarship on aboriginal populations and reviews the nature of the basic disagreement over the size of those populations. Seven regional studies follow.

The essay by Ángel Rosenblat on Hispaniola, translated from the Spanish, is a revised and expanded section of a monograph published in Mexico. It is an ardent defense of his estimates of low populations for the island. Geographer David R. Radell finds support for very large populations in Nicaragua by examining documentary evidence on the Indian slave trade from that country to Panama and Peru. William T. Sanders, an archaeologist and cultural ecologist, provides the most detailed counter argument to date against the high population estimate (25,200,000) for central Mexico by Borah and Cook, followed by alternative calculations based on archaeological, ecological, and historical research. Daniel E. Shea, also an archaeologist, applies statistical techniques to obtain a conservative population total for Peru. Geographer Jane Pyle reviews the documentary record of Indian populations in Argentina and concludes that numbers were much greater than those derived by the Argentine historians who utilized the same record. Denevan's study of Amazonia, a revision of an article originally published in Brazil, takes an ecological approach by estimating representative aboriginal populations for the different habitats, thereby deriving potential total populations. Anthropologist Douglas H. Ubelaker examines the unpublished notes of James Mooney in the Smithsonian archives on North American tribal populations. In the introductory section of each part of the volume, each of these essays is reviewed in more detail in a regional context.

The time period concerned is that of initial contact and subsequent depopulation. Most of the articles pertain to the sixteenth century, the main exceptions being those on Amazonia and North America, where European reporting and influence were either minor or were delayed until the seventeenth and eighteenth centuries. Thus, "1492" in the title of this book is used in a symbolic rather than an absolute sense. The terms "native" and "aboriginal" are used here to refer to the conditions of Indian groups just prior to either direct or indirect contact with Europeans. Such conditions clearly persisted until much later in some regions than in others. No attempt has been made to include material on pre-Columbian populations. Archaeologists, however, have been giving considerable attention to the reconstruction of prehistoric populations, utilizing data on settlement, subsistence technology, and ecology (e.g., S. F. Cook, 1972a).

Increasing research on the historical demography of the Americas resulted in several interdisciplinary conferences in the 1960s. A session was held on native populations at the 35th International Congress of Americanists in Mexico City in 1962 (Miranda, 1964). At the 37th International Congress of Americanists at Mar del Plata, Argentina, in 1966, a symposium was held on "Historical Demography: New Contributions and New Methods," which featured a prolonged debate between Borah and Rosenblat. Revisions of the papers presented by Borah and by Denevan and a portion of Rosenblat's are included in this collection. In 1968 a session was held on "The Historical Demography of Latin America" at the Fourth Congress of the International Economic History Association in Bloomington, Indiana, and nine of the papers were later published in *Population and Economics,* edited by Paul Deprez (1970). The importance of scholarship on aboriginal demography is attested to by the interest shown in these international sessions, by the associated upsurge in publications on the topic, and by the intensity of the arguments which the new research has generated.

We are now in a period of marked disagreement about the size of former Indian populations, both regionally and for the hemisphere, with a strongly realized need for resolution based on better techniques and evidence. Relevant research is accelerating, with contributions from varied disciplines. The introductory discussions, essays, and the bibliography presented here can serve both as an overview of past estimates, methods, and conflicts and as indicators of new approaches and perspectives.

January 1976   WILLIAM M. DENEVAN

Acknowledgments

Financial assistance for various phases of the preparation of this book was received from the Graduate Research Committee and the Ibero-American Studies Program of the University of Wisconsin, Madison. The Cartographic Laboratory of the University of Wisconsin, Madison, was responsible for the funding, design, and preparation of the maps and figures. Secretarial services including part of the typing were provided by the Department of Geography; particularly helpful was student assistant Lynn Larson Douglas. The translation of the Rosenblat article was done by the editor with the assistance of Elizabeth López-Noël. The quotes from the chroniclers within the article were translated by Lloyd Kasten. Other translations of quotes are by the essay authors. The Newberry Library, Chicago, kindly provided a print of the De Bry engraving used for the frontispiece.

The concept for an essay collection on native populations, but not specific essays, had its genesis at the Conference on Population Problems and the Development of Latin America, chaired by David Chaplin and held in Madison, Wisconsin, in May 1968. A session was included on "The History of Population Change in Latin America," with participation by Woodrow Borah, Herbert Harvey, David Sweet, William M. Denevan, and John L. Phelan as moderator. An initial objective of a large anthology of reprinted articles on the historical demography of Latin America was pursued with Herbert Harvey, but proved impractical. A more modest collection of mostly original essays was subsequently assembled.

Many scholars in geography, history, and anthropology have contributed to the content of this book in one way or another. Some of them were to have had essays here but regrettably had to be left out. Original plans were to include articles by Carl O. Sauer and Sir J. Eric Thompson, whose deaths in 1975 terminated long and monumental careers in cultural historical geography and Mayan archaeology, respectively. At the time of his death in 1974, Sherburne F. Cook was preparing an article reviewing the population of North

American Indians, which would have been included. Woodrow Borah, Henry F. Dobyns, Ángel Rosenblat, Andrew H. Clark, and John L. Phelan were bulwarks of encouragement from the beginning. Woodrow Borah and Henry F. Dobyns reviewed the introductions and made many useful suggestions, as did five anonymous referees for the manuscript and Arnold Strickon of the University of Wisconsin Press Editorial Board. Much of my own thinking and knowledge about native peoples of the Americas reflects instruction at the University of California, Berkeley, under Carl O. Sauer, Erhard Rostlund, James J. Parsons, and John H. Rowe.

It is sometimes said that it is easier to write a book than to edit one, and I almost have to agree, having shepherded this through several quite different versions, and, accordingly, through different authors, referees, editors, and masses of detail and correspondence. My particular thanks are extended to the essay contributors for their own efforts and for their patience over several years. And to Susie, Curt, and Tori for encouragement and forbearance and for keeping things going when I couldn't.

January 1976   W. M. D.

PART I Estimating the Unknown

"Estimates of the native population of the Americas of the Conquest period made by competent scholars have an incredible range of difference" (Steward and Faron, 1959: 51).

INTRODUCTION

How many Indians were there? No one will ever know, but can't we at least agree on whether there were few or many? Apparently not yet, for on few questions of history do so many authorities continue to differ so greatly. The reasons for attempting to know are numerous and important. It would not be an overstatement to hold that almost every major investigation of pre-Columbian cultural evolution and ecology, of the European conquest, and of colonial social and economic history must ultimately raise the question of Indian numbers. Thus, the effort to determine those numbers continues, and as the quality of the research improves, the trend is toward acceptance of higher numbers.

Europeans came into abrupt confrontation with previously little-known or unknown populations throughout Asia, Africa, and the Pacific, as well as in the Americas. The problem of estimating numbers at the time of initial contact might seem to be the same for all these areas, but such is not the case. Asia and Africa were in constant contact with Europe, if only indirectly, whereas the Pacific and the Americas were isolated, or nearly so. As a result, there was a very rapid decline of native peoples in the New World and the Pacific[1] following exposure to Old World diseases, but not in Asia and Africa.

1. For discussions and further references on contact populations and their decline in Hawaii, Polynesia, New Guinea, Australia, New Zealand, and other Pacific areas, see Borah (1964), W. H. R. Rivers (1922), Schmitt (1972), Oliver (1962), Jacobs (1971), and Keesing (1941: 43–65). Schmitt's article carries a warning to all historical demographers: the frequency with which population figures are "garbled," or incorrectly copied, and the consequent importance of relying on original sources.

1

Most of the decline of population in the Americas and the Pacific occurred before systematic counts of people were possible.

A history of the various estimates for the aboriginal population of the Americas is provided in the first essay in this collection. The author, Woodrow Borah, is probably the most prolific and controversial of the active scholars in the field of New World historical demography. Here he briefly reviews the debate over the size of Indian populations—the major protagonists, their arguments, and their figures. He then outlines the main issues about which there is disagreement: the nature of pre-Columbian Indian society; interpretations of history; and in particular the evidence, its reliability, the nature of its treatment, and the validity of the results.

Borah's own inclination toward high estimates is clear, but he provides sound guidelines for one who would venture into this uncertain realm of scholarship. He stresses that the margin for error is potentially great, that the problems of analysis are not unique to the New World, and that more detailed local studies are essential but that the results are not necessarily transferable to other regions. To what magnitude of accuracy can the aboriginal population ultimately be estimated? Borah suggests someday arriving at a hemspheric figure with an error of from 30 to 50 percent, but only after decades more of careful research.

RECENT HEMISPHERIC ESTIMATES

In recent years, there have been numerous general discussions of the question of the size of the native American population at the time of European conquest.[2] The most comprehensive is the 1966 essay by Henry Dobyns, an anthropologist, who previously carried out research on the aboriginal demography of Arizona (1963a) and Peru (1963b). He summarizes the estimates and methodology for both the hemisphere and subregions. A primary objective is "to analyze some major methodological reasons why estimates of aboriginal American population have yielded a picture of small scale preconquest human population in the Western Hemisphere" (Dobyns, 1966: 396). Particular attention is given to the low estimates of Kroeber, Rosenblat, and Steward (Table 0.1 below), and he reviews methods which have produced substantially larger figures. He concludes that the main reason for the low estimates, other than the general distrust by many scholars of early estimates

2. For example: Chaunu (1964), Lipschutz (1966), Dobyns (1966, 1976), Borah (1970), Borah and Cook (1972), Stewart (1973: 29–55), M. J. MacLeod (1973: 1–20), Sánchez-Albornoz (1974: 32–36), and Jacobs (1974).

and censuses, is the failure to take into account massive depopulation, mainly as a result of introduced disease, from the time of initial European contact to the time of the first reasonably reliable population information, a period amounting to from a few to many decades for most regions.

Proceeding from this conclusion, Dobyns presents a new calculation of the hemispheric Indian population by deriving a ratio of the degree of decline from the time of contact to the population nadir (the date of recovery; about 1650 for most regions). He determines depopulation ratios for tribes or small regions for which there is reasonably good information, and he then comes up with a rough overall average of 20 to 1, or a population decline of 95 percent. Applying this to the nadir populations for the major regions, he obtains a total aboriginal population of 90,043,000. (A projection using a ratio of 25 to 1 results in 112,553,750.) The article by Dobyns was published in *Current Anthropology*, where the procedure is to send manuscripts in final form to reviewers whose comments are published with the article along with a response from the author. Most of the reviewers (24 in all) commend Dobyns' review and discussion of the literature, but several are critical of Dobyns' own calculations, pointing out the great range of depopulation ratios from region to region and the lack of enough valid ratios to arrive at any reasonable hemispheric average.

Another recent high estimate for the contact population of the hemisphere is that by Borah (1964: 381) of "upwards of one hundred million." This is an

Table 0.1
Some Previous Estimates of Aboriginal American Population, ca. 1492[a]
(in millions)

	Kroeber	Rosenblat	Steward	Sapper	Dobyns
North America	0.90	1.00	1.00	2.00– 3.50	9.80–12.25
Mexico	3.20	4.50	4.50	12.00–15.00	30.00–37.50
Central America	0.10[b]	0.80	0.74	5.00– 6.00	10.80–13.50
Caribbean	0.20	0.30	0.22	3.00– 4.00	0.44– 0.55
Andes	3.00	4.75	6.13	12.00–15.00	30.00–37.50
Lowland South America	1.00	2.03	2.90	3.00– 5.00	9.00–11.25
Hemisphere total	8.40	13.38	15.49	37.00–48.50	90.04–112.55

[a]Modified from Steward (1949: 656), with Kroeber corrected and Dobyns added. Sources: Kroeber, 1939: 166; Rosenblat, 1954: 102; Steward, 1949: 656; Sapper, 1924; and Dobyns, 1966: 415.

[b]Honduras and Nicaragua only. Guatemala and Salvador are included with Mexico, while Costa Rica and Panama are included with lowland South America.

intuitive figure based on a lifetime of research rather than on a group by group summation. Chaunu (1969: 382) accepts 80,000,000 to 100,000,000. Denevan (1966c) and Jacobs (1974: 123) have suggested that a total between 50,000,000 and 100,000,000 is reasonable. A lower but still substantial figure of no less than 33,300,000 is accepted by the respected Swedish historian of Latin America, Magnus Mörner (1967: 12).

While most scholars now believe that the low totals of Kroeber (8,400,000) and Rosenblat (13,380,000) are unreasonable, they still are not ready to accept the high numbers of Dobyns and Borah. Given that, "in the year 1500 Europe from the Atlantic to the Urals had a population estimated at perhaps sixty to eighty million souls,"[3] it is not surprising that higher figures for the Western Hemisphere are protested. Rosenblat (1967) stands by his original figures and has been a continuing critic of Cook and Borah. The archaeologist William Sanders (see Chapter 4 in this volume) has derived large estimates for central Mexico, but they are well below those of Cook and Borah. A demographer, William Petersen, is not impressed with the demographic methodology of Dobyns and of Borah and Cook.[4] So the basic disagreement about the relative size of the aboriginal population of the New World continues, and this disagreement is a major focus of each of the essays in this collection.

CAUSES OF DEPOPULATION

The main objective of this collection is to examine the question of the size of aboriginal populations. However, since the rate and degree of depopulation after European contact are criteria often utilized for calculating original populations, it will be useful to review the causes of depopulation. Were these causes of such a nature as to account for the rapid and massive declines some scholars argue for? The answer seems to be in the affirmative.

Most historians now agree that introduced disease was the major killer of New World Indians and seems to be the only way to explain the rapidity of

3. Borah (1976: 49); also see Jacobs (1974: 123–24) and M. J. MacLeod (1973: 18).

4. "They typify the all too common indifference to demographic expertise: the authors use nonprofessional techniques to generate from dubious data conclusions that they seemingly find attractive just because of the presumed [demographic] disasters" (Petersen, 1975: 241). Petersen, however, weakens his own position by uncritically accepting Kroeber. For a reasoned defense of the techniques of historical demography used by Cook and Borah, see their *Essays in Population History* (1971–74) and Borah's essay in this volume.

decline in many areas.[5] This is confirmed by hundreds of reports in the documentary record. Single epidemics reduced villages by half or more, and the people of many tribes were completely wiped out in a few decades. The process has been documented in modern times in Amazonia, where isolated groups still lack either resistance or immunity.[6]

Crosby (1967), an "anthropomedical" historian, has described the nature and impact of introduced disease, particularly smallpox.[7] As he points out, prior to the great European voyages of discovery most diseases in fatal form "tended to be endemic rather than epidemic." Isolation, such as that of the American Indians from the Old World, rendered populations very susceptible to catastrophic epidemics from diseases introduced from overseas. The major killers included smallpox, measles, whooping cough, chicken pox, bubonic plague, typhus, malaria,[8] diphtheria, amoebic dysentery, influenza, and a variety of helminthic infections (Borah, 1976: 60). The few important viral diseases of the American Indians prior to 1492 included infectious hepatitis, encephalitis, and polio. Venereal syphilis was clearly present.[9] Yellow fever has generally been believed to have been introduced from the Old World, but the reservoir of yellow fever among South and Central American monkeys (Pavlovsky, 1966: 145–46) and historical evidence (Pedersen, 1974) suggest otherwise. Chagas' disease was apparently a widespread endemic killer in the New World (Shimkin, 1973: 279–81). For a discussion of other endemic diseases see Dobyns (1976).

Although smallpox was not present on Hispaniola until the end of 1518, thereafter mortality from Old World diseases was universal and rapid in the New World when and where Europeans appeared, until some resistance was acquired by the seventeenth century and after. The swiftness of epidemic death, often occurring decades and even centuries before the first estimates and counts of populations, particularly confounds our efforts to determine

5. "The invasion of New World populations by Old World pathogens constituted one of the world's greatest biological cataclysms" (Dobyns, 1976: 22). Crosby (1972: Ch. 2), among others, suggests that the European introduction of new diseases, causing massive native mortality, was a major reason why the Europeans conquered the Americas so easily.

6. For example, over 1,000 Tapirape Indians were reduced to 147 between 1890 and 1939 mainly by smallpox, influenza, and yellow fever (Wagley, 1940). A group of Sabané Nambicuara were reduced from 300 to 21 between 1931 and 1938, mainly by an epidemic of pneumonia (Dobyns, 1966: 409–10).

7. Earlier, general studies include Stearn and Stearn (1945) and Ashburn (1947).

8. A post-Columbian introduction of malaria to the New World is disputed by some scholars. For a recent argument in support of a late arrival and a discussion of the problem, see Wood (1975); also Dunn (1965).

9. See "The Early History of Syphilis: A Reappraisal" in Crosby (1972: 122–64).

original numbers. Depopulation from disease even preceded the arrival of Europeans in some areas, as has been claimed for Peru (Dobyns, 1963b) and as probably occurred in much of the interior of Amazonia and North America. The literature on the introduction and impact of diseases is considerable.[10]

It must be emphasized, however, as is done by Shea (Chapter 5 here) and especially by Friede (1967), that epidemics did not have a uniform impact within a region, depending on settlement pattern, degree of isolation, population density, climatic conditions, and other factors. Borah and Cook (1969) found a significant variation in Mexico between altitude and rate of population decline, and they have more recently suggested a similar pattern in Colombia (Cook and Borah, 1971–74: 1:411–29). The same seems to have been true in Peru (C. T. Smith, 1970).

The contribution of nondisease factors to demographic decline is treated in Kubler (1942: 633–39), Radell (Chapter 3 here), Sauer (1966: 202–4), Unrau (1973), and Sánchez-Albornoz (1974: 51–60). These factors included military action (between Europeans and Indians, Indians allied with Europeans against Indians, and tribe against tribe), mistreatment (torture, overwork under forced labor-especially in the mines, and massacre), starvation [11] or malnutrition from breakdown of subsistence systems, loss of will to live or reproduce (suicide, infanticide, abortion, lowered vitality), and slave shipments to other lands. Keen (1971: 353), among others, sees a recent "tendency to accept uncritically a fatalistic 'epidemic-plus-lack of acquired immunity' explanation for the massive decline of Indian populations, without sufficient attention to the socioeconomic factors . . . which predisposed the natives to succumb to even slight infections." For Hispaniola, and presumably elsewhere, Cook and Borah (1971–74: 1:409) "agree that disruption of native society and the introduction of new, unusual, and harsh systems of exploitation undoubtedly had a severe effect," in addition to the effect of disease.

10. For example: Aschmann (1959: 186–89), S. F. Cook (various, including 1937, 1939, 1946b, 1955a, 1973a), Dobyns (1962, 1963b, 1966: 410–12), Duffy (1951), Friede (1967), Kubler (1942: 630–33), McBryde (1940), Sánchez-Albornoz (1974: 60–64), Sauer (1935: 11–13; 1966: 204), Shea (Chapter 5 in this volume), Simmons (1966), and J. E. Thompson (1970: 52–54). For studies of disease in tropical South American tribes, see Neel (1971) and relevant articles in PAHO (1968). For bibliographies and information on health and disease of North American Indians, see Barrow et al. (1972); also Dobyns (1976) and Jarcho (1964).

11. Las Casas (1957–58: 5: 146) stressed that starvation in Nicaragua occurred because the Indians were not able to plant crops and the Spaniards took the available maize for themselves, probably a common occurrence in the early decades throughout the New World. A documented study of White-induced famine leading to extinction in North America is that of the Kalapuya by Ratliff (1973).

A reason for decline not usually considered is the reduction of the population of some cultural groups to a level at which traditional marriage pools were inadequate to provide eligible mates. This has been significant among the Cahuilla in California (Harvey, 1967) and the Tapirape in Brazil (Wagley, 1951). The decline of North American Indians in the nineteenth century, even though by then a certain degree of disease resistance had been acquired, is well known. See, for example, "The Destruction of the California Indian," by S. F. Cook (1968: see also 1970).

Despite the disagreement about the size of the New World Indian population, there is little doubt about the massive and rapid drop in that population in the sixteenth century.[12] The discovery of America was followed by possibly the greatest demographic disaster in the history of the world. And unlike past population crises in Europe[13] and Asia from epidemics, wars, and climate, where full recovery did occur, the Indian population of America recovered only slowly, partially, and in highly modified form. In 1650, the native population numbered only about 4,000,000 south of the United States (Dobyns, 1966: 415). It has subsequently increased greatly in some regions and for some groups. The total "recent" Indian population, considered racially, not culturally, of Latin America is estimated at about 18,000,000 by Salzano (1968: 60–61). The Indian population of the United States, as determined by the 1970 census, was 792,730 (United States, 1972: 293), but is probably around 1,000,000 according to Jacobs (1973: 47). Despite recent population increases, most Indian cultures have become extinct or nearly so. Many of those groups that have survived remain threatened with extinction for much the same reasons as in the sixteenth century: disease, inhumanity, misguided "salvation," and racial and cultural mixing to the point of non-recognition.[14]

METHODOLOGICAL SYNTHESIS

Given the incomplete, inaccurate, or nonexistent documentary evidence for the many aboriginal groups in the Americas at the time of European arrival

12. One dissenting voice is that of Petersen (1975: 241, 235–36), who suggests that much of the presumed decline of Indian populations actually reflects migration and an absorption into racial mixture.

13. See the discussion by M. J. MacLeod (1973: 1–20) of the Black Death in Europe, including a comparison of the impact of epidemics in Europe and the New World.

14. For recent surveys of current Indian numbers and situations in South America, see Dostal (1972).

starting in 1492, how may the size of populations at least be approximated?[15] A wide variety of methods are available and have been utilized with varying degrees of success. These are discussed in detail by their practitioners and by their detractors. Some degree of overview is provided particularly by Dobyns (1966) and by Borah (1970). A brief synthesis follows.

The basic and most direct evidence of numbers is documentary. This can be evaluated and adjusted as judged appropriate, and it can be analyzed statistically to obtain projections for larger areas, other groups, or other dates. In addition, there are indirect forms of evidence which can be used to help corroborate documentary numerical evaluation and projections thereof.

Documentary Evidence

The direct written evidence on population numbers consists of (a) estimates by Europeans, both contemporary and in later memoirs, of regions, tribes, number of settlements, settlement size, warriors, adult males, persons in other categories, size of migrations, slave exports, degree of mortality; (b) counts by Europeans, including censuses (usually for taxation) and church or mission records (converts, baptism, etc.); and (c) native estimates and counts, both contemporary and recollected, of tribes, warriors, families, or tributaries.

Whether taking original figures at face value or adjusting them, the modern scholar is on shaky ground. The earlier the figure, the larger the region it pertains to, and the more it is an estimate than a count, then the less confidence there tends to be in it. (In contrast, however, we tend to have excessive faith in modern censuses.) The usual procedure, then, is to modify the original figures accordingly, giving particular attention to evaluating source reliability, adding for unknowns, and giving consideration to available corroborative evidence. The result may not be too wide of the mark depending on the data and depending on one's assumptions. The expression "dead reckoning" sometimes applied to this procedure (Dobyns, 1966: 401) seems appropriate.

The low figures arrived at by Mooney, Kroeber, Rosenblat, and Steward can be attributed not to their basic sources but to their assumptions that early estimates were invariably exaggerated and must therefore be shaved, that relatively little decline occurred before the availability of counts and good estimates, and that the first counts and estimates apply to the full areas or groups concerned. Indirect evidence suggesting higher figures is often simply discounted or ignored. Examples are numerous, and the reader is referred to Dobyns (1966) and the various essays in this collection.

15. For a general discussion of the problems and methods of estimating population, see Grauman (1959).

In contrast to the foregoing "subtractive method" is the "additive method" (Dobyns, 1966: 408), which has resulted in substantially higher figures. Adjustments of original figures are still made to a large degree by "dead reckoning," that is, a scholar's best judgment, but under a different set of assumptions. Numbers are added for Indians known or estimated to have died prior to the dated population, to have moved out of the area under consideration, and to have not been included in the recorded population. Aschmann (1959: 145–80), for example, does this for Baja California.

Projection Methods

Regardless of whether a contemporary figure is accepted at face value or subjected to either subtraction or addition, most of the data available for the period of initial contact are very incomplete.[16] They tend to become progressively more complete, as well as more reliable, with time. Consequently, to estimate contact populations, projections both spatial and backward in time are necessary, and a variety of extrapolation or projection techniques are employed in many of the recent calculations. Basic assumptions are that there was a decline dating from contact times and that there was a degree of uniformity in population density within areas of similar culture and environment. The resulting figures are usually very high, and these methods are as much or more subject to criticism as are other methods.

Area projection. If population is known for a portion of a region and other evidence indicates that the rest of the region had a similar density, then a projection can reasonably be made. Likewise, if the ratio of change between two dates is known for a portion of a region, then the same ratio can be applied to the rest of the region, other conditions being similar. These are major techniques of Borah and Cook in utilizing incomplete tribute records for Mexico.

Depopulation rates ("bichronic ratios"). Given reliable counts for the sections of a region at one point in time and reliable counts for some sections at an earlier date, a rate of population change can be derived and applied to all sections. Dobyns (1966) worked with regional depopulation ratios from original contact to population nadir to arrive at an average rate of decline for

16. Borah (1970: 179) usefully applies the concept of "protohistoric populations" to this situation: "Protohistoric populations in America may be defined as those Indian groups which underwent change though European influences that reached them through other Indian tribes or through perhaps unrecorded, perhaps fairly infrequent European landings, incursions, and explorations." What happened to the native population during this period is, of course, at the core of the problem of determining the original population.

the entire hemisphere. Also, given a known rate of depopulation between two dates, that rate can be projected backward to earlier dates. Cook and Borah (1957: 466), for example, obtained a population of 25,300,000 for central Mexico in 1519 by projecting back the depopulation rate for a period with only nonepidemic disease, the years 1550 to 1570. However, rates of change also changed. If data for three or more dates are available, then changes in the rate of change can be calculated. Coefficients of change are discussed in "An Essay on Method" by Cook and Borah (1971–74: 1:73–118).

Given their own population calculations for six dates (1605, 1595, 1580, 1568, 1548, and 1542), Borah and Cook (1963: 4) used different types of curves to extrapolate 1519 populations for central Mexico of 32,000,000, 40,000,000, and 50,000,000, and later (Cook and Borah, 1971–74: 1:115) 27,650,000 or 27,615,000. They emphasize, however, the need for more regional studies to uncover erratic fluctuations not revealed in curves for larger areas and countries.

Projection of counts of portions of a population. Much of the best statistical data consists of counts or calculations of warriors, adult males, heads of households, or, more frequently, tribute payers consisting of males between certain ages. Hence to project a total population it is necessary to calculate the number of people each such person represents. The average arrived at is obviously critical. Borah and Cook (1963: 67) used 4.5 persons for the average family size in 1519 in central Mexico, but others would accept a somewhat higher or lower figure. And an average derived for one region is not necessarily applicable to another.

Conversion of tribute amounts to population. Much of the data for central Mexico consists of Spanish tribute assessments, for which the quotas per tributary, making possible a determination of the number of tributaries, may or may not be known. The treatment of this material is discussed by Cook and Borah in their 1960 monograph. For calculating the pre-Conquest (1519) population, all that is available are pictographic summaries of the tribute records of the Triple Alliance of Tenochtitlán, Texcoco, and Tacuba (Borah and Cook, 1963). Average quotas of different materials per tributary family had to be determined, along with relative value of the commodities, frequency of payment, average family size, exempt populations, and adjustments for areas outside the imperial tribute system. Decisions about these matters are subject to judgment, and variations in them significantly alter the population totals derived.

Age-sex pyramids. If the age-sex structure of a population is known for a date not too long after initial contact, then anomalous age groups can be indicative of intervening demographic events and even earlier population numbers, as is demonstrated for Peru by C. T. Smith (1970).

Basically, then, projection methods must be used to convert portions of populations into full populations. Criticism of these methods comes easy, but it should be kept in mind that similar methods of sampling are used today, without challenge, by the United Nations to derive populations for the less developed countries. And even sophisticated census organizations in the Western nations, including the United States Bureau of the Census, use surprisingly small and not always valid samples for interim estimates and other purposes.

Corroborative Evidence

There are several forms of nondocumentary demographic evidence that, while not capable of precision, are indicators of relative population and thus are very useful for corroborating documentary and projection methods. These are discussed in some detail by Borah (1970). Some of the problems in using these techniques are mentioned by Petersen (1975).

Social structure. There has been increased emphasis in recent years on the general relation of population density to social complexity and level of cultural evolution (Carneiro, 1967; Harner, 1970). The more advanced societies invariably have relatively dense and large populations. The converse is not always true, however, as witness the substantial California Indian populations of hunters, gatherers, and fishermen and the dense aboriginal populations of intensive horticulturalists in highland New Guinea.

Archaeology. Indicators of population that survive in the archaeological record include number of houses (Haviland, 1969), settlement size and dwelling space utilized,[17] structure size and complexity in terms of labor required, quantity of artifacts such as pottery residues (S. F. Cook, 1972b), remains of wild and domesticated plants and animals, and soil chemical changes.[18]

Food production. Documentary or archaeological evidence is often indicative of size of fields, number of fields, area under cultivation, yields per unit of cultivated land, and amount of food in storage or paid in tribute or produced in a region. All such evidence can provide clues to population.

17. The considerable literature on this technique includes Cook and Treganza (1950), Naroll (1962), Cook and Heizer (1965a; 1968), MacNeish (1970), and Plog (1975).

18. See Cook and Heizer (1965b), Eidt (1973), Eidt and Woods (1974).

Intensive agriculture and relic fields. As argued by Boserup (1966) and others, agriculture generally becomes more intensive, in terms of frequency of cultivation, as population density increases. Hence, documentary, archaeological, and aerial photographic evidence of forms of intensive agriculture such as irrigation canals, terraces, raised fields, and sunken gardens is evidence of populations sufficiently dense not to be supported by more extensive forms of land use such as hunting and gathering or shifting cultivation. There is considerable evidence of former intensive agriculture in the form of remnants of millions of agricultural fields. Such relic fields can be measured and converted into rough populations (e.g., Denevan, 1970b; B. L. Turner II, 1976). Dating is difficult, however, and it cannot be certain if all the fields in an area were used simultaneously.

Carrying capacity. Knowing environmental conditions and the subsistence technology employed, it is theoretically possible to calculate the number of people a region could support (Allan, 1965; Carneiro, 1960; Zubrow, 1975). This is an imprecise index, however, since both the environment and the technology are readily subject to change, but it is nevertheless useful as an indicator of relative potential population. Careful evaluation of carrying capacity may well show that claims that the technology-environment systems of certain areas could not support large populations are unwarranted. Variations of this approach occur in Denevan (Chapter 7 of this volume, Baumhoff (1963), and H. P. Thompson (1966).

Environmental modification. Drastic modifications of vegetation, soil, and hydrology may be indicators of prolonged and intensive human occupation. See, for example, S. F. Cook (1949a, 1949b, 1963), Johannessen (1963), Denevan (1961), and Sternberg (1975: 32-33).

Skeletal counts. In some rare situations, it is possible to calculate village sizes from analysis of skeletal remains in cemeteries (Howells, 1960; Ubelaker, 1974).

In summary, the best information for estimating aboriginal populations consists of actual counts of portions of total populations. Mathematical techniques can be applied to convert such data into total populations or to project estimates of earlier populations. We can expect historians to uncover or reexamine more numerical material in the future and to apply more rigorous analysis to such material. The resulting estimates can be corroborated to varying degrees by a wide variety of nondocumentary techniques, and such techniques can provide an indication of relative populations where historical records are absent.

CHAPTER 1 **The Historical Demography of Aboriginal and Colonial America: An Attempt at Perspective**

Woodrow Borah

The debate over the size of human populations in pre-Columbian America and the changes in them during the centuries of European domination has long been characterized by wide differences of opinion and much fervor. In recent decades the debate continues, if anything with greater participation and, one suspects, with no diminution of emotion. One can distinguish within it a series of questions: What have been the numbers of people in America from the arrival of the Europeans to the beginning of the nineteenth century— that is, during the colonial period? What is happening and has been happening in the present day to the Indians as a distinct group in terms of numbers? Although none of these questions can be declared of easy answer, the last, with its needs for an exceptionally elusive clear definition and its involvement in problems of cultural assimilation and passing from one group to another, may turn out to be the least soluble.[1] Involved also in the debate are differences over method, evidence, and basic philosophy that have much to do with the positions taken.

Previously unpublished paper presented at the 37th International Congress of American-ists, Mar del Plata, Argentina, September, 1966. A few minor changes have been made in the original paper by the author and editor, and the author has added a short addendum.

1. See the discussions, for example, in Steward and Faron (1959: 456–58) and in Rosenblat (1954: 1:17–35, 137–70).

At this point, it may be well to borrow from the millennial wisdom of rhetoric and examine the discussion as a whole in an attempt to get perspective on it. The reader may recognize that I am having recourse to the categories of formulation customary in debating briefs: the history of the question, the major points at issue, the kinds of evidence available for decision, and the extent to which and terms in which answers are possible.

The basis for dispute was furnished initially in the first years of European penetration and conquest as the Europeans reported dense populations for many areas. Las Casas, for example, in an estimate which has become famous or notorious, reported that a count of the area of Hispaniola under Spanish control in 1496 showed approximately 1,000,000 Indians; by adjustment for areas not under Spanish control and with due attention to comparative density, he arrived at a total figure of more than 3,000,000.[2] Gonzalo Fernández de Oviedo (1959: 3:353) estimated the aboriginal population of Castilla del Oro (Panama) and southern Central America at 2,000,000. Even though Bernal Díaz del Castillo (1960: 1:79) objected scornfully to the reports of numbers by López de Gómara, especially of warriors opposing the Spaniards, his own reporting on the province of Soconusco (now southwest Mexico) gave a population of 15,000 *vecinos* in 1525, which, he stated, by 1568 had shrunk to fewer than 1,200 (Díaz del Castillo, 1960: 2:402).

In its present forms the debate really began to take shape in the eighteenth century with the beginnings of critical history. Writers at that time examined early testimony and evidence of all kinds, testing by comparison with what they knew of Indian culture and social structure, in an attempt to arrive at some determination of probability.[3] The two positions that emerged are exemplified in the comments of Clavijero and of William Robertson, the Mexican Jesuit accepting an estimate of 30,000,000 for pre-Conquest Mexico, the Scottish writer scornfully declaring that the Spanish had found sparse settlements of barbarians which, in their surprise at seeing even modest structures, they turned into populous, civilized realms with great stone temples and palaces.[4] The conquerors were also led to hyperbole, wrote Robertson, by desire to enhance the reports of their services to their king.

There is little need to trace the controversy through the multitude of estimates and the long discussions since the middle decades of the eighteenth century.[5] An indication of a few of the estimates in our own century should suffice. Some of the better-known higher estimates of pre-Conquest aborigi-

---

2. Las Casas (1957–58: 2:51–52). Las Casas here gives the basis for his estimate.
3. See the discussion in Rosenblat (1954: 1:99–101, 283).
4. Robertson (1777: 2:293–302, 409–50, 459–61, 483–86); Clavijero (1964: 2: 561–70). The latter essay has a long review of evidence and discussion down to the middle of the eighteenth century.
5. References are spread through the pages of Rosenblat (1954: Vol. 1).

nal population by scholars earlier in the century were made by Spinden, Means, and Rivet. Spinden (1928: 660) greatly influenced by his knowledge of the Mayan area, estimated 40,000,000 to 50,000,000 Indians for America in 1492 and 50,000,000 to 75,000,000 around the year 1200 of our era. Rivet (1924: 12:601) arrived at a similar estimate of 40,000,000 to 50,000,000 Indians for America in 1492. Means (1931: 296) estimated the population of the Incan empire alone at 16,000,000 to 32,000,000. The most impressive and careful statement was by the famous German scholar Karl Sapper (1924: 95–104). On the basis of technology, resources, and comparative examination of extent and densities of human occupation, he estimated 37,000,000 to 48,500,000, or about 40,000,000 to 50,000,000 Indians for approximately 1492, of whom 12,000,000 to 15,000,000 were in Mexico, an equal number in the Andean area, and 5,000,000 to 6,000,000 in Central America. These scholars, it should be noted, were all specialists of what one might call the areas of high culture.

Contradiction of these estimates came quickly from a group which derived much of its initial inspiration from studies of America north of the Rio Grande, admittedly an area of considerably lower density of population and of what one might call lower culture. James Mooney prepared a series of careful estimates of aboriginal population north of the Rio Grande, tribe by tribe, which added up to a total pre-Conquest population of 1,150,000. His figures were published posthumously in 1928. In 1931 the famous anthropologist A. L. Kroeber adjusted Mooney's estimates by reducing the calculation for California in accordance with his own studies, with a result of 1,020,000 for America north of the Rio Grande. Considering even this estimate too high, he then reduced the figure to 900,000. Admitting candidly that he knew little of America south of the Rio Grande, Kroeber then used rough calculations of density of settlement to arrive at calculations for the various regions. His total for the population of America about A.D. 1500 was 8,400,000, with Mesoamerica and the Incan empire each having approximately 3,000,000. In a thoughtful discussion, Kroeber pointed out that there was little evidence for any decision in the matter, that accordingly he had chosen deliberately low estimates, and he declared that only careful regional studies would give better answers. He recognized that Carl Sauer's study of the Indian populations of northwest Mexico offered another approach and posed a serious challenge to his own low figures (Kroeber, 1939: 131–81, esp. 166, 177–81).

Kroeber's monograph was not published until 1939.* In 1935 Ángel Rosenblat published a study of the aboriginal population of the New World from

*Editor's note: A summary of the population section was published as an article by Kroeber in 1934.

1492 to 1930 which was then the most detailed review of the discussion of varying estimates. His estimate for all of America in 1492 is 13,385,000. When this figure is placed against his estimates for later periods, it is clear that Rosenblat's calculations discount the reports of massive decreases except for the West Indies, and that, in general, he would attribute the decline in aboriginal population to racial mixture and assimilation. The contribution of Rosenblat, even more than his estimates, was a review of the discussion and much of the material then known to exist. Two further editions of the work in 1945 and 1954 and a commentary in 1967 have held to the original calculations but have incorporated much of the new material published.[6] Because of its relative comprehensiveness and convenience, the monograph of Rosenblat is probably that most consulted by people wishing information on estimates of aboriginal population.

The lower estimates characterize the *Handbook of South American Indians,* although there are considerable differences between John Rowe and George Kubler for the Andean area. Julian Steward used the lower figure advanced by Kubler in his calculations of the pre-Conquest Indian population of South America to arrive at 9,129,000 for that continent and a total of 15,590,000 for America.[7] The more recent text by Steward and Faron (1959: 334–40) repeats the same estimates for South America, Central America, and the Antilles.

The impact of these far lower estimates may be seen in revisions by Sapper in 1935 (published in 1948) and Rivet in 1952. Sapper discarded all attempts at an estimate for the temperate areas of North and South America and carefully reexamined his original calculations for tropical America. His estimate of 31,000,000 for the hemisphere meant a shaving down for most regions and a drastic reduction in his figure for the West Indies.[8] Rivet (1952: 2:946) frankly accepted a low total for the hemisphere of 15,500,000.

Meanwhile other scholars, including an especially active group which got much of its stimulus from Carl Sauer (1935, 1948), were accepting Kroeber's challenge for careful, detailed local studies. Most of the work of these scholars has centered on parts of Mesoamerica and has utilized tribute and missionary counts, which increasingly have been brought to light.[9] Such work

6. Rosenblat (1954: 1: esp. 9, 102, 105, and 122–24). The table on p. 122 and the graphs on p. 123 are especially important for Rosenblat's position on movement of population and racial components within such movement.

7. Steward (1946–59). The estimates of the contributors are the basis for the calculations of Steward (1949: 655–68). Differing estimates in the *Handbook* are by Rowe (1946: 184–85) and Kubler (1946: 334–40).

8. Sapper (1948). Because of the Spanish Civil War, publication was delayed from 1935 until 1948.

9. Much of the work has been published in two series of the University of California Press: Ibero-Americana, and Publications in Geography.

was foreshadowed by Camavitto (1935: 218–43, esp. 242) and Miguel Othón de Mendizábal (1946–47: 3:309–35). The now well-known study by Sherburne F. Cook and Lesley Byrd Simpson (1948) estimated the pre-Conquest population of central Mexico alone at approximately 11,000,000 and made a series of estimates for post-Conquest population in various years. Their calculations indicated a decline by the mid-seventeenth century to a low of 1,500,000 total population and subsequent recovery by the end of the eighteenth century to a total population of 5,200,000, which then included a substantial number of non-Indians and mixed-bloods. Cook's (1949a, 1949b) notable studies on the Teotlalpan and on the evidence for prolonged and serious soil erosion in central Mexico brought new supporting evidence for the existence of large populations. Other works on Lower and Upper California[10] also yielded higher estimates than Kroeber's. One interesting monograph by Simpson (1952) gave evidence for massive replacement of man by domesticated animals as a result of rapid depopulation during the sixteenth century in Mexico. Since 1957 a series of new studies by Cook and myself have reexamined even larger masses of tribute material, with very careful attention to the contemporary rules of assessment. We have derived even larger estimates for the pre-Conquest population of central Mexico—of the order of 25,200,000.[11] On the basis of our own and similar work, I have made an admittedly hasty and general estimate extending similar proportions to America, and have suggested that we might well find in the end that the population was upwards of 100,000,000 (Borah, 1964; also 1962b). Henry Dobyns, applying a proportion of decline to a residuum averaging 2 percent for populations that did survive, has recently come to an estimate for America of perhaps 90,000,000 to 112,000,000.[12]

It is clear that the controversy over the size of the pre-Conquest population continues unabated. The dispute extends automatically to the course of population movement in the colonial period and to the question of what has happened to the Indians from 1492 to the present.[13] We may group the various opinions into a number of camps. There is first a major division into those who find that there was a substantial decrease in Indian population after the coming of the Europeans and those who deny such a massive

10. On Lower California: Meigs (1935: 133–42), S. F. Cook (1937: 14 et passim), Aschmann (1959); on Upper California: S. F. Cook (1964).

11. Cook and Borah (1957; 1960); Borah and Cook (1960; 1962; 1963). The 1962 item is a Spanish version of a paper delivered at the 11th International Congress of the Historical Sciences, Stockholm, 1960. It summarizes work done to 1960.

12. Dobyns (1966). Dobyn's paper gives a careful and very thoughtful review of past work, the techniques of estimate employed, and the problem of the state of each Indian population at the date of earliest report.

13. This may be seen from the discussion in Rosenblat (1954: 1).

decrease as a general phenomenon. Kroeber (1939: 160) and Rosenblat (1954: 1: esp. 122–23), for example, belong to those who deny massive and general depopulation. So, too, would Bailey Diffie (1945: 178–89, 446–47) with his declaration that the "idea of a great decline was postulated on an allegedly enormous pre-Conquest population which never existed." Within the perhaps majority group of those who accept substantial or massive decline, there is a further division into those who postulate relatively small and those who postulate relatively large pre-Conquest populations. Here there is really a range from Steward (1949) and Kubler (1946: 334–40; 1942) through John Rowe (1946: 184–85) to the much larger estimates of Sauer, Simpson, Cook, Dobyns, myself, and others.

It is also clear that the disagreements are much greater on the size of pre-Conquest populations, and that for the size of populations in America after the close of the sixteenth century and for the movement of populations since then there is less disagreement. For Mexico, for example, almost all scholars accept an estimate fairly near that of Humboldt for the end of the colonial period, but disagree on the rate and direction of change in the seventeenth century.

Clearly any such range of disagreement as I have indicated involves many issues and highly variant assessments of evidence. Let me list the more important issues, as I see them, and then point to the differences over evidence. I must warn, however, that there is a complex series of assessments by scholars rather than a simple polarization into two camps. People arriving at the same conclusions on population may give different answers on some of the issues.

1. The nature of pre-Columbian Indian society. Involved in the disagreements are questions of the complexity of social structure, extent of social stratification, division of labor, and the extent and manner of production of a surplus from primary production. The range of opinion runs from those who would see merely more elaborate chiefdoms in Mesoamerica and the Andes to those who see highly complex social structures. Robertson (1777) in the eighteenth century and Bandelier (1879) in the nineteenth century would lie at one extreme; Kroeber and Steward are in an intermediate position that would accept elaborate social structures and, therefore, substantial surplus of primary production for the areas of advanced culture. Cook, Simpson, and I would agree with Prescott (1936) on the existence of highly complex societies having at their disposal a huge surplus from the small surpluses created individually by a horde of peasant families (Cook and Borah, 1963). For Mexico and Peru, the picture would not be too dissimilar to pharaonic Egypt. Another form of the debate on this set of issues, for Mesoamerica at least, is the question whether or not the Indians had true urban centers, except admittedly for a few such as Tenochtitlán, or whether the towns were mere

ceremonial centers of such low concentration of civic and intellectual inter-change that they could not fulfill the same functions as the urban centers of the ancient eastern Mediterranean. The extremes would be Ronald Spores, who denies the extensive existence of urban centers,[14] and Alfonso Caso (1964), who finds urban centers widespread and points to the existence of large-scale territorial units of some kind worthy of the name of empires even for Teotihuacán and the culture of La Venta. At issue here, *inter alia,* are matters of density of human occupation, for the densities postulated by upholders of low estimates would not maintain elaborate social structures.

2. Interpretations of history. Here we deal with an especially complex series of disagreements over interpretations of the world, past and present.

a. The idea of progress. The idea that the present is superior to the past has an interesting corollary that earlier periods of time must have had smaller populations than later ones, especially if the earlier population postulated would be nearly equal to or larger than a present-day one. The opposing view is likely to emphasize fluctuations and even cycles.[15]

b. The European conscience. The decades through which we have lived have been the period of the relinquishment of much of direct European political control over other parts of the globe and the reassertion of old native sovereignties or the emergence of new ones searching for ties to traditions antedating the European dominance. Liberation, a consciousness of past exploitation for the profit of the imperial country, and the need for achieving a viable Europeanized and economically developed structure lead to a series of views that strongly influence interpretations.[16] The general category may be broken into a number of elements which overlap considerably.

(1) Reparation for historical and material wrongs to native peoples. The destruction of a large native population and highly organized native political and social structures is held to mean greater European guilt because of conquest and domination; conversely, the existence of a smaller native population which underwent less loss or none at all, and the existence of more primitive social and political structures are held to diminish European guilt.[17] In Marxist terms the issue may be stated as determination of the

14. Spores (1964: 6–9, 65–66, 124–31). That this view is not unique may be seen from Coe (1961).

15. The objection to larger populations in earlier periods relative to later ones shows up repeatedly in private and semipublic discussion, and tends to be associated with relative lack of concern with present uses of land. The opposing group tends to be concerned with problems of destructive use of resources and excessive population. Simpson was chided by Cline (1962: 263–64) for his neo-Malthusian views.

16. See the discussion by Konetzke (1963: 7–11).

17. In this connection see the remarkable essay by Lewis and Maes (1945: esp. 115–18); also Gamio (1942).

extent of capitalist damage to innocent native peoples.[18] The Marxist statement is especially useful for countries such as the Soviet Union since the fires
of revolution have purged the guilt incurred through similar treatment of
native peoples (although not American ones) by preceding regimes.

(2) *Indigenismo* and the search for a non-European basis of national
origin and identification. This subcategory is really self-explanatory. It oper-
ates in some countries of America but not those in which there has been
massive implantation of new populations. Attitudes will function as in subcategory (1) above.

(3) Exaltation of the European. The countercurrent to categories (1)
and (2) is an emphasis upon the European contribution to former possessions
and depreciation or lesser emphasis upon previous native society and its
contributions to the new national state (Cuevas, 1946–47: 1). For Spain the
discussion rapidly touches upon the *Leyenda negra* and the opposed *Leyenda
blanca.* An especially interesting and intricate series of attitudes are manifest
in the devotees of Las Casas, who tend to emphasize the Spanish conscience
and humanitarian impulses, with Las Casas as a principal figure, but are
usually not prepared to accept the large aboriginal populations and their
brutal destruction as reported by Las Casas himself.[19]

3. Evidence and treatment. With this category we come to the most
obvious series of disagreements, those which concern what is evidence, the
extent to which it is trustworthy, what are the appropriate methods of
treatment, and the extent of reliability of results.

a. The reliability of contemporary reports and other contemporary
indications and their analysis. For the areas of Spanish penetration especially,
the earliest reports and other forms of evidence such as statements on tribute
assessments and delivery tend to give very large populations indeed and
indicate shattering decline in the first decades of European domination.
Many, if not most, scholars have tended to discount such figures or arbitrarily
revise them sharply downward to an extent that constitutes repudiation;
many have substituted a new figure derived through tribal analogy with the
North America of the eighteenth and nineteenth centuries or a figure given as
suitably low without much explanation. Kroeber, with his customary percep-
tion, summarized the problem well for the opposing points of view.[20] On the
one hand:

> Whoever uses Spanish figures seems almost always to reach higher
> populations than modern ethnologists. The kernel of the problem lies here.

18. See Markuzon (1957); Al'perovich (1964: 54, 58, 60–61, 71–72).
19. Much of the recent literature is reviewed in Hanke (1964). See further the two
classic works on the Black Legend: Juderías Loyot (1917) and Carbia (1943).
20. Kroeber (1939: 179–80). See also the discussion in Rosenblat (1954: 1) and the
very interesting review in Dobyns (1966).

Shall we pin more faith on contemporary Spanish opinions, or on those of professional ethnologists who often have not seen an Indian of the tribes they deal with?

On the other hand, continued Kroeber, most ethnologists rely upon certain assumptions:

1. The vast majority of figures by contemporaries are too large. This fact will be generally admitted. The problem is to know when the exaggeration is slight and when it is unreasonable. In general, documentarians tend to cling to the more moderate figures given in the records, ethnologists to distrust them generically. Where Sauer shaves sixteenth- and seventeenth-century statements, I am likely to reject most of them outright.
2. Competent ethnologists with interest in concrete fact are able to correct the statements of contemporaries which relate to population size. This assumption may or may not be true, but is evidently made by American anthropologists who have concerned themselves with the subject. The basis of the assumption is not clear. It may be little more than professional distrust of lay opinion. But again, this may be sound.

Of a piece with the attitude of ethnologists as defined by Kroeber are two more rules of thumb of considerable currency today, namely, first that all European explorers on coming into contact with other peoples overestimated their number, usually by substantial margins,[21] and second, that since sixteenth- and seventeenth-century Europeans were characterized by a relative lack of statistical sophistication they could not count large numbers or handle fairly complex governmental administration and finance with reasonable accuracy (Mauro, 1961: 8). What is under debate here is not merely the reliability of statements of number but also that of the testimony to be derived by analysis of tribute counts and assessments, censuses and *padrones,* and church and other registers of vital statistics.

b. The validity of calculations by present-day scholars who discard contemporary evidence or rely on evidence of such date that there may well have been massive alteration of the aboriginal population. The first part of this subcategory has been discussed above. The second concerns the weight to be given to reports of Indian populations of such date that either directly, or by transmission of disease and other factors through native channels of communication, the population may have suffered substantial change. The question may be restated concretely as: To what extent does a count or estimate of an Indian population in California in the mid-nineteenth century[22] or of that in Mojos in 1680[23] deal with pre-Conquest density

21. This point is made explicitly by Petersen (1961: esp. 337–38).
22. S. F. Cook (1955a; 1956: 111 et passim). See also the discussion in Dobyns (1966).
23. Steward (1949: 662). See the discussion in Denevan (1966b: 112–20).

undisturbed by European diseases, trade, and pressures generated by European penetration of other areas?[24] Much of Mooney's work on North America and Kroeber's on California is at stake in this question.

c. The value of estimates derived by studies of occupation and land use.[25] A still-continuing series of attempts at solution has been based upon studies of technology, resources, and archaeological evidence of occupation. The studies are not simple and rest upon development of a set of techniques that is just under way. The range is from such work as Sapper's to the studies of production and output for Yucatán and the Tabasco coast. It includes the new work on alteration of complexes of biota and successions of complexes, especially of plants, by biogeographers. All of such work involves questions of operation of factors and validity of results. The discussion has proceeded with less heat and more attention to solving problems.

Thus far I have examined categories of disagreement, or issues, as I would assess them. Are there categories of agreement? There is certainly agreement that the entire series of questions is complex and that for the entire hemisphere we are far from reaching full possession of the data and command of the techniques necessary for solutions. Yet the situation is far from hopeless. Let me turn now to an exploration of the possibilities of eventual solution. I shall do so in terms of kinds of evidence and their treatment and of the extent to which answers are possible.

Let me comment initially that certain methodological considerations seem inevitable. Detailed regional analysis is obviously better than hemispheric generalization in advance of such analysis. In the end, such analysis is the only way to arrive at a solution. The presentation of a statement for a tribe or a relatively small region, without rigorous examination of date, circumstance in which the statement was made, and the relation of date to direct and indirect European influence, however, does not constitute analysis. We must take into account the possibility of massive alteration of populations once Europeans appeared upon the scene, even if only as traders or casual explorers, and also the possibility that epidemics, territorial pressures, and changes in technology set loose by the Europeans traveled far in advance of

24. See the general discussion of these aspects in Dobyns (1966). The reorganization of Indian life in the tribes of the Great Plains through introduction of firearms and of horses secured by interchange among the Indians themselves after an initial European importation into New Mexico may be cited further (Secoy, 1953).

25. Much of the literature is summarized in two volumes of essays reviewing America, region by region: Willey (1956), and Jennings and Norbeck (1964). The first volume has a general bibliography; the second has much larger ones at the end of each essay. Additional and important material on the New World will be found in Heizer and Cook (1960). For the Lowland Maya region, which has been the focus of sustained work by more scholars, see Sanders (1962–63), which has a very useful bibliography at the end of the essay.

their actual presence.[26] These lines obviously apply to the dead-reckoning method of Kroeber and Steward. Furthermore, in all methods most scholars resort to comparative approaches. One such approach is to take a fix in time, whether in this century or in some other, and apply proportion. Dobyns has coined the term "bichronic method" for this. Its use seems inevitable since so much of our data is fragmentary and for the earliest periods not likely to become of complete coverage. Another comparative approach applies estimates or data on density of occupation for one region to another region. If technology, resources, and kind of occupation are similar, the method has validity. If they are not, it is questionable.[27] The most interesting application of this method is the good-neighbor policy in historical demography which accords approximately equal postulated populations for the sedentary Indians of Mexico and those of the Incan empire. There would seem to be some need for justification.

When we begin to examine evidence and appropriate methods of treatment, we find that there are really two major categories, often handled separately, but not mutually exclusive. At some future date they should corroborate and verify each other, especially for estimates of pre-Conquest population.

The first category of evidence consists of studies of resources, technology, settlement patterns, and social structure. The data cover such matters as soils, terrain, climate; the food available through gathering, hunting and fishing, presence or lack of domesticated animals, cultivation of plants known to have been used; techniques of cultivation, their yields and their consequences in erosion; patterns of human occupation in villages and towns; and finally the indications of social surplus or lack of it that one may derive by examination of classes of the population not directly engaged in primary production. The techniques of treatment are drawn from geography, the life sciences, and geology. Of late, chemical analysis has become increasingly important (Cook and Heizer, 1965b). An earlier instance of the use of this category of evidence

26. Thus the Atlantic coast of the United States was visited by explorers, fishermen, and traders long in advance of actual settlement. Robert Heizer has suggested (in oral discussion) an interesting system of classifying Indian cultures as prehistoric, proto-historic, and historic. Prehistoric would mean no possibility of European influence; historic, culture after substantial European contact; and protohistoric, an intermediate period in which European influence would reach the Indians through channels or by casual and very infrequent contact with Europeans.

27. The very real problems of maintenance of social structure in the low densities proposed by Kroeber (1939) for areas of high culture are partly masked by use of averages per hundred square kilometers. If the densities are brought to average per square kilometer or square mile, the difficulty becomes much clearer. See the discussion relative to the Old World in Steward and Faron (1959: 51–54).

is Karl Sapper's 1924 and 1935 (1948) estimates of population for America. Even under the pressure of the writings of Mooney, Kroeber, and Rosenblat, his examination of technology, density of population, and evidence of extent of occupation led him to cling to a revised estimate of 31,000,000 for tropical America. More recently the studies of production, soil exhaustion, and yield in Yucatán and Tabasco, some sponsored by the Carnegie Foundation and others carried on independently, have begun to supply the beginnings of a sound foundation for the Lowland Maya region.

This category of studies of human occupation has an obvious link to archaeology, which brings evidence on extent of fields and settlements, trade, and nature of religious and political structure. A good deal of evidence is being accumulated for the Andean region, the Amazon, and for Mesoamerica. One of the most interesting contributions is an essay by MacNeish (1964).

Another set of studies, which at first sight may not appear to fit within the category of studies of human occupation but really has within it extraordinary potential, is that of biogeographical analysis: evidence of changes in complexes of fauna and flora, and examination of plant and animal successions. Such studies are yielding us new knowledge on the activity of man and domesticated animals and in the end seem likely to yield a good deal of evidence on length and density of human occupation.[28]

All of these kinds of studies have a most promising potential but are also complex. They demand the application of techniques drawn from many fields of knowledge, and are likely to give fairly slow yield to general questions. To illustrate by merely one kind of difficulty, the determination of total number of households within an archaeological site leaves the further question how many were occupied at any one time. Similarly, data from one or even several sites leave unanswered the question of application to a region. It is impossible to excavate all Yucatán or enough of it to arrive at an answer at this time.

The second major category of evidence is documentary—contemporary testimony of all kinds that has come down to us in written records which may lie hidden in archives and libraries or which may have been brought to light and be known to scholars. This category is one of historical evidence and requires for proper study the application in full of very elaborate and exacting techniques of verification, painstaking reading, interpretation in the light of close knowledge of administrative systems and units of measurement used at the time, and of cross-comparison. They are the techniques that have been developed for the examination of historical materials over the centuries

28. Examples of studies of successions of biotic complexes are Richards (1952), Nye and Greenland (1960), Pacific Science Association (1958). For a brilliant application to America, see Johannessen (1963) on Honduras; also Denevan (1961) on Nicaragua, and Gordon (1957: 57–78) on Colombia.

from Lorenzo Valla, the Bollandists, and the school of Saint-Maur to the present.[29] To give an illustration, it simply will not do to continue to cite the estimate of population for Tenochtitlán given by the Anonymous Conqueror after the studies of Federico Gómez de Orozco have indicated that the work is a compilation prepared in Italy, probably by Alonso de Ulloa,[30] nor to continue to cite 60,000 inhabitants on the strength of the Anonymous Conqueror after critical comment that the statement is either misstatement or deliberate reduction from the usual one of 60,000 houses.[31] Similarly, in making estimates for Tenochtitlán, scholars will have to indicate whether their calculation covers Tenochtitlán alone or includes Tlaltelolco, in what after all were twin cities.[32]

For convenience in discussion, we may divide the historical materials into two subcategories: those giving evidence on populations at the time of European contact and some decades afterward (for much of Spanish America, say 1492–1600), and those on later centuries. For central Mexico, for example, there is a very real divide in nature of materials and the problems of treatment that falls in the years 1558–1560 (Cook and Borah, 1960: 5–32). For other regions, the divide may come in different years, but is likely to exist. For yet other regions, the divide may be between a later period for which there is documentary evidence and an earlier one for which there simply is none. However, our ignorance of the existence of records does not necessarily mean that there are none. For, despite a good deal of search and publication, the bulk of the documentary evidence remains to be unearthed.

For the study of populations in what one might call the first century of European contact, there is, at least for some regions, a bewildering variety of documentary evidence: accounts and estimates of eyewitnesses, records of

29. As embodied in such manuals as Bernheim (1903), Langlois and Seignobos (1898), and Samaran (1961).

30. Anonymous Conqueror (1961). See pp. 23–33, which contain Gómez de Orozco's revised study of the authorship of the account.

31. Anonymous Conqueror (1961: 61, note 57). The English translation by Saville (Anonymous Conqueror, 1917: 61) gives 70,000.

32. The very thoughtful study by Toussaint, Orozco, and Fernández (1938), based on examination of the "plano en papel de maguey" and sixteenth-century maps of Mexico City, arrived at an estimate of 60,000 for Tenochtitlán. Since the authors set the area of Tenochtitlán at 7.5 square kilometers, it is clear that they exclude Tlaltelolco, or half the urban area. The sixteenth-century maps, superimposed upon maps of present-day Mexico City, give an area for the twin cities of roughly 16 square kilometers. See especially pp. 50, 64–70, 71–74, 85–105, and maps. Incidentally, dwellings on the causeways and *chinampas* beyond the urban circuit as set for Mexico City would not be included within the 16 square kilometers.

For a most interesting critical examination of the bases of estimates of the population of the Incan empire, which applies techniques of historical verification, see Wedin (1965).

tribute levy and other administrative activity yielding direct and indirect evidence on number, missionary and church records of various kinds, and even records from native administration and recorded native tradition. In examining such material, what has been said about taking into account alteration through direct and indirect European influence must be borne in mind. One must also apply the normal techniques of verification and cross-checking that would be used for any historical work. Thus, in general, accounts of numbers in battle, especially if reported by combatants, tend to be unreliable. On the other hand, statements of numbers of warriors and workmen levied are much more likely to be accurate.

Our most important records for much of Spanish America are probably the remains of direct counts and of assessments for labor and tribute. These, nevertheless, present a series of difficulties which may be illustrated by the instance of central Mexico. There, for the earlier years, when tribute assessments and even population counts were not linked directly to a relatively uniform system of classification and ignored substantial parts of the population as exempt for varying reasons, the use of such materials requires careful analysis of kinds of statements and type of treatment necessary to arrive at a common and interchangeable form. We are plunged at once into the difficulties that beset the historical demographer studying Medieval and Renaissance populations in Europe: the basis for the count or assessment, exact territorial coverage, exemptions, the factor of adjustment for family or household to reach numbers of persons, and possible fraud or carelessness leading to over- or under-assessment.[33] Even counts giving numbers of persons may omit substantial categories, such as the nursing infants.[34] A complex and almost bewildering series of calculations and adjustments is necessary to make allowance for such matters; the calculations and adjustments in turn must be based upon close study of the society, the administrative system, and the circumstances of the making of the count or assessment. It is no wonder that people unacquainted with such techniques or with methods of historical verification are tempted to dismiss all such studies as mere legerdemain.[35] Perhaps more important is the inescapable consequence of the length and complexity of calculations and adjustments, namely, that the margin of error steadily widens. Yet, in the end, if we are to arrive at some idea of populations on the eve of the European penetration and

33. The fundamental work is Mols (1954–56), which gives a detailed and comprehensive review of problems of evidence. It should be supplemented by two studies by Russell (1958; 1965), each with bibliography.
34. See the discussion and description of the forms of statement in the *Suma de visitas* (Borah and Cook, 1960: 75–103, 119–45).
35. See, for example, Spores (1965).

immediately thereafter that is to be more than mere guess, we shall have to accept historical evidence and historical analysis.

For the period after the first decades of European penetration, the later colonial period, the documentary materials available improve steadily with recency down to the upheaval of the Wars of Independence. Despite great regional variation in survival, in general there are available huge masses of records, although by and large they have been left to gather dust. Counts for purposes of tribute, labor, and church administration continued to be taken, and were made upon fairly uniform bases at least within each region. In the eighteenth century in Spanish America, the imperial government attempted to have the first general censuses taken. For Mexico, we know of three such attempts during the eighteenth century: 1742–1748, 1777, and 1793. The census of 1777, at least, was general for Spanish America (Konetzke, 1965: 99–101). Another enormous source of data is the parish registers of birth, marriages, and burials, which, at a time varying from region to region, began to be kept during the last third of the sixteenth century and continued throughout the colonial period.[36] Despite huge losses during the upheavals of past centuries, there remain in many regions long runs that reach back to the middle of the eighteenth century or even to the end of the sixteenth.[37] The parish registers were kept with varying faithfulness, but locked up within them is a wealth of demographic data. I need merely point to the increasing use of them in Europe for demographic study. The now famous study of Crulai (Gautier and Henry, 1958) used what is considered the best technique, namely, reconstructing families. This may not be possible for much of Mexico where the use of a few surnames in large populations makes identification of family impossible, nor for much of the rest of America. On the other hand, a great deal can be done with baptisms, ages at marriage and death, numbers of marriages, and numbers and causes of deaths.

In terms of a highly sophisticated study of population, with elaborate statistical analysis using the best actuarial methods, even the records of the later colonial period may not give rise to enthusiasm among demographers as

36. The registration of baptisms and marriages was made compulsory by the Council of Trent in 1563. In 1614, the *Rituale Romanum* made compulsory registration of deaths and confirmations. Parish registers, however, antedate these requirements in Europe (Henry, 1965: 436–37). In Mexico the First Provincial Church Council of 1555 directed that baptisms and marriages of Indians be recorded so that there might be a record in case of doubt. In 1585 the Third Mexican Provincial Church Council made mandatory keeping of registers of baptisms, marriages, and burials for all (*Concilios provinciales primero y segundo, celebrados en . . . Mexico,* Mexico City, 1769), clause 32 of decrees of First Council; *Concilium mexicanum provinciale III,* Mexico City, 1770, Liber 3, Titulum 2, [Article] 2.

37. Such has been our experience with parish registers in the Mixteca Alta in Mexico.

distinguished from historical demographers. In such terms, there is little firm ground until the twentieth century. In our time, beginning at varying years for each country, there is usually a civil register or its equivalent with reasonably complete coverage, and there are reasonably complete and sophisticated censuses. However, that is not true even today for all countries of America (Collver, 1965), and even in countries with the best registration of vital information and most careful censuses, certain questions still cannot be answered with any certainty. Let me mention one: How many Indians are there in America today by any definition that will receive general acceptance as valid? On the other hand, if one accepts broader tolerances, much can be done with available materials.

I come now to the second part of this discussion of the possibility of finding answers. In terms of the categories of evidence and treatment indicated above, to what extent and in what terms are answers possible? The matter is not simple, and discussion of it must take into account a series of limitations that are often ignored.

First, even the most sophisticated statistical analyses using quantitative data gathered by the best methods available today have within them considerable margins of error. The more the number of agents and agencies entering into the gathering and processing of materials, the wider are the margins of error. The best of present-day censuses, for example, are claimed to have within them margins of error that are relatively very narrow—from 2 to 4 percent. Poorer ones will have larger margins. A simple test of checking the number of children in the first year of life against those one, two, three, and four years old is apt to give interesting perceptions on the care with which present-day censuses are taken. Furthermore, the introduction of better methods of processing data through the punching of cards has actually introduced the additional errors made by the operators of the punching machine. In other words, no census is accurate down to the last digit or even to the last ten thousand; the statement of number down to the last digit postulates an accuracy that is not there. Other quantitative data on births, marriages, deaths, imports, exports, production, and so forth have the same difficulties. The discrepancies between official figures for imports of gold into the United Kingdom and official figures of other countries for exports of gold to the United Kingdom have become proverbial.[38]

Second, there are problems inherent in all work on historical demography that are inescapable in studies for pre-Conquest and colonial populations. We are dealing with what the French have termed Old Regime populations, that is, ones subject to violent downward movement because of the ravages of

38. The remarkable, sobering essay of Morgenstern (1963) should be read with care by all who would deal in figures. See especially pp. 33–34, 40–43, 140–63.

famine and epidemic, and to recovery which might be slow or rapid until the next disaster struck. In these circumstances, estimates for specific dates require also some idea whether or not disaster had just struck or was about to strike or whether the population was then in the upward movement of recovery or on the increase because of an unusual period without disaster (Helleiner, 1965; Goubert, 1960: 1:25–84). (Let me hasten to add that for the period immediately after the appearance of the Europeans or their influence in any region, the entrance of Old World diseases meant a steady hammering downward for some decades.) Furthermore, an examination of current work in European historical demography should demonstrate quickly that fragmentary evidence and insufficient knowledge of forces at work make definite answers difficult everywhere. Medievalists are debating at this point whether the decrease in population of the later Middle Ages began with the outbreaks of the Black Death in the middle of the fourteenth century, or actually began earlier in a population which had increased beyond its long-term powers of support (in effect, the Cook-Simpson-Sauer-Borah thesis in another context).[39] For the eighteenth century, students of British demographic history are debating vigorously the appropriate calculations for birth and death rates and the dating and reasons for the great increase in the population of England and Wales that began some time in the eighteenth century. Did the Industrial Revolution provide sustenance for millions who came into existence because of an as yet unexplained drop in death rate, or did the population respond to the opportunities and need for labor of the Industrial Revolution by breeding up to the new level of subsistence possible? Perhaps the most remarkable aspect of the discussion in the United Kingdom, as in so much discussion of New World historical demography, is that it takes place without examination of other areas. In the eighteenth century, much of Western Europe showed the same phenomenon of shift from an Old Regime population to a New Regime one, and that without the Industrial Revolution.[40] Historical demography over the world would seem to have its difficulties, not all of them completely necessary.

Third, work to be well based must involve careful local analysis. That may seem to contradict the preceeding paragraph but does not do so. Reference to other regions and other times for comparative data and for ways of verifying one's postulates and results is desirable. Extrapolation from one region to

39. Hallam (1961); Titow (1961); Slicher van Bath (1963: 87–90, 132–44). The matter is discussed at some length by Postan (1966: 548–70) and Genicot (1966: 660–94).

40. See the essays embodying differing points of view in Glass and Eversley (1965). For a vigorous revival of the theory of improvement in medicine and therefore a drop in death rate, see Razzell (1965). Glass and Eversley reprint studies of continental European population; see especially Helleiner (1965).

another without proving the appropriateness of the extrapolation is of dubious value. I have mentioned the odd good-neighbor policy in historical demography that postulates relatively equal pre-Conquest populations for sedentary Mexico and the Incan empire. Similarly, more confusion than light is cast by reasoning from temperate America north of the Rio Grande to other American regions of different resources, technology, and human occupation. One would hardly estimate the probable population of India by reference to the tribes of northern Siberia.

After these caveats, what is possible with evidence that we know is likely to be available and with techniques of treatment we now have? (New techniques that opened new ways of treatment or even made use of new evidence would change perspectives greatly.) Here again, we should distinguish between populations on the eve of European penetration or shortly thereafter and those of the later colonial period. For those of the first century, it seems likely that the most we can hope for is estimates of the order of magnitude. Although we owe much to Rosenblat's (1954: 1:103) careful assembly of materials, his statements that his estimates of pre-Columbian population in aggregate are not off by more than 20 percent is best characterized as illusion. Sapper[41] admitted the margin of error in his estimates to be perhaps 50 percent; Steward (1949: 664) thought his figures could be off by from 10 to 100 percent; Kroeber (1939: 166, 181) admitted the possibility of 100 percent or more. Since estimates for the hemisphere now range from 8,400,000 to over 100,000,000, one is inclined to suggest that probable margins of error are very large. They undoubtedly can be made smaller although it seems unlikely that they can ever be brought to the accuracy of present-day censuses or even the smaller margins of error possible in work on the later colonial period. We may in the end come near the 20 percent margin postulated by Rosenblat, but that will take decades, if not generations, of careful assessment of local evidence and the putting together of carefully arrived at regional estimates into a hemispheric total. Personally I should regard an estimate for the hemisphere that came within from 30 to 50 percent as an achievement.

The situation changes, of course, as records become fuller. It is possible to estimate the population of central Mexico in the 1560s, for example, with far greater accuracy and considerably narrower margins of error than for the same area in 1519. For the eighteenth century, estimates can be made that are even more accurate and have still narrower margins of error. Cross-checking and careful verification of data, as well as use of the techniques that are now becoming common in historical demography, can yield relatively reliable results. However, there will still be margins of error and they are

41. The margin is inherent in Sapper's (1924) estimate of about 40,000,000 to 50,000,000.

likely to be distinctly larger than those claimed for a Western European census today. The results will, nevertheless, be valid within reason and most useful.

That many of the possibilities I have indicated are being explored, at least to some extent, is clear if one looks at work done during the past quarter of a century. Again, work of a kind closer to standard current demography—i.e., studies of birth rates, death rates, size of family, age of marriage, and age of death, etc.—has not been done even though for the colonial period the materials do exist for many regions and centuries. The bulk of the work has been on gross numbers and changes in them. Careful, local studies on numbers are sufficiently numerous and are increasing to such an extent that a paper of this length can mention only samples. For South America, one can point to careful research in documents by a number of scholars: Juan Friede[42] for tribes within Colombia; Rolando Mellafe (1965) at the Instituto de Investigaciones de Historia de América, Santiago, on Peru; John Murra and the Casa de la Cultura del Perú, who have taken up John Rowe's interest in documents and are doing indispensable spadework by searching out and publishing the documents that will make possible firmly based research on Andean populations.[43] A combination of documentary research and the techniques of biogeography may be found in the study of the Sinú Valley of Colombia by Gordon (1957) and of the Indians of the Llanos de Mojos, in northeastern Bolivia, with their adaptation to flooded lowlands, by William Denevan.[44] Indeed, perhaps a good measure of the fact that there has been advance in knowledge can be gained by the comparison of the paucity of information on the Indian cultures of the Amazon Valley in the *Handbook of South American Indians* and the far greater knowledge that has been gained since then by excavation, exploration, and documentary research.[45]

For the West Indies and regions north of the Isthmus of Panama, one can point again to much careful local work. Documentary materials have been especially explored for central Mexico by Carl Sauer, Lesley Simpson, Sherburne Cook, and myself, and in that exploration the techniques for examining fiscal materials have been brought to yield.[46] Aschmann (1959), Spicer

42. For example, see Friede (1963), with its impressive documentation of movement of native population.

43. Espinoza Soriano (1964). The materials for the demographic history of the viceroyalty of Peru in the sixteenth century may turn out to be more complete and better than those for Mexico.

44. Denevan (1966b: 120) suggests 350,000 as a reasonable estimate of probable pre-Columbian aboriginal population in Mojos, based largely on the use of ridged fields.

45. Evans (1964); Denevan (1966a). For the region near Mojos, see Vázquez-Machicado (1957).

46. These have already been cited in preceding notes, as have most of the works that follow. I should point, in addition, to the fine work of Kelly and Palerm (1952).

(1962), and Cook have explored documentary materials, in combination with geographical and biological evidence, in work on northwest Mexico, the southwestern states of the United States, and Lower and Upper California. Archaeology and biogeography are being brought to yield for Yucatán and parts of the Mexican plateau in a steadily progressing series of studies that stem from the Carnegie-sponsored ones for Yucatán and are now associated, among others, with the names of Willey, MacNeish, and Heizer. The new work on the urban area of Teotihuacán by Millon (1964, 1970), with its surprising result of a maximum of about 20 square kilometers of urban settlement at peak, opens many new doors and reinforces the indications of long cyclical movements of population change in Cook's study of the Teotlalpan. Finally, one must mention the brilliant combination of close use of documentary evidence, including maps, and biogeography in Carl Sauer's (1966) examination of the first years of Spanish exploration and exploitation in the West Indies.

Whatever the problems of evidence and analysis, careful regional studies are being carried out in increasing volume. Our great need now is to search out the evidence, test it with care, and let it lead us where it will.

ADDENDUM

The foregoing essay was written in 1965, with only minor changes subsequently. It remains valid, but the emotionally charged questions centering about the size and nature of the aboriginal population of America at the coming of the Europeans—referred to perhaps fondly by Ángel Rosenblat as *La Polémica*—continue to attract attention and work. Recent advances in archaeology and geography have indicated approaches and lines of inquiry that may shed light rather than heat: quantitative methods of analysis of archaeological sites; the study of diet, disease, and longevity; new examination into matters of density of urban populations and occupation of what were thought to be less-used interspaces.[47] Completely new has been the discovery of the extensive areas of raised fields in both highlands and lowlands, of which *chinampas* are one variation, with the implication that these fields, a technique for cultivating areas subject to flooding, must have meant population pressure against available food.[48] This kind of study has

47. Acsádi and Nemeskéri (1970) use data on skeletons in archaeological sites for the development of tables of life expectancy for prehistoric and historic populations. The method can easily be applied to the New World. For discussion of Mayan urban densities in Yucatán, see Haviland (1969) and Cook and Borah (1971–74: 2:3–4).

48. Denevan (1970b); Parsons and Bowen, 1966; J. J. Parsons, 1969; Smith, Denevan, and Hamilton (1968). As anthropologists and geographers look for such fields, they are finding them throughout the Americas.

become possible only with the development of aerial photography. A further suggestion for an approach, not as yet well developed, lies in chemical analysis of soils and the examination of complex colloidal clays, since some of the elements in the latter must have come from the excreta of large animals. What large animal could have supplied the organic ingredients for the deep deposits along the banks of the Amazon (Sternberg, 1975: 32–33)? Additionally, a body of anthropologists, largely under the leadership of William T. Sanders, has advocated applicaton of another technique basically consisting of rating areas as to comparative density of occupation and then applying a multiplicative factor (Sanders, 1970; Bray, 1972–73: 166–67). The major problem lies in the multiplicative factor, which can only be arrived at by complex calculations involving inevitably a substantial element of personal preference.

Some of the more prominent recent studies may be listed here: Sherburne F. Cook and myself, responding to a challenge by Rosenblat, have published a study of the aboriginal population of Hispaniola which arrives at a range of which 7,000,000 to 8,000,000 would be the midpoint (Cook and Borah, 1971–74: 1:376–410). The study is based upon careful textual criticism of early reports and comments, using the methods developed by Lorenzo Valla, the editors of the *Acta Sanctorum,* and the school of Saint Maur—in short, methods accepted universally by historians (see note 29). At nearly the same time, a celebrated Belgian scholar, Charles Verlinden, published an estimate of 55,000 to 60,000 Indians as the aboriginal population of the island. The Indians, he declared, lived a nomadic existence in clearings, despite the explicit contemporary testimony to the contrary.[49] For Amazonia, we now have two notable studies, one published in this volume, the other in typescript only (Sweet, 1969). Both represent the best work to date; both have come into existence in a rapidly changing scholarly effort which is uncovering new evidence.

Perhaps the major development in the study of aboriginal populations at and shortly after the appearance of the Europeans has been a remarkable series on regions of Colombia by Colombian scholars, most of them students of Jaime Jaramillo Uribe. The Audiencia of New Granada (covering most of what is now Colombia) made careful and fairly frequent tribute counts, starting almost at the moment of conquest. The series, preserved in the Colombian national archive, may be the best of its kind in Latin America. The studies all arrive at large populations, which declined more slowly than those in Mesoamerica and the Caribbean islands but over a longer period. [50]

49. Verlinden (1968). "D'autre part les Tainos ne pratiquaient qu'assez peu l'agriculture et vivaient très pauvrement de chasse et de pêche." In this regard, see the contemporary testimony quoted at length in Cook and Borah (1971–74: 1:376–410).

50. See the discussion and citations in Cook and Borah (1971–74: 1:411–29). To the works cited there should be added Fajardo M. (1969), Colmenares (1970), and the

They are summarized by Germán Colmenares (1973: 47–75), who puts the aboriginal population of Colombia at 3,000,000, a considerable increase over Kroeber and Rosenblat.

Finally, for Mesoamerica, an area embracing much of Central America as well as much of Mexico, estimates by William T. Sanders, applying his own factors of density of occupation, propose 12,000,000 to 15,000,000. [51] Recent studies of control of water in the lakes and streams of the Valley of Mexico and adjacent regions, all testifying to a degree of sophistication and complexity hitherto unsuspected, give massive support to high estimates for central Mexico (Palerm, 1973; Rojas R. et al., 1974). Finally, studies of vital characteristics for towns of central Mexico in the seventeenth century indicate substantial population decline still in progress at the beginning of the century that came to an end in the early or middle decades of the century. [52] The trend is clearly linked to the sixteenth-century decline and may be held to be the final phase of it.

---

articles by Jaramillo Uribe, Hermes Tovar Pinzón, and Juan Friede in *Anuario colombiano de historia social y de la cultura* (Vols. 1–5, 1963–70).

51. Sanders (1970: 423–30); Sanders and Price (1968). The exact degree of disagreement between these estimates and the Cook-Borah ones is not easy to gauge since the territories are of different extent, but in general Sanders accepts the Cook-Borah postulates of zonal difference in attrition although he rejects their calculations of tribute exemption and general attrition, 1519–1531. At a guess, adjustment of his calculations to the 500,000 square kilometers of central Mexico, as defined by Cook-Borah, would yield an estimate of 5,000,000 plus by one method and nearly 10,000,000 by another.

52. See Vollmer (1973), Morin (1972, 1974), and Calvo (1973).

PART II

The Caribbean,

Central America, and Yucatán

*"All that has been discovered up to the year forty-nine [1549] is full of
people, like a hive of bees, so that it seems as though God had placed all, or
the greater part of the entire human race in these countries"* (Bartolomé de
Las Casas, in MacNutt, 1909: 314).

INTRODUCTION

Reconstruction of sixteenth-century native population patterns for tropical
lowland Middle America is particularly difficult because of an extremely
rapid decline and only fragmentary reporting during the early contact period
(Denevan, 1970c). The high-low ranges of the various estimates are generally
greater than for any of the other regions of the hemisphere. For example,
estimates for Hispaniola in 1492 vary from less than 100,000 up to
8,000,000.

The debate over the magnitude of New World native populations properly
begins with the publication in 1552 of the *Brevísima relación de la destruición de las Indias* by Bartolomé de Las Casas (1957–58: 5:134–81; MacNutt,
1909: 311–424). Las Casas arrived in Hispaniola in 1502 and served as a
priest after 1512, traveling widely both in the Caribbean and on the mainland. He is known for his outspoken defense of the Indians against inhumane
treatment, and he wrote of millions of Indians dying at the hands of the
Spaniards within a few years. He claimed a total mortality of over 40,000,000
by 1560 (Las Casas, 1957–58: 2:549). The picture painted in the *Brevísima
relación* is bloodcurdling, seemingly one of the greatest of all genocides. The
sort of atrocities described certainly did occur, as they are mentioned by
many others; however, numbers aside, Las Casas gave little consideration to
introduced diseases, over which the Spaniards had little control, as the
probable major factor in native population decline. The *Brevísima relación* is

35

a propaganda tract, and was so considered by contemporary Spaniards, while Spain's European enemies quickly translated and circulated it, thereby contributing to the "Black Legend" of Spanish terrorism in the New World. Most historians discount the population estimates in the *Brevísima relación* as serving only to support the crusade by Las Casas. Recently, however, there have been calls for a reexamination.[1]

Are the early estimates to be taken at face value or not? Were they gross falsifications, as vigorously argued by Rosenblat? The figures of Las Casas, Oviedo, and other chroniclers are invariably said to be much too high as a result of ulterior motives or because their authors magnified their own deeds by exaggerating the number of natives (Steward and Faron, 1959: 51; Rosenblat, 1954: 1:101). However, an *a priori* assumption of intentional exaggeration for any reason or because of ignorance is not justified. The chroniclers' early estimates for central Mexico were also high, and they have been substantiated, at least in part, by the work of Borah and Cook. In treating the initial Spanish activities in the Caribbean (1492–1519) in *The Early Spanish Main,* Sauer (1966: 65) argued convincingly that the chroniclers had no reason to distort their population estimates, and that they were well qualified to make estimates: "There was neither reason of vanity nor of practical ends to inflate the native numbers." Cook and Borah (1966) make the same defense in their article on the credibility of contemporary testimony in Mexico. And M. J. MacLeod (1973: 18) argues that those claiming the conquistadors were lying "have a heavy burden of proof placed upon them." A reasonable approach would seem to be to use the contemporary estimates as points of departure, rather than either to accept or to reject them without good cause.

HISPANIOLA

Hispaniola is of particular concern for the historical demography of Latin America because it was there that the first New World settlements were founded by Columbus, and it was from there that we have the first reports of very large native populations and their massive mistreatment at the hands of

---

1. Gibson (1964: 403) concludes that "the substantive content of the Black Legend asserts that the Indians were exploited by Spaniards, and in empirical fact they were." Dobyns (1973) concludes that "the 'Black Legend' was not very legendary." Borah (1976: 55), however, stresses that the Spaniards were no more and no less cruel than other Europeans at the time, and that the main destroyer of native peoples was introduced disease. Among the many discussions of the Black Legend, see Keen (1969, 1971) and Hanke (1971) for contrasting points of view and for further references.

the Spaniards. For Hispaniola, the lines in the debate over high and low native populations are clearly drawn in the studies, on the one hand, by Sauer and by Cook and Borah, who tend to accept or exceed Las Casas, and on the other by Rosenblat, who, in the following essay, is very conservative. Sauer (1966: 65–69) cited several Spaniards who gave figures for Hispaniola, or part of it, of "over a million" or 1,100,000, probably on the basis of an apparent census of adults for tribute purposes made in 1496 by Bartholomew Columbus on orders from Christopher Columbus, after severe depopulation in 1494–1495; Las Casas said the original population in 1492 had been 3,000,000 to 4,000,000 (1957–58: 2:52, 217). Sauer has been accused of reviving the Black Legend, whose strength at times seems to rest more on the size of the original native populations than on what happened to them. He has been sharply criticized in reviews by Spanish historians such as Salvador de Madariaga (1966), who sees Sauer as overly influenced by Las Casas, who is himself one of the most controversial figures of the Conquest period.

In a recently published essay, "The Aboriginal Population of Hispaniola," Cook and Borah (1971–74: 1:376–410) reexamine much the same evidence as covered by Sauer and others, but they derive a figure of 3,770,000 Indians for 1496 on the basis of the Columbus count and from this they derive a figure of 8,000,000 for 1492. These calculations are even more controversial[2] than their 25,200,000 for central Mexico (Borah and Cook, 1963).

Rosenblat's essay here is a reaction to Sauer and to Cook and Borah as well as to other recent studies by Pierre and Huguette Chaunu and by Verlinden. In particular, he maintains that there is inadequate evidence for the supposed census of 1496. He stands fast on his figure of 100,000 (or 80,000 to 120,000), which he first proposed in 1935. This figure is based on the report by Las Casas of 60,000 inhabitants in 1508–1510 and allows a decline of only 20,000 to 60,000 since 1492. Rosenblat makes the telling point that a higher rate of decline could not be expected since the first epidemics on Hispaniola did not occur until 1517–1518. Cook and Borah (1971–74: 1:409–10), however, maintain that there was disease among the Spaniards from the first voyage of Columbus on. Sauer presented other explanations for depopulation, the most important of which may have been ecological: the Spaniards suppressed hunting and fishing, which supplied most of the protein in the native diet.

The situation for Cuba, which apparently had a less dense population than did Hispaniola, is discussed by Dobyns (1966: 409). For the Caribbean as a whole in 1492, most recent estimates are well below 1,000,000. Rosenblat (1954: 1:102) gave 300,000; Steward (1949: 664) gave 225,000; and Dobyns

2. See the reviews of Cook and Borah (1971–74: 1) by Mörner (1973), Denevan (1973), and Dobyns (1973).

(1966: 415), whose other regional figures are very high, originally gave 443,000 to 553,750.[3]

CENTRAL AMERICA

The sixteenth-century chroniclers reported substantial populations in most of Central America, particularly on the Pacific coastal plain where there were rich volcanic soils from Guatemala to Costa Rica, and also in Panama (Castilla del Oro). Las Casas (1957–58: 5:146) said that more than 500,000 Indians were carried from Nicaragua as slaves to Panama and Peru and that the Spaniards killed another 50,000 to 60,000 in battle. Diego de Herrera in a letter to the emperor reported 600,000 Indians in Nicaragua in the 1520s (CS, 9:384–96). Oviedo (1959: 4:385) stated that over 400,000 Indians were removed from Nicaragua. Another equally generalized but possibly more meaningful indication of dense native populations on the Pacific Coast of Nicaragua are the reports of massive baptisms by the priests with the first explorations in the early 1520s. Oviedo (1959: 4:385) mentioned 100,000 baptisms by Gil González Dávila and others.

An examination of the Nicaraguan Indian slave trade is made here in the essay by Radell, mainly using the *Colección Somoza* (CS) documents. He concludes that the early sixteenth-century population of western Nicaragua, including Guanacaste (now in Costa Rica), "may have exceeded 1,000,000"; that the volcanic soils of the region could easily have supported such a number; and that available information on the slave traffic indicates that it was quite possible for as many as 500,000 Indians to have been removed, as claimed by Las Casas. Under Governor Pedrarias Dávila, starting in 1526, the slave trade was Nicaragua's main economic activity. Radell indicates that by 1535 as many as 20 ships were transporting Indians to Panama and Peru from Nicaragua with an estimated total of up to 210 trips a year carrying an average of 350 slaves each. The trade continued into the 1540s and was halted only by depopulation.

The size of the Nicaraguan slave exports is also examined in a recent study by Sherman (1979), who arrives at a much more conservative estimate of about 50,000 from all of Central America between 1524 and 1549. Sherman believes that only a small number of ships were involved during the early part of the period, that during the later years heavy cargo demands for space

3. Dobyns (1973) now sees these figures as much too low and accepts the Cook-Borah estimate for Hispaniola.

reduced that available for slaves, that there is no evidence that the *average* slave capacity of ships was 350 or 400, that the number of round trips to Peru per year by each ship was only one or two due to wind conditions, and that there is little evidence for large slave-hunting expeditions. A position intermediate between Radell and Sherman is that taken by M. J. MacLeod (1973: 52), who concludes that "a total of two hundred thousand Indians for the whole Nicaraguan slaving period appears to be conservative."

Oviedo (1959: 3:241) in the sixteenth century estimated the population of Castilla del Oro to have been 2,000,000, and he knew the area well, including the official records. In a recent ecological study of Panama, C. Bennett (1968: 36) reduced Oviedo's figure by one half. Las Casas (1957–58: 5:153) reported that 4,000,000 or 5,000,000 Indians died in Guatemala between 1524 and 1540. Benzoni (1967: 163) reported 400,000 Indians in Honduras in 1524.[4] In contrast, and at the other extreme, several modern scholars suggest much smaller populations. Rosenblat (1954: 1:102) gave a contact population for all of Central America of only 800,000, and Steward (1949: 664) gave only 736,500. M. J. MacLeod (1973: 71, 93, 332) cites specific reports of 30,000 tributaries in Soconusco (now part of southwestern Mexico) at contact; 12,000 to 14,000 tributaries in Verapaz (north-central Guatemala) in 1544, well after first contact; and 80,000 Indians in Costa Rica in 1563, long after first contact. Veblen (1974: 322, 334–35) estimates an early sixteenth-century population for Totonicapán (highland Guatemala) of 50,000 to 150,000, based on reports by Alvarado in 1524 and taking into consideration a major epidemic in the highlands in 1520.

Besides those of Radell and Sherman, there are only a few detailed regional studies for Central America which examine and evaluate the early estimates, such as the preceding, and other forms of evidence. The best known is that of Barón Castro (1942: 105–24), who estimated an Indian population for El Salvador of at least 116,000 to 130,000. This is based on the size of the invading army of Pedro de Alvarado in 1524, an estimate of the magnitude of the opposing Indian armies, an estimate of the proportion of warriors to the total regional population, and an extension of the result to the rest of El Salvador, allowing for an error of 10 percent. Daugherty (1969: 105–21) recently examined the same evidence, found Barón Castro excessively conservative, and raised the estimate to between 360,000 and 475,000. This does not seem unreasonable considering the other reports of dense populations in Central America.

4. Johannessen (1963: 29–31), believing that Benzoni was referring to tributaries, converted the 400,000 to a total of 1,200,000 for Honduras in 1524. Johannessen also mentioned a report in 1535 of "200,000 Indians," again presumably tributaries.

YUCATÁN

The demographic interest in Yucatán has been focused on the Classic Maya period, when population densities were undoubtedly substantial, and there has been less concern with the contact period other than the assumption of a significant earlier decline associated with the abandonment of many of the large ceremonial centers. Sir J. Eric Thompson (1970) countered the belief that the Mayan Central Area (central and southern Yucatán including Petén) was largely deserted when the Spaniards arrived, and he presented evidence for areas of relatively dense populations separated by very sparse populations, with indications of depopulations of 90 percent or more mostly within less than 100 years after contact, mainly from epidemics. He attributed much of the postcontact mortality to the introduction of malaria. Thompson, however, declined to estimate the total contact population of the region.

The contact population of northern Yucatán, including Quintana Roo, has recently been reevaluated by Lange (1971b), making use of previously unpublished and seldom-cited theses by Jakeman (1938), Hester (1954), and Edwards (1957). Documentary evidence indicates that the coastal area in particular contained large Mayan cities, dozens of which numbered over 5,000 inhabitants. Lange obtains a figure of 2,285,800 persons for 1528 for a total area of about 30,000 square miles, giving a density of about 77 persons per square mile. He believes that the resource base was adequate to support such a density, taking into consideration crop diversity, evidence for intensive cultivation,[5] a strong reliance on semiwild and wild foods (such as the ramón nut), and particularly an intensive utilization of marine resources (Lange, 1971a). For all of Yucatán, Cook and Borah (1971–74: 2:38) on the basis of a careful review of the documentary evidence arrive at a figure of only 800,000 for 1528, but this is some years after a major smallpox epidemic which may have started as early as 1500. Another recent study by H. O. Wagner (1968: 102; 1969: 185) obtains an estimate for 1492 of 8,000,000.

Whatever the original populations, there can be no doubt about an extremely rapid decline in the tropical lowlands of Middle America. The calculations of Borah and Cook (1969: 181) indicate a depopulation ratio of 48 to 1 on the tropical Mexican coasts during only the first 50 years of contact, or over five times as rapid as in the highlands. Edwards (1957: 128, 132) determined a decline equal to 28 to 1 for the island of Cozumel (Mexico) between 1518 and 1587. These ratios are low, however, compared to those of other areas where there was near extinction within a few years.

---

5. The use of agricultural terraces and raised fields has been associated with the Classic Maya, but it is not known if these techniques continued into the sixteenth century (B. L. Turner II, 1974).

Even if the very conservative estimate by Rosenblat of only 100,000 is used, the depopulation rate for Hispaniola was still tremendous (400 to 1 in 48 years) because only about 250 Indians were left by 1540 (Cook and Borah, 1971–74: 1:401). The large native population of Jamaica was gone by this time and that of other islands nearly so. Sauer (1966: 284–85) discussed the reports of only scattered Indian villages left in Panama by the late sixteenth century. The rapid declines of the population of Yucatán and El Salvador are described by J. Eric Thompson (1970) and Daugherty (1969: 128–34), and only 8,000 Indians were left in Nicaragua in 1578 according to Bishop Antonio de Zayas (see Radell, Chapter 3 below).

The reasons for the more rapid population decline in the lowlands are not entirely clear. The introduction of Old World tropical diseases such as malaria, which were less destructive in the highlands, is generally thought to have been a major reason for the difference. On the other hand, the main highland killers, smallpox and measles, may have been even more virulent in the lowlands. Some viruses tend to survive better in warmer climates. Also, different dietary patterns may have been the key factor. In the lowlands, where starchy tubers were the staples, malnutrition would have been more likely to have occurred when hunting and fishing, the main protein sources, were disrupted by Spanish labor demands than in the highlands where maize and beans (Mesoamerica) or potatoes with *quinoa* (Andes) provided balanced diets.

CHAPTER 2 **The Population of Hispaniola at the Time of Columbus**

Ángel Rosenblat

All historiographical work carries within it the proclivities of its authors. It is not unusual for research to lead to the opposite of what had been anticipated; it is, nevertheless, more common for the scholar to slant facts and even figures in order to reach preconceived conclusions. There is no more malleable material than statistics.

The study of the American Indian population from 1492 to the present is one of the most striking examples. The Spanish Conquest and colonization, an event inspiring passionate polemics confounded by legend, is on trial. Also involved is the question of the magnitude of the pre-Conquest Indian populations, which some people feel should be expressed in high figures even though this does not seem justified.

When I first touched upon this theme 40 years ago (Rosenblat, 1935), my concern was a purely linguistic one. What were the indigenous languages spoken at the time, and how many people used them? The topic led me unwittingly into the past, where I found the figures of Humboldt for 1810 (Nueva España census of 1791–1794) and of Juan López de Velasco for

From *La población de América en 1492: Viejos y nuevos cálculos,* El Colegio de México, México, 1967, pp. 7–23, 82–84. Copyright by El Colegio de México. Reprinted with permission of the publisher and author. The text was translated by William M. Denevan, with the assistance of Elizabeth López-Noël. The passages quoted from the chroniclers were translated by Lloyd Kasten. The English text has been reviewed, revised, and corrected by the author, who has also added several new pages of text as well as new note information and addenda. Based on a paper presented at the 37th International Congress of Americanists, Mar del Plata (Argentina), September 1966.

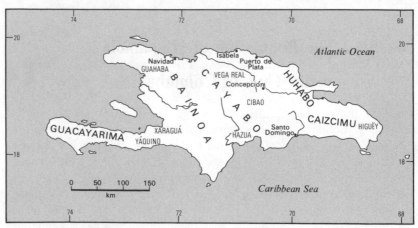

Map 2.1. Hispaniola at the time of Columbus. Based on maps in Sauer (1966: Figs. 7, 9, 11, 12, 13).

1570. I wondered then if it would be possible to start with the present and work back little by little to the first moments of the discovery and Conquest. It seemed foolhardy to attempt such a survey, and I resisted the temptation. But time and again I would come across different calculations, beginning with those of Las Casas and proceeding on up to the modern ones of Sapper, Spinden, Rivet, and Kroeber, in addition to the various other figures that were proposed for each region of America. Thus I felt impelled to pursue the topic, in spite of the inherent dangers. I thought that the old, rather impressionistic calculations could be confronted with an historiographical *modus operandi,* reaching out gradually from the present to the past, from the known to the unknown, so as to take that leap into the dark which is part of all ventures into the unknown, with a minimum of risk.

I must declare categorically that I was not carried away by an inclination to glorify or justify the work of Spain in America. I was a good deal younger than I am today, and as an Hispanic American I had thoroughly absorbed an unreserved condemnation of the Conquest. At no time did exaltation of the conqueror appear in my work. On the contrary, I identified far more with the anguish of the indigenous population, and I was deeply impressed with the words of Juan Montalvo, the great Ecuadorian writer: "Had my pen the gift of tears, I would write a composition entitled *El Indio*, and the world would weep." Today I feel that if the historian were given the gift of drawing tears, all of history would make the world weep.

As it was, if instead of the 3,000,000 or 4,000,000 Indians Las Casas ascribed to Hispaniola—the figure being a weapon in his ardent plea for the Indian and not based on statistical evaluation—I only admitted to there being

100,000, it was not in order to defend the enterprises of Columbus or Ovando. I have considered the regrettable process of extinction of those 100,000 Indians, and it scarcely seems that explaining the extinction of 100,000, instead of 3,000,000, implies a glorification of colonization.

In any event, all figures are subject to distortion. If instead of the 4,000,000 that I calculated for central Mexico in 1519, 25,200,000 are accepted, as Borah and Cook maintain, then Hernán Cortés' enterprise of venturing out with 500 men to conquer that immense world, at least twice as populated as any European state of the times,[1] is transformed into a super-human deed with no equal in the world's history.

Everything, as we see, has its counterpart. The only solution is to confront problems as they appear, shutting our ears to siren songs and eluding dangers. If in fact I did derive moderate and even low figures for the 1492 population, it was not because I had intended to do so. The data I had about the Conquest allowed no other choice, unless one were to assume vast and horrible killing, which requires a macabre imagination and which I found unacceptable given the known extermination techniques of the sixteenth century.

Of course, a study such as mine (the last edition came out in Buenos Aires in 1954 under the title *La población indígena y el mestizaje en América),* which covers the whole hemisphere from Greenland to Tierra del Fuego, was bound to have serious deficiencies. My work was fundamentally intended to stimulate more detailed monographic studies on each region.

A series of such studies confirmed my figures in general. Julian H. Steward (1949) in a serious work based on the analysis of each cultural area of South America arrived at results very similar to mine. That was the first period of reaction. But there followed a second period of open opposition to my figures. I have followed this new trend [*nueva ola*] with much interest. Should I admit that my *Población indígena* is outdated, pushed aside by new research? Let us try to look at the matter calmly. To do so, I will consider here one of the two cornerstones of the new reaction: the population of Hispaniola in 1492.*

Faced by the exaggerated figures of the original sources, I calculated 100,000 Indians on Hispaniola at the time Columbus arrived. Cook and Simpson (1948: 39) maintained that if the testimony of respectable witnesses

---

1. Wagemann (1949: 78) calculated that in the year 1500 Germany had 12,000,000 inhabitants; France, 13,000,000; England (with Wales), 3,000,000; and Italy, 10,000,000. Spain had some 10,000,000.

*Editor's note: Rosenblat's (1967) critique of the second "cornerstone of the new reaction," which is not included here, is of the monographs in the University of California Press series Ibero-Americana by Lesley Bird Simpson, Sherburne F. Cook, and Woodrow Borah, on the aboriginal population of central Mexico in 1519.

could be so easily discarded, all history would have to be rewritten as interpretations are made later. The truth is that history is continually being rewritten, and that all past testimony is subject to contemporary criticism. Swallowing past testimony whole, as one would swallow an oyster, does not make history.

This is even more true where numbers are concerned. I have at hand the inscription from Thermopylae copied by Herodotus 30 or 40 years after the event: "Four thousand men of the Peloponnesus once fought here against 300 myriads" (that is, against 3,000,000 Persians). Herodotus calculated that Xerxes had taken 5,283,220 people to Greece, including ship crews and transport and auxiliary personnel, but not including the women who prepared food, the concubines, the eunuchs, and so on.[2] He did not ignore the problems of provisioning all these people and also of feeding the horses, beasts of burden, and dogs that accompanied the army, but he stuck to his figures. Delbrück (1900–1902: 1: Ch. 1),[3] obviously a historian of our times, calculated that as the head of the army approached Thermopylae, the rear guard had not yet reached the Tigris. Rabelais (1944) had already made mocking parody of this kind of figure in the sixteenth century in *Pantagruel* (Bk. 2, Chs. 26, 28, etc.) and *Gargantua* (Bk. 1, Ch. 26, etc.). Delbrück believed that the Persian army probably had some 20,000 fighting soldiers, and that including ancillary elements the army might have mustered some 60,000 or 70,000 men. It is not, then, a question of conflict between old and new data but one of determining whether or not past figures are historically consistent and how they arose to begin with.

Statistics, as a discipline, is a recent development. Even today, when one's sense of numbers is formed in childhood along with elementary notions of local, provincial, and national geography and with the counting of election results, how many people have a real feel for numbers, and what value should we impute in any case to sets of data that can be used as counterarguments to each other every time there is disagreement? I also have on hand a newspaper article about the Tarahumara Indians of Mexico, written toward the end of September 1966. The inhabitants of Lafayette, Louisiana, disturbed by

2. Herodotus (Rawlinson, 1859–60: 4: Bk. 7, Ch. 186). In Chapter 60 he said that Xerxes, at Doris, had counted the land army of the combined allied nations, obtaining a total of 1,700,000 men. Then, in Chapters 184–87, Herodotus reported that between Sepias and Thermopylae, since new forces had been incorporated, Xerxes again counted the combined land and sea forces and obtained a total of 2,641,610 combatants. Including camp attendants and sailors, he arrived at the total of 5,283,220.

3. Delbrück reduced the Greek army to 6,000 hoplites. He analyzed many analogous cases of inflated armies and losses in battle (including those of recent times). Laffont (1965: 1:52) said that Plato was closer to the truth than Herodotus in attributing to Xerxes 300,000 infantry and 60,000 cavalry, a figure which also appears to be enormous. Carlos Beloch (in Goetz, 1932–36: 2:92–93) did not believe that the Persian army exceeded 50,000 fighting men.

reports of the daily deaths of hundreds of these Indians through hunger and weakness, as a result of drought the previous year, floods in 1966, and the subsequent decline of hunting, sent down ten freight cars of food, medicine, farm tools, and machinery. The Mexican government stopped the convoy, maintaining that the report was exaggerated and that it could care for the Indians on its own. The Jesuit priest who had initiated the campaign denied emphatically that 100 or 200 Indians died daily, reducing the number to one or two a day. (It is calculated that in all there are about 30,000 to 50,000 Tarahumara Indians, half of them living in regions that are inaccessible even today.) Another Jesuit, head of the Chihuahua state mission, declared that it was true that the Tarahumaras were suffering from malnutrition, and that from one to three Indians, mostly children, died daily. Which of these reports lends itself to statistical calculation?

Pierre and Huguette Chaunu tried to rehabilitate the old figures by posing the problem of Hispaniola's population in a work of monumental size entitled *Séville et l'Atlantique (1504—1650)*. "The testimony of all the conquerors," they say, "agrees: Hispaniola was densely populated. In no other part of the Antilles did our witnesses portray the same impression of strength and number. Confidence may be placed in them, this time at least" (P. and H. Chaunu,1955—60: 8:497). The confidence is based on the testimony of "all the historiographers" from Las Casas to Fernández de Oviedo, those two opposite poles of Indian historiography. "Dominican theologians, doctrinaires of natural law and Christian equality among men, that philosophy so often confused with its principal interpreter, the gifted Fray Bartolomé de las Casas; the 'anticolonialists' of the sixteenth century (we dare to add); and the Aristotelian humanists of Sepúlveda's school, of which Oviedo is the perfect representative," all concurred, they say, in the curious figure of 1,100,000, or more than 1,000,000. First of all, let us see if this is true.

Las Casas said in *Historia de las Indias* (1957—58: 2:396—99 [Bk. 3, Ch. 94]) that the Hieronymites who had arrived in Hispaniola in 1516 to free the Indians consulted the opinion of Franciscans and Dominicans. Padre Bernardo de Santo Domingo spoke for the Dominicans. He had been in Hispaniola since 1510 and was, according to Las Casas, "the most accomplished scholar." In three days, he wrote a treatise in Latin against the destructive character of the *encomienda* system (apparently dated April 18, 1517). Las Casas summarized Padre Bernardo's accusation, which he said was signed by the principal monks of the Dominican convent, as follows:

> He proved in the following manner that it was true that through the *repartimiento* and the *encomiendas* of the Indians given to the Spaniards, all perished and suffered the aforementioned harm. The first time that the Indians of this island of Hispaniola were counted, it was said that there had been found on it 1,100,000 *vecinos,* and that when the same padres of Santo Domingo came to this island, which was in the year 1510, he said

that absolutely everyone had been counted, and only 46,000 were found; and then, a few years later, they were counted again, and 16,000 were found; and at the time he was writing this treatise there were only 10,000. Concerning the other islands, he proved the same.

Thus, according to Padre Bernardo, there were 1,100,000 *vecinos* at the time of the first repartimiento. In the terminology of the times, "vecino" meant head of the family. This gives an equivalent of at least 4,400,000 inhabitants. Isn't it fairly obvious that this is an attack on the encomienda, which the Dominicans considered unlawful and tyrannical, and on the *encomenderos* and governors, whom they were always threatening with eternal condemnation? It is evident that the figure has no statistical value.

Las Casas was not at all satisfied with the small figure of 1,100,000 inhabitants. He said so quite clearly (Las Casas, 1957–58: 2:51–52 [Bk. 2, Ch. 8]):

The number of people who inhabited this island was countless, and this is what the old admiral wrote to the king and queen. The archbishop of Seville, Don Diego de Deza, who lived in those days, told me that the admiral himself had told him he had counted 1,100,000 souls. But these were only the people around the mines of Cibao, those who dwelt on the great Vega and nearby, on whom was bestowed the gold-filled bell as tribute, as was stated previously. The 1,100,000 possibly included some of the Indians of the province of Xaraguá, whose people gave as tribute cassava bread and cotton, both spun and unprocessed. But, I believe, without fear of being wrong, that there were more than 3,000,000, because in those days they did not take into account the province of Higüey, nor Haniguayaba and Guacayarima, nor Guahaba and other portions of the island.

More pathetically, he then reiterated, on speaking of the arrival of the treasurer Pasamonte in 1508 (Las Casas, 1957–58: 2:106 [Bk. 2, Ch. 42]):

When this treasurer came . . . there were, counting all the Indians on the island, 60,000 people. Thus, from the year 1494, in which their misfortune began, . . . until the year 1508, a total of 14 years, there perished over 3,000,000 of the people that had been there, from wars, from being sent as slaves to Castille, in the mines, and from other calamities. Who among people to be born in future centuries will believe this? To me, myself, who is writing it, and who saw it, and who knows most of it, it now seems that it was not possible.

He likewise insisted (Las Casas, 1957–58: 2:217 [Bk. 3, Ch. 19]):

There were on this island at the time, when concern and confusion prevailed over the making of laws in Castille [1512], something like 20,000 Indians, men and women, large and small, and I truly believe that the number was even less. These remained from the 3,000,000 to 4,000,000 who lived in their towns, peacefully, with their lords and kings and in all abundance, having more than enough of all necessary things, unless it was the light of faith. I speak truly because I saw it.

He gave the same figure in the *Brevísima relación* of 1552 (Las Casas, 1957–58: 5:136): "that having seen more than 3,000,000 souls on Hispaniola, there are no more than 200 of the native people left"; and he repeated it in the *Historia* on every possible occasion.[4] He did the same in his *Apologética historia* (Las Casas, 1957–58: 3:65 [Ch. 20]): "I truly believe that those we found alive surpassed 3,000,000 or 4,000,000." Egypt, he said, had 3,000,000 at the time of Ptolemy; the island of Hispaniola, which is larger, "clearly must have had a much greater number of people than the 3,000,000 or 4,000,000 reported."

The same thing is repeated in a series of reports. In a letter to the emperor, December 15, 1540, he made the encomienda responsible for "what has been done to the 3,000,000 souls that were just on the island of Hispaniola, plus another 3,000,000 on the other islands." And immediately he repeated this (Las Casas, 1957–58: 5:79): "May Your Majesty be pleased to ask how many people we saw on the island of Hispaniola alone, on which there were 3,000,000 souls."

But at times it would seem to have been the same to Las Casas whether there were 3,000,000 or 4,000,000 or only 1,000,000. In a letter dated October 15, 1535, written to a court personage, he said (Las Casas, 1957–58: 5:65): "They took them away from their lands to go and get gold . . . this was the most powerful reason why all the people of the island of Hispaniola perished, and they killed 1,100,000 souls, which I saw there with my own eyes, and there are on it now only the Indians of Enrique."[5]

If he arrived on Hispaniola in 1502, and in 1508 there were only 60,000 Indians left, as he said (Las Casas, 1957–58: 2:261 [Bk. 3, Ch. 36]) ("not vecinos, but young and old, women and children"), it is a little hard to believe that he could have seen 1,100,000 *with his own eyes*. In any event, there is that often repeated figure again.

The figure comes from Dominican sources and would not seem to date prior to 1510, the year in which the Dominicans reached Hispaniola. We have already seen that Las Casas took it from the Latin treatise of Padre Bernardo de Santo Domingo, written in 1517. The Dominicans of Hispaniola again insisted on it in a letter dated December 4, 1519 (CDI, 35:203–4; see Rosenblat, 1954: 1:294–95):

4. See Las Casas 1957–58: 2:259–61 (Bk. 3, Ch. 36), etc.
5. Nearly the same was said in *Memorial de remedios para las Indias* in 1518 (Las Casas, 1957–58: 5:33): "of the 1,100,000 souls that were on the island of Hispaniola, the Christians have left no more than 8,000 or 9,000, for they have killed the rest."

The people who could be counted, 1,100,000 persons, were all destroyed and dispersed, and today there are not even 12,000 souls, great and small, old and young, healthy and sick. We learned that there had been that many from the governor, Don Bartolomé, brother of the old admiral, God rest his soul, for he himself counted them at the command of the admiral when they once tried to impose tribute on them. . . . A priest going from here to the court to testify on the same subject to the most Christian king, Don Fernando, may God preserve him in His glory, said before the bishop of Burgos that the Indians who had been on this island numbered 1,100,000 and that there were no longer left but about 11,000. He said that he did not believe that there had been that many; however, he well knew there must have been 600,000. Whether there were 600,000 or over 1,200,000, as many of those who came at the beginning asserted, they have said that this entire island was as populated as the land of Seville.

So there are at least two different versions with respect to the source of this figure. First, the admiral had told the archbishop of Seville (who told Las Casas) that he himself had counted those 1,100,000 souls. Second, Bartholomew Columbus had counted them, on orders from the admiral, when they were subjected to tribute (this is the 1519 Dominican version). Had the figure been the result of a count, by Christopher Columbus or his brother Bartholomew, it is obvious that the bishop of Burgos would not have felt free to cut that number in half in the presence of King Ferdinand. Neither would there have been occasion for the statement of the Hispaniola Dominicans: "Whether there were 600,000 or over 1,200,000, as many of those who came at the beginning have asserted." Besides, it is inconceivable that Las Casas determined the population of Hispaniola by comparison with that of Egypt in Ptolemy's time.

The figures of Las Casas, as well as of his Dominican sources, represent an intentional, militant truth, not a statistical truth. And yet in the same *Historia de las Indias,* in which he spoke of 3,000,000 to 4,000,000 souls, there is a disconcerting passage, of great importance in my opinion. He summarized the tribulations of the Hispaniola Indians as follows (Las Casas, 1957–58: 1:293 [Bk 1, Ch. 106]):

Thus with the slaughter from the wars and the famine and disease which resulted from them, the troubles and oppressions which then followed, and especially from their inner sorrow, anguish, and sadness, it was believed that not one-third were left of the multitudes of people who had been on this island from the year 1494 to 1506. A fine harvest, and rapidly reaped!

In other words, "it was believed that" the multitudes of people on Hispaniola had been reduced to one-third from 1494 to 1506. If in 1508 there were only, as he says, 60,000 Indians counting men, women, and children, there could not have been very many more in 1506. Las Casas had forgotten the counts by Columbus and the millions of souls and came nearer to a statistical truth. At any rate, it is obvious he didn't adhere to consistent figures.

Let us next see what Fernández de Oviedo had to say (Oviedo, 1959: 1:66–67 [Bk. 1, Ch. 6]):

> All the Indians on this island were distributed by the admiral as encomiendas to the settlers who came there to live, and in the opinion of many who saw it and can speak of it as eyewitnesses, the admiral, when he discovered these islands, found 1,000,000 or more Indians, men and women, of all ages, adults and children. Of all these and of those born subsequently, it is believed that there are not at present, this year of 1548, among adults and children, 500 people who are natives and the offspring and stock of those first dwellers. This is because most of those here now are brought in by the Christians of other islands, or from the mainland, in order to make use of them.

It now can be seen that whereas Padre Bernardo de Santo Domingo, according to Las Casas, said there were 1,100,000 vecinos, that is, over 4,000,000 total inhabitants, and Las Casas himself talked insistently about 3,000,000 or 4,000,000 souls, Fernández de Oviedo said there were 1,000,000 or more people of all ages. The Chaunus (1955–60: 8:498) nevertheless saw a curious coincidence between the two figures: "It is a gold standard, with respect to Dominican demography, of the old historiography of the Indies," a notable coincidence because "it is difficult to imagine two spirits, two temperaments, two philosophies, more opposite than these." Fernández de Oviedo, whose *Historia natural* the Chaunus said is a "monument constructed to glorify the European colonization as the Spaniards saw it," would have, in their opinion, systematically dismissed high estimates.[6] The truth is that Fernández de Oviedo sometimes gave figures higher than those of Las Casas himself; he stated repeatedly, for example, that in the administration of Castilla del Oro and Nicaragua 2,000,000 Indians died during the 16 years of Pedrarias' rule (1514–1530). The Chaunus believe that if there had been differences in the Hispaniola figures, Fernández de Oviedo, "according to his thesis," would have chosen the lower figure. Polemics about the Conquest did, in fact, often become bitter, but we have not come across any discussion about the figures themselves. They were not a matter of speculation, but of pure illustration. Only in our time are we beginning to discuss them.

6. I think that the fundamental difference between Las Casas and Oviedo, as presented by the Chaunus, reflects the thinking of Manuel Giménez Fernández (1953–60), a work of great documentary value, but, in our opinion, excessively Manichaean.

In any event, whether or not there is agreement about 1,000,000 vecinos or 1,000,000 persons, what value should be ascribed to this 1,000,000? The Chaunus (1955–60: 8:500) felt that it was impossible to divide a population into encomiendas without some determination of the numbers involved, even if only crude, and so they accepted a "rudimentary inquiry of the *caciques,* as so often happened in Indian history." A count of this type, they added, always gave low figures because the caciques were wary of fiscal inquests and concealed true populations. Even so, they said that "the figure of 1,000,000 is based on a summary inquest. . . . It received the benefit of a general consensus that goes from Las Casas to Oviedo." Pierre Chaunu (1963: 79, 95) repeated the same idea later, that none of the figures in Las Casas' *Historia* was invented; they were of an administrative nature; the perfect agreement between Las Casas and Oviedo on the 1,000,000 Indians is a "supplementary guarantee of scientific objectivity."

We are not going to question all these statements, nor others which are not mentioned, for brevity's sake. Let us comment on one fact, however, that does matter very much. Was there ever a general inquest into the population of Hispaniola? Did Columbus himself order an Indian repartimiento, or did one take place in his time? Did an encomienda necessarily imply a count of Indians?

We have not found the slightest hint of that inquest or inventory in any of the documents of the period. Padre Bernardo's statement, which Las Casas recorded ("the first time that the Indians of this island of Hispaniola were counted"), and that of Fernández de Oviedo ("the opinion of many who saw it and can speak of it as eyewitnesses") belong to some oral tradition that probably goes back to statements made by Christopher Columbus, who was always very hyperbolical. (There is the testimony of the archbishop of Seville, Don Diego de Deza, to support this view of oral tradition.) To Columbus, who felt he had reached the Ophir of the Sacred Scriptures, Hispaniola seemed larger than England and Portugal (see Addendum 1) and could have provided Indian slaves "to Castille, Portugal, Aragón, Italy, Sicily, the islands of Portugal and Aragón, and the Canaries" (Columbus, 1892–94: 2:42). (For Columbus, lacking gold, Indians sold as slaves were the greatest wealth that he could offer to the Crown.) Nevertheless, he found only small villages of thatched huts. Only on the north coast did he get to see a village, on December 13, 1492, that he estimated had about 1,000 dwellings and some 3,000 inhabitants, who had all run away. The Indians evaded him so successfully that at one point he had to put the *hidalgos* to work on roads and ditches, thus gravely upsetting the social hierarchy.

Las Casas himself told how Columbus imposed the payment of tribute on the Indians in 1495. After a cruel nine- or ten-month campaign by the Spaniards, with some 200 foot soldiers, 20 horsemen, and 20 hunting dogs, the Indians submitted. Las Casas (1957–58: 1:291 [Bk. 1, Ch. 105]) reported:

> The admiral imposed [a tribute] of gold equal to the measure of a Flemish hawksbell every three months on all the vecinos over fourteen years of age in the provinces of Cibao and Vega Real and those living near the mines. King Manicaotex each month gave half a gourd full of gold which weighed three marks, which equal and are worth 150 gold, or Castilian, *pesos.* Everyone not residing near the mines was to contribute an *arroba* of cotton each.

Peter Martyr (1944: 47–48), who wrote his accounts the day following an interview, said nearly the same thing: each Indian between 14 and 70 years of age had to pay tribute "in the products of his region." But:

> They barely had strength to seek their food in the forests. . . . Most of the chiefs with their subjects, amid the rigors of need, presented only part of the promised tribute, humbly asking the admiral to take pity on their misery and to forgive them until the island returned to its original state, for then they would repay double the amount lacking. Of the Indians of Cibao, few kept their agreements since they suffered more hunger than the others.

Muñoz (1793: 238),[7] who examined all the Columbian documents, said that more than 20,000 pesos had been expected from each levy (there is no mention of millions), and scarcely 200 were collected in the first three levies. By 1496 the tribute collection had to be abandoned, the Indians having fled to the hills.

Las Casas (1957–58: 1:407–10, 419–21 [Bk. 1, Chs. 155, 160]) also mentioned the first repartimiento of Indians, "which later became known as encomiendas." Roldán, who had rebelled in 1498 when Columbus was in Spain, had more than 500 Indians serving him and his people. Bartholomew Columbus had to grant Indians to his men so that they would not join the rebels. These Indians were used to work the land and to man the fortresses and the towns. When Christopher Columbus returned and made a pact with the rebels, Roldán asked that King Behechío and his people, whom he now commanded, be ceded to him to work his lands. ("Neither a few nor many, as they say, but King Behechío himself, who was one of the greatest kings and

---

7. Muñoz maintained that the initial tribute was severe, and that the amount of the other two or three payments was less and then had to be abolished "in view of the low industry of those people." After the incursions of Columbus (in 1495) and the so-called pacification of the island, "much of the island was deserted, the fields abandoned, and the people dispersed in the rugged terrain." Then the men of Columbus captured 1,500 rebel Indians and took them to Andalusia to sell as slaves (the Crown ordered them returned to their island) (Muñoz, 1793: 243).

lords of this island, and all his court.") Columbus granted this request and made similar arrangements with the other rebels. "They asked for this or that lord and cacique, with all his people, to till their lands and help them farm; and in order to keep them content, in hopes that they would settle on the land at no cost to the king . . . these requests were liberally granted." In the same manner, Columbus apportioned caciques and their people among his own men, in order to keep them satisfied, as Columbus said, for a year or two. He gave them "the same plots of land prepared and worked by the Indians . . . one received 10,000 *montones* of *yuca,* another 20,000, a third a little more or less." And sometimes he would "join two or three Spaniards in a group and entrust to them some cacique who would till all their land so that they might later share the fruits of his labor." The Spaniards also forced the Indians to collect gold for them. We see that Columbus did not count the Indians, and that their apportionment did not imply a count of the population. The year was 1499, and in 1500 Columbus returned to Spain in chains.

It is evident then that the 1,000,000 figure that Las Casas (1,100,000 vecinos) and Fernández de Oviedo (1,000,000 or more Indians, men and women, of all ages) threw around, each in his own way, was not based on "quantitative sources now lost," nor can it be taken as "a firm basis for discussion" (Chaunu, 1960: 359–61). The figure undoubtedly persists as an oral tradition from the earliest years, very much in the style of Christopher Columbus. A million is a very tempting figure in all calculations, but it always carries with it a certain hyperbolic connotation. "More than 1,000,000" impresses us as being a slightly more pondered statement. And 1,100,000 (vecinos or souls, as the case may be), would seem to be the result of a serious tabulation (see Addenum 2). An analogous and equally fantastic tradition is to be found for Mexico and Peru. As there are still people who ascribe some value to this kind of figure, it is desirable that we give some attention to the matter.

Clemente Antonio Neve (1870: 451–52) used as a base a supposed "Estadística de Anáhuac" made, he thought, on the order of Hernán Cortés "after the taking of Mexico in 1519," which showed, he said, the existence of 600,000 families. Calculating six persons per family, he arrived at 3,720,000 inhabitants. But, protecting himself with an "it is maintained," he added another 900,000 families, and so reached 9,120,000 inhabitants. He was still not satisfied. Basing his argument on several other statements of "it is said," he concluded that the 30,000,000 that "various authors" have assigned to Anáhuac "are very exact." Not a trace of this "statistic" has been found, but Neve's calculations are repeated automatically.

A series of calculations of the population of the Incan empire is similarly based on a supposed general registration attributed to the archbishop of Lima, Fray Jerómino de Loaysa, which showed there were 8,285,000 Indians in 1551 (not including Chile and some provinces). Some refer to this as the "President Gasca census." As an extension of this legend, it was even said that Viceroy Toledo (1570–1575) had registered 8,000,000 Indians (it seems he only found 1,500,000). Humboldt has already shown that the famous Loaysa registration was fictitious (Rosenblat, 1954: 1:253–54). It is natural that the figures transmitted by oral tradition should seek a valid pretext: the count by Columbus, the statistics of Cortés, the registration by Archbishop Loaysa. This is especially so when the figures have a certain numerical precision, as with Licenciado Zuazo's [Çuaço] 1,130,000, or the 8,285,000 attributed to Archbishop Loaysa, or the 100,900 (the surprising part is the 900), that Fray Pedro Simón assigned to the ancient province of Tunja at the time of the coming of the Spaniards in his *Noticias historiales* of 1627.

Let us return to the Chaunus. Having "reconciled," as we have seen, Las Casas and Fernández de Oviedo with respect to 1,100,000 Indians for Hispaniola in 1494–1495, they were faced with the difficult problem of how that enormous population was reduced to 60,000 inhabitants by 1510, to 16,000 in 1520, to 10,000 about 1530, and to a few tens around 1570. At this point, they thought that the 1,000,000 so scrupulously counted by Columbus, and unanimously accepted by all the authors of old, may have had "a systematic error of the order of 100 to 200 percent" (P. and H. Chaunu, 1955–60: 8:504). That is, they took 500,000 as the point of departure for 1495. (Why do they suppose that a doubling is more tenable than a tenfold increase, which is so common?) And instead of the 60,000 ascribed to 1510, they assumed there were 100,000. (Besides the Indians that were subjugated, they said there remained in the interior "a trapped population that had taken refuge without hope of escape.") This was their "last concession to contemporary criticism."

Even so, to make the argument more credible (it is curious that they emphatically and continually denied credibility as a historical criterion), they thought that the pre-Hispanic population of Hispaniola, so large in number, was a simple enormous mass in a fragile, nearly artificial equilibrium, which was maintained in a kind of "state of super fusion." This population had reached a maximum density compatible with material and technical conditions, with a high mortality (the average age could not have been much higher than 20–they said), and a low birth rate (children were weaned at four years of age) (P. and H. Chaunu, 1955–60: 8:507). Under these conditions the unstable equilibrium could not survive the appearance of the Spaniards. Also, in order to make the decline from 500,000 in 1495 to the supposed 100,000 in 1510 even more credible, they introduced the effect of the epidemics and the cattle brought in by the conquerors. "Cattle literally replaced the Indians" (P. and H. Chaunu, 1955–60: 8:508). There is no doubt that the Europeans imported their microbes to Hispaniola very early, but it is odd that the first epidemic that is recorded is that of smallpox in 1517–1518, when there were only some 30,000 Indians on the entire island. And it would not seem that cattle, barely introduced during the 1494–1510 period, could be taken seriously as a factor in the painful process of Indian extinction on Hispaniola.

An estimate much lower than ours is that of Charles Verlinden (1968), a professor at the University of Ghent. His paper is mainly an analysis of the repartimiento of Rodrigo de Alburquerque (1864), made in Hispaniola between September 15, 1514, and January 9, 1515. This repartimiento is very important, since it is the first, or only, one remaining which is a detailed and complete account. In addition it was well prepared, with inquiries made by the council, mayors, investigators, and notaries. Nevertheless, the figures lend themselves to variable totals. Verlinden obtained 22,669 Indians under forced labor. Our own total is 22,336; Cook and Borah (1971–74: 1:381) obtain 22,644; and Saco (1932: 2:306) obtained only 20,995. Smedts (see Verlinden), a disciple of Verlinden, submitted the document to a thorough statistical analysis, and arrived at the total of 26,136 counted Indians. We have determined 3,109 children and old people, incomplete amounts since the numbers of children and elderly were not recorded in all the encomiendas; Saco calculated 4,545; Cook and Borah (1971–74: 1:383) obtained 4,704. Included are chiefs, who are listed in the document with their Christian names. Smedts added 556 Indians who, he said, were not included in the totals, and 5 percent more who presumably escaped the inventory (fugitives, those hidden, etc.), and arrived at a total of 28,000 Indians in all of Hispaniola in 1514. We also take into account the small proportion of women in the encomiendas, despite the previous battles which caused a major depletion of the men. (In Concepción they distributed 1,072 men and 880 women; in Puerto de Plata, 22 men, 16 women, 7 old people, and 5 children; Chief Juan de Vera had 18 men and 5 women; Chief Martín González had 27 men, 17 women, 13 old people, and 6 children; Chief Vega del Cutuy had 34 men and 18 women, etc. [Alburquerque, 1864: 62, 64]). It is clear that 60 encomenderos were married to chiefs' wives, who were not included in the inventory, but we also know that, at least from the time of Roldán, many of the Spaniards took Indian women as servants, cooks, or concubines (some even had Indian harems). We do not believe that the Indian servants and concubines were part of the repartimiento, and for this reason we arrived at a total figure of 30,000 (see our analysis of the repartimiento: Rosenblat, 1954: 1:113–14, 296–97). Serrano y Sanz (1918: 384) calculated 32,000, which seems more plausible to us today, and we accept it.

Verlinden's total for 1514 is 28,000. In addition he has, he says, one other precise figure: the repartimiento of Diego Columbus (the second admiral, governor of Hispaniola starting in 1508) which gave an inventory of 33,528

Indians in 1509 (CDI, 7:446; see Addendum 3). With only these two figures, Verlinden constructed his little statistical scheme. In five years, from 1509 to 1514, there was a decline of at least 5,500 Indians (33,528 minus 28,000 equals 5,528), but he allowed for 6,000. And since in 1509 17 years had passed since discovery, he arrived at a decline of some 20,000 Indians since 1492. He thus obtained a population total for Hispaniola of 55,000 to 60,000 inhabitants at the moment Columbus landed.

Even this amount seems to Verlinden to be too high, since he believed that Indian mortality increased over the years with the increase of the number of colonists, whose presence weighed more and more on the native population (see Addendum 4). Verlinden believed that the Taino practiced little agriculture and lived very poorly by hunting and fishing. He concluded that under such conditions the island before discovery could not have fed more than a very sparse population, and that it was the coastal concentrations of Indians that gave the completely erroneous impression of a dense population to the first whites.

Even though Verlinden's total is not very far from ours, it still seems inadequate. In the first place, he took as a base for the population of 1514 not the original figure of the repartimiento (22,669 Indians), but the result of an adjustment (28,000). On the other hand, for 1509 he took the original figure of the repartimiento (33,528) without adjustment. And this raises a question: If the 22,669 Indians (we obtained 22,336) imply a total population of 28,000 inhabitants, according to Verlinden, or of 32,000 according to Serrano y Sanz, which we now prefer, then what population total is implied by the repartimiento of 33,528 Indians for forced labor in 1509? If we apply the criteria of proportions, using our figure, then $22,336 : 32,000 :: 33,528 : x$, whereby x will equal 48,034. Or, in round numbers, and taking into account that in 1509 there were surely more Indians who had fled the repartimiento, we arrive at a total of some 50,000 Indians. This figure is not far from the 46,000 which the Dominicans counted when they arrived on the island in 1510, according to Padre Bernardo de Santo Domingo (Las Casas, 1957–58: 2:397 [Bk. 3, Ch. 94]).[8]

Thus, from 1509 to 1514 there was a decline of 18,000 Indians (50,000

8. This figure also is not far from the 60,000 (counting men, women, children, and the aged) which Las Casas several times emphatically affirmed had been encountered by Treasurer Pasamonte when he arrived on the island in November of 1508 (Las Casas, 1957–58: 2:106 [Bk. 2, Ch. 42], 261 [Bk. 3, Ch. 36]). The same even applies to the figures which Las Casas arbitrarily threw about: 60,000 in 1508; 40,000 in 1509 when Diego Columbus arrived; 13,000 or 14,000 in 1514 when Rodrigo de Alburquerque arrived (Las Casas, 1957–58: 2:261 [Bk. 3, Ch. 36]). If the figure for 1514 is incorrect, as we have seen from the results of the repartimiento for that year, then what confidence do the others deserve?

minus 32,000). This averages 4,500 per year for four years. If we take into account that the low date should not be that of discovery, 1492, but the year 1494, "when the destruction began," according to Las Casas, then we have 4,500 times 14 years, which equals 63,000 Indians. With the 50,000 we calculated for 1509, we still arrive at the rounded figure of 100,000, the same as we originally determined for 1492. Now it can be seen that our figure is not simply "impressionistic," as Verlinden characterizes it, but that it can be confirmed by the same method, excessively naive it seems to us, used by Verlinden, merely by applying more consistency. We originally arrived at the figure by an historical analysis of the extinction of the Indians of the Antilles (see Rosenblat, 1954: 1:109–18).

Therefore, even Verlinden's study confirms our calculation of 100,000 Indians for 1492 (with a margin of error of 20 percent). This is the figure which Karl Sapper sent me in 1935, which was derived by Gudmund Hatt of Copenhagen based on his archaeological excavations (see Addendum 5). It is also the number which can be inferred from the calculation of Kroeber (1934: 24), which assigned a total of 200,000 Indians to all the Antilles.

There is no doubt that the island's fertility permitted a larger population, even considering the unreliable *conuco* system (see Addendum 6). (The same was true of the immense North American territory, inhabited, nevertheless, by under 1,000,000 people before the arrival of the Europeans.) But the conquistadors found only dispersed Indian centers, and not a single large settlement. It is sufficient to follow Columbus' itinerary along the island's coasts, or his expeditions to the interior, to see the number of leagues he had to cover before finding a village clearing or a group of Indians in the midst of the tropical forest. Even Las Casas, in *Apologética historia* (1957–58: 3:156 [Ch. 46]), after expounding on Hispaniola's superiority over England, Sicily, and Crete, only spoke of small settlements: "It was the case that in this [Hispaniola] and in the forementioned islands [Cuba, Puerto Rico, Jamaica, and the Lucayos or Bahamas] there were to be found settlements of 100, of 200, and of 500 vecinos, I mean houses, in each one of which there lived ten or 15 vecinos with their women and children." And he described straw huts that were round and some 30 feet across. Peter Martyr (1944: 261), who collected detailed information from Andrés Morales, stated:

> *Haiti* means rugged in their ancient language, and so they called the whole island Haiti, naming the whole for a part . . . , inasmuch as this island in most places is horrifying because of the rough nature of its mountains, the black denseness of its forests, its fear-inspiring dark valleys, and because of the height of the mountains, notwithstanding the fact that in other places it is very pleasant.

The history of the entire first period—the hunger at Isabela, the tribulations of the first settlers of 1493 and 1494 (according to Fernández de

Oviedo, half the people of Isabela and Santo Domingo died of hunger and illness)—totally rejects the idea that the island could have been highly populated and rich. Furthermore, the Arawak culture which was on Hispaniola showed no evidence of dense centers of population, nor any social stratification greater than that of a succession of independent chieftains in any one of the islands or on the mainland.

That population of 100,000 inhabitants (the number may have reached 120,000) was in no way a simple amorphous mass, ready to disintegrate at the slightest puff. It offered resistance, beginning in 1492 with the destruction of Fort Navidad, to the extent that it was capable, and it always had the refuge of the forest. As a further sign of vitality, the Indians even erupted in a bloody insurrection from 1519 to 1533, which forced Spain to mobilize more soldiers than had accompanied Cortés in the Conquest of Mexico and which obliged the Spaniards to make a treaty.

ADDENDA

1. On December 23, 1492, Columbus estimated that Hispaniola was larger than England, and he stated that in all his 23 years of sailing (to England, Guinea, etc.) he had never seen a port like that of Hispaniola: "All the ships of the world could harbour therein" (Navarrete, 1954–55: 1:138; Columbus 1892–94: 1:71). On another occasion he estimated that Hispaniola was "larger than Portugal and its population double" (Columbus, 1892–94: 1:82). The province of Cibao alone seemed to him as big as The Kingdom of Portugal (Columbus, 1892–94: 1:170). In a letter from Lisbon dated March 14, 1493, he said: "The area of Hispaniola is equal to all of Spain, from Catalonia to Fuenterrabía" (Navarrete, 1954–55: 1:178). Even in his Relación of the third voyage, he again told the Crown (Navarrete, 1954–55: 1:206): "I subjected the island of Hispaniola, whose coast is greater than that of Spain and whose people are innumerable, so that all should pay tribute."

The area of Hispaniola is 76,286 square kilometers; Portugal, on the other hand, has 92,082 square kilometers. Great Britain, not including Ireland, has 142, 588 square kilometers. And continental Spain, without the Balearic and Canary Islands, has 494,946 square kilometers; but Columbus said that Hispaniola was further around than Spain, which has 3,318 kilometers of coastline. On his second voyage he reached the island of Jamaica, "the most beautiful ever beheld," and judged it bigger than Sicily (Columbus, 1892–94: 1,243). Jamaica covers 10,859 square kilometers and Sicily 25,461 square kilometers.

Columbus also assured the Crown of having seen from the coast of Hispaniola mountains "which seem to reach to the sky" (Columbus, 1892–94: 1:122–23).

Ramón Iglesia (1944: 17–49) explained all the reports of Columbus as being interesting information from a commercial man turned into a propagandist for the lands that he had discovered. The island of Cuba appeared to Columbus to be "larger than England and Scotland together" (Navarrete, 1954–55: 1:178); he believed it to be "the rich Cipango." On June 12, 1494, at a cape which he called Alpha y Omega (probably Cabo Maysi), where the continent began and ended, Columbus made his men swear before a notary that Cuba was a continent, threatening with death those who disagreed (Muñoz, 1793: 103; see Navarrete, 1954–55: 1:386–90).

Las Casas was to a large extent a victim of the illusions of Columbus and his figures. It is important to analyze his deductive and statistical methods. For example, let us take Chapter 20 of his *Apologética historia,* where the islands of England, Sicily, and Crete are compared with Hispaniola (Las Casas, 1957–58; 3:60–66).

He calculated the size of England using the claims of Julius Caesar (De *bello gallico*, Bk, 5), Pliny (Bk. 4, Ch. 16), Bede (*Historia ecclesiastica*), San Isidoro de Sevilla (Bk. 14, Ch. 6), Solinus, and Diodorus. On the other hand, of Hispaniola he reported: "The Admiral, who had sailed or gone all the way round, said that it was 700 [leagues] around, so that this island is wider and larger than England, or at least, to be honest it is not smaller." He again insisted on the immense population of Hispaniola: "To speak of the multitude of people who inhabit this island is like counting the waters that enter the sea; they were innumerable."

Later Las Casas compared the production and wealth of the two islands and concluded: "Overall, it seems that this island of Hispaniola is in no way inferior to England, nor less rich or precious; indeed it [Hispaniola] has many advantages in natural qualities, wealth, and healthful properties."

We shall pass over the comparison with the islands of Sicily and Crete (which is also based on the classical and the medieval writers) and the constant claims by Las Casas of the superiority of Hispaniola. Let us pause, however, to examine carefully his comparison between Hispaniola and the Kingdom of Egypt. For calculations of size he referred to the authority of Diodorus (Bk. 1, Ch. 3) and reached the following conclusion: "That kingdom, in the time of Ptolemy Lagi, according to Diodorus, numbered seven million men, and in the time of Diodorus there were three million souls; therefore since this island of Hispaniola has more than twice the area of Egypt, and finding it, as we do, so densely populated and of such excellent conditions, previously described at length, it is clear that it must have a greater number of people than the said three or four milion."

The comparison with Egypt is quite astounding. In truth Ptolemaic Egypt was the richest country of the world because of the inexhaustible fertility of its soil, which made possible the annual export of great quantities of grain, and because of its industry, which exported crystal, paper, wool, and colored tapestries. The population density was high (Goetz, 1932–36: 2:265–66).

In reality, it seems to us that the population figures of Columbus and Las Casas have the same historical value as all the other figures which we have assembled here. They result from the same illusion. And for this reason we challenge the Berkeley School and its eagerness to revive the old figures and "the testimony of reliable witnesses."

2. Peter Martyr (1944: 273), who collected information in 1516 from men who had returned from Hispaniola, reported: "The number of those unfortunate people is greatly reduced. Many say that at one time a census of more than 1,200,000 was made; how many there are now, I am horrified to say." The Hieronymite padres, who governed the island, were less precise when they wrote to Charles V on January 18, 1518 (CDI, 1:300): "At the time the Castilians entered this island there were many thousands, and even hundreds of thousands, of Indians on it, and, to our shame, such quick toll was taken of them that when we arrived a little over a year ago, we found as few of them as there are grapes left after a vintage." On the other hand, Licenciado Zuazo reached the height of precision in a letter to Monsieur de Xevres on January 22, 1518 (CDI, 1:310): "From what is known of past repartimientos, from the time of the old admiral up to our days, 1,130,000 Indians were discovered initially on this island of Hispaniola, and now they do not number 11,000 persons."

This figure (1,130,000 Indians) is taken as an article of faith by Carl O. Sauer in his recent work, *The Early Spanish Main* (1966: 66–67, 90, etc.). Sauer believed that the first census of the New World,[9] which escaped demographic attention, was undertaken in 1495–1496. That census or count,

9. This would have been the first census not only in the New World but in the entire world. It is true that ancient history spoke of censuses, but these "censuses" were simple counts of houses, of tributaries, or of citizens. The Emperor Augustus in A.D. 14 wrote: "In my Sixth Consulate (28 B.C.) I undertook, with my colleague Marcus Agrippa, a general tax census. This plebeian census, the first in 41 years, accounted for 4,063,000 Roman citizens. The last [next] census, which was organized with consular power under the Consulate of Caius Censorinus and Caius Asinius (8 B.C.), accounted for 4,233,000 Roman citizens. The third census, which was organized under consular power by the Consulate of Sextus Pompeius and Sextus Apuleius (A.D. 13) with the assistance of my son Tiberius Caesar, accounted for 4,936,000 citizens" (Goetz, 1932–36: 2:434). Still, Jacques Necker, the minister of finance under Louis XVI, maintained that "it is, of course, completely impossible to carry out a general census" (Wagemann, 1949: 8).

Man considered as a number is a preoccupation of modern demography. The first complete censuses in Europe were relatively recent: Sweden in 1749, United States in 1790, France and Great Britain in 1801, Russia in 1897, and the first Chinese census not until 1953–1954 (Wrong, 1961: 15).

he said, could have been undertaken by Columbus "only through the caciques, who were to be the collectors. To have exaggerated the number of their people would have put the caciques in jeopardy." One can only ask, at the very least, in what language and with what numerical system they could have given him such precise figures. But he further added (Sauer, 1966: 90): "The resultant figure of 1,130,000 was secured after a sensible reduction in native numbers had taken place," although he does not believe that this reduction could have been of the order of one-third between 1494 and 1496, as "Las Casas and Ferdinand Columbus agree." Also, Sauer said that the 1,130,000 of 1495–1496 only covered the tributary population, ages 14 to 70 years. To consider the whole population we would have to raise the figure to some 2,000,000. And since at that time contact had been made with no more than one third of the island (Sauer said that it was "a scant half"), the imaginary census would conjure up a population of some 6,000,000 inhabitants. This would still ignore the "sensible reduction" which had taken place as a result of the first contacts. If nothing else, he evidently exceeds the figures of Las Casas.

These calculations by Carl Sauer came from his view of native life (or did this view come from his demographic calculation?), which he summarized in the following manner (Sauer, 1966: 69): "The tropical idyll of the accounts of Columbus and Peter Martyr was largely true. The people suffered no want. They took care of their plantings, were dexterous at fishing and bold canoeists and swimmers. They designed attractive houses and kept them clean. They found aesthetic expression in woodworking. They had leisure to enjoy diversion in ballgames, dances, and music. They lived in peace and amity." This doesn't stop him from attributing syphilis to the Indians, for he does say: "An ancient disease of this part of the New World and of little damage to the natives, it gave savage punishment to Europeans" (Sauer, 1966: 86).

There is a passage that partly helps explain Sauer's attitude toward historical testimony. Peter Martyr (1944: 282), recording what was told him by the pilot Andrés Morales, who had explored Hispaniola in 1508 under Ovando, stated: "It seldom rains in Xaraguá, the kingdom of Chief Beuchío [Behechío], nor in Hazua, which is part of the Cayabo region, in an excellent valley with both salt and fresh water lakes, nor in Yáquino, a region of the province of Bainoa. In all these places with infrequent rains there are ancient ditches which they use to irrigate the land with no less ingenuity [non ineptiore ordine] than that of the inhabitants of Cartagena and Murcia in Espartaria." This is the only reference to irrigation in the whole of the Antilles (Las Casas copies this bit of information from Peter Martyr in his Apologética historia; 1957–58: 3:19–22 [Ch. 5]), but from it Carl Sauer (1966: 53) deduced: "The statement is terse and clear. This was no casual diversion of water but an extensive system of canals considered equal to those built by the Moors in Spain, and known as of ancient construction. Unfortunately, Morales did not explain." If Morales did not explain it, why did Carl Sauer deduce so much? And why did he say that Morales' "statement is terse and clear"?

I certainly believe it is necessary to qualify the statement by Peter Martyr, a person whom we have always idealized as a model humanist. Muñoz (1793: xii), who was so familiar with the documentation of the early period, said that "he was careless and lazy to an extreme, " and that "he was in the habit of writing impetuously as soon as he received a report . . . never reexamining it in order to make a revision."

Carl Sauer (1966: 58) even idealized the native food: "Plants provided the starch and sugar of native diet; animals supplied the protein and fat in admirable balance." That admirable equilibrium was "quickly and inadvertently" destroyed by colonization, in part because of "ignorance of diet" (Sauer, 1966: 202–3). To prevent escape, the Indians were forced to abandon hunting and fishing and the new generation lost the skill necessary to procure animal food for themselves. Sauer tried to partly explain the demographic catastrophe of Hispaniola this way. It must not be forgotten, however, that throughout the initial period there were scarcely more than 500 Spaniards on the island, the number increasing to some 2,000 in Ovando's time. If this extinction of millions of Indians took place between 1496 and 1508, what was this "new generation" that no longer knew how to hunt and fish?

Puerto Rico's population has also lent itself to hyperbolic calculations. In the seventeenth century, Vázquez de Espinosa (1948: 42) believed the island had had more than 600,000 Indians, not counting the women and children. Carl Sauer (1966: 158–59) did not find this hard to believe, because that figure coincided, he said, with the first calculations for Hispaniola, and both islands were similar in culture, climate, and soil. All the demographic calculations of his study are of this nature.

3. The figure of 33,528 Indians in 1509 does not appear in a letter by Cardinal Cisneros, as Verlinden says, but rather in the *legajo* of papers which the Hieronymite padres carried, together with instructions from the cardinal, on leaving Sanlúcar on November 11, 1516, to govern Hispaniola. There is actually a manifest dated September 3, 1516, signed in Madrid by Padre Bernardino de Manzanedo, one of the Hieronymites, of having received, by order of the cardinal, a packet of writings: "the account of the repartimiento of Indians made by Admiral Diego Columbus on Hispaniola, the account of the second repartimiento made by Alburquerque and Pasamonte of the same Indians, and a transcript and decree on how to enact the allotment of Indians by districts" (Serrano y Sanz, 1918: 355). Saco (1932: 2:306) assigned

33,523 Indians to the repartimiento of Diego Columbus, without doubt a printing error, which was the figure we recorded (Rosenblat, 1954: 1:297).

Diego Columbus received from King Ferdinand on August 14, 1509, authorization to make a new repartimiento (undoubtedly taking into account those made by Ovando). He was to divide up all the Indians on the island among the colonists, with 100 Indians going to each of the royal officials, 80 to married *caballeros,* 60 to married attendants, and 30 to the married farmer. The encomienda was to be for two or three years (see Verlinden, 1968: 637). Other information on the repartimiento of Diego Columbus (1509) is found in Serrano y Sanz (1918: 226–28).

4. In 1508, according to one of the documents concerning the repartimiento of Diego Columbus handed over to the Hieronymite fathers by Cardinal Cisneros, there were 715 citizens (vecinos) on Hispaniola (CDI, 7:446), equivalent, in our opinion, to a total of 2,860 Spaniards (using a multiplier of 4). It is necessary to add the residents who did not have the right of citizenship, which brings the total to some 5,000 Spaniards (a hypothetical figure). Las Casas (1957–58: 2:99 [Bk. 2, Ch. 40]) said that during the period of Ovando (referring undoubtedly to the final part, or perhaps the year 1508), the island was completely pacified and had, "as I heard, 10,000 or 12,000 Spaniards, many of them hidalgos and caballeros." Ovando had arrived in April of 1502 at the head of a spectacular expedition of 2,500 men (among them Las Casas, then a soldier). His rule (1502–1508) is considered the "Golden Age" of the colony. It is possible that the figure of Las Casas should be reduced by half, that is, to 5,000 or 6,000 Spaniards.

The repartimiento of Alburquerque of 1514 was made among 741 encomenderos (among them an Indian, a Negro, four convents, five hospitals, two churches, and some of the Iberian officials, such as the king, Bishop Fonseca, and Lope Conchillos, who was secretary to the king.) In addition there were 167 colonists who did not receive any Indians. Verlinden (1968: 644) calculated that in all there were some 1,035 colonists (men and women), and he accepted as reasonable a total of 1,200 Europeans, including children. The children, he said, were few, "because most remained in Europe." This total of 1,200 Europeans on Hispaniola is too low. It is essential to remember, however, that from the beginning Hispaniola was the base for Spanish conquest and colonization. As early as 1503 Balboa asked for 500 men from Hispaniola in order to continue his discoveries. The island provided a large part of the contingents of Ojeda and Nicuesa which colonized Darién and the mainland. In 1508 the expedition to conquer Puerto Rico, led by Juan Ponce de León, left Hispaniola; the expedition for Jamaica, under Juan de Esquivel, left in 1509; that for Cuba, under Diego Velázquez, left in 1511. It is certain that in 1514, the date of the repartimiento of Alburquerque, there were fewer Spaniards on the island of Hispaniola than in 1508. (It is possible that the expeditions mentioned also included Indian auxiliaries.)

The *Indice geobiográfico de cuarenta mil pobladores españoles de América en el siglo XVI* (Boyd-Bowman, 1964) identifies the origin of 404 vecinos of Hispaniola in 1514, and as the number identified represents just 20 percent of the total, we arrive at some 2,020 colonists. The Hieronymite fathers, upon arriving on Hispaniola, wrote Cardinal Cisneros on January 20, 1517 that they had encountered very few Spanish citizens and also few Indians (Serrano y Sanz, 1918: 552).

5. Karl Sapper, in a personal letter to me, dated December 22, 1935, discussing the figures for Hispaniola in my 1935 study, commented: "It surprised me that the Danish investigator Gudmund Hatt of Copenhagen, based on his archaeological studies, has calculated the population of Haiti [Hispaniola], as did you, at 100,000 persons, which appears to me to be too few in view of the well-developed agricultural works of the Taino, even though metal tools were lacking, as can be seen in the esteemed study of Sven Lovén (1924: 326 ff.)."

And in a letter dated February 19, 1936, he returned to the same question: "From the work of Sven Lovén it is seen that agriculture was very well developed and was adequate to support a multitude of people. Although it appears that there were no large cities, it is possible that the population had been very numerous, scattered in dwellings containing a few people each, such as I have seen in many parts of Central America. It is certain that there is insufficient data to calculate exactly the number of inhabitants during that remote time. The primitive houses, scattered in the mountains, did not leave archaeological remains which could indicate the number of people, and in general I believe that very little survives of the many ancient houses" (see Rosenblat, 1954: 1:296).

Nevertheless, in the paper sent to the 26th International Congress of Americanists held in Seville in October of 1935, he stated: "But Gudmund Hatt told me, on the basis of his excavations in Haiti, that, in his opinion, this island did not have more than 300,000 souls" (Sapper, 1948: 475). The proceedings of this Congress of Americanists, because of the Spanish Civil War, were not published until 1948, but the letter which Sapper sent me in 1935, concerning the 100,000 inhabitants calculated by Gudmund Hatt, was dated December 22, 1935, that is, after his Congress paper.

6. Contrary to Verlinden (1968), the island had a very rich agriculture. The Spanish found maize (the Indians ate the toasted kernels); yuca (from which they made cassava bread); the sweet potato (which had extraordinary success in Europe); *aje, yautia, lirén*, and *mapuey*, which are edible tubers; beans, hot

peppers, peanuts, and cashews; and fruits such as papaya, prickly pear, mammee, soursop, sweetsop, *guayaba, pitahaya,* star apple, hog plum, *jicaco, guácimo, guama,* plantains, pineapple; plus many other cultivated plants (see Oviedo, 1959: 1: Bks. 7, 8). All these products were adopted by the colonists. Hunting and fishing were in no way poor, and the Spaniards called attention to the large turtles, sharks, alligators, manatees, iguanas, *hutias,* and even the turkey, which had the Indian name of *guanajo* (called *guajolote* in Mexico, where it was more important). In addition, the great wealth of fish in the rivers and in the Caribbean must be taken into account. It is surprising that the Spaniards on the second voyage of Columbus could have died of hunger.*

*Editor's note: For a recent discussion of the population of Hispaniola, see David Henige, "On the Contact Population of Hispaniola: History as Higher Mathematics," *Hispanic American Historical Review* (1978), 58: 217–37.

CHAPTER 3 **The Indian Slave Trade and Population**

of Nicaragua

during the Sixteenth Century

David R. Radell

The Indian slave trade was colonial Nicaragua's principal economic activity during the second quarter of the sixteenth century, and the magnitude of this trade is an indication of the size of the native population of the province. These slaves were in great demand in Panama, Peru, the island of Hispaniola, and other early Spanish settlements where local Indian laborers were decimated by disease.

Nicaragua is divided physiographically, climatically, and culturally by the northwest-southeast trending backbone of the central highlands. Western Nicaragua was the main Spanish settlement area, and the area was exploited for its agricultural products, naval stores, limited mineral wealth, and above all for Indian slaves. In contrast, eastern Nicaragua, for the most part a rain-drenched forest land, was so isolated from the rest of the country during the colonial period that the Spanish were never able to control its native population effectively.

Western Nicaragua's pre-Columbian Indian population (including Guanacaste, now in northwestern Costa Rica) may have exceeded 1,000,000 and the region's fertile volcanic soils easily could have supported many more.[1]

The Indian slave trade in Nicaragua was initially examined by David R. Radell in his Ph.D. dissertation, "Historical Geography of Western Nicaragua," University of California, Berkeley, 1969.

1. Today (1976), with an estimated population of 2,100,000, Nicaragua is considered underpopulated. There is a shortage of agricultural labor, and abundant fertile land still remains unsettled.

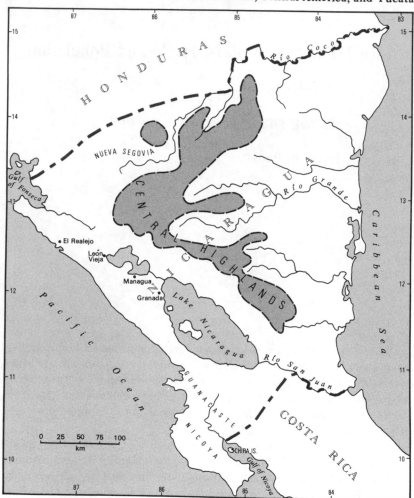

Cartographic Laboratory UW-Madison

Map 3.1. Nicaragua, 1524–1560

However, after the Spaniards arrived in 1523 the native numbers declined with tragic abruptness, so that within several decades no more than a few thousand Indians remained.

A major cause of depopulation in Nicaragua was the Indian slave trade. Las Casas (1957–58: 5:146) claimed that during the first 14 years of Spanish rule more than 500,000 Nicaraguan Indians were removed from the province as slaves. Oviedo approximated the number of Indians removed from Nicaragua at more than 400,000. He stated that Gil González Dávila, Bobadilla, Francisco Hernández, and others baptized about 100,000 Indians, but that more than four times that number were transported to other provinces of the Indies where they subsequently perished (Oviedo, 1959: 4:385). A letter written to the Crown by Herrera declared that from an aboriginal population of 600,000 not more than 30,000 remained alive in Nicaragua in 1544.[2]

Although the estimates of Las Casas, Oviedo, and Herrera are remarkably similar, these estimates have generally been considered grossly exaggerated. It seems incredible to suppose that 500,000 people could have been transported by the small number of Spanish vessels plying the Pacific Coast of the New World during the early sixteenth century. However, a reconstruction of colonial Nicaraguan slave traffic based on sketchy details from contemporary documents indicates that the initial estimates are plausible.

The Spaniards who conquered and settled Nicaragua were interested primarily in draining the province of its riches. Within one or two years following initial settlement the Spaniards had managed to separate the natives from their accumulated precious metals. With this means of support exhausted, colonists began looking for other profitable resources to exploit. Gold mining in the province was not impressive, and although agriculture in western Nicaragua was exceptionally productive, this activity did not possess the "get rich quick" appeal that had been the basis for Spanish exploration and conquest. The province's only major resource with potential to turn a handsome profit was the large, docile, but industrious Indian population. Quick to realize this potential, the barbarous but enterprising Nicaraguan governor, Pedrarias Dávila, began to nurture a colonial economy based on slave trading. After being replaced as governor of Castilla del Oro (Panama), where he had had previous experience and success in establishing slave marketing on the Isthmus, his infamous administrative skills were brought to Nicaragua in 1526.

Almost immediately the slave trade became Nicaragua's most profitable commerce. In western Nicaragua there were two human pools that could be tapped easily by Spanish slavers: the first, those Indians who were being subdued by exploratory and slaving expeditions; the second, those Indians already held as slaves by friendly native *caciques*.

Almost every exploratory expedition dispatched during the colonial period's first ten years was expected to gather Indian slaves. In addition, numerous Spanish raiding parties were organized exclusively for the purpose of discovering, conquering, and enslaving Indians. Often captive slaves were treated with extreme cruelty. During Martín Estete's expedition in search of the Río San Juan, captured Indians were bound by heavy neck chains; if one

2. "Carta que el Lic. Diego de Herrera, Juez de Residencia en Nicaragua, dirigió a S.M. informándole de la situación de la Provincia," Gracias a Dios, December 24, 1544 (CS, 9:384–96).

lost consciousness during the arduous journey, he was beheaded to free his body of shackles, thus enabling the expedition to continue with minimum loss of time (Herrera y Tordesillas, 1944–47: 5:189). The primary supply source, allegedly hostile Indians, was quickly depleted, leaving the central highland frontier area depopulated.

To replenish dwindling supplies of human cargo the slavers next turned to purchasing slaves already held by native caciques. Prior to the Conquest, hereditary native caciques possessed large numbers of slaves. After the Spaniards' arrival caciques in western Nicaragua who had remained friendly to the conquerors were permitted to retain many of their traditional privileges, including their right to hold slaves. In those places where an Indian council form of government had held power before the Conquest, the Spaniards usually appointed only one Indian to assume the general powers of cacique (Oviedo, 1959: 4:364). It was reasoned wisely by the Spaniards that it would be easier to control one man than a tribal council.

Motivated by profit in trade goods and fearing the well-armed slavers, native caciques readily sold their own slaves to the unscrupulous Spanish traders. The governor himself demanded that a supply of slaves be delivered every four or five months by these caciques (Las Casas, 1957–58: 5:146). Before long this second supply source had also been exhausted; yet the demand for slaves continued unabated. Few exported Nicaraguan slaves survived more than a few years in other provinces, and their demise promoted a continuous demand for replacements. To meet this demand the caciques were pressured into supplying the slave trade by every conceivable means remaining. Left with only a few household servants, the caciques were forced to sell the tribe's orphans and even freemen's children. From a man who had two children they took one and from a man who had three they took two (Las Casas, 1957–58: 5:146). So enormous was the demand for slaves that soon this supply also failed.

On May 26, 1536, a royal order was issued prohibiting the transportation of Indian slaves or freemen from Nicaragua to other provinces, and in 1537 a royal order prohibited slave sales by native caciques.[3] These orders were ineffective because royal officials derived an immense profit from slaving. When caciques were no longer able to supply enough slaves to meet the demand, slavers turned to kidnapping free Indians along with those who had been granted to Spanish colonists under the *repartimiento* system. Whereas many colonists complained bitterly of their Indian losses, many others sold their Indian wards illegally to slavers. Complaints of kidnapping continued to reach the Crown throughout the 1540s.

At first all slaves were carried to the Isthmus of Panama where they were traded and sent to other parts of the New World. At least one shipload of

3. "Cédula de la Reina," Madrid, May 26, 1536 (CS, 3:442–43).

Nicaraguan slaves is known to have arrived in Panama in 1526 (Borah, 1954: 4), and Las Casas (1957–58: 5:146) indicated that for the next six or seven years five or six ships were exporting slave cargoes from Nicaragua.

By 1528, under the successful promotion of Pedrarias, the slave trade had become Nicaragua's most profitable economic activity. A letter sent by Francisco de Castañeda[4] to the Crown describing conditions in the province of Nicaragua in March of 1529 listed five ships engaged exclusively in the slave trade between Nicaragua and Panama. Although slave shipments were considered private enterprise, all shipowners listed were Crown officials. One ship's joint ownership was in the hands of the Crown and the governor of Tierra Firme; one belonged to Alonso de Cáceres, the royal treasurer, and his partners; another was the property of Pedrarias; the remaining two ships belonged jointly to Francisco Pizarro and Diego de Almagro. A sixth ship being completed in Nicaragua at the time was the property of Ponce de León and Hernando de Soto.

For at least six more years the number of ships engaged in the Nicaraguan slave trade continued to increase. In 1533 and 1534 it was reported that the number of ships exclusively engaged in the Nicaragua-Panama slave trade had grown to fifteen or twenty (Herrera y Tordesillas, 1944–47: 7:8). By 1535 twenty ships were said to be carrying human cargo to both Panama and Peru from the shores of Nicaragua.[5] Many of the ships engaged in this commerce were still owned either openly or secretly by colonial officials. In addition, in return for the use of the royal branding iron, officials themselves collected one-fifth of all slaves branded.[6] The failure of the Crown's official attempts to end the Nicaraguan slave trade can largely be traced to control of the profitable trade by local royal officials.

Estimating the size and capacity of ships engaged in the slave trade is difficult. Only incomplete ship registries for the years 1539 to 1544 have been found (CS). They are very brief and do not state the ship size or cargo carried. Only lists of crews and a few passengers are provided, and in some cases even destinations or points of origin fail to appear. Borah (1954: 66–69) has used crew size to help estimate approximate ship sizes engaged in the Mexico-Peru trade via the South Seas during the period 1550–1585. His estimates are helpful in approximating the size of ships registered in the Nicaraguan trade during the 1530s and 1540s. In fact, several ships registered in Peru in the 1580s seem to have been registered previously in Nicaragua in

4. "Carta con documentos del Licenciado Francisco de Castañeda a S.M.," León, March 30, 1529 (CS, 1:479–508).
5. "Información que hace a S.M. el Escribano Francisco Sánchez," Granada, August 2, 1535 (CS, 3:406–12). Indian slaves were wanted particularly in Panama to staff the routes across the Isthmus and in Peru for manpower for the Conquest.
6. "Carta de la Audiencia de Guatemala," Gracias a Dios, December 30, 1545 (CDN, 30–41).

the early 1540s. Nonetheless, crew size is a fallible index to ship size, and crew sizes varied in registries for the same ships on different voyages. However, crew size remains the only index available to indicate the size of ships registered in Nicaragua in the 1540s.

The *Santiago,* owned by Pero [Pedro] Sánches Dalva and Pedro de la Palma, when registered in April 1542 had a crew of thirteen, including a master pilot, boatswain, notary, steward, four unclassified seamen, and five Negro cabin boys. However, the following year this same ship sailed again with a crew of only eight.[7] One of the largest ships listed in the early registries seems to have been the galleon *San Esteban de la Cruz*, owned by Pedro de los Rios. When registered for a trip to Peru from Realejo, the port for León, in 1542, it carried a crew of twenty-two: master, pilot, boatswain, steward, ten seamen, and eight Indian hands—four female and four male.[8] Based on estimates by Borah, the *San Esteban de la Cruz* was probably 150 to 200 tons, and the *Santiago* probably was of 60 to 100 tons. Many of the other ships listed were probably of 30 to 60 tons (Borah, 1954: 66–69). Larger ships are definitely known to have been built at Realejo a few years later,[9] and it is possible that a few of the ships engaged in the Indian slave trade were larger than those listed.

Only one reference has been found that states the slave-holding capacity of a ship engaged in the Nicaragua-Panama slave trade. In 1535 a ship is reported to have left Nicaragua carrying 400 slaves, not more than 50 of whom survived the journey.[10] This report was quoted by the Crown as justification for the 1536 *cédula* prohibiting the Nicaraguan slave trade. Although this voyage's death toll is shocking and is probably exceptional, there is no reason to believe that the number of Indians listed for shipment was anything but average. Nevertheless, in the absence of other stated ship capacities, it seems prudent to consider this figure exceptional and reduce the estimated average number of slaves per voyage to 350. This estimate also seems reasonable when it is compared to a report that in 1533 Governor Francisco de Castañeda left Nicaragua taking with him 200 Spanish settlers and more than 700 free Indians on five ships.[11] The Spaniards probably voyaged aboard three ships and the Indians aboard two.

7. "Registro del navio Santiago," León, April 26, 1543, and July 17, 1543 (CS, 10:485; 9:39).

8. "Registro del galeón San Esteban de la Cruz," Xagueyes, July 12, 1542 (CS, 10:516-18).

9. For a discussion of the early colonial shipbuilding and port function of Realejo, see Radell and Parsons (1971).

10. "Información que hace a S.M. el Escribano Francisco Sánchez," Granada, August 2, 1535 (CS, 3:406–12).

11. "Petición que Diego Núñez de Mercado, Alcalde de la Fortaleza de la Ciudad de León, presentó al Consejo de las Indias," Madrid, November 16, 1541 (CS, 7:151–224).

In estimating the number of trips per ship each year, the general length of journey has been taken into consideration and a liberal allowance made for repairs, bad weather, and other delays. Throughout the legalized slave-trading period the Gulf of Nicoya served as the primary shipping station for Nicaraguan slaves; Realejo was not opened to commerce until the mid-1530s. Castañeda reported that the Panama-Nicaragua round trip to and from the island of Chira in the Gulf of Nicoya generally required 16 to 20 days and in exceptional cases 30 days in all but the worst weather.[12] Only in the last year or two before prohibition of the slave trade in 1536 did Realejo become a competitor, and then mainly to accommodate Peruvian demands. Allowing for delays and repairs, it is estimated that ships engaged in the nonstop Nicaragua-Panama commerce could average 12 round trips per year. For those ships engaged in the Nicaragua-Peru trade, two round trips per year represent a conservative estimate of the frequency of service to Nicaragua. Table 3.1 is a reconstruction of the potential volume of Nicaraguan slave-trade traffic before the trade was outlawed in 1536.

It is not impossible that 450,000 Indians were exported within the initial ten-year period. If the actual slave cargoes were somewhat smaller or the voyages somewhat less frequent than estimated, it is only of academic significance because the Nicaraguan slave trade did not end with the stroke of a pen in 1536. An illegal commerce in Indian slaves continued for an additional ten years or so. In 1540 charges were issued against Rodrigo de Contreras claiming, among other things, that he had been responsible for the shipment of more than 2,000 free Indian natives of Nicaragua to Peru and the North Sea (Caribbean) Coast, of whom only 100 survived. In addition, he was accused of selling free Indian women to the sailors at Realejo, determining price on the basis of beauty.[13]

The limiting factor in this trade proved to be neither royal legislation nor ship capacity but rather the failure of supply. The disappearance of all Indians who could be purchased or kidnapped caused numerous complaints by colonists, clergy, and even royal officials, some of whom were themselves secret partners in illicit slaving operations.

Many Indians also perished from warfare, starvation, and disease. Las Casas (1957–58: 5:146) stated that 500,000 to 600,000 Indians died as a result of warfare. Furthermore, he said that on one occasion Indians were unable to harvest their maize crop because repartimientos were shifted from one *encomendero* to another; as a result 20,000 to 30,000 were said to have starved

---

12. "Carta con documentos del Licenciado Francisco de Castañeda a S.M.," León, March 30, 1529 (CS, 1:479–508).

13. "Capitulos de cargos, formulados por Francisco Sánchez contra Rodrigo de Contreras, Governador de Nicaragua," Panama (CS, 6:103–16).

Table 3.1
Estimated Yearly Potential of the Nicaraguan Slave Trade, 1527–1536[a]

Year	Ships on Panama Run	Number of Trips per Ship	Ships on Peru Run	Number of Trips per Ship	Total Slave Trips from Nicaragua	Number of Slaves Exported
1527	2	12	0	0	24	8,400[b]
1528	5[c]	12	0	0	60	21,000
1529	6[c]	12	0	0	72	25,200
1530	8	12	0	0	96	33,600
1531	11	12	0	0	132	46,200
1532	14	12	0	0	168	58,800
1533	17[d]	12	2	2	208	72,800
1534	17	12	2	2	208	72,800
1535	17[e]	12	3	2	210	73,500
1536	17	6	3	1	102	35,700
Totals					1,280	448,000

[a]This table attempts to present the numbers of slaves that could have been carried by sea from Nicaragua in order to see if the estimates by early chroniclers are plausible. All figures, except those annotated, are estimates based on the few available documented citations as well as the general description of the trade as discussed in this chapter.

[b]Calculated on the basis of 350 slaves per ship. This is a reduction of the only contemporary report of a slave cargo size of 400 in 1535 ("Información que hace a S.M. el Escribano Francisco Sánchez," Granada, August 2, 1535, in CS, 3:406–12).

[c]Based on information in "Carta con documentos del Licenciado Francisco de Castañeda a S.M.," León, March 30, 1529, in CS, 1:479–508.

[d]Using a figure of 17 for the estimate of 15 to 20 by Herrera y Tordesillas (1944–47: 7:8).

[e]Based on "Información que hace a S.M. el Escribano Francisco Sánchez," Granada, August 2, 1535, in CS, 3:406–12.

to death. In 1533, Governor Francisco de Castañeda (Pedrarias' successor) told the Crown that more than 6,000 Indians had succumbed to a single measles epidemic. He also related that free Indians were fleeing and others were being illegally carried away by ships without license. The governor warned that the Indian supply would last scarcely four years if conditions were not remedied.[14] Later that year, when Rodrigo de Contreras became

14. "Carta a S.M. del Adelantado Don Pedro de Alvarado sobre varias puntos acerca de la población de Nicaragua" (signed, Licenciado Castañeda), León, May 1, 1533 (CDI, 24:192–203).

governor, the hypercritical Castañeda departed for Peru, taking 200 Spanish settlers and more than 700 free Indians with him on board five ships. During Casteñeda's governorship 80,000 Indians, excluding slaves, died or fled the province in four years.[15]

The problem of native depopulation became so serious that there was scarcely any labor for mining. Near the northeastern frontier of the central highlands, unconquered Indians continued to harass the settlers and miners of Nueva Segovia for many years.[16] Many mines were abandoned for lack of Spanish supervisors, who feared hostile Indians, and because of a native labor shortage. As a result, in 1537 the Crown agreed to reduce the king's fifth to a tenth for a period of ten years.[17]

In the absence of any contemporary contradictory sources, there seems little reason to doubt the remarkably similar contemporary estimates by Las Casas, Oviedo, and Herrera. It is likely that between 1527 and 1548, 450,000 to 500,000 Indians were removed from Nicaragua by the slave trade. During the same period an additional 400,000 to 600,000 Indians under Spanish domination probably died of disease, in war, or fled the province. A further unknown number, perhaps 200,000 to 250,000, residing unsubjugated in the central highlands was to be decimated during the ensuing period of 20 to 30 years.[18]

In the tribute assessment of 1548 for western Nicaragua, 11,500 tributaries were listed.[19] If this total is multiplied by the factor 3.3—a figure used by Borah and Cook (1960) for converting tributary numbers (taken from the *Suma de visitas de pueblos* of about 1548) to population totals in central Mexico—the 1548 population of western Nicaragua under Spanish domination would be estimated at 37,950. This estimate is remarkably similar to the 1544 Herrera estimate of 30,000.

The population appears to have declined still further during the remainder of the sixteenth century. In 1578 Bishop Antonio de Zayas estimated a native population of 8,000 for the province of Nicaragua; he stated that the region had become so poor that no *oidor* from Guatemala had visited the province in

15. "Petición que Diego Núñez de Mercado, Alcalde de la Fortaleza de la Ciudad de León, presentó al Consejo de las Indias," Madrid, November 16, 1541 (CS, 7:151–224).

16. "Carta a S.M. del Adelantado Don Pedro de Alvarado sobre varias puntos acerca de la población de Nicaragua" (signed, Licenciado Castañeda), León, May 1, 1533 (CDI, 24:192–203).

17. "Real Cédula expedida en Monzon," September 5, 1537 (CS, 5:224-25).

18. See Denevan (1961: 283) for more information on the population history of the central highlands.

19. "Diligencias de la distribución de los tributos de los pueblos de Nicaragua, practicadas por los oidores de la Real Audiencia de los Confines," San Salvador, November-December 1548 (CS, 14:357–85).

twelve years.[20] By that time most of the remaining Indians near the frontier had also perished.

In conclusion, it appears that the native population of western Nicaragua declined, as a result of slavery, war, and disease, from more than 1,000,000 in 1523 to less than 10,000 within a period of only 60 years.

20. "Carta del Obispo de Nicaragua y Costa Rica, Fray Antonio de Zayas a S.M. el Rey, sobre el estado de su diocicesio," León, January 12, 1578 (Peralta, 1883: 556–59).

PART III Mexico

"The total of our regional estimates for the population of central Mexico on the eve of the Spanish Conquest is 25.2 millions, which should be understood to be an estimate with a wide margin of error" (Borah and Cook, 1963: 88).

". . . Puzzling because their analysis leads the reader to the almost inescapable conclusion that it can't be done!" (Sanders, 1966).

INTRODUCTION

CENTRAL MEXICO

For central Mexico[1] there is more detailed statistical evidence, primarily tribute (tax) records, available for the size of aboriginal populations in the sixteenth century than for any other major region of the Americas. In the area of high civilization, all indications are for a population numbering in the many millions when Cortés arrived in 1519. The total is, nevertheless, very controversial, for the tribute records are incomplete, projections must be made from them in both time and space, and conversions must be made of tribute to tribute payers and of tribute payers to total people. It is not only the analysis of the data by modern historians that may be subject to question, but also the reliability of the data. The literature on the size and decline of the aboriginal population of central Mexico is considerable and the contributors numerous; however, it is dominated by the research of three Berkeley scholars—Simpson, S. F. Cook, and Borah—who have painstakingly uncovered and analyzed masses of numerical material.

---

1. As defined in the publications of Simpson, Borah, and S. F. Cook, central Mexico includes "Mexico from the Isthmus of Tehuantepec to the northern border of sedentary [Indian] settlement in 1550" (Borah and Cook, 1963: 3, end map).

77

The methodological contribution of Simpson, Cook, and Borah lies in the statistical treatment of incomplete tribute records for various periods of the sixteenth century. The analysis of such data was pioneered for central Mexico by Kubler (1942), who made use of the *Suma de visitas de pueblos* (1905) for 1547–1551 and other *encomienda* lists for 1569–1571 and 1595–1597. He made no attempt, however, to project back to the contact population of 1519. Kubler believed that the *encomenderos* over-reported tribute amounts, making the tax lists unreliable,[2] although he considered them still useful for estimating relative changes. His sampling resulted in the conclusion that the Indian population increased between the epidemics of 1545–1547 and 1575–1579, a conclusion not supported by the later research of Cook and Borah. Kubler did recognize a major overall decline from 1519, and the last section of his article discusses the impact of this decline on both Indian and Spanish societies. Kubler evaluated the various types of evidence for determining population movements (changes in relative density through time) in the sixteenth century. This discussion should be compared with that by Cook and Borah (1968) on the same topic. Kubler was much more critical of the reliability of the tax lists and believed that the data are too incomplete for determining total populations. Simpson, Cook, and Borah, of course, later developed techniques for estimating total populations from such incomplete lists.

The work of the "Berkeley School" need not be discussed here at length. It has been summarized by Borah and Cook (1969). It has been reviewed favorably by Dobyns (1966) and more critically and in detail in the following essay by Sanders. And it has been repudiated at length by Rosenblat (1967: 23–81), who stands by his original estimate (4,500,000 for all of Mexico; 1954: 1:102).[3]

See Cook and Borah (1960: 15–32) for a detailed description of their methodology for analyzing three types of data: actual counts of tributaries or other groups; tribute assessments for which the quota per tributary is known; and tribute assessments for which the quota per tributary is not known. For further discussions of their treatments of data, see Borah and Cook (1963) for the handling of pre-Conquest fiscal materials to estimate the aboriginal population of 1519. Also, see the chapters on method in Cook and Borah's *Essays* (1971–74).

Cook and Borah in 1968 examined the contemporary testimony by missionaries, soldiers, administrators, and other chroniclers on sixteenth-

2. Cook and Simpson (1948: 4) assumed error for the opposite reason, while Borah and Cook (1960: 7) believed that the *Suma de visitas* give "an accurate picture of central Mexico."

3. Rosenblat's 1967 critique is primarily directed at Borah and Cook's 1960 and 1963 monographs. For a response, see Borah (1968).

century Indian populations, testimony discarded by Kroeber, Rosenblat, and others as being mostly unreliable. Cook and Borah compare the reliability of different categories of evidence, and find that their own research agrees "in general with the ideas conveyed by early testimony." As a test, they compare their own results for 1519 with the responses to the *Relaciones geográficas* general questionnaire of 1577, which includes statements on pre-Conquest populations (PNE, Vols. 3–7). They find "reasonable agreement" between the two sets of figures.

The Berkeley thesis, arguing for quite large populations, is primarily contained in four now famous monographs in the Ibero-Americana monograph series (Cook and Simpson, 1948; Cook and Borah, 1960; and Borah and Cook, 1960, 1963), along with regional treatments of the Mixteca Alta (Cook and Borah, 1968) and west-central Mexico (Cook and Borah, 1971–74: 1:300–375). These monographs are particularly useful, and are capable of independent evaluation, because methodologies are usually clearly stated and because much of the relevant statistical data is presented in appendices. Cook and Simpson (1948) obtained an estimate for central Mexico in 1519 of 11,000,000 utilizing three different methods: baptismal figures, army sizes, and the ratio of the 1565 population (based on various tax lists) to that of 1519. Subsequently, as more tribute materials became available, estimates were derived for several other dates in the sixteenth century, particularly important among them being 6,300,000 in 1548, based on the *Suma de visitas* tribute lists for about half the towns in central Mexico,[4] and a 1532 figure of 16,800,000 based on a projection from 1568 (Cook and Borah, 1960: 47). On this basis, the rate and degree of decline determined by Cook and Simpson was apparently too low. Various projections from 1532 back to 1519 yielded populations of from 32,000,000 to 50,000,000, which seemed too high.

In their 1963 monograph Borah and Cook examined pictographic summaries of the tribute records of the Aztec empire and from them derived a 1519 population of 25,200,000, or a range between 20,000,000 and 28,000,000, depending on the figure used for average family size. Borah and Cook judge this figure to be a rough calculation but nevertheless supportive of their dense-population argument; and they consider such a population (average density of 125 per mi^2) to have been ecologically feasible in terms of pre-Conquest habitat and technology.[5] But as might be expected, the reaction in some historical circles was one of disbelief. The variables, the use of ratio and proportion, the interpolations, the seemingly arbitrary decisions were too many (e.g., Sanders, 1966). (Or was the total simply too high?)

4. The original figure given for 1548 by Borah and Cook (1960: 115) was 7,800,000, an error corrected in Cook and Borah (1960: 110).

5. Sanders (1966 and Chapter 4 here) does not agree.

Much of the reaction was emotional, and few of the critics, other than Sanders and to a lesser extent Rosenblat, have taken the time to examine the evidence and the methodology. Actually, the main methods of Cook and Borah, at least in their earlier studies, have become widely accepted (Mörner, 1973: 109). Also, it is interesting to note that scholars who will not accept 25,000,000 find figures between 10,000,000 and 15,000,000 not unreasonable (e.g., West and Augelli, 1966: 236). Such scholars were rare when Cook and Simpson postulated 11,000,000 in 1948. While their higher figures for central Mexico may be questioned, Simpson, Cook, and Borah nevertheless have brought about a radical revision of aboriginal demographic history not only in Mexico but throughout the hemisphere.

The population estimates for sixteenth-century central Mexico by Borah and Cook (1963: 4, 88) are as follows:

1519	25,200,000	1580	1,900,000
1532	16,800,000	1595	1,375,000
1548	6,300,000	1605	1,075,000
1568	2,650,000		

In *The Population of the Mixteca Alta, 1520–1960* (1968) Cook and Borah shift from a consideration of all of central Mexico to an examination of population for a small region therein from pre-Conquest times to 1960, an example of the kind of intensive local research they believe should be carried out in Mexico as well as elsewhere in the New World. In a chapter on population change from 1520 to 1590, they show changing rates of depopulation and calculate a 1520 population of 600,000 to 700,000, using three different methods. By 1590 the population was only 57,000.

The results of the Borah-Cook research for different dates is summarized in their 1969 article, "Conquest and Population." They provide a good, short review of the types of quantitative data available, the methods used to estimate population for a particular date and to determine the rate or changing rates of depopulation, and the social, political, and economic implications of massive depopulation. A major conclusion is that there were differing rates of depopulation from 1518 to 1568 in different climatic zones, with a much greater decline in the tropical lowlands.

William Sanders, in the essay that follows, makes a detailed evaluation of the Simpson, Cook, and Borah studies and for the most part finds their results unacceptable. First, he believes, as did Kubler, that the various available censuses and tax lists are far from accurate. Second, he questions the ability to derive a reliable conversion ratio of *casados* (married men) to the rest of the population. Third, for the period prior to the *Suma de visitas* he finds the ranges in taxes paid to be so great "that population calculations from the tax assessments would be virtually useless." Fourth, "the weakest argument in the studies conducted by Cook and Borah on sixteenth-century demography lies in their statistical manipulations to arrive at a figure for the tax-exempt population of 1548."

In reviewing the specific Simpson, Cook, and Borah monographs, Sanders discounts the 1948 study on the grounds that the clerical and military estimates used are much less reliable than Cook and Simpson believed. The reliability of Indian informants and other sources is also questioned, as well as what specific administrative levels the tax records refer to. The difficulties of converting tribute to tributaries and tributaries to total population are emphasized. The use of the Aztec tribute list in the 1963 Borah and Cook monograph is also criticized. Sanders notes that the authors themselves point out the main difficulties. He lists seven major problems with the treatment, basically concluding that the relationship between tribute and population is "exceedingly tenuous."

Sanders next presents an alternative calculation of the population in 1519 based on the archaeological, ecological, and documentary research of his Pennsylvania State University Teotihuacán Valley Project. He focuses on the "Central Mexican Symbiotic Region," a much smaller region than that studied by Simpson, Cook, and Borah (it is a part of their Region 1). This is a core area consisting of the Basin of Mexico and immediately adjacent areas. Sanders accepts the Cook and Borah figures for 1568 and compares them regionally with those for the first half of the twentieth century, excluding large urban centers, finding the two populations about the same. For the 1530s, he examines several estimates and censuses for the districts of Cholula and Tepoztlan, and arrives at populations under half those obtained by Cook and Borah. A basic assumption by Sanders is that very steep curves of depopulation during the early years are unreasonable, especially since "major" epidemics did not, in his opinion, occur until the 1540s.

Sanders obtains a population for the Central Mexican Symbiotic Region by using data in a census document signed by Ochoa de Luyando for the 1550s, containing apparent references to figures for the 1530s, plus other evidence for Mexico City and Tlaxcala. Using the resulting estimates for 1540 and 1532, plus those of Cook and Borah for 1568, the curve of decline is projected back to 1519, arriving at a total of 2,634,723 to 3,081,983, or an average of about 2,900,000 (Table 4.9; Fig. 4.4). The Borah and Cook population for the same area in 1519 would be 6,400,000. If the same ratio for the two estimates (2,900,000 and 6,400,000) is applied to the full region of central Mexico, for which Borah and Cook obtained 25,200,000, then Sanders' total for central Mexico would be 11,400,000.[6] Such an extrapolation, however, does not take into consideration the differences in ecology,

6. Elsewhere, Sanders gives an estimate of at least 5,000,000 to 6,000,000 for the full Aztec empire in 1519 (Sanders, 1972: 116) and 12,000,000 to 15,000,000 for all of Mesoamerica, from central Mexico into northwest Central America (Sanders and Price, 1968: 77).

population, and decline rates between the upland region studied by Sanders and the central Mexico of Borah and Cook, which includes tropical lowland regions.

Sanders then examines the population of the Teotihuacán Valley in detail, utilizing several different censuses. A total of 135,000 is obtained for 1519 in comparison to the 320,000 that can be derived from Borah and Cook. Sanders' total for the valley is close to that of 1910, a similarity considered to provide support for his figure over that of Borah and Cook, since Sanders believes that, overall, aboriginal agricultural potential was equal to that of the early twentieth century. A section-by-section examination of the valley suggests that a population of 150,000 to 175,000 could have been supported (supplied with sufficient maize). Sanders' 1519 total of 135,000 thus allows for land in other crops besides maize and for a surplus for trade and taxation. Given this argument, the Borah and Cook total becomes "absolutely impossible." This conclusion assumes that more intensive cultivation (in terms of both yields and frequency of cropping) than granted by Sanders did not exist, which is not necessarily true. There is increasing evidence that in many parts of the world agricultural productivity was significantly greater in the past than today, and that the differences are not always due to subsequent environmental deterioration.

Finally, Sanders examines the demography of districts and towns in the Valley of Mexico, including the city of Tenochtitlán, for which he accepts 150,000 to 200,000 for the island city proper in 1519, supported largely by intensive *chinampa* agriculture.[7]

Of the various other studies of the aboriginal population of central Mexico, most are cited in Dobyns (1966) or in Borah's essay here. Also, see Sauer's (1948: 59) calculation of a minimum of 140,000 Indians in Colima about 1523, and Gerhard's (1975: 343) figure of 850,000 for Morelos in 1500 and 600,000 in 1524. Particular mention should be made here of the research by S. F. Cook (1949a, 1949b, 1963) on the erosional history of central Mexican valleys, which has provided evidence for changing settlement, accelerated erosion due to excessive cropping and deforestation, and relative populations. One conclusion is that the native population of central Mexico had exceeded the carrying capacity of the land and by the end of the fifteenth century "was doomed even had there been no European conquest" (Borah and Cook, 1967: 719–20). It has been suggested that one manifestation of this was Aztec human sacrifice and warfare (S. F. Cook, 1946a). Another, related conclusion is that excessive pressure on the environment was

7. Teotihuacán was also large, with an estimated probable population of 125,000 and possibly a population exceeding 200,000 at its height in A.D. 600 (Millon, 1970: 1080).

only temporarily eased by the native depopulation and was soon renewed by overgrazing of Spanish livestock whose numbers increased as human numbers decreased and as Indian agricultural lands ceased to be farmed (Simpson, 1952). By 1610 the human population had decreased to about 1,000,000 (Borah and Cook, 1963: 4), whereas the population of cattle, sheep, and goats had risen to about 8,000,000 (Simpson, 1952: ii).

NORTHERN MEXICO

Northern Mexico is a vast, arid region, and there is little likelihood that it ever had a great aboriginal population, although densities were locally high along rivers and the coast. Nevertheless it was the scene of a major confrontation between Carl Sauer (1935) and Alfred Kroeber (1939: 177–78). By carefully examining and cross-checking documentary materials, Sauer was able effectively to challenge Kroeber's low totals of 100,000 for the northeast and 100,000 for the northwest (Sauer obtained 540,000 for the northwest), and thereby raise doubts about Kroeber's estimates for other regions. Kroeber opposed Sauer "with the generic supposition that the Spaniards counted or estimated excessively," but conceded that if Sauer was right "all our figures for the American Southwest must be far too low." The debate is discussed in some detail by Dobyns (1966: 398, 403–4) and need not be repeated. It should be emphasized, however, that research by Dobyns (1962, 1963a, 1976), plus that of Ezell (1961: 17), suggests that even Sauer's figures, at least for some groups such as the Yaqui and Northern Pima, were too conservative, since losses from early epidemics were not fully considered. Dobyns (1976: 18) suggests a total of 930,000 for Sauer's area.

Sauer was one of the first to convert "warriors, families, baptisms, and other items" into total populations, a technique which is now common. Not only were documents cross-checked, but comparisons were made with present populations in the same areas. Estimates were considered in the light of resources, subsistence, and material culture on the basis of detailed field work by Sauer in most of the areas concerned.

The debate over populations in Baja California is similar to that for the region covered by Sauer; however, the anti-Kroeber position is backed up by several detailed regional studies: Kniffen (1931: 51) for the Colorado delta area; Meigs (1935: 133–42) for the northern peninsula; Cook (1937: 1–19) for the entire peninsula; and Aschmann (1959) for the central desert. Kroeber questioned Meigs' figures for all of Baja, which add up to 33,000 (0.57 per mi^2 or 0.22 per km^2) on the assumption that the area could not have supported "more than a fraction" of the density of American California (0.85

per mi^2 or 0.33 per km^2 according to Kroeber, 1939: 178). Yet Cook, averaging results from four different methods, obtained an even higher total of 41,500 for just the Jesuit mission area in the south.

Aschmann (1959: 178) obtained an average density of 1.12 per square mile (0.43 per km^2) for perhaps the least hospitable sector of the peninsula. (Meigs' average for the more favorable north was 1.15 per mi^2 or 0.44 per km^2.) Aschmann's central area total of 21,000 is based on the recorded maximum populations in the missions. To these he added documented numbers of deaths just prior to a mission count, of Indians shifted from one area to another, of converted Indians in settlements outside the missions, plus an estimate for unconverted Indians. The methodology is sound, generally being based on actual counts rather than estimates, except for the unconverted Indians. As Aschmann acknowledges, however, the maximum recorded populations used are for dates well after initial contact. Hence they do not take into consideration early depopulation, so that Aschmann's totals are too low for pre-Spanish conditions. Disease was the major cause of depopulation, with the Indians "dying off almost as rapidly as they were reduced" (Aschmann, 1959: 244). If Aschmann's density is extended to the full peninsula, a total of 62,300 is obtained.

Although the area and population concerned are relatively small, the Aschmann study effectively demonstrates that population densities of over one person per square mile (0.39 per km^2) are possible under aboriginal conditions of subsistence in very poor environments such as deserts. The same must be assumed for the more favored tropical rain forests. Both environments, considered by some scholars to have been virtually empty, cover vast areas of the New World, and even average densities of only one person per square mile would result in total populations numbering in the several millions.[8]

Thus the totals for Mexico tend to loom large, especially for the central highlands, but with substantial populations also in the deserts and tropical lowlands. Even the moderate estimates for Mexico are higher than most of the maximum estimates for comparable regions in North and South America. Is this a correct comparison, and if so why the difference, or are there major errors in the estimates for either Mexico or the other regions? In the essay that follows, William Sanders challenges the high figures for central Mexico by Cook and Borah, but his own estimates are still relatively large compared to other regions of the hemisphere.

8. An average of one person per square mile (0.39 per km^2) for all 48 contiguous states in the United States would equal 3,022,260 persons, and for the Amazon Basin would equal about 2,564,000 persons.

CHAPTER 4 **The Population of the Central Mexican**

Symbiotic Region, the Basin of Mexico,

and the Teotihuacán Valley

in the Sixteenth Century

William T. Sanders

One of the major objectives of the Teotihuacán Valley Project was to establish a relative, possibly an absolute, picture of population distribution and history in the valley. We are convinced that there is a positive correlation between societal evolution and demographic processes, and we view the project as a test of this theoretical position. During the Classic, Postclassic, and post-Conquest periods the central plateau of Mexico played an extraordinarily dominant role in the cultural history of Mesoamerica. It was in this area that the largest cities and states were found, and the growth of these cities and states, to a great degree, determined the course of Mesoamerican history over a period of 2,000 years. This dominance was mainly the product of demographic factors and processes. Within the plateau is a core area where agriculture was intensive, population was heavily concentrated, and where the great Classic and Postclassic cities were located. It includes the Basin of

This article originally appeared as part of a mimeographed report by W. T. Sanders, A. Kovar, T. Charlton, and R. A. Diehl, *The Teotihuacán Valley Project, Final Report, Volume 1: The Natural Environment, Contemporary Occupation and 16th Century Population of the Valley*, Occasional Papers in Anthropology No. 3, Department of Anthropology, The Pennsylvania State University, University Park, 1970, pp. 385–457. The author has deleted several of the original tables, and he rewrote the section on the special problem of Tenochtitlán; he and the editor have made minor revisions and corrections in the text.

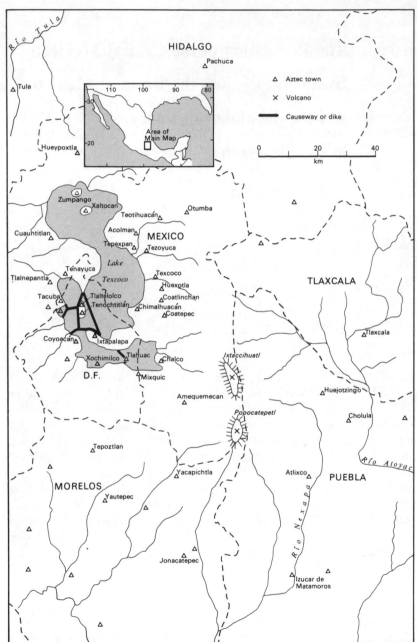

Map 4.1. The Central Mexican Symbiotic Region. Based on Sanders and Price (1968: Fig. 10).

Mexico and adjacent areas in southern Hidalgo, southwestern Tlaxcala, the western third of Puebla, and the state of Morelos. Sanders (1956) has referred to this area as the Central Mexican Symbiotic Region (Map 4.1).[1]

In this essay we will attempt to reconstruct the political demography of the Central Mexican Symbiotic Region, the Teotihuacán Valley, and the Basin of Mexico for the year 1519. The evidence will be based on documentary sources from the sixteenth century, checked against Charlton's (1970) studies of present-day agricultural systems and Diehl's (1970) analysis of recent population history and distribution. In a later study we will test the conclusions against our data from Aztec archaeological sites. Moving one step further we hope to use the Aztec population data as a yardstick to measure the population of the Teotihuacán Valley in earlier periods. We will, we hope, be able to present a picture of population size and distribution for all of the major periods of human population of the valley. The significance of these demographic patterns with respect to cultural process will then be analyzed in detail.

THE POPULATION OF CENTRAL MEXICO, 1530–1595: THE COOK, BORAH, AND SIMPSON STUDIES

In 1948 Cook and Simpson published a monograph entitled *The Population of Central Mexico in the Sixteenth Century*. In this study they utilized Spanish secular and ecclesiastic tax lists and censuses to establish a population datum for the year 1565 for the region of Mesoamerica they call "central Mexico." This includes the area embraced by approximately the states of Vera Cruz, Oaxaca, Guerrero, Puebla, Tlaxcala, Morelos, México, Hidalgo, the Distrito Federal, Michoacán, Jalisco, Colima, and Nayarit, plus small portions of Zacatecas, Querétaro, and San Luis Potosí. They also attempted to arrive at an estimate for the population in 1519 based on statements as to the population of communities and provinces, the size of Indian armies, and the number of conversions made by missionaries during the first decade after the Conquest. On the basis of these data they arrived at a population figure of 4,409,180 for 1565 and 11,000,000 for 1519. Utilizing these two datum points and data from other censuses for a small sample of communities ranging in date between 1553 and 1571, they calculated a curve of popula-

1. For the locations of Aztec towns and provinces mentioned here but not shown on Map 4.1, see Map 2 and other maps in Gibson (1964) and the end map and Appendix 3 in Cook and Simpson (1948). Aztec place names on Map 4.1 and in the text usually follow the spellings in Gerhard (1972).

tion decline between 1519 and 1565. By using the same procedure, plus overall census calculations by the Spanish authorities themselves, they also calculated a population curve for the period between 1565 and 1607.

The report produced a lively controversy with respect to their estimates and methodology and stimulated a great number of subsequent papers and monographs by Cook and Borah.

In 1960 Borah and Cook published *The Population of Central Mexico in 1548*. This study was primarily an attempt to utilize the *Suma de visitas de pueblos* (1905) to establish a reasonable population figure for the midpoint of the sixteenth century.

In the same year Cook and Borah published a monograph entitled *The Indian Population of Central Mexico, 1531–1610*. In part this was a reevaluation of the Cook-Simpson study of the population in the 1560s, with corrections of errors in the earlier study (primarily in the elimination of overlaps of census data and changes in conversion ratios). They also examined the rather scanty and highly variable tax data from the Second Audiencia (1530–1536) to establish a population estimate for the 1530s, and they reexamined the data from the period between 1570 and 1610 to establish population estimates for two datum points, 1595 and 1605.

In 1963 Borah and Cook, in a third monograph, attempted to use the *Codex Mendoza* (1938) and the *Matrícula de Tributos* (n.d.) (two surviving copies of the tax list of the Aztec empire) to achieve a population estimate on the eve of the Spanish Conquest. On the basis of these documents they estimated a popluation of 25,200,000 for central Mexico, with a possible range of between 18,000,000 and 26,300,000, a figure approximately double the estimate of the Cook and Simpson study.

The population of central Mexico between 1519 and 1607 as derived from these studies can be summarized in the list given below.

Date	Cook-Simpson (1948)	Date	Cook-Borah (1960, 1960, 1963)
1519	11,000,000	1519	25,200,000
1532	–	1532	16,800,000
1540	6,427,466	1548	6,300,000
1565	4,409,180	1568	2,650,000
1580	–	1580	1,900,000
1597	2,500,000	1595	1,375,000
1607	2,014,000	1605	1,075,000

The Cook-Borah studies resulted in a sizable reduction of the figures for the period between 1565 and 1607, but, on the other hand, a considerable increase in the estimates for the period between 1519 and 1548, as compared to the Cook-Simpson figures. The implication here is one of a much steeper decline as compared to the earlier study.

We will now examine the sources for their estimates and discuss their population figures and the methodology for deriving them.

Sources of Data

Within a decade after the fall of Tenochtitlán the Spanish institutions of church and state were introduced into central Mexico. Prior to the establishment of the First Audiencia in 1528 no formal tax structure was established. During part of that time Cortés was governor of the newly conquered territory and was primarily occupied in military expeditions to pacify outlying provinces and in the reconstruction of Mexico City as the colonial capital. He exacted informal taxes in labor, goods, and services from a number of towns in central Mexico during the period of his governorship. The church was primarily concerned with a program of missionization by mass baptisms, and accurate data utilizable in population estimates were not compiled.

During the First Audiencia (1528–1530) a formal tax system was established. The old Indian states were converted into tax districts; each consisted of a center or *cabecera* and dependent settlements variously called *aldeas, sujetos, barrios,* or *estancias.* The majority of these tax districts were made tributary to the Crown; the balance, 180,000 Indian tributaries in all according to one estimate (Gibson, 1964: 61), were assigned to 30 *encomiendas.* No standard tax ratios were established, and the amount of the tax exacted per capita by Crown and *encomendero* varied considerably from tax district to tax district. Excesses within the system were notorious and were the basis of continuous complaints by the Indians. The constant abuse and injustices resulted in an acrimonious debate between Nuño de Guzmán, president of the audiencia, and Bishop Zumárraga. The tax system was apparently modeled on the aboriginal pattern, which seems to have had the following characteristics.

A large tax-exempt class existed that included nobles by birth, nobles by military achievement, and various types of serfs or *mayeques,* some attached to the state, others to the temples, others to private estates. There were also variations in the kinds of taxes paid by the tributary population. Craftsmen and merchants were exempt from corvée labor and taxes in agricultural produce. The bulk of the population consisted of peasant farmers who paid taxes in agricultural produce, labor for public construction, and household services in the houses of the nobles.

The structure was slightly remodeled for Spanish use. The encomendero received goods (salt, cloth, lumber), agricultural produce, corvée labor for house construction and agriculture, and daily household services and goods in the form of firewood, processed and cooked food, poultry, and servants. Comparable services and goods were exacted by the Crown. The hereditary Indian nobility was tax exempt and its members were allowed to maintain their estates and attached serfs, the latter being also tax exempt with respect to Crown and encomienda. Some of the tax-exempt population formerly assigned to temples and palaces were reassigned to the church and municipal governments and continued their tax-exempt status. Also tax exempt were the old and infirm.

The First Audiencia was extremely unpopular and was finally replaced by the Second Audiencia, which functioned from 1530 to 1535. During this period a serious but apparently unsuccessful attempt was made to correct the abuses of the tax system. Between 1528 and 1535 two minor epidemics (Gibson, 1964: 448) occurred, which resulted in some population loss, consequently aggravating the Indians' problems of tax payments. Taxes were revised in some cases, particularly in the Crown holdings, and a central register of taxes was established called the *Matrícula de Tributos* (n.d.). Generally speaking, however, the reforms were not too effective (Zorita, 1941: 171; see quote below).

In 1536 the office of viceroy was created, in part to provide a more effective executive and judicial structure for New Spain. The first viceroy, Antonio de Mendoza, held office until 1550. During his administration a minor epidemic occurred in 1538, followed in the period from 1545 to 1548 by a series of epidemics of major proportions that ravaged the colony and resulted in an extremely heavy loss of life. This was followed by another minor epidemic in 1550. This enormous loss of life produced serious economic hardships, and the period is rife with Indian complaints about their inability to meet the tax schedules established by the Second Audiencia. After the 1545–1548 epidemics the situation became so serious and tax payments were so far out of balance in relationship to population that a census was conducted of the population and an investigation of the tax rates made. The investigation was conducted by special emissaries sent by the Crown, in part based on "on the spot" censuses made by them, in part by information derived from local informants. The census took approximately four years to complete (1547–1551) and the final report was a document called the *Suma de visitas de pueblos* (1905). The tribute schedule contained in the *Suma* is mostly that established by the Second Audiencia; the population census dates from the time of the investigation. Borah and Cook converted the various goods and services into the contemporary monetary scale and by a comparison of taxes and population demonstrated that there was wide variation in the amount of tax paid per capita—from 2.01 to 63.2 *reales*! This simple fact dramatically illustrates the ineffectuality of the Second Audiencia and Mendoza's administration in correcting abuses and their complete inability to keep tax schedules in a reasonable relationship to population.

The *Suma* contains information on 1,200 cabeceras and their tax districts (probably about half of those in existence in central Mexico at that time). Unfortunately, the census itself was only a partial one; in the majority of the towns only *tributarios,* or tribute payers, were counted, and tax-exempt groups were excluded from the census.

In 1551 Mendoza was replaced as viceroy by the first Luis de Velasco. The *Suma* was completed during the two years that witnessed the change of command. A number of complaints as to the accuracy of the census led to a series of rechecks in the 1550s, and during the same period tax schedules were revised on the basis of the various censuses. Such reforms were carried out primarily on the Crown holdings and then only incompletely.

In 1556 Philip II ascended the throne of a bankrupt kingdom. In order to raise funds for the royal treasury a new tax law was promulgated in which all exemptions, except the *caciques,* or native dynastic chiefs, and their immediate families, the aged, and the infirm, were abolished, and for the first time a standard head tax was established. After several revisions an annual tax of one *peso* of gold and half a *fanega* of maize per year was set for each married man. Widows, widowers, and unmarried adults were classified as half tributaries and were taxed at a rate of one-half that of married men. Between 1557 and 1576 the new tax reforms were extended over the entire area of central Mexico. The tax lists from this period and particularly from after 1565 can therefore be easily converted to total population.

During the period from 1556 to 1576 the tax structure remained stable, frequent censuses were taken, and taxes were periodically readjusted. None of these records, however, has survived in complete form.

The period between 1556 and 1576 was also one of relative economic prosperity, but minor epidemics (1550, 1558, 1559, 1563–1564, and 1566; Gibson, 1964: 448) continued to plague the Indian population. As a result of the problems engendered by this further population loss and other fiscal problems, Philip ordered a new assessment of the population and of natural resources based on data compiled by investigators and local officials between 1575 and 1580. Unfortunately the censuses coincided with the second major epidemic of the sixteenth century; a series of diseases ravaged the country between 1576 and 1581 with the result of extremely heavy loss of life. Gibson also reports subsequent epidemics of minor proportions in 1587–1588, 1590, 1592–1597, and 1601–1602.

At approximately the same time as the establishment of the cabecera-sujeto administrative district, the church instituted its own administrative system which included three levels in descending order of size: *arzobispado, obispado*, and *parroquia*. The parroquia was equivalent to what in English one would call a parish. It included a main church with a resident priest and a series of smaller dependent churches called *visitas* that were visited on a regular itinerary by the parroquia priest. In many cases, but not all, the parroquia coincided with the cabecera-sujeto district, the parroquia church being located in the cabecera and the visita churches in the dependent settlements. Periodic censuses were conducted by ecclesiastic authorities, at least after 1560, and this body of independent data can be directly compared to the tax censuses. The ecclesiastic censuses are as variable in content and terminology as are the tax documents, however, and some censuses include only adult married males, others the number of confessees (males over 14, females over 12), and still others the entire population over four years of age.

Cook and Borah (1960: Ch. 2) examined a great number of the sixteenth-century civil tax lists and ecclesiastic censuses and assigned a letter key to identify them. The *Suma,* for example, is identified as Source A. In this study we have used this key, and the reader is referred to their descriptions of each source.

There are a number of problems involved in the utilization of these sources to derive reasonably accurate estimates of the sixteenth-century population. These may be described as follows.

The Accuracy of the Censuses

One problem that Cook, Simpson, and Borah have greatly underestimated is that of the accuracy of the censuses. Even in cases where no intentional fraud was involved we suspect considerable inaccuracies. In many parts of central Mexico the settlement pattern was extremely dispersed and census taking must have encountered considerable difficulty. As they point out, not all of the censuses were conducted by the Crown inspectors: they were frequently based on local officials and informants. Furthermore, even in areas where the population was nucleated into a relatively small number of large settlements, it is doubtful that actual "on the spot" counts were made in all of the sujetos or visitas. Even in contemporary Mexico, in areas of dispersed or nucleated settlements, censuses are not entirely reliable, and under the conditions of sixteenth-century transportation and communication the problem was even more acute.

Cook, Simpson, and Borah to the contrary (and their own treatment of the subject reveals this), there were both incentives and opportunities for fraudulent censuses. The history of the sixteenth century was one of rapid population decline and a continuous struggle by the Indians to reduce their tax loads, counteracted by attempts by the Crown and encomenderos to keep the status quo. Cook and Simpson, basing their argument on the famous dispute between Cortés and the Crown over the size of his encomienda, contended that most figures when inaccurate were repressed rather than exaggerated. The Cortés estate, however, was an exceptional, perhaps unique, case. He had originally requested as his encomienda almost the entire Basin of Mexico, the most densely populated area in the newly conquered territory. This request was rejected by the king, who was afraid of the possible political power Cortés might exercise with such an estate, and he was finally awarded an encomienda that included the modern state of Morelos, the Valley of Toluca, southern Vera Cruz, the Valley of Oaxaca, and the Tacubaya-Coyoacán zone near Mexico City. The official census of this huge territory was only 23,000 *vasallos*. Secret investigations revealed that the actual figure was several times higher, and apparently Cortés intentionally suppressed the real figures to distract the attention of the Crown from his huge holdings.

Most encomiendas, however, were quite small, and the encomenderos in fact exaggerated the census data to support their litigation against a reduction of the tax schedule. This procedure, combined with Indian attempts to show population loss, resulted in a stream of legal suits and investigations by audiencia and Crown officials. Obviously we are faced here with a very complex situation in which census frauds were expectable in both directions, with Indians attempting to show population loss, encomenderos attempting to stabilize tax rates based on earlier censuses, and investigators in an extremely exposed position between the factions.

Zorita discussed in detail the problems of census taking, and the following quote illustrates the methods:

> Some encomenderos were accustomed, when counting their people, to designate officials from the village, or elsewhere, to accompany those who made the accounting. By pleasing them with gifts, or by other ways, every means possible was made to obtain a large show of people. The same was done by the encomenderos personally, and it is known, as I have determined from my own investigations, that they bring people from nearby villages and say that they had come to live there, and these are then counted as tributaries. The census completed, or when convenient, these people return to their native homes or go elsewhere, and thus their tribute obligations are placed on those who remain in the village (Zorita, 1941: 171).

With respect to the Crown dependencies, perhaps the problem was less acute. But even in those cases we really have scanty information on the techniques of census taking. In some investigations the Indians themselves provided the census taker with the data. We grant readily, as Cook and Borah argue, that the Indians prior to and after the Conquest did keep accurate population statistics; but how do we know that they did not provide the Spanish investigator with a doctored or falsified census? The motivation was there, and unless the investigator conducted a house-by-house count, deception would have been relatively easy. Furthermore, some investigators were in fact accused of overzealous devotion to Crown interests, and offered exaggerated census figures. We refer specifically to the series of censuses conducted by Vasco de Puga in the region around Mexico City in the 1560s. He in turn accused the church of depressing its censuses to protect the Indians from taxation by the state.

Wholly aside from the problems of the accuracy of the censuses, there is the problem of completeness of surviving records, omission of remote districts or communities, and particularly the problem of overlapping administrative districts. In one case, and there are others, the problem is particularly acute.

Prior to the Conquest, Texcoco was the center of an enormous tributary domain that rivaled that of Tenochtitlán. The political structure of this domain was similar to that of the Aztec. It was divided up into a great number of semiautonomous cabecera-sujeto states, each with its own government headed by its own hereditary ruler who ruled his state with little interference from Texcoco. All paid an annual tribute to Texcoco, and other than that little political integration was achieved. An exception to this rule of semiautonomy was a large, continuous, compact territory that included 14 small states plus the core state of Texcoco itself. All but three of these 15 states were located within the Basin of Mexico, east of Lake Texcoco (the exceptions were Tulancingo, Huachinango, and Xicotepec). The population of this area shared a tradition of common origin, dialect, and name, and the territory was referred to as Acolhuacan. The rulers of the 14 subject states were all related to the Texcocan royal family and acted as an advisory council.

After the Conquest the Texcocan royal family attempted unsuccessfully to claim cabecera status over the entire former tributary empire, and, failing in this endeavor, over Acolhuacan. Finally they settled for an extended domain that included the core state of Texcoco plus Huexotla, Chiautla, Coatlichan, and Tezoyuca, all in the immediate area. In some of the post-Conquest sixteenth-century censuses it is not entirely clear whether the data refer to the core state or the extended domain. Cook and Simpson, for example, took census data that undoubtedly meant to refer to the extended domain and applied them to the core state. With respect to references to the Conquest period, the problem is even more acute, as shall be demonstrated at a later point.

Conversion Ratios

The data assembled by Cook, Borah, and Simpson on post-Conquest sixteenth-century population may be for convenience grouped into two major types. One involves actual population figures or tax assessments levied at a time when the quota per tributary was standardized. The population estimates after 1556 are based primarily on this direct evidence. For the period from 1531 to 1556 there are very little direct population data. An exception would be the *Suma de visitas,* but the rates of tribute per capita at that time were not yet standardized. Their method in such cases was indirect, and consisted of a calculation of the *monetary value* of the various goods and services exacted as tax (based on Borah and Cook's 1958 study of price indices for the sixteenth century); from these data population was calculated based on an *assumed average quota.*

Direct data. One of the problems in utilizing the direct data is that of the conversion of the category of persons actually counted to the total population. The earliest document that gives population figures extensively is the *Suma.* The data from town to town in the *Suma* are extremely variable. In some documents the count is of *casados, vecinos,* or tributarios. Borah and Cook (1960) demonstrate that at the time of the *Suma* these terms were synonymous and all referred to an adult married male taxpayer. Subsequent to 1556, however, the definition of a tributario changed. A whole tributary referred to an adult married male taxpayer; *viudas* (widows), *viudos* (widowers), and *solteros* (unmarried adults) were classified as half tributaries. The result was that the term tributario no longer corresponded to a casado or vecino in the later census periods. In order to establish a ratio between the various types of tributaries for calculations of total population in the period after 1556, Borah and Cook (1960) tabulated data from a number of towns where more than one category was given. In a sample of 81 cabecera districts (from documents ranging in date between 1540 and 1570) the total number of casados was 47,761, of viudos 8,994. The overall ratio of casados to viudos was therefore 1.0 : 0.188. The problem of the ratio of casados to solteros was considerably more difficult, since there was apparently great variation in the age and residential status on the one hand and the tributary status for the term soltero on the other. In some censuses only tributarios solteros were counted (prior to 1556). In others, the count includes all solteros. Complicating the picture is the fact that tributario soltero status was assigned in different towns at different ages. In some cases only solteros living in separate households were taxed, a pattern that might well have acted to perpetuate the extended family. In others, those residing with their parents were taxed as well. Borah and Cook (1960: 81–82) tabulate the data (primarily from the *Suma*) as shown below.

Category	Number of Towns	Ratio to Casados
Tributarios solteros	12	0.103
All solteros above 12 years	12	0.274
All solteros above 8 years	3	0.832
No age or status given	102	0.039–1.435

The data are so variable and indefinite that an overall conversion ratio could be established only with considerable reservations. On the basis of the data, however, Borah and Cook (1960: 88) settled on an overall ratio of 0.11 tributarios solteros per casado. They then state: "Thus for every one hundred casados, there were twenty-three viudos and eleven solteros, each of whom paid tribute at a lower rate." In the tabulation of total population for the later censuses they considered that there were 1.17 times as many tributarios as casados, or 0.855 times as many casados as tributarios. In their calculations for earlier censuses they simply equated tributarios with casados.

In order to establish the ratio of casados to total population Borah and Cook surveyed a number of documents, particularly the *Suma,* where categories of population other than casados, viudos, and solteros were given. The pre-Conquest Aztec states apparently did take complete censuses, except that they excluded children below three or four years of age. This pattern apparently continued into the sixteenth century after the Conquest. In the *Suma* one-fourth of the cabecera districts provide data for categories of population other than casados. The number and designation of categories from document to document are extremely varied and at times vague. Categories frequently given are casados, viudos, viudas, solteros, *muchachas,* and *niños.* Occasionally the source explicitly states that the count includes all persons (presumably including the children below three or four years). Borah and Cook (1960: 89–95) tabulate the data as shown below.

Group of Towns	Number of Towns	Ratio of Casados to Rest of Population
A	12	2.79
B	23	2.95
C	92	3.19
D	91	2.96

The ratio is very consistently about 3.0, suggesting that the looseness of phraseology was an idiosyncracy of scribe rather than of the census procedure, and that in all cases the census was meant to include all persons above three to four years of age. Borah and Cook then used an average ratio of 3.0 to convert casados to population above three to four years of age.

In one set of reports in the *Suma,* that of the region of Tehuantepec, a complete census was taken including children below three to four years of age. Those children made up 11.24 percent of the total population. Borah and Cook cite the 1940 census of Mexico in which the children below four years made up 11.4 percent of the population. On the basis of these calculations they then arrived at a conversion ratio for casados to total population of 3.3.

In the ecclesiastic documents the problem is relatively simple, since the census was based on either the casado or a category called *gente de confesión.* As the sources made clear, this category included all males above 14 years of age and females above 12. Using the 1930 census of Mexico, Cook and Simpson (1948: 12) found that this age category comprised 62.6 percent of the total population. In their later studies Cook and Borah used ecclesiastic documents only sparingly, primarily to check figures from the secular tax lists or to fill out lacunae.

Generally speaking, the censuses made later in the sixteenth century were of considerably greater reliability than the earlier ones; rechecks were frequent and there is agreement between church and state in many cases. Population data for the first half of the sixteenth century, however, are highly suspect, and any calculations based upon such data must be used with considerable caution and reservation.

Indirect data. For the period prior to the *Suma* there are very few direct census data. Borah and Cook (1960) established population figures for 1548 based on the *Suma*, and then (Cook and Borah, 1960)) attempted to establish a population figure for the period of the Second Audiencia (1532) based entirely on the quantity of the tax. It must be emphasized that the earlier taxes were not based on a standardized per capita formula. Their method involved two basic steps: (1) the conversion of the various kinds of goods and services, first to a relative scale, then to an absolute scale in terms of the Spanish real; (2) the conversion of this total tax in reales to population. With respect to the first step, they assembled data from documents to establish a relative scale of values of goods in the early sixteenth century. They were also able to establish a monetary common denominator in terms of the Spanish currency. The major problem lies in the second step. Cook and Borah on the one hand have emphasized the fact that there was considerable variability in the quotas paid per tributary family from town to town, and the courts were full of complaints of the inequalities of the system. They argue, however, that the tribute exacted must have had some relationship to tributary population, and that it must have been within the capacity of the population to pay. We agree, but what does the term "some relationship" mean, and what is meant by the "capacity of the population to pay"? When the *Suma* investigations were conducted, the range of tax per capita from town to town varied from 2.01 to 63.2 reales per tributary as noted previously, presumably the result of a great number of causes of which variation in population decline and inequalities in the tax structure were primary. With ranges this great, we argue that population calculations from the tax assessments would be virtually worthless. One could even make the assumption that, without the effective controls established after the 1550s, *even the minimal average tax found in the* Suma *of 2.01 reales was excessive in proportion to living-cost standards for the early sixteenth century.*

In their subsequent discussion Cook and Borah disagree with themselves (they have to if a population figure is to be derived), since they argue for a relatively narrow range of tax variation in an attempt to establish an average payment per married taxpayer. They settled on a figure of 1.5 reales per tributary for 1530 and used this as a base for population calculations. This figure is based on the following arguments.

During the sixteenth century there was a steady rise in the prices of goods. Cook and Borah were able to establish a price curve based on data between 1551 and 1571. They then projected the curve backward and arrived at a figure of 2.0 reales per casado for the 1530s as a reasonable per capita tax in terms of existing living-cost standards for that period. They then proceeded to test this figure, using a sample of three communities for the period 1526–1536 in which the source provides data on both taxes and population. The range of tax per capita is from 0.47 to 2.09. (The very low figure, however, is from the *Codex Kingsborough* [1912] and relates to the town of Tepetlaoxtoc, in which all population estimates for the early sixteenth century are certainly excessive.) They also based their estimate on an extremely vague statement by Zorita, referring to the *pre-Conquest* tribute and dating around 1565, to the effect that:

> As for the third question, about the value of tributes in terms of gold pesos, this cannot be clearly established, for in those days [before the Conquest] each tributary gave little and what he gave was of little value among them although worth much today. It is certain that now one tributary pays more than six did then, and one town now gives more in pesos than then did six towns of those that gave tribute in gold, and because the tribute did not cost the labor that it does now it was not valued as highly; but as far as one can guess, everything that a tributary paid, even including service, was not worth more than from three to four reales (Zorita in Cook and Borah, 1960: 25).

The statement was clearly not meant to be exact, yet Cook and Borah take the ten reales average tax paid in 1565 per tributary, divide by 6, and arrive at an average of 1.67 reales average tax for 1519. They then argue, on the basis of the sixteenth-century price curve, that the three to four reales in 1565 would probably be worth one real in 1519, and that their 1.5 figure (see below) for 1530 is therefore reasonable.

Finally, their estimate is based on a statement by Bishop Sebastián Ramírez de Fuenleal to the effect that in 1532 the most common annual tax levy was strips of cotton cloth ("una pierna de manta"), in some regions given every 80 days, four such piernas making up one manta per casado. The price of such a manta in Mexico City at that time, from other sources cited by Cook and Borah, was 2.17 reales. In fact, however, no town paid only mantas, and their tax included other items; furthermore the majority of the towns paid taxes in goods other than cotton cloth. It is possible, but in view of Indian complaints it is doubtful, that taxes in cloth were based on a regular rate since Indian techniques of production were too primitive to permit a very wide range of variability, but there is no reason to assume this was true of other commodities. Ramírez de Fuenleal's statement probably relates to an ideal condition, possibly in reference to more equitable pre-Conquest native tax rates, but the history of litigation by the Indians conclusively demonstrates that it was never effectively applied in the post-Conquest period.

The Nontributary Population

The only document prior to the 1556 tax reform that provides abundant direct population data is the *Suma de vistas*. A number of writers (Kubler, 1942; Cook and Simpson, 1948; Borah and Cook, 1960) have noted that the population figures in the *Suma* are consistently and strikingly lower than those reported in later censuses. Kubler suggested that the census was accurate and that there was a population increase in the decades of the 1560s and 1570s following a sharp decline between 1519 and the date of the *Suma*. Borah and Cook, however, have argued for a continuous decline throughout the sixteenth century, a position which is better supported by the documentary sources and with which we concur. The explanation for the lower *Suma* figures, as Borah and Cook demonstrate, lies in the fact that only taxpaying families were included in the *Suma* count, and with the exception of a few documents all tax-exempt families and individuals were excluded. A major problem therefore exists: the size of the tax-exempt population. The weakest argument in the studies conducted by Borah and Cook on sixteenth-century demography lies in their statistical manipulations to arrive at a figure for the tax-exempt population in 1548.

To establish a ratio of tax-exempted to taxed population, they first examined 11 documents (of the 1,200) in the *Suma* that provided population figures for both categories. On the basis of these 11 cases (of which 9 were located in Nueva Galicia), they calculated an average of nontributary to tributary population of 35 percent. Then they make the assumption, with no justification from statements in the *Suma,* that this nontributary population did not include nobles or mayeques but only people living in the "free *calpullec,*" who were exempt. They also make the assumption that 10 percent of the population were nobles (we think this figure is much too high, also), bringing the total non-mayeque elements in the nontributary population to 45 percent.

They then deal with the size of the mayeque population separately. On the basis of a sample of only six communities (none from the *Suma*) where a total count was made that included mayeques, they estimate an average of 35 percent mayeques. One of the major problems in applying these averages to the total sample (aside from the extremely small size of the base sample) is the fact that Indian society was far from uniform and the mayeque class was found apparently only in some areas. We suspect that the pattern was even more complicated than Borah and Cook imagined, and that mayeques were not necessarily present in all communities within a region; the mayeque status was apparently the product of conquest (pre-Hispanic), which means that they were common only in politically powerful communities. Borah and Cook assume that mayeques were present in all communities in the central plateau and portions of Oaxaca and were absent in all the other areas. On the basis of this assumption and the averages calculated above, they derived the following formulas for converting the *Suma* census to total population:

> For the central plateau and Oaxaca
> | | |
> |---|---|
> | Tributary population | 43% |
> | Exempt nobles and *calpulli* population | 22 |
> | Exempt mayeque population | 35 |
> | | 100% |

For the rest of the area of central Mexico

Tributary population	65%
Nontributary population	35
	100%

We find these arguments extremely tenuous and reject the assumptions upon which they are made. The samples are much too small to establish averages for the huge area embraced by the *Suma,* and the assumption of uniformity of social structure over such a huge region is unsupported. The assumption that the *Suma* statements about nontributaries refer only to free calpulli members is also unwarranted. Only one *Suma* document (Izúcar) in the entire central plateau area contains data on the nontributary population, the only sample we have that includes the tax-exempt elements! The Izúcar document simply reads that in the town there were "five barrios with 484 casados who did not pay tribute." The term barrio here cannot be assumed to mean only free calpulli members. It refers to a physical and administrative unit that included sections or wards of communities or isolated settlements and was frequently applied to mayeque settlements as well as free calpulli communities. In his study of Aztec social structure, Carrasco (1964) demonstrated that the nobles of a community were usually members of a single barrio or calpulli, and his detailed study of Tepoztlan supports this (as well as the fact that the mayeques were structured into barrios). Consequently the nontributary population in the Izúcar document could have included all nontributaries—free calpulli members, mayeques, and nobles. (The nontributaries there made up 34.8 percent of the census.)

In the case of their tabulation of mayeques from the six communities, the range was between 11.4 and 57.0 percent, an extraordinary range for so small a sample that certainly casts suspicion on the averages they used as a reasonable basis for calculations of mayeque population over the entire plateau. The range points out another interesting facet to the entire question of the size of the mayeque population. The rapid reduction of the population during the sixteenth century generated problems for the Indian noble serf holders as well as for the Spanish encomendero and the king. They responded by a regularized procedure of illegal conversion of free calpulli members to mayeque status. The result was an increase in the ratio of mayeques to total population and a rash of suits against the nobles by encomenderos and Crown investigators. The calpulli member himself apparently entered into such contracts willingly, expecting, and in most cases receiving, a lighter tax burden than was exacted by his Spanish masters. In all probability the percentage of mayeques steadily *increased* during the period from 1519 to 1556 (at the latter date the mayeque system was abolished). Furthermore, we would expect great variability from town to town related to variations in population decline, to the economic significance of the mayeque class, and to the political sophistication of the noble class from community to community.

One cannot therefore assume that the process was regular (see Gibson's 1952 revealing account of the ability of the Tlaxcalans to manipulate the Spanish bureaucratic structure, as contrasted to other Indian groups).

Our only good data on mayeque population, in the sense that it is at least based on a large sample, is the statement (cited by Borah and Cook, 1960: 71) that there were more than 100,000 mayeques in the area of the audiencia of Mexico. Borah and Cook calculate a proportion of mayeques to the total population of only 10 percent (this is approximately the percentage reported for the 1550s in *Nuevos documentos relativos a los bienes de Hernán Cortés* [Cortés, 1946] for the town of Yecapixtla in a census that was so detailed it included even the names of each mayeque and of the noble whom he served!). Borah and Cook accept the figure for 1563 but argue that the mayeque population probably had declined faster than the free calpulli populations because of their depressed economic status. We see no justification for this argument at all and would even run the argument in the opposite direction—i.e., that the Indian noble was probably a less stern tax master than either the Crown or encomendero and certainly no more exacting. Furthermore, we have presented an argument that the mayeque class was increasing, for the reasons cited. At any rate, the figure is obviously a gross estimate and should be used with extreme caution. If it is close to the truth, then the total exempt classes of 1548 need not have comprised more than 20 or 30 percent of the tributary population in the area where the mayeque system was in vogue, a figure far below Borah and Cook's 57 percent for the central plateau and Oaxaca and 35 percent for the remaining areas.

THE POPULATION OF CENTRAL MEXICO IN 1519:
THE COOK, BORAH, AND SIMPSON STUDIES

In 1948 Cook and Simpson attempted to estimate the population in 1519 from two sources: (1) the estimates of conquistadors as to the number of enemy warriors they fought, and the populations of towns and provinces they conquered; and (2) clerical estimates of conversions made during the decades of intensive proselytization following the Conquest. We feel that estimates based on such data are of very dubious value. Our criticism centers on two assumptions made by the authors, that the estimates are based on relatively reliable data, and that the Spaniards lacked motivation to alter whatever data were available. We disagree with both of these assumptions, and, Cook and Simpson to the contrary, the extraordinary divergence of opinion on Indian population sizes found among the sources cited by them supports our position.

The Clerical Estimates

During the 1520s approximately 45 Franciscan monks conducted a series of trips through the country on a great soul-saving mission. The Indians gathered in enormous crowds at various places along the route and the monks conducted mass baptismal services. It is worth quoting Cook and Simpson (1948: 19–21) in full on the statements by the priests as to the number of people baptized:

> In 1531 the Bishop of Mexico, Fray Juan de Zumárraga [García Icazbalceta, 1881: 57 ff.] stated that by that time more than a million persons had been baptized. Later, Motolinía [1914: 105] said that between 1521 and 1536 more than four million souls were baptized. This figure is raised to 5,000,000 by Mendieta [1945: 2:124], who adds that by 1540 it had risen to not less than 6,000,000. The analysis of baptismal figures by Motolinía is the most detailed that we possess and is worth citing *in extenso* to demonstrate the sincerity, if not the statistical competence, of this famous missionary. He uses two methods, which are summarized below.
>
> a) By priests. In 1536 there were sixty Franciscan priests in all New Spain. (The other orders had not yet baptized many Indians, according to Motolinía.) In addition, forty others had been there, but of these twenty had returned to Spain and twenty had died. Five of these no longer present had baptized about 100,000 each, or 500,000 in all. Forty of these still present had likewise baptized about 100,000 each, or 4,000,000 in all. The total would be about 4,500,000. Torquemada [1943–44: 3:156], writing at a later date, supports Motolinía by citing names: according to him, Fathers Cisneros, Caro, Perpiñán, and Facuencia performed more than 100,000 baptisms each, and Father Motolinía, 300,000.
>
> b) By regions. Motolinía specifies the following towns and provinces:
> 1. México, Xochimilco, Tlamanalco, Chalco, Cuernavaca,
>   Yecapixtla, Huaquechula, Chietla .... +1,000,000
> 2. Texcoco, Otumba, Tepeapulco, Tulancingo, Cuautitlán,
>   Tula, Xilotepec .... +1,000,000
> 3. Tlaxcala, Puebla, Cholula, Huejotzingo, Calpa,
>   Tepeaca, Zacatlán, Hueytlalpa .... +1,000,000
> 4. South Sea Coast .... +1,000,000
> 5. Converted since this calculation was made   500,000
>   Total 4,500,000
>
> Motolinía thought this estimate too conservative and hazarded the opinion that the number reached 9,000,000. However, if we allow an additional 500,000 to account for regions not covered in his list, we get 5,000,000. A further million baptisms between 1536 and 1540 would yield Motolinía's [1914: 107–8] figure for that date.

The account indicates that no accurate counts were made, and that the monks disagreed among themselves as to the number. Motolinía himself apparently placed little faith in such figures since he stated that over

4,000,000 were baptized, but that the real number could have been as high as 9,000,000. Yet Cook and Simpson did accept the numbers and used them as a basis for their population estimates! The lack of preciseness in such estimates is understandable. No records were kept, and one suspects a pardonable amount of excess zeal. In short, the clerical estimates of baptisms are worthless as the basis for population estimates.

The Military Estimates

The same objections to the use of clerical estimates apply with even greater vigor to estimates based on the size of Indian armies stated by the conquistadors who fought with or against them in the various campaigns between 1519 and 1521. First, there is the simple problem of establishing the size of the territory from which the warriors were gathered. Cook and Simpson argued for example, that the enemy forces at Otumba were composed of warriors drawn from Tenochtitlán and the mainland settlements west of Lake Texcoco, and they used the figures as a basis for calculations of population from that portion of the Basin of Mexico. Díaz del Castillo (1927: 264), however, stated that they came from all the towns around the lake including Texcoco.

Second, there is little basis for the extraordinary faith the authors had in estimates made by Cortés. His legal position was exceedingly precarious throughout the Conquest (particularly prior to the Narváez expedition; Narváez was specifically commissioned to imprison him for disobedience), and the tone of his letters was clearly calculated to impress the Spanish king. After the Conquest he was constantly in trouble over his political ambitions, and his biography, written by López de Gómara (1964), was obviously a propaganda device to improve his position at Court. Furthermore, there is the very serious question as to the possibility of making even rough approximations of the size of Indian armies.

Finally there is not fundamental agreement, Cook and Simpson to the contrary, on the part of the various documentary sources as to the number of men in the native armies. For example, the estimate of Díaz del Castillo of the size of the Indian armies that attacked the Spaniards in Tlaxcala is 40,000 and 50,000. Corresponding estimates by Cortés are 100,000 and 149,000! These discrepancies are shown in Table 4.1.

Estimates of Town and Provincial Populations

Somewhat more useful are the statements by the Spanish sources concerning the populations of towns and districts. The same problem of intentional manipulation of the data, however, may be assumed for these figures. With respect to the bases of the figures, Cook, Simpson, and Borah argued that the

Table 4.1

Sizes of Indian Armies according to Various Spanish Sources[a]

Armies	Cortés	Díaz del Castillo	Anonymous Conqueror	López de Gómara	Herrera	Ixtlilxochitl	Oviedo
Tlaxcalans							
Battle 1	100,000	40,000	over 100,000	80,000	150,000		
Battle 2	149,000	50,000		150,000			
March to Cholula	100,000	1,000	40,000	100,000			
Assembly following Otumba battle					200,000		
Tepeaca campaign	25,000	4,000		40,000	56,000		
Siege of Tenochtitlán	45,000	16,000 20,000		60,000	30,000 60,000 110,000	25,000	
Aztecs and Allies							
Second march to Tenochtitlán	150,000						
Battle of Otumba				200,000	200,000		
Siege of Tenochtitlán						300,000	

Texcocans				
Military resource of province				
Siege of Tenochtitlán	50,000	50,000	200,000	58,000
Total Indian Allies of Cortés				
Siege of Tenochtitlán				
Initial	75,000	24,000	100,000	200,000
Final	150,000	over 100,000	200,000	300,000	130,000
Indian Allies of Cortés				
Southern Campaign	100,000	120,000	100,000	

---

[a]Information derived from Cook and Simpson (1948: 22–30). See that work for documentation.

105

Indian states took population censuses for the purposes of taxation, and that careful records were kept. We agree, but the questions are: Did Cortés have access to such records? How was the information relayed to him? Did the Indians give him reliable data? Or did they exaggerate the figures to discourage him? (The cacique of Tzaóctlan's statement that Montezuma had 30 vassals—each with 100,000 warriors—is the case at point.) Or did Cortés simply estimate on the basis of his impression of the size of the community? And finally, regardless of the sources of information, how much did he doctor the figures to magnify his exploits and achievements? It seems to us that Cook and Simpson grossly underestimated the problems of utilization of such data.

Ultimately, there is the even more serious problem of what the figures refer to. In Aztec times the population was organized into a great number of small states, each consisting of a central town and dependent villages and hamlets. This was the largest stable political unit within which the social contract of obligations and privileges among the various social classes was accepted and legal. The Spaniards in referring to the rulers of such states called them *los señores naturales*—the natural lords. Historically, one or another of these states would conquer its neighbors and exact an annual tribute. But this was paid only as long as the conquerors were able to enforce it. Generally speaking, the local political system was unmodified by this suzerainty. Aside from these conquest-states, above the level of the local states were what might be called ethnic provinces—provinces within which were a number of politically autonomous states that shared a common dialect, name, and tradition of a single origin based on a migration myth. Within the Basin of Mexico there were a number of these groups: the Acolhuas, Chalcas, Xochimilcas, Tepanecas, and the Culhua-Mexica or the Aztec. The few cases where more highly integrated, supralocal political systems did emerge in the history of central Mexico involved these ethnic provinces. We have noted the case of Texcoco and the ethnic province of Acolhuacan.

After the Conquest the Spaniards converted most of the local states into tax districts, retaining the old central Aztec town as the cabecera. The tax and census data of the post-Conquest period refer to the population of the tax districts, except in cases where a community-by-community census was provided.

In many cases of Conquest-period population figures, it is not clear which of these levels is intended. In their 1948 publication Cook and Simpson *assumed* that estimates of populations of "pueblos" by Cortés and other Conquest period accounts refer to the *local state,* and on page 37 these estimates are compared with their calculations of the population in 1565 of the equivalent post-Conquest tax districts. They then argued that the rate of decline revealed by a comparison of the two figures is a reasonable one. It is quite clear in most cases from the context and wording, however, that Cortés and others referred only to the *cabeceras or towns, not the entire districts*. In the case of Huaquechula, Cortés explicitly stated that there were 5,000 to 6,000 vecinos in the town and as many more in the surrounding province. The wording of many of the other statements by Cortés or his biographer, López de Gómara, is such that the figures obviously refer to towns, not districts, as the following quotes illustrate.

In this city of Yztapalapa [Ixtapalapa] live twelve or fifteen thousand inhabitants. It is built by the side of a great salt lake, half of it on the water and the other half on dry land (Cortés, 1971: 82).

After staying there four or five days, I left them all very pleased and went up the valley to the town [locale] of the other chief I spoke of, which is called Ystacmastitán [Ixtacamaxtitlán]. His territory consists of some three or four leagues' extent of built-up [alluvial] land, lying in the valley floor beside a small river which runs through it. On a very high hill is this chief's house, with a better fortress than any to be found in the middle of [half of] Spain, and fortified with better walls and barbicans and earthworks. On top of this hill live some five or six thousand inhabitants with very good houses and somewhat richer than those living in the valley. Here likewise I was very well received, and this chief said that he was also a vassal of Mutezuma [Montezuma] (Cortés, 1971: 56–57).

Most Powerful Lord, in the preceding chapters I told how at the time I was going to the great city of Temixtitan [Tenochtitlán], a great chief had come out to meet me on behalf of Mutezuma, and, as I learnt afterwards, he was a very close kinsman of Mutezuma and ruled a province called Aculuacan [Acolhuacan], next to the territory of Mutezuma. The capital of it is a very great city which stands beside the salt lake; and by canoe it is six leagues from there to the city of Temixtitan, and by land ten. This city is called Tesuico [Texcoco], and there are as many as thirty thousand inhabitants in it. It has very remarkable houses and temples and shrines, all very large and well built; and there are very large markets.

In addition to this city he has two others, one of which is three leagues from Tesuico and is called Acuruman [Acolman], and another six leagues away which is called Otumpa [Otumba]. Each of these has three or four thousand inhabitants. The aforementioned province and dominion of Aculuacan has many other villages and hamlets and very good lands and farms. This province borders on one side with the province of Tascalteca [Tlaxcala], of which I have already spoken to Your Majesty (Cortés, 1971: 96–97).

The wording from the references would also suggest that Cortés was supplying his own estimates, not figures based on Indian informants, since the latter would probably provide data for the entire political district, not just the central town. This is also indicated by the fact that Cortés at times gave the population in vecinos, at times *casas,* and apparently used the terms synonymously, as they were in contemporary Spain. He probably did not realize the Aztec tendency for multifamily residence. This last fact presents even more serious problems in calculations of population from the Conquest sources. All writers, including Cook and Simpson, have used as conversion ratios for populations given in counts of houses, four to five persons per casa or per vecino. The documentary evidence, however, is conclusive as to the custom of multifamily residence. Borah and Cook (1960: 96–97) found a number of documents in the *Suma* that give data on the ratio of casados and of *personas* to casas in 1548. The data are tabulated in Table 4.2.

Within the México-Hidalgo area, the average household membership was 2.93 married men and 6.34 people, excluding children below four years of age. Calculating for them, the average house contained approximately seven persons, not four to five. Carrasco's (1964) intensive study of a Tepoztlan document dating from the Second Audiencia revealed an average 1.5 casados per casa and a household population of 5.6 persons (also probably excluding children below four). A document (ENE, 2:124) in reference to Cortés' estate in the Toluca Valley based on a secret investigation states that the 20,000 casas in the area contained 50,000 casados, or an average of 2.5. If we apply these ratios to the figures given by the conquistadors we arrive at impossibly high populations. For example, the cabecera of Acolman in the Teotihuacán Valley would have had a population of 21,000 to 28,000 inhabitants (3,000 to 4,000 casas). The archaeological remains indicate a town of no more than 4,000 or 5,000 inhabitants. (These calculations assume that the size of the extended family remained constant between 1519 and 1548, which is by no means certain.)

Finally, the various documentary sources are *not* in substantial agreement

Table 4.2
Ratios of Casados and Personas to Casas, 1548

Area	Number of Tax districts	Ratio of Casados to Casa	Number of Tax Districts	Ratio of Personas to Casa
México-Hidalgo	60	2.93	17	6.34
Oaxaca (except Zapotecas)	50	1.67	12	4.67
Morelos-Guerrero	8	1.67		
Puebla	56	1.26		
Vera Cruz	14	1.48		
Oaxaca-Zapotecas	45	1.30		
Jalisco-Nayarit			35	6.21
Michoacán			53	5.23
Sinaloa	33	1.75		

Source: Borah and Cook, 1960: 96–97.

as the authors claim (except where one copied from the other). Tlaxcala (in this case the province) is variously estimated at having a population of 50,000, 150,000, 200,000, and 500,000 vecinos. The population of Texcoco is variously estimated at 8,000, 20,000, 30,000, 70,000, and 140,000 casas or vecinos. For Ixtapalapa there are estimates of 8,000, 10,000, 12,000, and 15,000 casas, and for Tenochtitlán from 60,000 inhabitants to 60,000 casas or vecinos to 120,000 casas or vecinos. Tables 4.3 and 4.4 summarize the data.

What is even more disconcerting in the use of such estimates to achieve a population figure for central Mexico is the fact that many of them are based on one primary source, Cortés. (This is even true of Torquemada, 1943–44, who seems to have simply used a regular procedure of doubling Cortés' figures!) Peter Martyr's (1912: 2:64–148) figures were obtained from various emissaries sent by Cortés to the court; López de Gómara (1943) wrote his biography of Cortés under Cortés' direction; and most of the others restated the figures provided by Cortés and his biographer. The only other independent sources are Díaz del Castillo (1927), who provided very few population figures, and the Anonymous Conqueror (1941), who is the source of the sharply divergent and highly controversial statement that Tenochtitlán had 60,000 inhabitants. Finally, although Díaz del Castillo provided us with very little demographic data, he completely rejected the estimates of the size of Indian armies, towns, and provinces provided by Cortés and his biographer, as the following quotes from his book clearly indicate.

> Gómara also greatly exaggerates the numbers of our Indian allies, and the population of the country beyond all reason; for it was not the fifth part of what he represents it. According to his account there would have been more thousands here, than inhabit all Castille; but where he has written eighty thousand we should read one thousand. All this he has done in order to make his narrative the more agreeable (Díaz del Castillo, 1927: 25).

> I Bernal Díaz del Castillo, regidor of this loyal city of Guatemala, and author of the following most true history, during the time I was writing the same, happened to see a work composed by Francisco López de Gómara, the elegance of which made me blush for the vulgarity of my own, and throw down my pen in despair. But when I had read it, I found that the whole was a misrepresentation, and also that in his extraordinary exaggerations of the numbers of the natives, and of those who were killed in the different battles, his account was utterly unworthy of belief. We never much exceeded four hundred men, and if we had found such numbers bound hand and foot, we could not have put them to death (Díaz del Castillo, 1927: 272).

Table 4.3

Comparison of Populations of Indian Localities according to Various Spanish Sources[a]

Locality	Martyr (casas)	Mendieta (vecinos)	Hernández (casas)	Anonymous Conqueror (habitantes)	Cortés (vecinos)	López de Gómara	Ixtlilxochitl (vecinos)
Ixtacamaxtitlán	5,000–6,000				5,000–6,000[b]	5,000 vecinos	
Tlaxcala (province)		200,000			500,000	150,000 vecinos; 50,000 vecinos	
Texcoco (town)	30,000	30,000			30,000		70,000
Texcoco (province)	many towns; 3,000–4,000				150,000 (hombres)	"as many as Tenochtitlán"	
Nameless town in Tlaxcala	3,000				3,000 (casas)	3,000 casas	
Huejotzingo		80,000					
Teotihuacán		2,000					
Cholula (center)	20,000					20,000 casas	
Cholula (suburbs)	20,000					20,000 casas	
Amecameca (province)	20,000				20,000	20,000 vecinos	
Mixquic	1,500				1,000–2,000		
Tláhuac	2,000 (vecinos)				2,000	2,000 fuegos	
Ixtapalapa	8,000				12,000	10,000 casas	
Culhuacan	8,000				15,000		

Mexicalcingo	3,000		3,000	4,000 casas
Coyoacán	6,000		6,000	6,000 casas
Huitzilopochco	4,000		4,000–5,000	5,000 casas
Tenochtitlán	60,000	60,000		60,000 casas
Hueyotlipán	4,000	60,000		4,000 vecinos
Huaquechula (town)	6,000		5,000–6,000	5,000 vecinos
Huaquechula (province)			10,000–12,000	
Itzocan	3,000		3,000–4,000	3,000 casas
Acolman			3,000–4,000	
Otumba			3,000–4,000	"a trifle less than Texcoco"
Zautla			5,000–6,000	30,000 vasallos;
Zumpancingo				20,000 casas
Basin of Mexico	50 towns; many of 5,000 casas, others over 10,000			50 towns; many of 5,000 casas, others over 10,000
Aztec empire				30 vasallos; each one with 100,000 guerreros

[a]Sources: Martyr, 1912: 2:64–148; Mendieta, 1945: 2:59, 203; Hernández, 1946; Anonymous Conqueror, 1941: 42; Cortés, n.d.: 1:146–278; López de Gómara, 1943: 1:155–341; Ixtlilxochitl, 1952.
[b]Including Huejotzingo.

Table 4.4
Torquemada's Classification of Population Centers[a]

First Class (over 100,000 casas)

Tenochtitlán	120,000 casas, in each casa 1, 3, 4, 10 vecinos
Texcoco	140,000 casas, but some barrios 3 to 4 leagues from center

Second Class (over 20,000 vecinos)

Cholula	20,000 vecinos in city, 20,000 more in suburbs
Huejotzingo	35,000 to 40,000 vecinos
Tepeaca	Over 30,000 vecinos
Xochimilco	Over 30,000 vecinos
Chalco	Over 30,000 vecinos
Tlalmanalco	Over 30,000 vecinos
Amecameca	Over 30,000 vecinos

Third Class (10,000 to 15,000 vecinos)

Otumba	Xilotepec
Tlacopan	Ixtapalapa
Azcaputzalco	Huitzilopochco
Cuauhtitlan	Coyoacán
Tepexic	Toluca
Tula	Cuernavaca

Fourth Class: villas or aldeas
(below 1,000 vecinos)

[a]Source: Torquemada, 1943–44: 1:249–312.

The Aztec Tribute List

In 1963 Borah and Cook attempted to establish a new population estimate for central Mexico on the eve of the Spanish Conquest. The approach was similar to Cook and Borah's calculations of the population in the 1530s. They used the tribute estimates of the Aztec empire as contained in three surviving documents, the *Matrícula de Tributos* (n.d.), the *Codex Mendoza* (1938), and the "Scholes document" (Scholes and Adams, 1957), to establish the size of the population in 1519. For descriptions of the three documents, see Borah and Cook (1963: Ch. 3). Their discussion of the use of this material to arrive at population estimates is particularly puzzling since the authors themselves provide us with a detailed and excellent analysis of all the problems and objections to such use. Their own analysis leads the reader to the almost inescapable conclusion that it cannot be done! The major problems seem to be the following.

(a) The tribute collected by the Aztecs was not based upon a head count, and the relationship therefore between taxes and population is an exceedingly tenuous one.

(b) The Aztec rulers intentionally gave the conquered groups differential treatment: some were heavily taxed, others had only military obligations. The basis of this differential treatment seems to have been primarily one of relative degree of resistance to the initial Aztec demand for tribute.

(c) The tribute was levied in kind, varying in particular goods from province to province. In some areas feathers were paid, in others honey, or cacao, or maize, etc. There is no indication in the sources that any master plan of relative values among types of goods (certainly not in terms of provincial population) ever existed. There are post-Hispanic references to the relative values of goods, and it is these which the authors use to establish a common denominator. It is very probable, however, that such relative values varied from market to market, season to season, and year to year, and certainly post-Hispanic values cannot be applied to the pre-Hispanic period. In the sources there are statements dealing with the post-Conquest period to the effect that agricultural production had declined sharply since the Conquest and that the price of foodstuffs had increased relative to Spanish currency and Indian barter patterns. The ratios then are clearly not applicable to the pre-Hispanic period.

(d) In many cases Texcoco and Tenochtitlán exacted tribute from the same district, but the authors use only the Tenochca tribute list.

(e) The authors argue that a certain proportion of the population of the local conquered state was tax exempt and that the Aztecs' tribute burden would be imposed therefore on only a certain percentage of the population. This argument is not entirely defensible since the Aztecs were exacting tribute from states, not people, and the ruler of each state was responsible for payment. How the ruler arranged the collection of this tribute among his dependents is not known and is really immaterial. The authors assume that the tribute was based on a rough population approximation and that it was based on the number of taxpayers in each conquered state—an assumption completely unwarranted. They then apply their estimates of the relative proportions of taxpayers to nontaxpayers in 1548 (and we have questioned their figures in this regard) to the population of taxpayers they calculate from the tax list to obtain a total population. Wholly aside from the fact that the actual size of the tax-exempt class is not known for 1548, we have no proof that the relative proportions were the same in 1519. One could argue that the tax-exempt classes were both larger and smaller in 1519, and it would be virtually impossible to prove it, one way or the other. In favor of a larger percentage would be the facts that the tax structure was pre-Hispanic in origin, that it was in conflict with Spanish objectives, and that pressures from the Crown and encomenderos would result in a gradual reduction of the tax-exempt class. On the other hand, we have cited evidence to suggest just the opposite trend, that the Indian nobility attempted to increase their mayeque personnel at the expense of the free calpulli population.

(f) There are disagreements in the three sources as to the amount and frequency of tribute.

(g) Borah and Cook cite documentary evidence in reference to taxes paid to the "natural lords" by their dependents to suggest a standard tax rate. We agree. In all probability local taxes (within the local, legal, taxpaying state) were based on a census and the tax did relate to population. All statements by the Spaniards with respect to the imperial tribute, however, emphasize the inequalities of the system. The imperial tribute was just that—tribute, not in any sense a tax; it was considered as an abuse by the tribute payers; and it was based on a variety of factors, as we have indicated. Granted, the tribute had to be within the capacity of the population to pay, but again we raise the question, what was the capacity to pay?

In summary, we feel that the population estimates of Cook and Simpson and Cook and Borah of the population in 1519 are based on extremely unreliable data and we question the appropriateness of their methodology. In the next section alternative possibilities for the population in 1519 are discussed.

THE POPULATION OF THE CENTRAL MEXICAN SYMBIOTIC REGION IN 1519: A REEVALUATION

We will now attempt to derive an estimate of the population of a portion of the area studied by Cook, Simpson, and Borah for the year 1519. Our methodology will consist of the following steps.

1. All documentary evidence points toward a substantial population loss between 1519 and 1595. There are no dissenting sixteenth-century sources on this point. If one can establish with reasonable accuracy a population for the area at some time during the post-Conquest portion of the sixteenth century, then this provides at least a minimal population for 1519. The earliest date for which this is true is 1568. The methodology will consist first of the establishment of the population for that year.

2. This population figure will then be compared with modern censuses[2] of the same area to test its reasonableness.

3. We will utilize the relatively accurate sixteenth-century censuses that postdate 1568 and the scattered but apparently reliable data from test areas

2. México, 1901–1907, 1918–1920, 1925–1928, 1932–1936, 1943–1948, 1952–1953, 1962–1964.

prior to 1568 to establish a population curve. This curve will then be extended back to 1519.

4. We will test these estimates by a more intensive examination of one small area, the Teotihuacán Valley. In this final step the approach will be multiple: sixteenth- and twentieth-century censuses will be used, Charlton's (1970) study of agricultural productivity for the region will be tested against the estimates, and some archaeological survey data will be examined.

To recapitulate, Cook and Simpson (1948) established a population figure for all central Mexico of 4,409,180 for 1565. Cook and Borah (1960) revised these figures downward to 2,649,573, or approximately 2,650,000. They then qualified the figure, suggesting a probable range of from 2,500,000 to 2,800,000. This figure is reasonably accurate, as are the estimates they calculated for the period subsequent to this time. A dependable population curve could then be established between 1565 and 1568 and between 1605 and 1607. From their calculations we have estimated a population of approximately 1,000,000 for the Central Mexican Symbiotic Region in 1568.

For the period prior to 1568 their estimates are completely unreliable. If one assumes that the *Suma* census was accurate, and the paucity of corroborative censuses makes this assumption dangerous, then all that can really be said is that there were approximately 2,940,000 taxpaying Indians and their dependents in central Mexico in 1548. The Borah-Cook (1960: 114–15) estimate by the utilization of the various formulas discussed would raise this to 6,300,000 to account for the tax-exempt elements; their figures for the Central Mexican Symbiotic Region can be calculated at 2,500,000. The total percentage of tax-exempt elements could have been as low as 20 to 30 percent, however, in the areas where mayeques were present. If this percentage of tax-exempt elements is used, it would result in an approximate population figure of 3,530,000 to 3,820,000 for central Mexico in 1548, disregarding the probability that mayeques were absent as a class in many towns. For the Central Mexican Symbiotic Region the application of this percentage figure results in a population of 1,500,000; this recalculated population would still allow for substantial population loss between 1548 and 1565 and yet would be far below the Cook-Borah estimates. We are not, however, insisting on these figures, since we have already expressed our opinion as to the reliability of the earlier censuses.

We reject outright Cook and Borah's estimate of the population of central Mexico during the First Audiencia, including in our rejection both the figures and the methodological assumptions and procedures upon which they are based. Although the Borah-Cook 1548 estimate is high, a reasonable curve of population could be projected, by utilizing it, back to 1532. Between 1532 and 1548, however, they estimate a drop of from 16,800,000 to 6,300,000, and we are very skeptical of a loss of 10,000,000 people in a period of only 16 years. This figure of 16,800,000 for 1532 offered by Cook and Borah is a critical one, since it would provide a minimal population for 1519—that is, only 13 years removed from that date—but we feel it is much too high.

The 1568 Population

As stated previously, the earliest reliable estimates of population offered by Cook and Borah date from the 1560s. In Table 4.9 (see p. 130) their data for that decade have been summarized (1568 populations) for the Central Mexican Symbiotic Region. In the table the cabecera districts have been grouped into larger units equivalent to the twentieth-century judicial districts. (For a tabulation by cabecera districts, see Sanders, 1970: Table 4.) This has been done to facilitate comparisons of contemporary censuses to those of the sixteenth century. The contemporary *municipios* correspond only roughly or not at all to the sixteenth-century cabecera districts, and the problem was to find a territorial unit large enough to reduce gross discrepancies in the size of the units being compared, yet smaller in size than a modern state. The use of the judicial district was a happy compromise, and it was relatlvely easy to equate sixteenth- and twentieth-century territorial units by this means. The judicial districts, furthermore, coincide rather well with ecological units.

The total population for the Central Mexican Symbiotic Region in the decade of the 1560s, after 40 years of decline, can be calculated at approximately 1,000,000 with an overall density of approximately 40 per square kilometer or 100 per square mile. In order to test the reasonableness of these calculations, those figures may be compared with the population of the same area according to a number of twentieth-century censuses. (See Sanders, 1970: Tables 6, 7, and 8 for tabulation of these data.)

In comparing the sixteenth-century and twentieth-century censuses, a number of precautions must be taken. Up until 1900 Mexico was still a predominantly agrarian state. Prior to this time the population size and density from area to area reflected primarily local ecological processes. Between 1900 and 1960 there was an enormous growth in the population of Mexico City (from 500,000 to 5,000,000), and the growth of the city has stimulated the growth of population throughout the central plateau, particularly in the Basin of Mexico. Many one-time farmers living in small communities have become industrial workers commuting into the city. In some areas commercial agriculture has replaced subsistence farming in response to the growth of the urban market. Most of this development, however, has occurred since 1930, and therefore the 1900 and 1910 censuses should still reflect a population distribution that was linked primarily with local ecology. Areas particularly affected by the urban growth of Mexico City are the districts of Cuauhtitlan, Tlalnepantla, and all of the Distrito Federal except Milpa Alta, but perhaps no area in the Basin of Mexico has been unaffected. Urban growth of Puebla, Pachuca, and Cuernavaca has undoubtedly had effects on population distribution in their immediate rural hinterland as well. Aside from the growth of major population centers, lesser urban development in Jojutla and Cuautla in the state of Morelos and in Atlixco and Matamoros in Puebla has stimulated population movement and growth. The following comparative evaluation, district by district, may be made.

Cuauhtitlan. The 1568 population corresponds very closely to the 1900, 1910, and 1930 censuses. Since 1930 the population has climbed very rapidly, presumably in response to the growth of the factory complex at Cuauhtitlan and on the north slope of the Guadalupe range.

Chalco. All of the modern censuses show figures strikingly higher than those compiled by Cook and Borah. The density of 25.2 persons per square kilometer for the mid-sixteenth century is surprisingly low and at first sight we felt something was wrong. The clue is provided by Document 546 (ENE, : 10: 33–40), where intensive investigations of tax abuses by Vasco de Puga demonstrated that the mayeque system was still actively functioning in Chalco as late as the 1560s. He claimed that the official count of 13,000 tributaries could be increased to 20,000 if the mayeques were included. He also pointed out that the *number of mayeques had steadily increased in the province since the Conquest.*

Otumba. This area has apparently stabilized in population, with very little increase between 1900 and 1950. The total range of the densities varies from only 38.8 to 47.3 per square kilometer. The 1568 density can be calculated at 47.43. For reasons to be elaborated later, we feel that Cook and Borah have overestimated somewhat the 1568 population of this district, but our recalculated figure still falls close to those of the modern censuses.

Texcoco. The population of this district between 1900 and 1930 was approximately two-thirds that of Cook and Borah's estimate, and the 1568 level was achieved only as late as 1940. Texcoco, however, contained a large Conquest-period city, and contemporary Texcoco is a small town of between 8,000 and 10,000 inhabitants, substantially smaller than the Aztec town in 1519. Allowing for this urban decline, therefore, the rural population for 1568 was comparable to that for the period between 1900 and 1930.

Tlalnepantla. Contemporary Tlalnepantla has a population far in excess of that in 1568, and here the reasons are clear. Much of the urban expansion of Mexico City has been northward into this area, and much of the population in recent censuses can be considered as urban in way of life. Furthermore, one suspects that in the sixteenth century much of the land on the north and west shores of Lake Texcoco was controlled and utilized by people residing in Mexico City, leaving only a small area for a resident rural population.

Zumpango. The figures for the 1900–1950 censuses are all fairly close to those compiled by Cook and Borah for the 1560s. The lower figures for 1900 and 1910 may relate to the loss of the lake as an ecological resource with the difference being made up in the 1950 and 1940 censuses by urban occupations.

Xochimilco. The 1568 population figures are considerably lower than all twentieth-century censuses for this portion of the Basin of Mexico (37,268 compared to from 61,809 to 81,241). Since 1930 a substantial percentage of the population of the area has become urban in mode of life; people live in the old peasant village but work in the growing metropolis. Even as late as 1900, when Mexico City still had a population of only about half a million inhabitants, the population was still 70 percent larger than was the case in 1560. Unlike Chalco, for Xochimilco there is little reason to doubt the accuracy of the figures that Cook and Borah cite, and they check closely with special investigations conducted by the Crown.

Mexico City and environs. This is the area most drastically affected by twentieth-century urban growth of the capital, and even as early as 1900 and 1910 much of the surrounding population was urban in mode of life. Of course this was true in the sixteenth century as well; such towns as Coyoacán, Ixtapalapa, Azcaputzalco, and Tlacopan (Tacuba) were major urban communities linked by causeways to Tenochtitlán. Nevertheless, even excluding Mexico City from the comparisons, in this area there were two and a half times as many people living in peasant communities in 1900 as compared to 1568.

Tula and Pachuca. The 1568 figure for southern Hidalgo compares very closely with the censuses from the twentieth century, if we exclude the city of Pachuca, a mining and industrial center, from the picture.

Tlaxcala. There is no breakdown by areas, but only a total population estimate for the province for the sixteenth century. The overall density can be calculated as slightly higher than that for the 1900 and 1910 censuses for the same area as the modern state and is very close to the 1940–1950 figures.

West Puebla. For the West Puebla area the districts have been sorted into two groups (excluding that which includes the city of Puebla) for comparison. Cholula and Huejotzingo form one group, and contemporary densities approximate very closely those for the middle of the sixteenth century. Sixteenth-century Huejotzingo would be somewhat below contemporary figures and Cholula somewhat above, but one cannot be entirely sure that the administrative borders were comparable to the modern district, and this difference may be more apparent than real. The population for Atlixco and Matamoros, on the other hand, is twice as high in recent censuses as for the mid-sixteenth century.

Morelos. The total population of the state of Morelos in the 1560s was very close to that in 1900, but with a somewhat different distribution. The sixteenth-century population was heavily concentrated in the northern half of the state, particularly in areas above the 1,400 meter contour. This bias is still reflected in the twentieth-century censuses but is considerably less pronounced.

Generally speaking, then, the twentieth-century censuses, particularly the 1900 and 1910 censuses, approximate very closely the population figures given by Cook and Borah for the 1560s, with two major exceptions. One is an area located close to Mexico City, where recent urban growth has resulted in a densely settled suburban strip with heavier densities in the twentieth century; the other is a band of settlement extending from Morelos into West Puebla and located between 1,000 and 1,400 meters above sea level, in other words, an altitudinal strip which lies below most of the area. The Cook-Simpson-Borah studies demonstrate conclusively that population decline occurred at a much faster rate in lower-lying areas than in the uplands. The fastest and most catastrophic losses were in the tropical lowlands, in areas below 1,000 meters above sea level. The major factors seem to have been the addition of malaria to the more generally distributed smallpox, measles, and whooping cough epidemics, which caused frightful mortality in all areas. These studies indicate that the decline of population in the coastal areas between 1519 and 1568 was seven times as fast as in the central plateau, and that the decline in areas of intermediate altitude was approximately twice as fast. We do not accept the actual rate of decline between 1519 and 1568 given by Cook and Borah, but the ratios between the various ecological zones are probably approximately correct. If so, then the much lower figure for the 1560s for the band between 1,000 and 1,400 meters above sea level is explicable.

In summary, our survey of recent censuses demonstrates that the population in the first half of the twentieth century, excluding the large urban centers and their immediate rural fringe, was approximately the same as that for 1568. The major factors that have operated to keep the contemporary population below the 1519 level are as follows:

1. Post-Conquest deterioration of the environment resulting from sheet and gully erosion of slopes, loss of the lakes as a resource, and loss of water

resources for irrigation as result of erosion, drainage of the lakes, and capture of water sources for urban centers.

2. Slow recovery from the epidemics of the sixteenth and seventeenth centuries.

3. Social and economic institutions of the seventeenth, eighteenth, nineteenth, and early twentieth centuries, which resulted in a consolidation of small, intensively cultivated holdings into large, extensively cultivated ones, a process that retarded population recovery.

Earlier Censuses

By a combination of direct statements by Cook and Borah (1960) and Borah and Cook (1963) and *ratios* based on their data, the populations for the various levels of territory discussed in this study are tabulated in Table 4.5.

In Figure 4.4 (see p. 129) the curve of decline for the Central Mexican Symbiotic Region is presented according to the Cook-Borah estimates. Immediately apparent is the extraordinary steepness of the curve between 1519 and 1540. There is a slight deviation from a linear curve between 1565 and 1540 as well, but particularly dramatic is the shift during the early decades. This is all the more surprising since the first major epidemic occurred in the 1540s, and an equally severe one occurred in the 1570s. One would expect a slow decline between 1519 and 1540 and then a rapid increase in the curve of decline between 1540 and 1595.

We have compiled data for a number of areas that provide a much more reasonable picture of the rate of the population decline between 1530 and 1580. One of the most consistent pictures emerges from Cholula (see Sanders, 1970: Table 9).

Table 4.5
Sixteenth-Century Populations for Mexico from or Based on
Cook and Borah[a]

Year	Central Mexico	Cook-Borah Area 1[b]	Central Mexican Symbiotic Region	Basin of Mexico
1519	25,200,000	10,907,000	6,400,000	2,560,000
1532	16,800,000	7,992,307	4,600,000	1,840,000
1540	6,300,000	4,120,000	2,400,000	960,000
1568	2,650,000	1,707,758	1,000,000	400,000
1580	1,900,000	1,233,032	780,000	310,000
1595	1,375,000	770,649	450,000	180,000

[a]Cook and Borah, 1960; Borah and Cook, 1963.
[b]The central plateau.

Between the late 1550s and 1571 there are six separate estimates of population for Cholula, with a total range of variability of between 11,786 and 13,640 tributaries, a rather remarkable agreement. The data suggest, furthermore, *considerable stability in population even though no less than five minor epidemics occurred during that span of time* (see Gibson, 1964: 449). Following the great epidemics of the late 1570s it dropped to 9,000 vecinos. In the article "Descripción de Cholula," written by Gabriel de Rojas (1927), a figure of 15,000 vecinos was estimated for the late 1540s. The population for the same period given in the *Suma de visitas* is 9,340 tributaries. Presumably the Rojas figure refers to the total population, tributary and nontributary, which would suggest a nontributary population of approximately 40 percent of the total, tributaries making up 60 percent. For earlier figures there is a statement in a document dated 1531 (ENE, 16:9, Doc. 96) that the district had 20,000 *hombres de guerra*. If we assume an equivalence of casados with hombres de guerra, the population declined 25 percent between the two dates. For the Conquest period almost all statements derive from a figure given by Cortés. Cortés (López de Gómara, 1943: 1:198) cited a figure of 40,000 casas in the city and dependent territory. Rojas converted this to vecinos. Both these figures would seem high if the 1531 population estimate is reasonably accurate. The total population, assuming the figure refers to casas (and multiplying by a factor of 7), would be 280,000; assuming vecinos, the population can be calculated at 132,000 (3.3 conversion ratio). The figure for 1531 would be but 66,000, and we would have to assume a reduction in a ten-year period to either one-half or one-quarter of the Conquest figure to accept them. The rate of decline here seems extremely excessive. The figure of 280,000 would be closest to the curves plotted by Cook and Borah (1960: 55). There is one document from 1544 that suggests a more conservative population figure (ENE, 4:137, Doc. 233). It states that the province once had 25,000 hombres de guerra. This could be a possible variant of the same 1531 figure or it may refer to 1519. If the latter is assumed, then a population for Cholula of 82,500 can be calculated for the time of the Spanish Conquest. These figures have been plotted on Figure 4.1. The curve very closely approximates the more conservative curve plotted on Figure 4.4 (see p. 129) for the Central Mexican Symbiotic Region, and again it casts considerable doubt on Cook and Borah's estimates. It would seem highly unlikely that the district of Cholula had a population exceeding 100,000 in 1519.

Another district for which we have some reasonable estimates from early in the century is Tepoztlan. Cook and Borah calculate the population in 1595 at 4,890 and for 1568 they estimate 7,498. If Cook and Borah's curve for the central Mexican area is correct, Tepoztlan should have had a population of 34,490 inhabitants in the 1530s. Carrasco (1964) reports an extraordinarily detailed house-to-house census that dates from 1537. In the case of the central town, all residents were counted and even their kin relationships noted! The total population in 1537 was only 12,062. It is possible that the figure excludes children below four years of age, but even allowing for this the population was still only 40 percent of that calculated from the Cook-Borah curves (Fig. 4.2).

There is an undated document (ENE, 14:115, Doc. 825) that may provide a key to calculations of early sixteenth-century population. The document is signed by Ochoa de Luyando, who was apparently a census taker conducting a tax investigation for the Crown. The census covered a large area including the districts of Huejotzingo, Cholula, Tlaxcala, Chalco, Texcoco, Xochimilco, and the City of Mexico. The document has two sets of population figures, one pair for each district. One set of figures, with two exceptions (Mexico City and Tlaxcala) is approximately double the other. The higher figures are cited in the main part of the document. The lower figures occur as notations on the left margin. The form of the document is reproduced below, using Huejotzingo as an example, to clarify the following discussion.

| Tributaries: 25,000. As appears in the last census which was made in this city of Guaxocingo [Huejotzingo], the Indians that are found there number 11,325. Don Luis de Velasco (Signed). | The town of Guaxocingo, two leagues from the volcano, has 25,000 tributaries. It pays rent to your majesty of 8,000 fanegas of maize, extracting from it the *diezmo* and selling it at three reales each, amounting to 2,700 pesos of common gold. They could pay without difficulty 29,337 pesos, 4 *tomines* of common gold, extracting the other tributes as stated above, and not assigning a tribute of more than eight reales of silver and half a fanega of maize as a minimum for each tributary in the villages of the encomenderos. | That which they pay in tribute. 2,700 pesos | That which they could pay in tribute. 29,337 pesos, 4 tomines |

The lower figure it will be noted, has the signature of Don Luis de Velasco, the viceroy, at the end. The figure for Huejotzingo is the only exact figure of the set and a total of 11,325 is almost exactly the figure of 11,318 cited by Borah and Cook (1960: 66) for the 1558 investigation of the town. The smaller population figure on the left signed by the viceroy then clearly refers to the decade of the 1550s and was part of the investigation we noted during the final years of Velasco's administration. This raises the question as to the

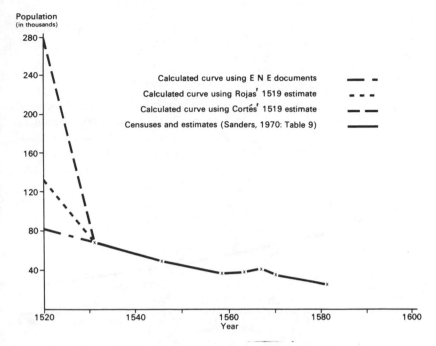

Figure 4.1. Cholula: Sixteenth-Century Population History

origin of the larger figures. They almost certainly refer to some earlier census. The document gives the actual tax paid by the district and *suggests the amount that could be paid with a uniform head tax.* The taxes paid relate definitely to the period of the Second Audiencia; for example, Chalco's tax is given in this document as 8,000 fanegas of maize, which was the Second Audiencia tax assessment for Chalco. The problem is, to what date do the population figures refer? The figures cited for Cholula and for Huejotzingo of 25,000 tributaries each are very close to figures of 20,000 to 30,000 hombres de guerra cited for the same districts in Document 96. The sense of Document 825 seems to be that Luyando had made a population estimate of the various districts in the 1550s based on the earlier Second Audiencia census, and that Velasco's investigators revealed a considerably lower figure, presumably the product of population decline between 1531 and 1560. If we make this assumption, then we have a major source from which to plot population decline between the two dates. The data are particularly important since they involve a large population and territory and not a single tax district as in the cases cited above. In Table 4.6 the data for this document are summarized and compared with the Cook-Borah 1568 figures (see also Fig. 4.3).

The figures from Tlaxcala and Mexico City have been separated because they do not vary for the two censuses. In summary, if we assume that the

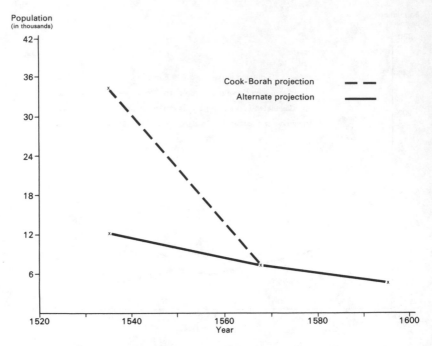

Figure 4.2. Tepoztlan: Sixteenth-Century Population History

larger figures refer to the Second Audiencia censuses, then the five districts (excluding Tlaxcala and Mexico City) had a population of approximately 400,000 in 1530–1535, and declined to 200,000 by the late 1550s, and declined further to approximately 160,000 by the late 1560s. If the curves of decline plotted from these test cases are correct, then it seems likely that the 1530–1535 population of those areas in central Mexico above 1,500 meters above sea level (all but Tepoztlan were above 2,000 meters) was between 1.5 and 3.0 times that for 1568. Cook and Borah estimate a ratio of 4.6 to 1.0. The best data are from Cholula, which would suggest either a 1.8 to 1.0 or 2.0 to 1.0 ratio, dependent on whether the 1530–1535 population was 20,000 hombres de guerra or 25,000 tributaries. The large sample from Document 825 yields a ratio of 2.5 to 1.0. We would therefore suggest that the population of the high elevated portions of the Central Mexican Symbiotic Region in the 1530s was between 2.0 and 2.5 times that for the 1560s, with the exception of Tlaxcala and Mexico City. We also suggest that Cook and Borah's assumptions that the population in the 1,000 to 1,500 meter band declined at approximately double the rate of areas above 1,500 meters is correct. If these assumptions are accepted, then the 1530–1535 population can be tabulated as shown in Table 4.7.

Table 4.6
Demographic Analysis of Document 825 as Compared to Cook-Borah
1568 Estimates for the Same Region

Province	1530–1535 Population[a] (tributaries)	1555–1560 Population[a] (tributaries)	1568 Cook-Borah[b] Population (total)
Chalco	45,000	22,000–23,000	40,490
Cholula	25,000	13,000	35,772
Texcoco	25,000	12,000–13,000	25,212
Xochimilco	20,000	12,000–13,000	31,018
Huejotzingo	25,000	11,325	26,285
Total calculation	140,000 × 2.8 = 392,000	70,325–73,325 × 2.8 = 196,910–205,310	158,777
Tlaxcala	50,000 × 2.8 = 140,000	50,000 × 2.8 = 140,000	165,000
Mexico City	20,000 × 2.8 = 56,000	20,000 × 2.8 = 56,000	52,000

[a]ENE, 14:115, Doc. 825.
[b]Cook and Borah, 1960: Appendix.

125

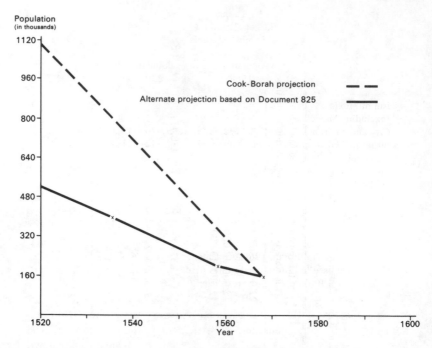

Figure 4.3 Sixteenth-Century Population History of the Area Included in Document 825 (ENE, 14:115), excluding Tenochtitlán. This area includes the districts of Huejotzingo, Cholula, Chalco, Texcoco, and Xochimilco. Data from Table 4.6.

Mexico City presents a number of problems. The city in 1568, following Cook and Borah (1960: 63), had 52,000 inhabitants and the attached ward of Tlaltelolco had 14,982, or a total of 66,982 inhabitants. It is not entirely clear in Document 825 whether the figure of 20,000 tributaries includes Tlatelolco, but it probably does not. At any rate this figure of 20,000 is repeated for the earlier period, indicating population stability during the span of time between 1531 and 1568. On the other hand, the census data for the communities on the immediate lakeshore suggest a much faster rate of decline than in most areas at that elevation. Ixtapalapa in 1568, for example, had a population of only 1,972, Mexicalcingo 621, Churubusco (Huitzilopochco) 1,320, and Azcaputzalco 5,082 (Cook and Borah, 1960: Appendix). Although Cortés' absolute figures for the Conquest are unacceptable, the fact that he assigns Ixtapalapa 12,000 vecinos, Churubusco 4,000 to 5,000, and Mexicalcingo 3,000 to 4,000, as compared to 60,000 casas for Tenochtitlán, would indicate a considerably higher population in 1519 than our graph projections (Fig. 4.3) would suggest. In all probability two factors operated to produce the rapid decline of lakeshore settlements around Tenochtitlán. First, the city itself was characterized by population stability. This could only

Table 4.7
Calculated 1530–1535 Population for Part of Central Mexican
Symbiotic Region

Area	Population in 1568[a]	Population in 1530–1535	Ratio
Basin of Mexico (excluding Mexico City and environs)	294,535–297,335	589,070–743,337	2.0–2.5
Southern Hidalgo	128,721	257,442–321,802	2.0–2.5
West Puebla: higher elevations	80,332	160,664–200,830	2.0–2.5
West Puebla: intermediate elevations	38,103	152,412–190,515	4.0–5.0
Morelos[b]	153,599	460,797–614,396	3.0–4.0

[a]From Cook and Borah, 1960: Appendix.

[b]We have used an intermediate ratio here, since about one-third of the state lies above 1,400 meters, the rest below it.

have been the case if there was a relatively heavy immigration from nearby settlements. Second, the denseness of settlement in the city and nearness to the lakeshore and the fact that it was a center of Spanish control would engender a more rapid spread of epidemic diseases in contrast to rural areas with smaller or more widely spaced settlements, We have, therefore, excluded the Tenochtitlán area in Figure 4.3. Document 825 and the other data would suggest population stability for the city between 1530 and the later decades of the century, with a fluctuation of no more than between 60,000 and 80,000. With respect to the lakeshore communities, all one can say is that the decline was obviously much faster than in the plateau generally. If most of the loss in the smaller communities was the product of immigration into the city rather than differential disease rates, then a projected figure of 2.0 to 2.5 times 109,273, equaling 218,546 to 273,183, could be calculated for 1530–35 for Mexico City and the adjacent lakeshore areas.

For Tlaxcala the problem is more complicated. First there is the problem of the expansion of the territory of the Tlaxcalan province from a pre-Conquest area of only 1,200 square kilometers to a colonial province measuring between 2,700 and 3,000 square kilometers. It is not known precisely when the latter size was achieved or by what stages, but by the 1560s the expansion was complete. Population data between 1531 and 1596, therefore, do not refer to the same territory. Gibson (1952: 141) presented a table of population data from various sources. The figure of 50,000 tributaries is commonly cited for the period between 1531 and 1571 or its equivalent of 150,000 confessees (four different sources). Another source for 1569 cited 40,000 vecinos (which is approximately equal to 50,000 tributaries), and another cited 34,322 in 1557. The province was never carefully censused, and the figures are clearly approximations except for the figure of 34,322, which is an Indian census and includes only 75 percent of the province. This would suggest that the population of Tlaxcala between 1531 and 1571 clustered very closely to a total population of 140,000. Cook and Borah (1960: 67) estimate 165,000 for 1568. Along with these moderate estimates, Gibson cited three other sources with population figures ranging between 80,000 and 100,000 vecinos. Ochoa de Luyando in Document 825 was also aware of a 100,000 estimate but rejected it. Gibson felt that these three sources were biased, but that they might conceivably refer to earlier censuses. More probably the population did remain constant, and this resulted from two processes that apparently counteracted the effects of epidemics. First, the gradual increase of territory probably helped to make up losses. It is interesting that after 1571 the absolute population did decline to 24,000 tributaries in 1583, 16,000 in 1593, and 15,000 in 1596. A second process was migration into the province from outlying areas, stimulated by the relatively light taxation exacted from the Tlaxcalans as a reward for services during the Conquest. The province was free of encomiendas and was a Crown possession taxed at a rate of only 8,000 fanegas of maize per year. In Table 4.8 the relationships between the 1568 and the 1530–1535 populations in the Central Mexican Symbiotic Region, including Mexico City and Tlaxcala, are tabulated.

Table 4.8
Calculated 1530–1535 Population for Full Central Mexican Symbiotic Region

Region	Population in 1568[a]	Population in 1530–1535[b]
Basin of Mexico (excluding Mexico City)	294,535–297,335	589,070–743,337
Mexico City and environs	109,273	218,546–273,183
West Puebla: above 2,000 meters	80,332	160,664–200,830
West Puebla: below 2,000 meters	38,103	152,412–190,515
Morelos	153,599	460,797–614,396
Tlaxcala	140,000–165,000 (area 2,700–3,000 km²)	140,000–165,000 (area 1,200 km²)
Southern Hidalgo	128,721	257,442–321,802
Totals	944,563–972,363	1,975,927–2,509,063

[a]The basic data upon which the 1568 summary is based are found in Sanders (1970: Table 4), as derived from Cook and Borah (1960: Appendix), which is summarized here by region and by district in Table 4.9.
[b]The figures for 1530–1535 are ratio calculations (2.0–2.5 ratio).

The population of the Central Mexican Symbiotic Region, then, can be calculated at between 2,000,000 and 2,500,000 for 1530–1535 and the density at 80 to 100 persons per square kilometer. If Cook and Borah's estimates for the population between 1568 and 1595 are combined with our recalculations for 1540 and 1532 and the resultant curve of decline is projected back to 1519, then the population of the Central Mexican Symbiotic Region in 1519 can be calculated at between 2,600,000 and 3,100,000. See Table 4.9 for the tabulation summaries by region and district, and Figure 4.4 for the resulting population curves in comparison with Cook and Borah.

THE POPULATION OF THE TEOTIHUACÁN VALLEY, PAST AND PRESENT

We will now analyze in more detail the population of the Teotihuacán Valley, our primary area of consideration. We will attempt to establish a probable total population for the year 1519, a curve of population decline for the sixteenth century, a comparison of the sixteenth-century population with that

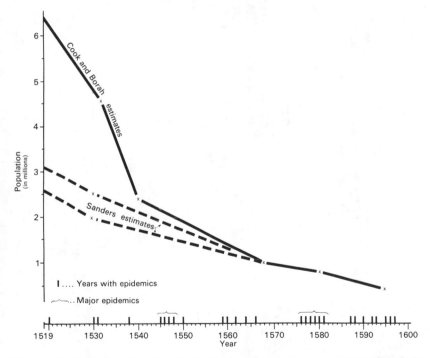

Figure 4.4. Central Mexican Symbiotic Region: Possible Sixteenth-Century Population Curves. For Cook and Borah, see Table 4.5; for Sanders, see Table 4.9.

Table 4.9

Summary of Sanders' Population Estimates for the Central Mexican Symbiotic Region during the Sixteenth Century[a]

	Area in km²	Population in 1568	Population in 1530–1535 (2.0–2.5 ratio)	Population in 1519 (2.7–3.0 ratio)	Density in 1519 per km²
Basin of Mexico					
Cuauhtitlan	590	33,486	66,972–83,715	90,412–100,458	153–170
Chalco	1,606	61,600–64,400[b]	123,200–161,000	166,320–193,200	104–120
Otumba	800	25,186[b]	50,372–62,965	68,002–75,558	85–94
Texcoco	1,100	76,220	152,440–190,550	205,794–228,660	187–208
Tlalnepantla	1,019	21,933	43,866–54,832	59,219–65,799	58–65
Zumpango	734	38,842	77,684–97,105	104,873–116,526	143–159
Xochimilco	792	37,268	74,536–93,170	100,623–111,804	127–141
Mexico City and environs	622	109,273	218,546–273,182	295,037–327,819	474–527
Subtotals	7,263	403,808–406,608	807,616–1,016,519	1,090,280–1,219,824	150–168
Southern Hidalgo					
Tula	1,451	67,364	134,728–168,410	181,883–202,092	125–139
Pachuca	1,591	61,357	122,714–153,392	165,664–184,071	112–116
Subtotals	3,042	128,721	257,442–321,802	347,547–386,163	118–127

Upper Atoyac Basin				
Huejotzingo	890	30,799	61,598–76,997	83,157–92,397	93–104
Cholula	777	49,533	99,066–123,832	133,739–148,599	172–191
Subtotals	1,667	80,332	160,664–200,829	216,896–240,996	130–145
Tlaxcala	1,200	140,000–165,000	140,000–165,000 (special case)	200,000–250,000 (special case)	167–208
Nejapa Basin (Puebla)			(4.0–5.0 ratio)	(guess estimates)	
Atlixco	982	19,206	76,824–96,030	95,000–115,000	97–117
Matamoros	1,703	18,897	75,588–94,485	95,000–115,000	56–68
Subtotals	2,685	38,103	152,412–190,515	190,000–230,000	71–86
Morelos			(guess estimates)	(3.0–4.0 ratio)	
Cuernavaca-Tetecala	1,767	51,061	153,183–204,244	200,000–250,000	113–141
Yautepec-Juárez	1,422	60,081	180,243–240,324	225,000–300,000	158–211
Morelos-Jonacatepec	1,765	41,058	123,174–164,232	165,000–205,000	93–116
Subtotals	4,954	152,000[c]	456,600–608,800	590,000–755,000	119–152
Totals	20,811	943,164–970,764	1,974,734–2,503,465	2,634,723–3,081,983	127–148

[a]The 1568 figures are from Cook and Borah (1960: Appendix) and the 1530–1535 and 1519 figures are ratio calculations, as indicated.

[b]Corrected from Cook and Borah (1960, Appendix).

[c]The total for Morelos for 1568 differs slightly from those in Tables 4.7 and 4.8 because two communities whose precise locations are uncertain have been omitted.

of the twentieth century, and finally we will discuss patterns of population distribution with regard to ecological zones and communities for the sixteenth and twentieth centuries.

Contemporary Population

Complicating the problem of ascertaining the population size of the valley is the fact that population censuses are recorded by municipio, whose boundaries correspond approximately or not at all to the limits of the hydrographic basin. The modern census data are summarized by Diehl (1970: Table 1). Each municipio consists of an administrative center called a cabecera and subject settlements variously referred to in the census as *pueblos,* barrios, *ranchos, rancherías, ejidos, haciendas, estaciones, campamentos, granjas, colonias* (see the paper by Diehl [1970] for a discussion of these settlement types). The survey area comprises approximately 650 square kilometers (including a section of the north slope of Cerro Gordo outside the hydrographic basin). In 1910 this area had a population of approximately 33,000; by 1960 this figure has ascended to over 57,000.

Sixteenth-Century Population

On the basis primarily of data compiled by Cook and Borah we have attempted to derive a reasonable estimate of the population of the Teotihuacán Valley in the sixteenth century (see Sanders, 1970: Table 11, for full presentation of these data). There are considerable problems in the collation of data to achieve reasonably accurate figures for the various points in time. A major problem is that the jurisdictions of the cabeceras constantly shifted in size during the century; Tepexpan, for example, had 10 estancias in the *Suma,* 13 in the *Relación geográfica* (Source O). Acolman had 6 and 27 respectively. A second problem is the incompleteness of the records, and finally there are disagreements even with respect to the later censuses.

If the data (from Sanders, 1970: Table 11) are converted into total populations, based on the Cook-Borah (1960) formulas, they can be tabulated as shown in Table 4.10.

Tepexpan. The *Suma* population (tributaries counted only) for the cabecera and ten estancias was 965 tributaries. Source B (refer to Cook and Borah, 1960: Ch. 2, for source descriptions), a tax list dating from 1560, cites 850 pesos tax with no data on the number of estancias. Source L, a tax document dating between 1565 and 1570, gives a figure of 1,579 tributaries. Between 1560 and 1565 Tepexpan shifted in status from an encomienda to a Crown colony, and its jurisdiction was at the same time expanded to include Temascalapa and other dependent settlements. We have been unable to find a

Table 4.10

Sixteenth-Century Population Estimates for the Teotihuacán Valley[a]

Community	1547–1551	1560	1563–1571	1580	1596
Tepexpan	3,184	2,805	4,421 (including Temascalapa)	2,660 (including Temascalapa)	
Temascalapa			2,699 (alone)		
Tequecistlan	775	666	1,722 1,182–1,294		773
Acolman	5,336	3,300	7,169 (partial count) 11,480 (complete count)	5,572	3,419
Teotihuacán	2,277	4,620	4,768 and 6,600	4,420	2,876
Chiconautla		429	1,478	1,232	
Tezoyuca			1,980		
Otumba, Axapusco, Oxtotipac		10,080	21,358 18,200 17,315		

[a]Town figures in Sanders (1970: Table 11) have been converted into total populations using formulas in Cook and Borah (1960).

parallel tax document that separates Temascalapa from Tepexpan, but an eccle-
siatic census for 1570 (Source K, *Descripción del Arzobispado de México*, PNE
3:43–47) assigns 615 tributaries to Temascalapa and its subject communities.
This would yield a balance of 964 for Tepexpan and its other subject settlements for 1565–1570. Cook and Simpson (1948: 54–55) cited a figure of only
543 tributaries from an Augustinian ecclesiastic tax list (Source H) for 1569–
1571. In this case, however, the figure probably refers only to Tepexpan and
a few estancias located several kilometers from the cabecera that were under
direct Augustinian control. Finally, the 1580 *Relación geográfica* provides a
figure of 950 tributaries in the cabecera and 13 estancias. This is approximately the same district censused in Source L. In summary, Tepexpan and
Temascalapa had a population of 1,579 tributaries in the 1560s, which
declined to 950 by 1580. The cabecera itself probably had a population of
approximately 400 tributaries in the 1560s.

Temascalapa. See Tepexpan.

Tequecistlan. The *Suma* figure the Tequecistlan is 235 vecinos, again
including only taxpayers. The district was unmodified throughout the sixteenth century, including the cabecera and only one estancia, Totolcingo.
Source B, dating from 1560, assigns only 220 pesos tax; apparently the
abolishment of tax exemptions had not yet affected the community. Other
censuses dating between 1560 and 1571 vary slightly and assign from 420 to
462 pesos or tributaries to the town. The *Relación geográfica* does not give a
population figure, but Document 745 (ENE, Vol. 13) dating from 1596
assigns 276 tributaries.

Acolman. The *Suma* census assigns Acolman 1,324 tributaries in the
cabecera and two nearby estancias and an additional 293 tributaries to four
others located further away. In 1580, the date of the *Relación geográfica*, the
cabecera had a district that included 27 estancias. Nearly all of the other
censuses are ecclesiastic and include only the cabecera and those estancias
served by the Augustinian monastery, not the entire civil tax district, making
comparisons difficult. Source H assigns 1,404 tributaries or 3,740 confessees
to the cabecera, 360 and 960 respectively to Atlatongo, 600 and 1,600 to
Chiapa, and 280 and 500 to Zacatepec, for a total of 2,564 and 6,840. Source
K corroborates these figures. Source B, dating from 1560, assigns only 1,000
pesos tax to the cabecera; the exemptions were apparently not yet abolished
at Acolman either. One census for the 1560s and 1570s (Source N, Velasco's
1571 geographical survey), probably includes a district comparable to that of
the *Relación geográfica*. It gives a figure of 4,100 tributaries for the "province." The 1580 figure is 1,990 tributaries. Finally, a civil tax document
(ENE, Vol. 13: Doc. 745) for 1596 assigns 1,221 tributaries.

In summary, then, we have three complete censuses for Acolman: 4,100 tributaries in 1571, 1,990 in 1580, and 1,221 in 1596.

Teotihuacán. The data are very unsatisfactory for Teotihuacán. The *Suma* partial census cites a figure of only 690 tributaries. In 1560 one encomienda tax census cites a figure of only 1,400 pesos, clearly not a complete census since Source L (1563) provides a figure of 1,655 tributaries, and Document E (1573) cites a tax of 1,703 pesos. The *Códice Franciscano* (1941), an ecclesiastic census, states that the cabecera and eight estancias had a population of 2,000 vecinos. Using the Cook-Borah formulas, the number of vecinos should be less, not more, than the number of tributaries. In 1563 Teotihuacán was still an encomienda community; by 1570 it had reverted to the Crown, and possibly the encomienda-Crown tax district was smaller than the ecclesiastic district. By 1580 the tax district had grown to 17 estancias with a total population of 1,600 tributaries. The same district had 1,027 tributaries by 1597. The data strongly suggest that the censuses prior to 1580 refer to a much smaller jurisdictional territory.

Chiconautla. The data for Chiconautla are by comparison uncomplicated. In 1560, 330 pesos of tribute are reported by Source B, and the community was, like Acolman, Tepexpan, and Tequecistlan, not yet affected by the tax reforms. Two more tax documents for 1571 and 1573 (C and E) both cite a figure of 538 pesos tax. The *Códice Franciscano* assigns 500 vecinos to the community. By 1580 the population had declined to 440 tributaries.

Tezoyuca. This community presents special problems. Although a cabecera, it was part of Texcoco's extended tributary district and separate tax censuses are unavailable. The *Códice Franciscano* assigned it and its two estancias (Nexquipayac and Ixtapan) 600 vecinos.

Otumba. The 1560 Source B reported only 1,600 pesos tax. For 1570–1571 there are five separate censuses; two are tax lists, two are ecclesiastic censuses, and one is Velasco's geographic survey. The civil tax lists (Sources E and C) reported taxes of 5,042 and 6,184 pesos respectively, a wide discrepancy. Velasco reported 6,500 tributaries in 1571. The *Arzobispado de México* census for 1570 reported 6,472 vecinos. The *Códice Franciscano* seems to clarify somewhat these discrepancies. It reports 4,000 vecinos in a cabecera and 20 "*iglezuelas,*" and adds that Axapusco and one sujeto had 700, Oxtotipac and three sujetos had 700, for a total of 5,400 in all. Both Axapusco and Oxtotipac had parroquia churches but were considered as sujetos of the larger parroquia church at Otumba. The *Arzobispado* document simply lists the two as sujetos and assigns Otumba a total of 29 sujetos—three more than the total of subject communities given by the *Códice Franciscano*. The three additional sujetos could have had a total population of 1,000 vecinos, thus explaining the discrepancy between the two ecclesiastic censuses.

The civil tax lists for 1570 excluded Oxtotipac and Axapusco, since they were separate districts. Axapusco and its sujeto Zaguala are assigned 695 pesos tax by Source E, approximately the population given by the *Códice Franciscano*. We have no data on the Oxtotipac tax.

In summary, the Velasco, *Códice Franciscano*, and *Arzobispado* documents all include Otumba, Oxtotipac, and Axapusco and assign a figure of around 6,500 vecinos or tributaries for 1570. The two tax documents refer to a smaller district that excludes Oxtotipac and Axapusco and vary from 5,042 to 6,184 pesos, a wide and unexplained discrepancy. The only data we have for a later period give a figure of 334 tributaries for Axapusco and Zaguala for 1597 (Source P).

With so much missing data we are forced to apply a system of ratios based on the rate of decline for those cases for which data are available. This is feasible only for the period after 1560, since all censuses prior to this are partial (including only tributaries). The ratio of the 1563–1571 population to that for 1580, based on Tepexpan, Acolman, and Chiconautla, is approximately 17 : 9 or 2 : 1. The ratio of the 1580 to the 1596 population, based on Acolman and Teotihuacán, is 10 : 6. If these ratios are applied to those communities with missing census data, the populations can be tabulated as shown in Table 4.11.

The population of the survey area then can be tabulated at about 50,000 in the late 1560s, 25,000 in 1580, and 15,000 in 1596. If the Cook-Borah ratios from the central Mexican region as a whole were applied, the population should have been 120,000 in 1548, 230,000 in 1532, and 320,000 in 1519. Our calculations would assign 75,000 in 1548, 100,000 to 125,000 for 1530–1535, and 135,000 for 1519.

Agricultural Productivity

The population of the valley in 1580 was very close to that in 1910. The 1950 population was almost identical to that of 1563–1571. In 1960 the population of approximately 55,000 exceeded all of the censuses dating from the last half of the sixteenth century. These comparisons, although they do not necessarily demonstrate that our calculations of late sixteenth-century population are correct, do make them plausible. What of our projection for the first half of the sixteenth century? Could the valley have supported a population of 75,000 in 1548, 100,000 to 125,000 in 1530, and 135,000 in 1519? Are Simpson, Cook, and Borah's much higher estimates possible in

Table 4.11
Recalculation of Population Data from the Sixteenth Century for
the Teotihuacán Valley

Community	1563–1571[a]	1580[b]	1596[b]
Tepexpan and			
Temascalapa	4,421	2,660	1,596
Tequecistlan	1,182–1,294	*591–647*[c]	773
Acolman	11,480	5,572	3,419
Teotihuacán	*8,960*	4,480	2,876
Chiconautla	1,478	1,232	*739*
Tezoyuca	1,980	*990*	*594*
Otumba, Axapusco,			
Oxtotipac	17,315–21,358	*8,657–10,679*	*5,194–6,407*
Totals	46,816–50,971	24,182–26,260	15,191–16,404

[a]From Table 4.10, except for Teotihuacán (see note b).

[b]Unitalicized figures are known populations, and italicized figures are estimates based on the average decline ratios for the towns with known populations (see p. 136).

[c]The calculated figure for 1580 for Tequecistlan is at variance with the trends in all other communities in that it is less than the 1596 population.

terms of the agricultural potential of the valley? We will now proceed to test these calculations on the basis of our data on agricultural productivity.

In order to do this, a number of basic assumptions must be made. First, we must assume that most of the food supply, at least the staples, were produced locally and that only small quantities were imported. All surrounding areas were at least as densely settled as the Teotihuacán Valley in 1519, and what surpluses were produced in those areas were more likely to have been channeled into major population centers like Texcoco and Tenochtitlán, rather than to markets in the small towns of the Teotihuacán Valley. In fact, one could more reasonably argue that the valley was essentially a rural, sustaining area for the major population centers and was, therefore, a producer and exporter of food surpluses.

Second, we must assume that the productivity of local races of maize used in the sixteenth century was comparable to that of races in use today. The little data available on maize evolution in central Mexico indicate that races comparable to those in use today were present in Postclassic times.

Third, we must assume that agricultural techniques in 1519 were at least as effective and the agricultural system as productive as those in use today. Some writers have, indeed, suggested that pre-Hispanic agriculture was less productive than that in post-Hispanic times. Kroeber argued this in his assessment of Mesoamerican population as a whole when he stated:

All these ratios are no proofs; but they do suggest that if our figures up to this point have been tolerably reasonable, the allowance of 3,000,000 for cultural Mexico is also reasonable and perhaps liberal. The actual population in 1500 A.D. may have been more. But it may also have been less. . . . But the illustration shows that we may not infer from present-day large populations to native large ones. And to assume that there was a large population, that this was reduced to a mere small fraction by the Conquest, and that then it built itself up again, is gratuitous. The Conquest no doubt did cause a shrinkage in numbers; but in the well-settled regions this effect seems to have been transient, and probably began soon to be made good by an increase attendant on the new experience of internal peace under Spanish colonial government (Kroeber, 1939: 159–60).

Gamio (1922:14) made a statement with similar implications: "The artificial production of this region, which comprises domesticated animals and vegetables obtained by cultivation, was doubtless much smaller prior to the Conquest than during the Colonial Epoch or the present time."

We disagree completely with this position. The introduction of winter wheat has increased the productivity of the lower valley by extending the growing season and permitting double cropping. This is, however, the only new plant that has directly affected productivity. Other crops simply replaced pre-Hispanic ones in the same areas. We see no reason to assume a priori that the introduction of the plow resulted in higher yields. The plow simply enables the farmer to cultivate more land, increases the production per family, and therefore elevates his standard of living. It does not necessarily result in an increase of *population density* or *regional productivity*. On the contrary, plow agriculture encourages extensive, rather than intensive, methods of cultivation. It may actually result in a decline of production per unit of land planted, as contrasted to hand tillage. (Note the shift from *cajete* to *al tubo* planting in recent times.) The densest rural populations today occur in portions of the Far East, where hand tillage is characteristic. Of course, if such hand cultivation were not accompanied by irrigation or terracing in pre-Hispanic times, the result would have been low productivity. Evidence of such techniques is conclusive for the Aztec period. One factor that conceivably might have resulted in lower yields in Aztec times was the lesser significance of domestic animals in pre-Hispanic economy, which would mean that fertilizers were therefore exceedingly scarce. Today, fields are kept in continuous cultivation by periodic application of animal fertilizers. There are a number of facts, however, which make us tend to disregard this consideration. First, the application of fertilizer today is neither general, consistent, nor regular. Second, the pre-Hispanic combination of *calmil* cultivation and terracing and the more extensive use of irrigation, particularly floodwater irrigation, would have made up for the deficiencies of animal fertilizers. All in all, then, the pre-Hispanic situation with respect to productivity did not differ strikingly from that today.

We lack good data on agricultural techniques and production for the upper valley. The following classification of the capacity of the valley with respect to agriculture therefore excludes this area.

Steep Slope and Mountain Areas:

Cerro Gordo	40 km²
North side, small hills	10
Patlachique and southeastern ranges	50
	100

Deep Soil Alluvial Plains:

Lower valley-delta	40
Middle and upper valley	30
	70

Gentle to Medium Slope:

Good conditions for terracing and floodwater irrigation

Cerro Gordo piedmont	60
South piedmont	30
	90

Poor conditions for floodwater irrigation or terracing

North piedmont	80
Total	340 km²

The alluvial plain of the lower valley and delta comprises 4,000 hectares of land, or 40 square kilometers. Of this 3,600 are today classified as irrigated land. In fact, as Charlton (1970) has noted, the declining yield of water from the springs has reduced the efficiency of the system. He also noted a considerable range of productivity between the lands of Atlatongo and Calvario Acolman (average yield from 1,875 to 1,350 kilograms). If we assume that the water output from the springs was 50 percent higher in 1519, as the recent declining yield of water suggests, then one could either apply the Atlatongo average yields to the 1,600 hectares under irrigation today or assume that the same pattern of pressure and competition for water operated in 1519 to spread the supply out over a larger area, say 5,400 hectares, and use the Calvario Acolman average. (This figure, however, would include some land outside the valley in the Texcoco plain.) There is the problem, of course, of the lower supply of fertilizers that complicates the picture. Considering all of these factors, we will assume continuous land use over the 5,400 hectares that comprise the lower valley, delta, and adjacent northern portions of the Texcoco plain, with an average yield of around 1,400 kilograms. The average ration of maize per year, assuming an 80 percent dependence on maize in the diet, would be around 200 kilograms for each individual. This means that a hectare of land would feed seven persons. The total population capacity of the irrigation system is therefore around 37,800. Of this total, 28,000 could be supported by the lands lying within the Teotihuacán Valley (i.e., 4,000 of the 5,400 hectares).

For the alluvial plain of the middle valley we have two possible productivity models. If we assume a system of floodwater irrigation comparable to that in vogue today, then the average yield would be close to 1,200 kilograms, including years of total crop loss and considering the variable conditions of canal and dam systems and their use. Under the ideal conditions characteristic of the hacienda-run systems of the late nineteenth and early twentieth centuries, the average would rise to at least 1,400 kilograms per hectare. This means that the plain could supply maize for a population of from 18,000 to 21,000. The alluvial plains of the delta, lower valley, and middle valley would therefore supply maize for a population of from 46,000 to 49,000 people.

If the model presented by Charlton (1970: 332) as to the nature and character of the middle valley alluvial plain in 1519 is correct, then the average yield would be similar to or slightly less than that of the adjacent terrace systems. This might reduce the maize producing capacity to as low as 12,000, more probably around 15,000, people, or a total of but 40,000 to 43,000 for the two plains. For the second-class lands—that is, lands lying in sloping areas but where the supply of floodwater for terrace irrigation was abundant—it is difficult to make calculations of productivity. Today, much of this area is severely eroded, and its overall demographic potential, therefore is low. From our test study of the Maquixco Strip (north slope of Cerro Gordo just north of the Teotihuacán Valley), we estimate the present-day condition of the land as follows: 10 percent steep uncultivated slope; 20 percent gentle slope, *tepetate* exposed; 35 percent gentle slope, severely eroded; 25 percent gentle slope, good agricultural land; and 10 percent deep soil terraces and *presas.*

Sixty-five percent of the land in this strip, then, is of marginal value to agriculture today, and this picture is generally true for the total area in question. Within the category of good agricultural land, Charlton (1970) estimates an average yield that varies from 1,000 to 1,700 kilograms per year. But these calculations do not include years of heavy crop losses through droughts or frosts. Even well-maintained terrace systems are characterized by a great deal of variation in age, erosion, deposition, and soil depth. Shallow soil terraces, or overcultivated lands, tend to suffer heavy crop losses in bad years, in some cases total losses. The average yield, therefore, including those years of heavy losses, over a long period of time probably does not exceed 1,000 kilograms. This would be particularly true during pre-Hispanic periods with the markedly reduced use of animal fertilizers. If we assume that the functioning part of the Maquixco Alto system was generally characteristic of the total ecological zone during Aztec times, and the Aztec settlement pattern data strongly suggest this, then this niche of the valley could have supplied maize for a population of perhaps 45,000 people.

For third-class lands—those lands that are situated on sloping terrain and without adequate floodwater irrigation sources—the average yield must have been considerably less. Generally speaking, these lands relied almost exclusively on rainfall for their humidity. The lack of irrigation water would also present much more difficult problems of maintenance of soil fertility, and we suspect that many of these lands either were not utilized for maize, were rotated, or were periodically rested. If all lands were rotated between alternate periods of cultivation and rest, or if the lands were rotated between maize and other crops like beans, and considering crop losses through frost and droughts, then the average yield of an individual parcel of land in this zone over a long period of time could not exceed 600 kilograms per hectare. This means that the 8,000 hectares could have supplied maize for only 24,000 people.

One of the problems in evaluating the demographic capacity of the valley is the possible utilization for cultivation of the steeply sloping areas of the Patlachique Range and the string of hills along the north side of the valley. Today this area is badly denuded of soil, and cultivation is restricted to small, scattered areas of level topography on or between the hills. Archaeological evidence indicates that during the Formative period the area was heavily utilized for agriculture. At the end of the Formative it was apparently abandoned as a major area of agricultural activities, and there is little evidence of its utilization throughout the succeeding Classic and early Postclassic periods. Aztec sites are few in number and small in size and are generally restricted to areas where there is evidence of contemporary cultivation. The implications of these data are that the Patlachique Range suffered heavy erosion during Formative times and was of marginal agricultural value in Postformative times. It was probably utilized primarily for hunting and gathering during the Aztec period.

In summary, the section of the Teotihuacán Valley included in the survey could have supplied maize for a total population of approximately 109,000 to 118,000 people. The capacity of the upper valley, an area somewhat smaller in size (approximately 300 km^2), is not known, but the productivity per hectare was certainly considerably far below that of the area considered. The alluvial plains are much smaller (they do not exceed 1,000 hectares) and much shallower with respect to soil depth than the alluvial plains farther down valley and are far removed from irrigation water resources. At least 50 percent of the surface of this area can be classified as third-class lands. All in all, it is difficult to see how more than 150,000 to 175,000 people could have been supplied with annual maize requirements from the total resources of the Teotihuacán Valley.

All of these calculations fail to take into account the amount of land planted in crops other than maize, or the fact that the population of the valley must have produced some surpluses for trade and taxation. With these considerations, Cook and Borah's population estimates, especially 320,000 in 1519, become absolutely impossible, and our estimate of 135,000 people for 1519 permits a model in which not all land was in maize and a substantial surplus was produced.

Another factor that would further reduce the population estimate arises from a statement by Juan Pomar that Nezahualcoyotl, the Texcocan king, diverted some of the water from the lower valley irrigation system for land around Texcoco. We have no way of knowing how much water was involved, but this diversion would have undoubtedly reduced the overall production of the lower valley (see Pomar in Zorita, 1941: 53).

Although our figures are considerably lower than Cook and Borah's, they still indicate a remarkably effective adaptation to the valley and to the intensity of land use, with an average density of approximately 200 per square kilometer.

THE POLITICAL DEMOGRAPHY OF THE BASIN OF MEXICO IN 1519

Districts and Domains

In 1568 there were 62 cabecera districts in the Basin of Mexico. These districts varied in population from 448 (Acolhuacan) to 52,000 (Mexico City). The average population was 6,513, and the average area was approximately 120 square kilometers. As was noted previously, the Spaniards converted most of the states in 1519 to cabecera districts. A few of the 1568 cabeceras were not former capitals; others were capitals a few decades prior to the Conquest, were conquered by the Aztecs and demoted to a subject status, and then were restored to their old rank by the Spaniards. Sometimes several rulers had their palaces in the same town. In such cases each palace was the center of an attached wardlike division of the town and a discrete rural domain. The Spaniards converted the separate domains into one and demoted the less powerful rulers to tributaries, considering the physical town as a single cabecera. Changes were also made in the specific territorial limits and alignments of subject villages of the former states, so that the 1568 cabecera districts did not correspond exactly. It would be virtually impossible, therefore, to make specific estimates of the population and territorial size of each domain in 1519. In the following summary we will attempt to provide estimates of average population size, based on our projected curves of decline.

The twentieth-century judicial district of Chalco corresponds roughly to the old province. Included in the twentieth-century district but not in the sixteenth-century province are the cabeceras of Coatepec and Ixtapaluca. The population in 1568, included those two districts, was 40,400 according to Cook and Borah (1960: Appendix). We have corrected this figure upward to 61,600 to 64,400. For 1519 our calculated estimate is between 166,320 and 193,200 (in both of these figures we have excluded Coatepec and Ixtapaluca). In 1519 there were ten domains in the province of Chalco. Of the ten, five were centered at the single town of Amecameca, three at Tlalmanalco, one at Tepetlixpa Chimalhuacán (the Chimalhuacán-Chalco of the 1560s), and another at Tenango Tepopula.

The average population of the domains was between 13,860 and 16,100 persons. If we make the assumption that few territorial changes were made by the Spaniards, then the bulk of the population, perhaps 50 percent, was subject to the three rulers of Tlalmanalco, perhaps 80,000 to 100,000 people. Most of the lakeshore plain, one of the most extensive in the Basin of Mexico, and the eastern *chinampas* were owned by Tlalmanalco so that this population is hardly surprising. The balance of the province was composed of gently sloping piedmont and steep hillsides.

The situation in the twentieth-century *delegación* of Xochimilco was much less complex. Most of the delegación equated with the old province of Xochimilco. The entire province was controlled by three rulers, all with their palaces located in the single town of Xochimilco. Not included in the old province, but included within the twentieth-century delegación, were Cuitláhuac, the capital of four rulers in 1519, and Mixquic, the capital of one. In the eight domains there was a total of 100,623 to 111,804 people in 1519, with an average population of 12,578 to 13,976. In the case of this area, there was apparently little shift in territorial boundaries after the Conquest, so that one can make some estimates of internal population distribution. The three domains of Xochimilco (those included in the 1568 cabecera districts of Xochimilco and Milpa Alta), applying our formula, had a total population of between 83,749 and 93,054 in 1519, or an average of 27,916 to 31,018 for each. The four rulers of Cuitláhuac shared a population of 10,495 to 11,661, or an average of only 2,624 to 2,915 per ruler. The single ruler of Mixquic was served by a population of 6,380 to 7,089 in 1519.

The two twentieth-century districts of Otumba and Texcoco correspond very closely to that portion of the old province of Acolhuacan which was located within the Basin of Mexico. In 1568 this area had 101,406 people. Our 1519 calculation is between 273,796 and 304,218. The history of the territorial limits and number of administrative units for this province between 1450 and 1568 is exceedingly complex, the product of political maneuvers by Texcoco both prior to and after the Spanish Conquest. At the time of the

Conquest there were rulers in twelve towns: Texcoco, Chimalhuacán, Coatli-chan, Huexotla, Chiautla, Tepetlaoxtoc, Tezoyuca, Tepexpan, Chiconautla, Acolman, Otumba, and Teotihuacán. A number of other towns had rulers in the mid-fifteenth century but had been converted by Nezahualcoyotl to direct tributary status. If we take the existing rulers in 1519, then the average domain included a population varying from 22,816 to 25,352.

Any attempt to relate the population figures to specific domains is fraught with particular difficulties with respect to this area. First, Texcoco succeeded in reducing the three former capitals of Chiautla, Coatlichan, and Tezoyuca to direct subject status so that Cook and Borah's 1568 population figure for Texcoco refers to this extended domain. The only source we have been able to locate that sorts out the four cabeceras is the *Códice Franciscano*. Bearing in mind that the ecclesiastic districts did not always coincide with tax districts and that one cannot be sure that either coincided exactly with the states of 1519, we would suggest a distribution of population in 1519 as follows: for Texcoco 43,200 to 51,000, Chiautla 6,750 to 7,500, Coatlichan 13,500 to 15,000, and Tezoyuca 4,050 to 4,500. To obtain a total figure for the Texcoco domain in 1519 we must also add the population of ten other states that had been demoted, some of which were reconverted to district status by the Spaniards. The post-Conquest changes in these territories would make it exceedingly difficult to sort them out, so we will simply offer here a reasonable estimate that the ruler of Texcoco must have had a direct tribu-tary population of approximately 100,000 people in 1519.

Those portions of Acolhuacan that lay within the Teotihuacán Valley have been discussed in the previous section. Our data would suggest a range in population of the 1519 domains of between 4,000 for Chiconautla to a maximum of 30,000 for Otumba (the figure for Otumba excludes Oxtotipac, Cuautlancingo, and Axapusco, which were direct tributaries of Texcoco).

Moving to the west central (i.e., the area west of Lake Texcoco) portion of the Basin of Mexico, the reconstruction of the political demography in 1519 is an even more difficult problem. Although the Spaniards emphasized the great size of the dual city of Tenochtitlán-Tlaltelolco in 1519, they also noted the presence of a number of large towns and numerous smaller settlements on the adjacent lakeshore plain and piedmont. With the exception of Tacuba and Coyoacán, which evolved into large suburbs of the colonial city after the Conquest, many of these towns had declined to the demographic status of small villages by 1568. We have previously suggested that this was the product of immigration to the city. As a consequence, the relative population distribu-tion of the cabecera districts in 1568 did not correspond at all to the domains in 1519. The population movement was probably local and internal, however, with respect to the district, and one can therefore apply the formula to the 1568 population of the entire district to obtain a total population for 1519.

The result is between 354,256 and 393,618. Of this, perhaps between 120,000 and 200,000 pertained to the joint cities of Tenochtitlán-Tlaltelolco and their dependent chinampa and mainland villages. The balance was distributed among ten domains, for an average of between 19,362 and 23,426 people each.

For the northwestern part of the basin (the districts of Cuauhtitlan and Zumpango), Gibson (1964: 66–68) notes that capitals were located at Tultitlan, Tepozotlan, Hueypoxtla, Tequixquiac, and Xilotzingo and that the former centers of Zumpango, Citlaltepec, and Huehuetoca had been reduced to direct subject status to Cuauhtitlan prior to the Spanish Conquest. The Spaniards restored them to cabecera status after the Conquest. Two other post-Conquest cabeceras within the area, Xaltocan and Tizayuca, had been reduced to direct subject status to Texcoco. Not included in Gibson's study were the colonial cabeceras of Apaxco and Teotlalpan, so we have excluded them. The total population of the two districts of Cuauhtitlan and Zumpango was 61,142 in 1568. Applying our formula, the population was between 165,083 and 183,426 in 1519. This population was subject to six rulers, for an average of 27,514 to 30,571 each. In fact, approximately 70,000 to 75,000 were tributary to the ruler of Cuauhtitlan, and the remaining five shared 95,000 to 110,000 tributaries, for an average of 19,000 to 22,000 each.

To summarize, in 1519 there was considerable variation in the size of the domains from a few thousand up to a possible 200,000 for Tenochtitlán. Although we cannot present a dependable grouping of these districts by population size, the mode would undoubtedly fall between 10,000 and 30,000. A few domains far exceed this size: Tenochtitlán, Texcoco, Cuauhtitlan, probably Tacuba (Tlacopan), and if we combine those domains that had their centers in the same town, Xochimilco and Tlalmanalco.

These demographic characteristics apply pretty well to the balance of the Central Mexican Symbiotic Region. Within the rest of the area there were several unusually large states (if we group those which shared the same cabecera) such as Cholula, Tlaxcala, Huejotzingo, and probably Quanahuac. The range and mode of the smaller domains was comparable to those in the Basin of Mexico.

Community Size

In our previous comparisons of the 1568 and 1519 populations we emphasized the point that the smaller the territorial unit, the more difficult it is to allow for local population movement and realignments of communities due to changes in territorial borders. It is primarily for this reason that we selected the twentieth-century judicial districts as our units of comparison. In our attempt to provide some impression of the population size of the pre-Conquest states, we worked with averages rather than attempting to apply our population decline ratios to individual cabecera districts, since we could not be absolutely sure that the old domains corresponded exactly to the post-Conquest districts.

Ideally, we would like to be able to calculate the population size not only for each state but for each of the central towns and all of the individual independent settlements, but there are a number of problems that make this a virtually impossible objective. We do know that in most domains only a fraction of the population lived in the central town. The percentage that lived in the center varied considerably, due only in part to the size of the dependent population. From the inception of their administrative system the Spanish state and church carried out extensive programs of relocation and centralization of population, so that numerous small settlements were abandoned. Although the civil *congregación,* as this policy was called, was not applied on a grand scale until after 1600 in the Teotihuacán Valley, it is quite obvious from a comparison of our Aztec settlement data with the 1580 map that numerous small settlements were abandoned prior to that time, in part the result of relocation by the church, and in part the result of less formal processes of local movement from marginal locations. As a result, there definitely was a total decline of population of the individual domains, but we are not able to assess its relationship to the population history of individual communities. In a separate monograph on settlement patterns, we will apply the Aztec period archaeological data to the problem and attempt to establish ranges, modes, and averages of population for the rural settlements in the valley.

For the Teotihuacán Valley we can make a rough estimate of the probable percentage of the population residing in the cabeceras of four of the states (Tepexpan, Chiconautla, Acolman, and Otumba), based on a comparision of estimates from archaeological data on the population of the cabeceras (see Sanders, 1956) and from documentary data on the population of the domain. The data are presented in Table 4.12.

Chiconautla, on the basis of both documentary and archaeological data, was a completely nucleated domain, and our independently derived estimate from the two sources of data conforms strikingly. With respect to the other three, between 12 and 22 percent of the population resided in the central community.

Spanish statements indicate that most of the cabeceras in 1519 in the Basin of Mexico were comparable either in political rank or population size to our four test cases from the Teotihuacán Valley. This would suggest that the smaller cabeceras in the basin ranged in population from 1,000 to 7,000 in 1519. In this category certainly would be included the following cabeceras:

Table 4.12
Calculated 1519 Population for Part of the Teotihuacán Valley

Domain	Population of the Cabecera (archaeological data)[a]	1568 Population (documentary data, total domain)[b]	1519 Population[c]
Tepexpan	900– 1,200	4,421	11,937–13,263
Chiconautla	2,500– 5,000	1,478	3,991– 4,434
Acolman	3,600– 4,800	11,480	30,996–34,440
Otumba	3,200– 6,400	12,000	32,400–36,000
Totals	10,200–17,400	29,379	79,324–88,137

[a]From Sanders, 1956.
[b]From Cook and Borah, 1960: Appendix.
[c]Calculated from 1568 figures, 2.7–3.0 ratio, total domain.

Chimalhuacán-Chalco, Tepetlixpa Chimalhuacán, Tenango Tepopula, Chimalhuacán, Chiautla, Tepetlaoxtoc, Tezoyuca, Tepozotlan, Tultitlan, Ecatepec, Tenayuca, Hueypoxtla, Jilotzingo, Tequixquiac, Tlapanaloya, and Coyoacán. At the opposite end would be the city of Tenochtitlán with an estimated minimum of 150,000 (see below). The others fall between these figures, but overwhelmingly at the lower end of the range. There are a number of problems. Cuauhtitlan possibly was somewhat larger than the group of small centers but there is no good evidence that it was, and we suspect Culhuacan, Azcaputzalco, and Tlacopan were larger also. Torquemada (1943–44: 1:249–312) classified them on the same level as Otumba, however, so there is a possibility that they were within the range. Huexotla and Coatlichan, on the basis of documentary data, would be relegated to the status of this lower group, but recent settlement pattern surveys made by J. R. Parsons (1971: Map 14) would suggest that much of the population of these domains was nucleated. If so, it would put the cabeceras in the 10,000 to 20,000 bracket. Other cabeceras of relatively small states were probably in this size bracket as well, since they were cases where most of the population was nucleated in the central town. Examples of these are Cuitláhuac, Mixquic, Ixtapalapa, Mexicalcingo, and Huitzilopochco, all chinampa communities.

There is another problem, however, in connection with the chinampa settlements. Recent archaeological surveys by Armillas (1971) indicate that most of the chinampa farmers resided on their holdings, so that most of the population was outside of the cabecera proper in what amounts to a ranchería (dispersed) settlement pattern. Because of the high level of productivity of chinampa farming, the density of rural settlement was unusually high (perhaps as high as 1,000 per km^2 in some areas), and a chinampa domain would appear as a single physical community from the air. In fact, since the domain borders merged, the entire chinampa area might appear as one huge settlement.

Other centers such as Texcoco, Amecameca, Xochimilco, and Tlalmanalco certainly exceeded 10,000 inhabitants. We have estimated the probable 1519 population of the core domain of Texcoco at 43,200 to 51,000. How much of the population resided at the center is not known. In a recent archaeological survey, J. R. Parsons (1971: 120) estimated a population of 25,000, or approximately half of the above total. In terms of the areal extent of the site, it certainly could not have exceeded a population of 30,000. Both of these figures are cited as the population of the city in 1519 by the sixteenth-century writers, but in terms of vecinos or casas rather than total population.

The Special Problem of Tenochtitlán

The population of Tenochtitlán (Mexico City) at the moment of the Spanish Conquest has stimulated considerable controversy over the years. Documentary sources provide us with three estimates. One is 60,000 casas, a figure derived ultimately from Cortés (López de Gómara, 1943: 1:231) and repeated by various later writers, the most common base from which modern writers have calculated the population. Another, the Anonymous Conqueror (1941: 42) cited 60,000 people, but the only original version of his work is in Italian, and it is possible that the translator misinterpreted the Spanish word vecino. Torquemada (1943–44: 286–88), with his usual zeal, cited a figure of 120,000 casas and then added that each casa contained one, three, four, and even ten vecinos or householders. Most contemporary writers have multiplied the Cortés figure of 60,000 casas by a factor of 5 to obtain a total population of 300,000. Even if Torquemada exaggerated somewhat the number of families per house, and we use the average of seven persons derived from the *Suma* as the size of an average household, the estimate of 60,000 casas would yield a population of 420,000. In fact, the urban character of the center with its large upper and middle class would seem to demand a higher average number. In Tepoztlan, a small cabecera, Carrasco (1964) reports the household of the cacique as comprising 23 persons.

In my original 1970 paper I attempted to estimate the population of the city on the basis of a series of assumptions. First I assumed that the famous Maguey map (Toussaint et al., 1938: 67) was a portion of the sixteenth-century but post-Conquest colonial city, that it was typical of the Indian portion of the city at that time, and that most of pre-Conquest Tenochtitlán had a comparable plan and population density. We then identified its location as near the colonial church of Santa María de la Redonda and estimated the population density of the area embraced by the map at 13,145 per square kilometer. The second assumption was that the total area of the city was 8 square kilometers, and that the type of settlement represented on the Maguey map covered approximately 5.75 square kilometers. The central, Spanish section, referred to in the sixteenth century as "La Traza," measured 2.25 square kilometers, and we assumed that it had a much lower density because of the higher social and economic level of the population living there and because of the presence of large civic and ceremonial structures. On the basis of these calculations, and checking against the censuses from the mid-sixteenth century, we estimated a population for early colonial Mexico City at approximately 80,000 and then assumed a comparable settlement arrangement size and density for Tenochtitlán at the time of the Conquest.

A recent study by Calnek (1973) demonstrates conclusively that the Maguey map does not in fact pertain to the city proper, but is a map of one of the chinampa settlements outside of the city and within Lake Texcoco. Furthermore, the city was probably at least 12 square kilometers in size. Although he does not discuss in detail the question of population estimates in the paper, he does offer a tentative estimate of 150,000 to 200,000 people for the Conquest city, a figure which we will accept here.

We might, then, reassess our position in the following way. The total population of the metropolitan area and satellite villages and towns would still be somewhere between 295,037 and 327,819 people (Table 4.9). Of this, between 150,000 and 200,000 resided in the 12 square kilometer island city and were probably, on the basis of Calnek's study, almost entirely nonagricultural in life style: professional administrators, nobles, priests, craft specialists, and merchants. The balance resided in the other island communities and lakeshore towns and villages (128,000 to 145,000 in all), and the entire complex of communities would have appeared from the air as a single great settlement (an impression heightened by the connecting causeways), the most massive concentration of settlement in Mesoamerican prehistory.

The Urban-Rural Ratio

In a previous section, we estimated the population of the Basin of Mexico in 1519 at between 1,000,000 and 1,200,000 inhabitants. It would be useful to be able to estimate the ratio of urban to rural population, or phrasing it more correctly, the ratio between cabecera populations and that of dependent settlements. We make this point because some of the people of the cabeceras were probably full-time farmers, and it is debatable whether these should be classified as urban simply because of residence in the cabeceras. This would be particularly true of the smaller cabeceras, where the majority of the population may well have been farmers. Our estimates of cabecera populations are summarized below.

Tenochtitlán-Tlaltelolco	150,000–200,000
Texcoco	20,000–30,000
Five third-level cabeceras, average population 15,000[a]	75,000
Forty fourth-level cabeceras, average population 4,000 to 5,000	160,000–200,000
Total	405,000–505,000

[a]Xochimilco, Amecameca, Tlalmanalco, Tlacopan (Tacuba), Ixtapalapa.

According to these calculations, nearly one-half of the total population of the Basin of Mexico resided in towns and cities in 1519.

PART IV South America

"The Inca *kept accurate population statistics . . . but the figures were nearly all lost at the time of the Spanish Conquest"* (Rowe, 1946: 184).

INTRODUCTION

The standard reference in English on the aboriginal population of South America is Steward's 1949 essay in Volume 5 of *The Handbook of South American Indians,* along with information in the individual tribal articles in the same collection. Steward acknowledged the influence of Kroeber and Rosenblat on his methodology, and in some instances he relied directly on Rosenblat. Steward used the "earliest data that appear to be reliable" and extended the density for one tribe to others with similar cultures and environments. He admitted to declines before the time of these estimates, so that his figures are "likely to be too small rather than too large," but he tended to regard the earlier declines as not significant; for example: "The neighboring Cocama retained nearly their native numbers to the present day."

Steward's failure adequately to consider previous decline has been pointed out by several scholars. In addition, the earliest "reliable" data that he did cite often reflect a poor utilization of or search for documentary evidence. Pyle, in her essay, makes this clear for Argentina. An almost classic example is the province of Mojos in northeastern Bolivia, for which Steward gave an estimate of 6,000 for the year 1680, whereas there is good documentation for at least 100,000 in 1690 (Denevan, 1966b: 116).

Steward calculated a total population for South America of 9,228,735,[1]

1. This total is from Steward's (1949: 664) Table 2, based on data in *The Handbook of South American Indians.* In Table 3 (p. 666) Steward without explanation reduced the total to 8,610,000 (South America only), increasing Ecuador from 500,000 to 1,000,000 but reducing some of the other regions significantly. In Table 1 (p. 656) Steward gave a total of 9,129,000 for South America although his totals for the Andes and the remainder of South America add up to 9,029,000. In a later description of the South American Indians, Steward repeated the total of 9,228,735 (Steward and Faron, 1959: 53).

151

nearly half of which was in the central Andes, in contrast to 4,000,000 by Kroeber (1939: 166), 6,785,000 by Rosenblat (1954: 1:102), and 39,000,000 by Dobyns (1966: 415). The resulting densities for Steward are quite low, a fact somewhat masked by his calculations in terms of persons per 100 square kilometers rather than per square kilometer. His density for highland Peru and Bolivia is only 3.9 per square kilometer. Steward misjudged the possibility for cultivation of the large tropical savannas when he said that the savanna populations were "extremely sparse" and contained only hunters and gatherers. Recent discoveries of relic savanna fields prove the contrary (Denevan, 1970b).

A basic question in New World historical demography, still unresolved, is whether the high-civilization regions of the Andes and central Mexico had populations of comparable size. Many scholars, such as Kroeber and Dobyns, arguing for either high or low totals, assume comparable numbers, while Phelan (1967: 44–45) and others accept much higher estimates for Mexico than for the Andes.

Regional demographic studies in South America have focused on the civilization of the central Andes for obvious reasons. Statistical data of the scope and detail of those utilized by Cook and Borah for central Mexico are scarce, however, or at least remain unknown or unused. There are some exceptions, such as the *Visita de Chucuito* (Espinoza Soriano, 1964), utilized by C. T. Smith (1970), the *Visita de Huánuco* (Murra, 1967–72), and the materials analyzed by Friede and Colmenares for Colombia. Other documentary regional studies are currently underway.

Estimates for the central Andes–the *audiencias* of Lima, Charcas, and Quito (coastal and Andean Peru, Bolivia, and Ecuador)–range from Kroeber's (1939: 166) 3,000,000 to Dobyns' (1966: 415) 30,000,000. Rowe (1946: 185) derived 6,000,000, probably the most frequently cited figure, by extending to the entire region the average rate of depopulation (4 : 1) for five provinces between 1525 (indirect evidence) and 1571 (census of Viceroy Toledo with additions up to 1591; Morales Figueroa, 1866: 61). Various Peruvian and other scholars have made different estimates, some of which are reviewed by N. D. Cook (1965). In addition, Cook examines the evidence and estimates for populations at later dates during the early colonial period. Cook himself originally accepted 6,000,000 for Peru alone but later (N. D. Cook, 1973: 304) calculated only 2,738,000 for Peru in 1530; this can be extrapolated to about 5,000,000 for the central Andes in 1520.

C. T. Smith (1970: 459) used the demographic data for ca. 1520–1525 (an Inca *quipu* census) and 1566 in the *Visita de Chucuito* of 1567 as a basis for deriving a figure of about 12,100,000, or double that of Rowe. Smith made some adjustments in Rowe's depopulation ratios for five provinces and added his calculations for Chucuito and also for Huamanga. His average depopulation ratio for the *sierra* is slightly less than that of Rowe, but applying his 1520–1525 tributary multiplier of 9 for Chucuito to all the provinces (Rowe used 5.1) results in his much larger total population. For the coast, Smith obtained a considerably higher depopulation ratio (58 : 1) than did Rowe (16 : 1 and 25 : 1). Smith stresses the great difference in depopulation ratios on the coast and in the sierra, and he also notes the probability of at least local population declines well before the arrival of the Spaniards. The four commentaries that follow the article by Smith (1970: 460–62) do not seem to be in marked disagreement with him. John Murra, however, raises important questions about our understanding of Andean social and economic categories in relation to attempts at quantification. For another, but more questionable, treatment of the Chucuito data, see Lipschutz (1966: 240–45).

Shea, in the following essay, takes a very conservative approach to Andean populations. His method is to calculate the annual rate of population change from 1581 to 1613 (0.00612 to 0.01151) and project this back to 1520, using a tributary multiplier of only 4.18 to 4.38. He obtains a 1520 total of 1,343,123 to 1,944,753 for Peru and 2,026,108 to 2,933,670 for the central Andes. However, this method and the similar one by N. D. Cook do not consider the possibility that the early decline rate was much greater than during the period 1581–1613, which would have meant a larger 1520 population. Shea believes that epidemic behavior in the Andean environment was much different than that in central Mexico, resulting in a slower population decline, and that considerable decline may have taken place during the Inca period prior to the Spanish Conquest. Also, he argues that a regional projection based on a later count for the same area is subject to considerable distortion if there had been massive migration from one region to another; such is suggested for early colonial Peru by Mellafe (1970).

Some idea of the size and decline of the population of the Bolivian altiplano and Cochabamba Valley is provided by Sánchez-Albornoz (1974: 45–47). In five provinces the number of villages before *congregación* (consolidation of villages) was 743 and the number after (in 1575) was only 35. Although the villages after congregación were substantially larger (range from 1,343 to 7,036) than immediately before (range from 44 to 548), there is every reason to believe that villages were considerably larger prior to the Conquest. (A conservative pre-Columbian average of 1,000 persons per village would provide a total population of 743,000 for only part of Bolivia, in contrast to 109,470 in 1575.)

Phelan (1967: 44–46) believed that the audiencia of Quito contained between 500,000 and 750,000 Indians on the coast and in the highlands at the time of conquest (plus another 200,000 in the eastern lowlands). Especially important, but unexplained, are indications that the Indian population did not decline significantly in the sixteenth century, except locally, in contrast to the situation in Lima and Charcas. Burgos-Guevara (1974) has argued for a population for the audiencia of Quito of 800,000 to 1,000,000 at the end of the sixteenth century. For a bibiography on the historical demography of Ecuador, Peru, and Bolivia, see Hamerly (1974).

For Colombia, estimates of the Chibcha population vary considerably. Steward (1949: 660) accepted only 300,000 (700,000 for the rest of highland Colombia), but other estimates range as high (surprisingly) as 1,000,000 by Kroeber (1946: 892). Eidt (1959: 378–82) reviewed the documentary evidence and concluded that an indication of 600,000 Chibcha was reasonable and could have been supported by the existing agricultural system. J. J. Parsons (1968: 29, also 194) found a total of 1,000,000 for the Antioqueño region to be reasonable. For more conservative interpretations, see the recent review of the aboriginal Colombian population by Jaramillo Uribe (1964). Colmenares (1973: 71) has recently estimated 3,000,000 for all Colombia.

There are several good regional studies of aboriginal populations in interior Colombia by Friede and Colmenares. For Tunja, using historical accounts, Friede (1965) calculated a total of 232,407 for 1537. Using a different method, Cook and Borah (1971–74: 1:417) obtained 283,000. For the Quimbaya, Friede (1963: 20) estimated 60,000 to 80,000 in about 1539; however Cook and Borah (1971–74: 1:421) obtained only about half as many. And for Pamplona, Colmenares (1969) provided data which were used by Cook and Borah (1971–74: 1:426) to estimate a minimum total population of 60,000 for 1532. Variation in the rate of population decline in the three areas suggested to Cook and Borah a significant difference between higher elevations (Tunja and Pamplona) and lower elevations (Quimbaya), such as they also found for Mexico (Borah and Cook, 1969).

For southern South America there have been few regional studies of aboriginal populations. Those that exist are generally superficial, as is suggested in the discussion of Argentina by Jane Pyle in this collection. She reviews previous calculations by Rosenblat, Steward, and Difrieri, all based on interpretations of sixteenth-century documents and chroniclers and finds them all conservatively biased, with reductions of the original figures substantial and arbitrary. She examines the same evidence, and in her judgment a reasonable total would be between 739,800 and 981,500, depending on the average family size.

For Amazonia, data on which to base estimates of aboriginal populations are probably more meager than for any other major region of the Americas except the Arctic. In fact, even estimates of current numbers of surviving Indians vary by 100 percent or more. Most of the decline of Amazonian people took place beyond the eyes of literate observers. The few regional studies that exist include those by Denevan (1966b: 112–20) for Mojos in northeastern Bolivia and by Sweet (1969) for Mainas in the northwest

Amazon; both areas were Jesuit mission provinces. Steward (1949) lists tribal estimates, but most are late and of little value. Denevan, in his essay here, attempts to estimate original populations by extending a known or calculated density for a group in a particular habitat type to the entire comparable habitat within Amazonia, on the assumption that resources and subsistence patterns were relatively uniform in each habitat. A total is arrived at for "greater Amazonia" of 5,100,000, an apparently high figure, but the density is only 0.5 per square kilometer. However, since it cannot be assumed that densities were uniform under similar resource-technology systems, this figure must be considered a reasonable minimum potential population rather than an estimate of actual population.

There are only a few estimates for Venezuela, southern Brazil, Uruguay, Paraguay, and Chile, other than the figures of Rosenblat (1954: 1:102, 278–320)[2] and Steward (1949). Some of the estimates for all of Brazil are listed by Onody (1970: 338–39). Blasi (1966) calculates 2,944,000 for 1500 on the basis of a density for an area of southern Brazil. Dobyns (1966: 415) cites evidence for high populations in Uruguay-Paraguay, where Portuguese slave hunters captured large numbers of Indians. The Araucanian population of Chile was estimated at 500,000 to 1,500,000 by Cooper (1946a: 694). The marginal tribes in the far south were probably never very numerous.

In conclusion, the striking characteristic of the demographic analysis of South America is the apparently much smaller Indian population in the Inca area and its slower decline, in comparison with the high-civilization region of central Mexico. It is possible, however, that the Andean population was larger but was struck down by European diseases which reached the Incas a decade or so before the Spanish Conquest, as argued by Dobyns (1963b). Certainly the Andes and South America in general have received less intensive study than has Middle America and hence offer a challenge to historical demographers.[3]

2. Rosenblat's figures for the South American countries are as follows: Colombia, 850,000; Venezuela, 350,000; Guianas, 100,000; Ecuador, 500,000; Peru, 2,000,000; Bolivia, 800,000; Paraguay, 280,000; Argentina, 300,000; Uruguay, 5,000; Brazil, 1,000,000; Chile, 600,000.

3. Two studies of aboriginal South American Indian populations have appeared recently. Noble David Cook examines six methods of calculation for Peru in 1530 and concludes that there were between 3 and 8 million Indians ("Estimaciones sobre la población del Perú en el momento de la conquista," *Histórica*, 1977, 1:37-60). John Hemming provides tribe by tribe estimates for the Brazilian Indians in 1500, arriving at a total of 2,431, 000 (*Red Gold: The Conquest of the Brazilian Indians*, Harvard University Press: Cambridge, 1978, pp. 485-501).

CHAPTER 5 A Defense of Small Population Estimates for the Central Andes in 1520

Daniel E. Shea

Since the conservative estimates of Ángel Rosenblat (1935, 1945, 1954), we have seen a steady trend of increasing size in determinations of the indigenous populations of the Western Hemisphere, culminating in the impressive work of Borah and Cook (1963) and Dobyns (1966). In general this trend is probably a desirable one; new problems and areas of research have been opened up, the Conquest period has been put into a new perspective, and perhaps our respect for non-European culture has been increased in proportion to the presumably enormous populations supported in pre-Conquest Mexico.

The picture in the Andean area has suffered in contrast with Mexico by virtue of a number of historical accidents. European man entered the Andean area later than Mexico, perhaps being preceded by his own diseases (Dobyns, 1963b), and European populations entered more slowly due to a much longer and more hazardous line of communication. Furthermore, intense civil war hindered the development of a stable bureaucracy, either civil or clerical, until relatively late in the sixteenth century. Thus the earliest and (possibly) most rapid decline of the Peruvian population is less well recorded than is the case in Mexico. The final difficulty is that although records of tribute in the

I wish to thank William M. Denevan for assistance, including obtaining documentary information otherwise unavailable to me. I would also like to acknowledge the generously extended expertise of John Finch, of the Beloit College Mathematics Department, who cleared up details and weaknesses of my understanding of the integration of equations in e. Neither, of course, is responsible for any errors of detail or calculation on my part, and both are to be commended for their patience.

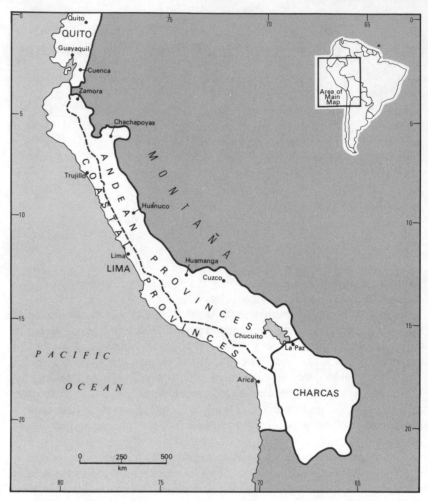

Cartographic Laboratory UW-Madison

Map 5.1. The Central Andes: *audiencias* of Quito, Lima, and Charcas, and the provinces of the Incan empire. Most of the towns shown were province capitals.

form of knotted cords were kept, Inca records are few and far between and almost totally untranslatable, in contrast with the Aztec tribute lists available to Borah and Cook for Mexico. The result is that estimates of the population of the Andean area at the height of the native empire (ca. A.D. 1520) are "projections" back in time from the latter half of the sixteenth century and early seventeenth century. These extrapolations are unsatisfactory for a variety of reasons, but principally because the large time gap involved introduces enormous possibilities of error, even with the best of all possible estimates for 1570 and later. Given varying assumptions about the available data, there are about as many estimates as there are students of the subject.

Based on decline rates from 1581 to 1613, a new attempt will be made here to recalculate the Indian population of the central Andes (Peru, Bolivia, and Ecuador, or roughly the *audiencias* of Lima, Charcas, and Quito) in 1535 and in 1520 and thereby to defend the position that numbers were relatively low.

This essay attempts to discuss some of the major considerations implicit in employing a mathematic model to estimate the size of the Andean population at the time of the Spanish Conquest. It is to be remembered that any form of such calculation is a model, even that involving the most elementary arithmetic, and that one function of such models is to sharpen our perceptions of the processes occurring in that population, as well as to calculate a reasonable figure. With this in mind, a model is proposed that satisfies the general criteria of population dynamics as well as the specific criteria of the Andean area. (The mathematical method I employ for estimating population is described in Addendum 1). First, however, a critical discussion is provided of other models, often derived from studies of other areas, that have been used to estimate Andean populations in the sixteenth century.

PREVIOUS CALCULATIONS OF DECLINE RATES
AND CONTACT POPULATIONS

A number of recent authors, notably Dobyns (1966), have projected decline rates for the Andean area comparable to those for Mexico on the assumption that the same diseases must have caused essentially the same mortality rate in both areas. Dobyns has demonstrated the existence of a large number of epidemics (1963b; see also Lastres, 1951), and we have no reason to suspect that the Andean peoples had any more resistance to European diseases than the Mexicans. It appears certain that the European-introduced diseases had some fairly important effect on the Andean population. However, there is still a questionable ethnological assumption involved in this sort of reasoning. Not all the vectors of a disease are specific to the disease organism itself; population size and density, rates of interpersonal contact, indigenous sanitary habits, and culturally determined avoidances, choices of water source, methods of food storage, and a whole host of other factors can accelerate or hinder the progress of a disease. Even already existing diseases in local areas are of some significance. A recent epidemiological study of four Peruvian towns reveals enormous numbers of diseases and toxic situations, some of which, like hookworm and amoebic infections, are probably pre-Hispanic

(Buck, Sasaki, and Anderson, 1968: 66–67). There is no telling, given sixteenth-century diagnoses, how often such infections were confused with smallpox or other European diseases. It seems to be true that epidemics of one disease follow another, as though any disease produces weakness that leads to susceptibility. It also seems true that people rarely have two epidemic diseases at once, and almost never have three; disease organisms are in competition for the available hosts. Therefore, local diseases can affect susceptibility to an incoming disease, even in areas where we may suppose no natural immunity to the new disease. Also to be considered, when the question is focused on the Andean area, is the matter of altitude. Relative lack of oxygen and carbon dioxide, relatively higher incidence of solar energy, and the other effects of altitude may affect the human organism and make it more susceptible, or alternatively, it may affect the disease organism to the human's advantage.

Buck, Sasaki, and Anderson (1968: 29–31, 48–49, 55, 64, 66, 79) discuss a number of physiological conditions, diseases, and disease vectors that show either regional or altitudinal variation. For example, the disease vectors from the order Diptera have four superfamilies and 166 families recorded in Peru. Of these, 53 families were observed for the four localities of the study. Of these, the single family Culicidae (mosquitoes) has 46 species observed in the four localities. Twenty-nine species of the Arthropod family Tabanidae were observed. Most members of the order are potential disease vectors but of varying diseases. Furthermore, the species and frequencies of species vary regionally and altitudinally (Buck, Sasaki, and Anderson, 1968: 29–37).

The underlying assumption of Dobyns' and similar arguments, which imply that since the disease organism is the same all other vectors, cultural and environmental, are identical or unimportant, is not a tenable position.

Elementary Model

The proper information, such as age distribution and differential suscepti-bility coefficients, is lacking for a thorough analysis of comparative cases such as Mexico and the Andean area. However, even with such scanty information, a very elementary mathematical model should indicate some of the differ-ences involved in the two cases. The distribution of the population of the central valley of Mexico is described in a fashion adequate for our purposes by Gibson (1964: 49, 89). Villages were distributed around the valley, with concession made to the topography, but nevertheless in a more or less random and even distribution. These villages were linked to larger villages by a centralized tax-collecting system, and to one another by five-day markets. The larger villages (*cabeceras*) were linked directly to Mexico City by the tax-collecting system and by a number of other cultural factors such as markets, political affiliation, and the Aztec trader/spy system (*pochteca*). Given the introduction of smallpox into Mexico City, it is difficult to imagine a system that could be better designed to spread the disease. Smallpox (or any other disease) should have spread out from Mexico City in ever widening concentric circles. The infection rate would be some mathematical function of πr^2, since the number infected would be proportional to the area of the circle. Of course, the radius of the circle, r, would be some function, perhaps logarithmic, of the infection rate of the disease. In contrast, the Andean population is notorious for its linear distributions. Andean villages were, and still are, strung along the east-west running rivers of the coastal area, and distributed northwest-southeast along the highland intercordilleran valleys and plateaus (see James, 1959: Map 54). The distribution of the Peruvian population might be likened to a comb, with its back lying along the Andes and its teeth pointing toward the Pacific. Smallpox or some other virulent disease would spread rapidly along such a population distribution, but not nearly as rapidly as in the Mexican situation. If we make the assumption that exactly the same disease is introduced into the two areas at the same time, with a rate of propagation (coefficient of virulence times percentage of susceptibility) r, the infection rate in the Andean area will be rt (t being time), while that in highland Mexico will be $\pi r^2 t$. Thus the rate in Mexico will be $3.141r$ greater than in the Andean area. And, if the disease is virulent (i.e., r is a large number), the death rate in Mexico will be considerably larger, both relatively and absolutely. The percentage of those dying will be greater, and the absolute numbers might be greater by an order of magnitude or more.

This sort of analysis suggests an additional problem, namely that circular reasoning is involved in population estimates based on projections by rate of change. Larger populations will have areas of higher density in which disease will be propagated more rapidly. Larger populations will suffer more from famine and attendant woes of epidemics because larger numbers of people will be removed from work in the fields. Certain diseases do not reach epidemic proportions unless a large enough population is available to propagate the disease faster than some critical rate, a sort of "critical mass." In short, larger populations will have higher rates of decline due to more virulent disease, and smaller populations will have lower rates of decline. Furthermore, as a large population declines, becoming a smaller population by definition, its rate of decline declines (i.e., a logarithmic curve is involved), below its rate at some previous (or subsequent) time, creating a vicious circle for one who tries to estimate earlier populations. This makes the analysis of declining population a difficult and frustrating job. Unless they illustrate critical points or factors of the decline, even very good historical records may be insufficient or even irrelevant.

Population Profiles

A possible way out of the above dilemma is to begin with relevant biological criteria like the population profile. Sixteenth-century statistics, of course, do not provide this sort of information, but C. T. Smith (1970) has made a reasonable case that such information from later censuses could be usefully applied to the earlier data. The 1567 census for the province of Chucuito (Espinoza Soriano, 1964; C. T. Smith, 1970) permits reconstruction of a simple population profile for the province, and although the profile differs in a number of significant aspects from the modern one, this sort of analysis is worth the effort. This approach is particularly logical for attempting to set up some sort of ratio between total population and adult tribute-paying male population, which overcomes the problem of early censuses being head counts of male taxpayers only. By this method Smith arrives at a multiplier of 9 for estimating the total central Andean population from the recorded taxpayer head count. Application of this multiplier leads to an estimate for about 1520 of 12,139,498 (C. T. Smith, 1970: 459).

Smith deserves praise for a conscientious and ingenious approach, which ought to be applied elsewhere and should produce new and useful results. Nevertheless, however valid Smith's multiplier of 9 for the province of Chucuito, it is a questionable procedure to apply it too liberally to the entire area. The very source Smith used was originally ordered as an investigation into the fact that the Indians of Chucuito were richer than those of the surrounding area (Espinoza Soriano, 1964: 5). Since Chucuito was a Crown *encomienda,* it may be fair to suppose that the reason was that the Crown was more lenient with its Indians than with those of the private holders, or even that appointed Crown officials were more lax in exploiting the Indians to the king's benefit than the private holders were in their own interests. Smith's multiplier of 9 ultimately rests on the assertion (C. T. Smith, 1970: 456) that the tribute age was from 30 to 50 or from 30 to 60 years. If men were held for tribute either earlier or later in their life-span, then the ratio would change. Presumably other areas were more stringent with or more exploitative of their Indians, and this means that the ages and therefore the ratios would be different. Longer periods of tribute paying would result in more men in the tribute-paying group, and the multiplier would be smaller. We may regard Smith's multiplier of 9 not as a reliable indicator of population, but as an upper limit.

In the attempt to test the validity of Smith's ratio, an additional pessimistic observation was made: no other multiplier seems to work either. In 1628 Vázquez de Espinosa (1948: 644–70) supplied us with an elementary population profile of the central Andes. His categories (*mozos* or *muchachos, viejos, tributarios,* and *mujeres*) are not very sophisticated by modern demographic standards, but they are sufficient to test ratios of the sort Smith proposes (see

Addendum 2). Testing a few areas, particularly the south coast specifically associated with Chucuito, by the technique known as "chi-square" (hereafter χ^2), I came up with some interesting results. The χ^2 values were far, far out of line for any stable or even normally producing population. Row and column totals were used in the computation of expected values, so that if any sort of consistent relationship existed between the relative sizes of the categories the results of the test would indicate only random variation about a consistent ratio. Instead, the χ^2 values were unusually large, indicating strongly nonrandom variations. Even disease, while it might kill enormous numbers, does not kill males in greater numbers than females, and if it killed either old or young in greater proportions than adult middle-aged individuals, then the entire mozo (or muchacho) or viejo columns would be equally affected, so that column totals would automatically incorporate the correction in the results. The only answer is that there is no regular relationship among the numbers of other categories of the population.

There are probably several contributing factors to this discrepancy. In telling the king about the problem of the *reducción* in Peru, Miguel de Monsalve (1604: 13–14) had an interesting analysis of the problem. It seems that while men left their villages periodically to perform the tribute labor, it was the women who most disrupted the reducción system by their own departure. In the man's absence, the Spaniard, often the *corregidor,* took advantage of the woman. Occasionally this took the form of sexual exploitation, but more frequently it was simply a matter of forcing her to pay the tribute of the husband in his absence. This obliged her to operate the entire agricultural enterprise, forcing her to do the work of two people, including the work of a man. Monsalve did not mention that this put her in a socially anomalous position with regard to the other villagers, as well as forcing her to cross traditional lines of division of labor. Whatever the principal cause, however, Monsalve insisted that it was the women who left the reducciones. In some cases the husband never returned, but if he did he found his wife gone. The husband's choice was clear. He could leave to find his own wife, or to find another, but in either case he would leave if at all possible. Neither husband nor wife, after such an experience, would be likely to reenter reducciones, or reenlist on the tax lists if it could be avoided. Monsalve placed most of the blame on the competition for labor between the private *encomendero* and the royal tribute labor in the mines, but in some areas, especially the coastal areas associated with Chucuito (Espinoza Soriano, 1964: 63), trading expeditions might very easily have produced the same household situation; once a man left home for whatever reason, the exploitation of his wife would cause her to leave.

Both corregidores and *curacas* were involved in the tribute-collecting system and computed the tribute lists. These lists were irregularly changed after the census of Viceroy Toledo (Monsalve, 1604: 7–8, 10, 14, 16, 25), and we may assume that a variety of graft techniques were employed in the tribute collection. The most probable situation is that the lists were under-reported, since the discrepancy would be divided between the tribute collectors. If the lists were under-reported, not only did the revenue go into the corregidor's or the curaca's pocket, but unlisted individuals could be used as personal servants in violation of the Crown law (Monsalve, 1604: 18–19, 25–26; Melchor de Navarra y Rocaful, 1859: 253). Curacas did not have a motive for carefully reporting deaths, since the proceeds of Indian states went, legally or illegally, into their pockets (Monsalve, 1604: 15–16). Of course, the extent to which this sort of skulduggery went on is problematic, but it did occur and may have occurred in very different degrees in neighboring towns. The net result is that there is no reason to believe that any sample of the Peruvian population has any sort of consistent relationship between tributaries and total population.

Coastal Populations

It is interesting that Rowe found that apparently the coastal populations declined more rapidly than the highland ones (Rowe, 1946: 184). Since the coastal areas west of Chucuito may have been involved in this decline, there is some reason to consider this matter; and since Dobyns used a disease-theory explanation of decline, it is relevant to Dobyns' hypothesis as well. Monsalve's account of the reasons for which Indians left encomienda areas may be relevant, as well as his observation that the Indians had no pride whatever about living in properly habitable places (towns) and would cheerfully abandon them for the distant villages and even the open country itself (Monsalve, 1604: 7, 10, 33). Since the women were a cause of the movement, and there was some movement into areas outside the control of Spaniards, it is possible that the Indians simply moved up into the higher reaches of the valley or all the way to the highland areas. Perhaps it is important to remember that the population distribution in these coastal valleys is linear, and any movement on the part of Indians, including the seeking of new wives as a result of desertion or death of spouses, would not have been into the desert or into the sea. Highland populations could move in all geographic directions, and on the large scale their movements would statistically cancel out. In the coastal valleys, however, any reasonable amount of population movement must be up and down valley. Since down valley is toward the sea, there are definite limits, with the result that there was a "boundary effect," and the net change of population was toward the highlands. The important and virtually unanswerable question is, what part of the difference in highland-coastal population decline is accounted for by this boundary effect? There does not seem to be any way that the question can be answered, and, if we cautiously assume the worst possible situation, it may account for all the difference. If so, we have no reason to assume that the coastal areas were harder hit by disease than any other area, nor any reason to believe that figures for any coastal area can be used to derive a ratio of tributary to total population.

Cultural and Historical Adjustments

Noble David Cook (1965) has attempted to deal with some of the cultural and historical factors involved in the decline of the Peruvian population, and he has created a picture of a long, slow decline in which disease, but also factors such as increases in the Spanish population, in the number of mixed bloods ("Castes"), in European livestock, in infant mortality, and in famine, all interacted to produce a general decline in the native population. One of his more interesting calculations resulted in a chart in which the percentage of Indians, Castes, and Whites is depicted for the period from 1530 to 1950 (N. D. Cook, 1965: 96). His point is well taken that the decline in the Indian population is highly correlated with the increase in the Caste and White populations. In all probability some Indians were joining the Caste classification. In any case, the White and Caste populations were exploiting the Indians, and certainly one factor in the decline is the rate of exploitation.

Figure 5.1 should give a better idea of the direction of these population changes. The White and Caste groups increased at a literally explosive rate, while the initially much larger Indian population declined steadily in response. It is interesting that Cook's estimates of the Indian population from 1754 to 1725 almost exactly match Rosenblat's estimates of the Caste groups for the same period. The exact match is probably coincidental, yet the fact that the rate of population increase was the same, and was the same as the rate of increase of the White population, is probably significant. By 1750 the great age of migration was past and the rate of increase of the White population was primarily a matter of natural increase, as was also that of the Caste population. If the Indian population was also increasing at this time at the same rate, it is a general population increase that is indicated. This is in harmony with N. D. Cook's (1965: 93) own conclusions and with those of Kubler (1946: 336) who considered 1720 to be the nadir of the Andean population curve.

A NEW ESTIMATE OF THE POPULATION FOR 1535 AND FOR 1520

Perhaps the best model of the early colonial period is one of ecological adaptation. It takes little imagination to see the Spaniards and Castes as either predators or parasites on the Indian population, and of course smallpox and

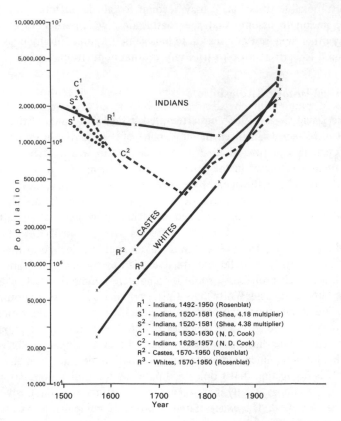

Figure 5.1. Calculations of Peruvian Population Fluctuation, 1520–1957. Sources: Indians, 1492–1950, Rosenblat in N. D. Cook (1965: 95); 1520–1581, Shea (this article); 1530–1630, N. D. Cook (1973: Table 10.2); 1628–1957, N. D. Cook (1965: 92); Whites, 1570–1950, Rosenblat in N. D. Cook (1965: 95); Castes, 1570–1950, Rosenblat in N. D. Cook (1965: 95).

other diseases were clearly parasitic on the Indian population. The rate of decline of the Indian population is a function of this sort of adaptation of several populations to one another simultaneously, a process of "co-adaptation" or "co-evolution." A good analytical or mathematical model would require more information than we have or could reasonably hope to get for the time period involved. Short of that, however, there is a fairly good method for dealing with population change, the system of the "natural" logarithms, based on the number $e = 2.71828 \ldots$. This constant, an invariant transcendental number like π, is defined as the limit of a function that is its own derivative. Having this unique relation to its derivative allows for a number of simplifications of calculation, as well as a number of interesting applications. One of the applications is to organic populations, since they satisfy the mathematical properties of *continuity* and of a function, e^x, that is a *derivative of itself.* Clearly an organism is continuous with its parent in biological terms, and a population is undoubtedly a derivative of itself at a previous time.

It is especially true that an integral of e over a period of time is a sensitive measure of population change, since like compound interest it takes into account the additional increments (or decrements) of population which are descended from increments (or not descended from decrements) of the previous generations (see Addendum 1). Being a continuous curve, it ignores the calculational difficulties of compound interest, yet will approximate very large numbers of slightly different rates of change. An integral in e would be some sort of measure of "people-years," which might be a difficult concept to absorb at first, but which reflects population over time and the effects that operate over time.

An integral approximation of the estimates of the total population of Lima, Charcas, and Quito from 1561 to 1720 by interpolation from Figure 5.1 gives an annual logarithmic decline rate of 0.00067. This is a decline of the total population including a declining Indian population and increasing populations of Whites and Castes. Even if the rather large estimate of the 1520 population by Smith (1970: 459) of 12,139,498 is used with an interpolation for 1720 of Rosenblat's curve of population decline (Fig. 5.1), the annual decline rate is only 0.00927. These are very small figures, both less than 1 percent. Of course this is a declining rate of decline, a logarithmic curve, and straight line percentages would be larger. Straight percentages would not take into account declining reproduction that results from loss of parents in previous generations.

These extremely small figures, indicating a low overall decline of the total highland population, are not conclusive because of probable errors in the estimates of the beginning and ending populations, and because of relative changes in the constituent populations. Nevertheless, such low figures do serve as a warning and an omen that the decline of the Indian population may not be nearly as precipitous as some have suggested, and if so, then high estimates of contact Indian population may be excessive.

It is clear from Figure 5.1 that the Whites and Castes were increasing explosively in numbers. However, until late in the colonial period these two groups were still small in absolute numbers, even with an explosive rate of increase, and the total number of Indians is a function of that absolute size as well as of the rate of change.

All estimates of which I am aware are ultimately based on numbers of tributary adult males in the Andean Indian population during the early colonial period. Tribute payers are, of course, only a segment of the Indian population, which is only a segment of the total population, but they are the segment that most interested early encomenderos and tax collectors, and therefore they were the most reliably reported group. It is here proposed that this group should be regarded as a statistical sample of a larger population, in the formal mathematical sense as well as the obvious biological sense. It is clear that some taxpayers evaded being counted, and criteria varied temporally and regionally as to who should have been counted; yet even minimal persistence by the tax collectors would have made the tributary count a "sample" in modern statistical parlance. Other categories of the population would almost certainly vary with greater random variation due to inertia and discrepancy in the counting procedure (for example, refer to the χ^2 results of p. 179). To the extent to which any sample can be used to estimate a parameter of the population from which it comes, integral approximations of the rate of change of the adult male population should be a fair measure of the rate of change of the total Indian population.

I should point out that the number of tributary males is a function in e of the number of their mothers. Thus using an equation in e of tributary males is automatically protected against certain errors which might arise because of sex imbalances in either the population or in the tribute count figures. Equations in e of this type are also automatically corrected for variations and limitations in biological fertility, as they represent a continuous curve of the *fertility* of the parent generation, which is dependent upon the number of females but varies with random differences from one female to another.

I first applied the approximation in e to the figures given by Kubler (1946: 334) for 1561, 1572, 1591, and 1628. These estimates all fall within the first century after the Conquest, and they have six possible combinations that might be used as estimates of the decline rate. Four of the six rates of decline are greater than 0.0040, and the mean of all six is 0.0049 per annum decline in the period 1561–1628. Similarly, a treatment of the same data as a problem in statistical correlation of logarithmic curves has a slope of 0.0045. In other words, judging from such a sample, we see that the average decline of the Indian population of the Andean area from 1561 to 1628 was about half of 1 percent per annum, compounded.

In editing this volume, Denevan has cautioned me to review such figures with great care, as there may be discrepancies in the estimates of total tribute figures that would modify the picture. There are in fact discrepancies within the standard available figures, which, although they do not alter my opinion that the rate of change of the Andean population was relatively low, do raise the rate somewhat. An example of the sort of difficulty is that Zavala (1973: 239) and Rowe (1946: 184) differ by 14,642 in their count of tributaries for 1571. A look at the original source used by Rowe (Morales Figueroa, 1866: 41–61), shows that Morales either incorrectly added or incorrectly copied the figures for Cuenca and Zamora, and the total error for the two provinces is the requisite 14,642. Zavala (1973: 238) introduces another question when he dates Toledo's census as 1581 instead of 1571, whereas Rowe (1946: 184) used 1571. Morales (1866: 41) stated that the figures were actually dated 1591, and some of the provinces are identified as *revisitas*, updating Toledo's census. Zimmerman (1938: 91–206) provided a history of Toledo's census, which did start in 1571 but which lasted until 1575 and may have been further delayed in some areas. The tributary totals given by both Zavala (325,899) and Rowe (311,257) differ considerably from that of Kubler (287,395). Kubler's (1946: 334) total is listed for 1572 and is taken from Vázquez de Espinosa (1948: 653, 670), but there is some doubt that this figure is for 1572; it may be for 1591 or even later, or be spread over several years. The technique described here, of estimating decline rates by logarithmic equations and then averaging the figures so derived, is not overly sensitive to variations in totals (14,000 in 300,000 is only about 5 percent), but could be seriously in error due to incorrect estimates of the length of the period in which the change took place.

N. D. Cook (1973: 11, 52) has done the most complete reanalysis of the available tribute figures, and he points out that areas visited by Toledo's census takers starting in 1571 were revisited in 1589 and 1591. Accordingly, a mean date for the census of Toledo as reported by Morales is the same 1581 used by Zavala. The census reported by Vázquez de Espinosa probably falls between the revisitas of 1591 and the 1628 date of his manuscript. A mean date would be 1609, but undoubtedly the Vázquez de Espinosa figures were heavily weighted by a census of the Lima area in 1613, and that would probably be the best mean date for that census, as is suggested by N. D. Cook (1973: 43).

An alternative is to use as estimates the averages of decline rates of towns and provinces. A random sampling of specific towns from Morales can be compared with their later size as given by Vázquez de Espinosa. The provinces of Lima, Cuzco, La Paz, Guamanga (Huamanga, now Ayacucho), and Guánuco (Huánuco) were among the largest and therefore received the most attention and so are utilized here. The decline rates derived for these provinces are shown in Table 5.1, and a graphic presentation is shown in Figure 5.2.

The mean of mean annual decline rates in Table 5.1 is 0.00614, and the mean of the decline rates of the total population of the five samples is 0.00598. Thus, despite considerable variation on a town-by-town basis, as well as differences between the town-by-town rates and in the rate for the area sample totals, there is good agreement that the decline rate is approximately 0.006. The moment coefficient of skewness for the town-by-town rates is −1.29666, and for the province-by-province rates it is −0.2753. The

Table 5.1
Sample Decline Rates for Peru, 1581–1613[a]

Province	Number of Towns in Sample	Weighted Mean Annual Decline Rate	Standard Deviation of Mean Annual Decline Rate	Annual Decline Rate of Total Population of Sample
Guamanga	10	.00916	.00598	.00967
Cuzco	14	.00630	.00953	.00398
Lima	24	.01019	.01854	.01264
Guánuco	8	.00940	.01077	.00564
La Paz[b]	10	−.00433	.01368	−.00201

[a]The 1581 data are from Morales (1866: 41–55); the 1613 data are from Vázquez de Espinosa (1948: 644–70).

[b]The sample of La Paz towns actually gained some tributaries during this period; hence the minus signs.

significance of the minus sign is that the mean which is used here is significantly less than the median. This is the principal difference between my figures and those of N. D. Cook (see the conclusion of this chapter).

Some improvement in calculating the mean annual decline rates can be made by weighting the samples in rough proportion as they contribute to the total census, thus providing a stratified sample. Guamanga represents about 11 percent of the total, Cuzco about 31 percent, Lima about 13 percent, Guánuco about 7 percent, and La Paz about 11 percent. This process leads to an estimate of a weighted mean annual decline rate of 0.00612 for this sample in the period 1581–1613 (32 years) but with a range of from −0.00433 for La Paz to 0.01019 for Lima.

The variation in estimates is interesting, since those for Lima and Guánuco are high but constitute 13 percent and 7 percent of the total number of tributaries in the census, whereas Cuzco contributes 31 percent of the total and has a mean rate of annual decline of 0.00630. However, Trujillo, which contributes 7 percent of the total, has a decline rate of .01690, almost three times the decline rate of Cuzco. (Trujillo is not included in the sample because of the difficulty of identifying towns.) This supports the conclusions of Rowe, C. T. Smith, and N. D. Cook that the rate of decline on the coast was significantly greater than in the highlands.

The La Paz sample has many towns that had exactly the same number of tributaries in 1613 as in 1581, which is almost certainly an example of tribute books that were not kept up-to-date. Probably several factors are at work here, but in gross terms remote provinces like La Paz had a minimal rate of decline due, at least partly, to bad bookkeeping, while some provinces were absorbing the migrants from other provinces, severely skewing the resulting

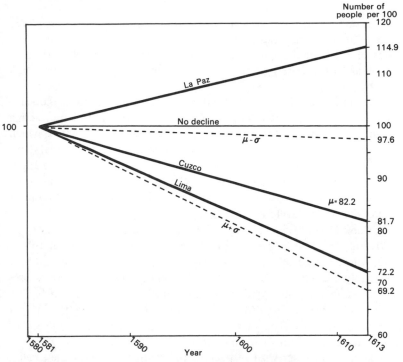

Figure 5.2. Comparison of Weighted Mean Annual Decline Rates for Peruvian Province Samples, 1581–1613 (see Table 5.1). For the purpose of comparing population declines, a standardized scale of 100 is used. Thus the populations indicated for 1613 are the number of people remaining per 100 present in 1581. To simplify the diagram, declines are not shown for Guánuco (74.0 in 1613) and Guamanga (74.6 in 1613). μ = mean of mean decline rates; $\mu + \sigma$ = μ plus one standard deviation; $\mu - \sigma$ = μ minus one standard deviation.

estimates. In fact an estimate of skewness of the decline rates for the towns is 1.296, and for the provinces is 0.275 when the skewness of a symmetrical normal curve is 0.0.

Skewness as an arbitrary number to describe the shape of a statistical curve is not very informative except on a comparative basis. The important point here is that the skewness of the estimate of the decline rate computed by province is 4.7 times the skewness of the estimate computed town-by-town in the several provinces. This indicates something akin to the famous method of unscrupulous politics called a "gerrymander." Gerrymandering can seriously affect the percentages of votes in a district merely by altering the boundaries of subdistricts in such a way as to balance large and small units against one another and minimize (or maximize) the voting power of one or the other. In this case the gerrymander is produced less by the artificiality of the Spanish provincial districts than it is by the difference in size between large and small settlements and by the differences in popularity of various provinces as places to migrate to or from. Undoubtedly this is a partial cause of some high estimates of pre-Columbian populations. This phenomenon will work most perversely against precisely those careful attempts to analyze population province by province.

This skewing means that the weighted mean, which in this case is 0.00612, must be carefully interpreted. The usual statistical operation of subtracting one standard deviation (0.00539) from the mean results in 0.00073, which can only be the minimal decline rate of areas, like La Paz, that have significant immigration. However, the mean plus one standard deviation, 0.01151, is an upper limit for 84 percent of possible decline rates computed in this way. It is most reasonable to assume that the actual decline rate is between 0.00612 and 0.01151.

N. D. Cook (1973: Table 10.1) gives tributary figures for Peru of 222,570 in 1580 and 152,424 in 1610. The decline rate calculated from this is 0.01262, which rounds to very nearly the same figure as my upper limit for approximately the same time period. Nevertheless, Cook consistently uses medians as estimators, and therefore his figures should be somewhat higher.

Sánchez-Albornoz (1974: 46) lists figures for the *congregación* of Upper Peru (Bolivia) in 1575. The mean size of towns before merger was 177 persons, whereas the mean size of merged towns was 3,173 persons. The ratio of the standard deviation with respect to the sample means of the smaller towns to that of the larger towns is 4.23 : 1.0. The Spaniards did not take over Indian towns randomly, but occupied the largest and richest first, and it is quite possible that a natural statistical gerrymander could occur which would raise certain percentage estimators by a factor possibly as great as 3. An additional explanation is that the later, larger towns were easier to police, which reduced the number of evasions of taxation, the number of changes of residence, and the number of changes of classification (i.e., from "Indian" to "Caste"), all of which inflate the estimates of the true population decline.

Once having settled upon a decline rate, it is necessary to decide what figure one is going to use to multiply the number of adult male tributaries to obtain the total population size. I repeat my earlier remark that the number of tributaries is a function of logarithms of base e of the number of females of the previous generation. The two factors cannot be arbitrarily separated because the decline rate is mathematically related to the multiplier factor. For example, a stable population must have some definition of a juvenile such that multiplying the adult population by 2.0 yields the total population. A declining population, however, would have a multiplier somewhat less than 2.0. Similarly, there should be about equal numbers of the genders in the adult population, so the multiplier of adult males to obtain the number of all adults ought to be 2.0 as well. An idealized stable population should have a total population that is 4.0 times the adult male population.

No real population ever has this ratio, of course, but it is a place to begin. Depending upon whether one uses the decline rate of 0.00612 or 0.01151, and depending upon a "generation" length of 15 or 30 years, the multiplier for the adult population to obtain the total population ranges from 1.416 to 1.824, with a median of 1.674. The first and third quartiles of this distribution are 1.750 and 1.540, and, in all probability, that should include the multipliers for the majority of the samples of the Andean population in question.

What was the ratio of adult females to adult males? Sánchez-Albornoz (1974: 45) gives some extremely exaggerated figures of 6 : 1 and 11 : 1, but it is my impression that he has misread his sources. Espinoza Soriano (1964: 204–6) and C. T. Smith (1970: 457) supply figures which show that the actual ratio of adult females to tribute-paying males ranged between 1.57 : 1.0 (Aymara Indians) and 1.53 : 1.0 (Uru Indians) for the Chucuito province in 1566. This would mean that the multiplier of adult male tributaries that gives the size of the adult population is about 2.5; and 2.5 times 1.674 is 4.185. If we take the quartiles as upper and lower estimates, then the multiplier should range between 3.85 and 4.38. This range is subject to a good deal of variation, however. For the Chucuito population Smith's own figure (1970: Table 3) is produced by a multiplier of 4.1, in the center of this range. The mean of ratios for the 1561 tribute list quoted by Zavala (1973: 238) is 3.76, which is on the low side of this range. Even the higher figures of N. D. Cook (1973: Tables 10.1 and 10.2) have a mean multiplier of 4.9, which is above, but only slightly above, this range. The range of multipliers in the Zavala figures is from 1.6 to 5.1. There are, of course, many sources of variance in this multiplier, ranging from disinterest of tribute officials in women and children to differential death rates of males due to tribute labor and conscription. Two things must remain as cautions however. First and foremost is the fact that males and females are conceived in nearly equal numbers, and reductions of males in any generation are not perpetuated in subsequent generations; killing males may reduce overall fertility, but it does not produce gender imbalances in subsequent generations. This elementary biological point should be obvious, yet some scholars appear to assume that sex imbalances are perpetuated. Second, the decline rate and the multiplier rate are not independent. If the population is declining rapidly the offspring generation is relatively smaller than the parent generation, so that if one opts for a high decline rate a smaller multiplier is reasonable, and if one opts for a lower decline rate a slightly higher multiplier is feasible. One cannot reasonably "have his cake and eat it too"; it is unreasonable to have both a high rate of decline and a high multiplier as well.

Using the 1580 tributary population as reported by N. D. Cook, his best estimate because it reflects Toledo's census, adding for Bolivia and Ecuador from Zavala's figures which are for a comparable year (1581), and using

Table 5.2

Population Estimates by Shea for Peru and the Central Andes for 1535 and 1520

Multiplier	Tributaries, 1580–1581	Total Population, 1580–1581	Type of Estimate	Decline per Annum	Total Population, 1535	Total Population, 1520
			Peru Only			
4.18 (median)	222,570[a]	930,343	mean	0.00612	1,225,314	1,343,123
4.38 (3rd quartile)	222,570[a]	974,856	mean plus one deviation	0.01151	1,636,377	1,944,753
			Central Andes (Lima, Charcas, and Quito)			
4.18	335,748[b]	1,403,426	mean	0.00612	1,848,393	2,026,108
4.38	335,748[b]	1,470,576	mean plus one deviation	0.01151	2,355,768	2,933,670

[a]For 1580, from N. D. Cook, 1973: Table 10.1.
[b]For 1580, from N. D. Cook, 1973: Table 10.1, with some additional provinces for 1581 added from Zavala, 1973: 238.

174

averages and statistically controlled upper limits, I have arrived at the estimates shown in Table 5.2. The estimated population for 1520 is offered in response to Dobyns' thesis that the population decline may have started that year with the introduction of smallpox from Panama.

CONCLUSION

I have proposed that a mathematical expansion in the natural logarithms, to the base e, be used to estimate the Andean population decline in the early colonial period, from A.D. 1535 to 1580, and also in the late pre-Columbian era, from A.D. 1520 to 1535. It is argued that this is appropriate both because it is the best model of compound and cumulative decline and because the mathematical criteria of continuity and integration make it a good model of organic population adaptation over time.

In addition, it is proposed that where estimates of population at different dates are available, equations in e be considered sample estimates of some true parameter of the population. Thus the mean and standard deviation of a group of such estimators should be a very good model of the true rate of change of a population.

This method applied to counts of tribute-paying Indians not only arrives at a good estimate of the true rate of population decline, but also, because of the skewing of the distribution of estimators, offers a reasonable explanation for the wide variety of rates of decline and multipliers that have been calculated in the past. Much previous work has been done with percentages or multipliers of population decline. Such figures often reflect the median or mode of the decline in the area for which they are calculated. They are inevitably skewed in the direction of the highest rates of decline within a locale and have no built-in compensation for the fact that some trading of population between areas was going on. These methods of calculation maximize statistical error.

Decline rates measured according to natural logarithmic curves are closely related to gender balance and juvenile population, and though a calculated decline rate does not specifically determine these other parameters, it does set limits on what is reasonable as an estimator for either of these calculators. In particular, decline rates of logarithmic curves implicitly include the female population, and place maximum limits on the size of the offspring generation.

The results of this sort of calculation (Table 5.2) produce answers for the Peruvian and central Andean cases that are disappointingly small. (The total population for Peru alone in 1973 was estimated by the United Nations to be 14,910,000 [*World Almanac.* 1975: 561].) As an archaeologist I am disappointed, since I would like to have a large Andean population as an explanation of the relatively high level of culture represented by the Incan empire. There are some consoling observations, however. The topography of the Andean area is sufficiently rigorous that epidemics could not as readily pass from one area to another as, for example, in central Mexico. One can still believe, with Dobyns, that Peru was ravaged by smallpox without necessarily accepting wholesale decline of the population except in local areas. And the environment carries another penalty, which is that very little land is readily arable. In the arid coastal regions of Peru the arable land under present technology is estimated at only about 2.1 percent of the total area (Peru, 1963). The percentage of arable highland surface area may be a little higher on the average, but certainly not higher than 10.0 percent, and as low as 1.0 percent would be valid for some areas.

It would be a major undertaking to calculate a ratio of population to square units of arable land, but it is clear that the population densities implicit in the low figures offered here are still high given the scarcity of arable land. There is also considerable archaeological evidence, which I will not review here, that Andean populations reached peaks earlier than the sixteenth century. Some of the peaks in specific localities were earlier by millenia, and while good estimates are not available, it is possible that some early populations were greater than during the Inca period, perhaps much greater. It is even possible that the decline of the Andean Indian population was a long-term process only slightly accelerated by the Spanish Conquest, and that the Incas themselves in the previous century had caused considerable loss of life. I know of no attempt to estimate the population dispersion and fertility suppression that resulted from the well-known Inca practice of moving whole populations to different geographic areas.

N. D. Cook's (1973) dissertation provides by far the best set of figures available for the Peruvian population in the first century after the Conquest. His estimate of 2,738,000 for 1530 is low compared to earlier published figures but not as low as those presented here. (His estimate can be extrapolated back to 1520 to reach a population of 3,426,958 for Peru and 4,990,563 for the central Andes.) The similarities and differences are significant. Cook uses expansions of e (= 2.718) as I do, and so his projections from the Toledo and later censuses are very similar. The annual rate of decline derived from Cook's (1973: Table 10.2) total populations for 1530 (2,738,673) and 1630 (601,645)—a 100-year decline ratio of 4.6 to 1—is 0.01516, in contrast with the high rate derived here of 0.01151. Much of his reasoning has the same merits or defects as what is presented here in terms of being a fairly good biological model of a reproducing population. Similarly, although Cook uses earlier and later censuses for a variety of estimates, his principal documentary tools, as are mine, are the Toledo census of about

1581 and the census reported by Vázquez de Espinosa of about 1613. The differences are subtle but significant. Cook (1973: 67, 69, 99) consistently uses medians, which give higher estimates than means, which I have used here. Undoubtedly there are instances in which the median is to be preferred as a statistical parameter; the mean, however, is normally the better estimator. In particular the mean is more reliable as a parameter of the total population because it represents the center of gravity of a sample, however badly it may be skewed.

Like N. D. Cook, I have used the median where the multiplier of tributaries to obtain total population is concerned. Nevertheless there are serious differences. Cook (1973: 99, Table 4.1) uses an estimator of range that has no justification that I know of. He employs both of the medians for 1570–1579 and for the 1600–1609 periods and then accepts an upper limit that is the higher of these plus 1.0 and a lower bound that is the lower of these minus 1.0. There is no reason to set the limit of one unit, and there is no statistical use of a double median. In addition, one of the numbers used by Cook (1973: 78) to generate a multiplier is his median childbearing ratio. This ratio does produce an interesting estimate of the parturition rate, by relating the number of children under age 5 to women in the 15-to-44 age bracket. I emphasize however, that these children do not necessarily become adult Indians, as they may not survive, and some of those that survive may "cross" and become Castes. The method proposed here relies on the logical necessity that a declining population has a smaller offspring generation than adult generation whether offspring are lost due to death or Caste change and regardless of parturition rate. (For a discussion of another method, see Addendum 3.)

N. D. Cook points out (1973: 37, 43–45) that Toledo's census causes an appearance of a higher than normal population because his population is raised above earlier censuses by more exact counting, particularly of *yanaconas*. This may result in additional skewing in those documents that Cook uses to project backward in time from the Toledo census, but certainly it adds to the skewing effect of earlier attempts to use the tribute lists. I therefore maintain that although Cook's estimates for 1580 and 1610 are the best currently available, his projections of earlier populations based on these are probably too high.

ADDENDA

1. I know of no specific case of the complete use of the method of calculation employed here, yet the use of various parts of it separately are

common. It is not unusual, for example, to use $f(x) = e^x$ either as a specific calculation device or as a mathematical model where populations are concerned, but rarely is this conjoined with the statistical estimation of x itself. Statistical estimates of rates are often used for change problems, but rates so treated are usually percentages derived from some calculation other than e^x.

What is done here is merely the conjunction of the two methods, with a good deal of (I hope) buttressing nonmathematical justification. The discussion in the text about the derivative properties of $f(x) = e^x$ is intended mainly for the nonmathematician, to provide a convincing argument that use of e^x is not merely number manipulation. The integral of e^x where a population is concerned can be best interpreted in nonmathematical terms as population-through-time, that is, "people years." However, population-through-time is itself a result of *all* the contributing factors to population change, including both those of the physical ecology and those of the social environment and the historical sequence of contingent events. The mathematical manipulation of e^x must therefore be regarded as a very good approximation of the sum total of all relevant factors affecting a population.

If rates derived from the $f(x) = e^x$ equation are computed for individual towns, if the averages of the rates so computed are used for the provinces in which the towns are located, and if the provinces are further averaged to obtain an estimate of the total decline rate, that average should be a very good estimate of population change. Thus, each rate, r, derived from a fitting of the curve e^x, is a sample estimate. The mean of such rates is a mean of sample estimates, and the mean of such means is, according to the usual theory of sampling, a very good estimator of the true rate of change of the "universe," the total population being sampled. Essentially the same calculation can be made either of two ways. First one may solve $P_1 = P_o e^{rt}$ for r, where r is the logarithmic rate of change, t is the time involved, and P_o and P_1 are the populations at the beginning and end of the time period in question. Having done this separately for several samples, the r's so derived may be averaged (strictly speaking, the *mean* calculated) and the standard deviation also calculated.

An alternative method is to calculate the slope of a regression line thru a series of points representing the populations of several towns at the beginning and end of a given period. The points represent the populations numerically not as the absolute size of the populations, but the natural logarithmic equivalents. This is the same as solving the equation

$$r = \frac{N \, \Sigma \, xy - (\Sigma x)(\Sigma y)}{N \, \Sigma x^2 - (\Sigma x)^2}$$

for r, where N is the number of towns involved, x is the number of years elapsed during the period, the y's are the logarithms (to base e) of the populations, and Σ is the usual capital sigma, symbolizing repetitive summation over the whole series.

It is entirely possible that these two methods of calculation are in fact algebraically equal in their results, although I know of no formal proof. They both give exactly the same results to seven decimal places for the sample populations I have used here, and they are close approximations of one another.

I do not expect everyone to agree with this method of calculation; it is fair to point out, however, that the arguable aspects of its validity lie less in the use of e^x, and the mean and standard deviation of rates computed from e^x, than in certain underlying presuppositions about the normality of distribution of r and the continuity of the population in time and space. In this regard, I maintain that the sources of error in the absolute figures, the tendency for people to shift from one town or province to another, and the deviations resulting from the discrepancies between different Spanish census takers tend to justify the assumptions of normality and continuity. These numerous small errors add and/or cancel in a variety of ways, contributing a deviation of small errors that is normal in distribution, and because the errors are small the results are a near approximation of continuity.

2. An example of a crude population profile from the census reported by Vázquez de Espinosa (1948: 657) is the south coast *corregimiento* of Arica, which shows the wide variation in the relative sizes of various subgroups of the population:

	Tributarios	Viejos	Muchachos (or Mozos)	Mujeres
Lluta and Arica	65	15	84	92
Tarapacá and Pica	950	121	981	2,035
Hilo	50	18	22	109
Tacama	525	50	493	979
Hilabaya	166	19	100	231
Totals	1,758	223	1,680	3,446

The χ^2 value for this set of figures is $\chi^2 = 89.6$, an extremely high value for such a small set of figures (more than 99.99 percent confidence). It is not possible to set reliable probability estimates to partial sums of a χ^2 calculation; however there is some significance in the fact that more than half the discrepancy is in the viejos and muchachos columns. The town of Hilo is particularly bad in this respect, having 12 more viejos than might be expected, and 25 fewer muchachos. All the population classes appear to be controlled by some nonrandom factors, but it is quite likely in this case that the *corregidor* is juggling the numbers of old men and young men to make the tax bill come out right.

The careful reader will note that the total given by Vázquez de Espinosa for the tributarios column is incorrect. It should be 1,756. The χ^2 calculations were made from the correct figure.

3. S. F. Cook and Borah (1971–74: 1:90) in their "Essay on Method" employ a different rate of population decline than that used here and that used by N. D. Cook. Instead of using natural logarithms, they use a factor ω calculated on the basis of two populations at different times and on the basis of the geometric mean of the two in the intervening period. As a "curve fitting" method, the ω of Cook and Borah is a legitimate calculation, and it should in most cases give results similar to those presented here in order of magnitude. However, the geometric mean is invariably smaller than the standard mean, and the division operation that Cook and Borah perform can be guaranteed to produce larger decline rates than other methods. Also, the numerator of the extrapolation equation used by Cook and Borah (1971–74: 1:90, 114) is a linear approximation of the derivative of one type of equation, and the denominator, the geometric mean, belongs to a slightly different but closely related equation. This not only leads to a higher decline rate, but contributes to the angularity of their graphs. Cook and Borah also favor the use of logarithms, but use base 10 logs, which are calculational conveniences, and unlike log base e are not based on a function that is its own derivative.

CHAPTER 6 **A Reexamination of Aboriginal**

Population Estimates for Argentina

Jane Pyle

A careful examination of the standard sources for estimates of the aboriginal population of present-day Argentina calls for a revision upward, to at least twice the currently accepted figures. In the following pages I will review the better-known secondary calculations of population estimates, summarize the arguments for reducing original estimates far below their face value, recapitulate original sources that give numerical estimates, and draw conclusions to support higher numbers.

SECONDARY SOURCES

Standard secondary sources dealing with aboriginal populations of South America, including Argentina, are Rosenblat (1945, 1954) and Steward (1949). A more recent treatment, limited to Argentina, is that by Difrieri (1961).[1] In these three works, estimates of the aboriginal population of Argentina ranged from 300,000 to 424,325 (see Table 6.1), although the latter should be reduced as it included Indians outside present-day Argentina. Each author pointed out the closeness of his estimate to one of the others (Steward, 1949: 655; Rosenblat, 1954: 320; Difrieri, 1961: 29). Elements of

1. For a review of Difrieri's study, see Pyle (1972). Another recent discussion of the aboriginal Argentine population by Comadrán Ruiz (1969: 19–22) accepts the figures of Rosenblat.

Map 6.1. Indian Tribes of Argentina. Based on Cooper (1946d: 15), Métraux (1946: 198), and Serrano (1947: end map).

Key to List of Tribes

1. Abipón (Frentón)	6. Charrúa	11. Guaraní
2. Araucano (Araucanian)	7. Comechingón	12. Huarpe (Guarpe)
3. Atacameño	8. Corondá	13. Humahuaca
4. Chaná	9. Diaguita	14. Juri
5. Chaná-salvaje	10. Guaicurú (Mbayá)	15. Lule

Table 6.1
Comparison of Estimates of Aboriginal Population, Argentina

Difrieri[a]		Steward[b]		Rosenblat[c]
Northwest	215,000	Diaguita	41,000	
Cuyo	18,000	Comechingón-Huarpe, etc.	52,550	
Pampa	30,000	Querandí	4,000	
Chaco	50,000	Eastern Chaco		
		Abipón and neighbors	50,250	
		Payaguá, Chané,[d] Mbayá	30,000	
		Western Chaco	186,400	
Mesopotamia	20,000	Paraná Delta	24,000	
Patagonia	10,000	Pampa-Patagonia	36,125	
Totals	343,000		424,325	300,000

[a]Difrieri, 1961: 29.
[b]Steward, 1949: 661–64. Includes some extension outside Argentina.
[c]Rosenblat, 1945: 81.
[d]Steward's Chané are not the Chaná of Uruguay. The Chané were located in the headwaters of the Río Pilcomayo in Bolivia just north of the area of Map 6.1.

the table are not strictly comparable. Difrieri used a regional breakdown, while Steward used cultural and regional groupings that did not respect later political boundaries. The principal differences arise in the Northwest and Chaco regions, partly because the original estimates varied so greatly and partly because estimates for the region around Santiago del Estero were sometimes included with the Northwest because of cultural similarities or colonial political organization and sometimes were included with the Chaco because of geography (Map 6.1).

The general problems of making population estimates for Argentina are of three kinds. The first is the relative paucity of numbers in firsthand accounts; the second is the possibility of exaggeration; and the third is the magnitude of change in numbers between the date for which an estimate is desired and the varying dates of sources used. Difrieri claimed to have used only sources that provided numerical evaluations: statistics of baptisms and ecclesiastical reports of heathen converted or of numbers of Indians, which are direct and

Key to List of Tribes, *continued*

16. Mahoma	22. Ona (in Tierra del Fuego)	27. Tehuelche
17. Mapení	23. Payaguá	28. Timbú
18. Mataguayo	24. Puelche	29. Toba
19. Matará (Amulala)	25. Querandí	30. Tonocoté
20. Mocoretá	26. Quiloazá	31. Yahgan (in Tierra del Fuego)
21. Ocloya		

reliable but incomplete; grants of *encomienda*; and censuses, which often have not been published. However, his citations were generally estimates by eyewitnesses. Soldiers and missionaries were expected to exaggerate, and government administrators may have overestimated or underestimated population to serve their purposes (Steward, 1949: 657). A weakness of using only sources with numerical estimates is in the omission of observed groups of unstated size, or in the inclusion of only the enumerated portions of larger groups. The datelines for the Argentine data constitute an additional weakness; most of the original sources are from late in the sixteenth century and extend into the seventeenth. For southern Argentina, the earliest numerical estimates were made still later, in the eighteenth and nineteenth centuries. Only small numbers of Spaniards were present in Argentina until the end of the sixteenth century, even on the periphery, and by the time the most complete firsthand accounts were written, the original population distribution could have been highly altered by disease, warfare, and migration, only some of which is documented.

FIRSTHAND ACCOUNTS

The earliest account for Argentina that included numerical estimates is the recollection of a German harquebusier, Ulrich Schmidl (1938), who sailed with Mendoza and remained in the Paraná-Paraguay area for twenty years. Schmidl was generous with estimates of population, especially in the early years. He described culture traits in detail for several groups. His service under Mendoza, Irala, and Núñez Cabeza de Vaca took him inland as well as far up the Paraguay River, but most of his history describing the interior refers to present-day Paraguay and Bolivia rather than to Argentina. Difrieri defended the relative sizes of groups that Schmidl reported. For the Pampa, for example, Difrieri suggested that the confederation of warriors (23,000) was not of unreasonable size, that the number reported for the Guaraní accorded with the seventeenth-century reports, and that concentration of usually nomadic Indians during the fishing season could have accounted for sizable numbers reported for an impoverished culture area (Difrieri, 1961: 27–28).

Sotelo Narváez (1931), a *conquistador* with early expeditions into the Northwest and later an *encomendero* in Santiago del Estero, was cited or copied by many later historians. He reported modest numbers of Indians in a letter to the president of the royal Audiencia of La Plata in 1582 and 1583. I submit that the reasons for which his figures are often cited are first because they were modest and second because he included all the important places of the Northwest, rather than just one or two.

Among the historians or chroniclers who worked from official statistics and reports, private papers, or personal observations were López de Velasco (1971), whose *Geografía* was written between 1571 and 1574; Canelas Albarrán (1586); and Vázquez de Espinoza (1948), who was in the New World between 1612 and 1621. Reports by missionaries began near the close of the sixteenth century and were incorporated into later histories. Torres (1927), first provincial for the Jesuit missions of the Río de la Plata, Paraguay, Tucumán, and Chile, reported population estimates in his annual letters, written between 1609 and 1615, and he quoted liberally from missionary reports. Rosenblat considered the numbers of unconverted Indians in the Jesuits' annual reports "always extremely exaggerated" (Rosenblat, 1945: 183).

Ramírez de Velasco (1915, 1931), Ribera (1915), and Albornoz (1939) were three of the governors whose estimates of population are reasonably complete. Ramírez de Velasco mounted several expeditions against the hostile Diaguita of the Northwest, and in his letter to the king of Spain in 1591 seemed to be exaggerating numbers in order to enhance his reputation, whereas in another in 1596 he seemed to be underestimating numbers in order to support his request for additional Indian laborers (Ramírez de Velasco, 1915, 1931). Ribera and Albornoz reported sizes of villages, as well as total numbers of Indians, presumably in encomiendas; their numbers are uniformly small.

Tables 6.3 through 6.7 recapitulate figures taken from original sources, most of which were cited by Rosenblat, who relegated all but global numbers to an appendix and did not explain how he calculated his estimate of 300,000, or by Difrieri, who cited documentary sources from various works. The tables represent a reasonably complete summary of published sources that contain estimates of the aboriginal population of Argentina.

DISCUSSION

The extreme range of estimates, late and variable datelines, indeterminate area encompassed by estimates, and small number of truly firsthand observations make analysis very difficult indeed. A single rule to be applied to various figures, such as an average of high and low or a consistent selection of highest estimates to suggest a maximum population, seems unwarranted by the data. The missionary figures especially seem inflated when compared with censuses of encomiendas, and without comparable data for each region averages computed from these extremes would overestimate and underestimate in unsystematic ways. The highest figures are not consistently exorbitant, although missionaries and their provincial superiors themselves suggested possibilities of exaggeration.[2]

Cognizant of these limitations, the author enters the lists in the game of estimation, and adopts the rule of "reasonableness." The various regional estimates are examined in relation to each other, to the context in which they were first given, and to the reporter's source of information.[3] The outcome of my pass at the game is tabulated in Table 6.2, and the reasoning for the estimates is summarized briefly in the pages that follow.

Penetration by the Spanish into present-day Argentina was sporadic and conquest slow. The Mendoza-Irala expedition advanced to Asunción in 1537, but the Spanish did not return to reestablish Buenos Aires until 1580; the Rojas expedition of 1542–1544 into the Northwest resulted in no permanent settlement; and advances from both Chile and Peru met great resistance through the sixteenth century. Towns were founded and lots and encomiendas were granted but left untended (Comadrán Ruiz, 1969: 1–18). The first Jesuits arrived in Tucumán from Peru in 1585, and the province of Paraguay was established in 1604. This state of flux is important to keep in mind while considering early estimates of native populatlon.

Northwest

Sixteenth- and seventeenth-century estimates for the Northwest are listed in Table 6.3. The estimates for Jujuy (San Salvador de Jujuy) comprehend the Atacameño and Humahuaca who inhabited the Puna and its large access canyon (Difrieri, 1961: 23). Serrano included the Mataguayo and Ocloya in this area as well (Serrano, 1947: end map). One encomienda, an early grant

2. The best example of this comes from outside the study area, in Uruguay, where a population of 20,000 families was reported: "And there is no need to imagine that there are more because those who say and have said that there are a hundred thousand Indians in this province have talked and are talking from Talanquera, without having seen either them or their lands, but only are informed by the Indians, who do not know how to tell the truth; of four they say there are many, and of a hundred, that they are as the grass in the fields" (Mastrillo Durán, 1929: 384, fn. 53). "They say" and "I'm told" introduce a number of estimates, and still more frequent are simply non-numerical adjectives–e.g., "many," "few," "a great many." Still, although they beg confirmation, the missionary estimates need not be dismissed out of hand; many are indeed reasonable.

3. Notably absent from consideration is an assessment of the cultural ecology of the regions of Argentina. Difrieri pointed out some of the environmental and cultural limitations of parts of the Argentine territory, but he did not pursue them in a comprehensive way. To my knowledge, basic information on the physical environment and cultural achievement of native peoples in Argentina has not yet been used to estimate population. Descriptions of cultural development, especially in agriculture, and limited firsthand knowledge of Argentina have colored my evaluation of the estimates given in Tables 6.3 through 6.7, but I am not now prepared to apply these factors systematically. That is the logical next step in pursuing the problem of aboriginal population.

Table 6.2
Aboriginal Population Estimates by Pyle for
Argentina, Sixteenth Century[a]

Region	Subtotals	Regional Totals
Northwest		61,000
Jujuy	3,000	
Salta, Calchaquí Valley	8,000	
San Miguel de Tucumán	3,000	
Catamarca-La Rioja	7,000	
Talavera de Esteco, Santiago del Estero	25,000	
Córdoba	15,000	
Cuyo		5,700
Pampa		55,000
Chaco		56,000
Riverine	34,000	
Interior	22,000	
Mesopotamia		10,000 + *33,000*
Paraná Delta	10,000	
Guaraní	*33,000*	
Patagonia		*10,000*
Total for Argentina		187,700 + *43,000*

[a]The figures given represent my conclusions regarding the estimates that appear in firsthand accounts of aboriginal populations. Those firsthand estimates are listed, by region, in Tables 6.3 through 6.7. In this table, estimates are for adult males, except those italicized, which include men, women, and children. This follows general practice and delays the question of an appropriate family size, which is discussed in the concluding section of this chapter.

by Pizarro to Juan de Villanueva, included ten villages of the Humahuaca, one of which numbered 500 Indians (Obando, 1931: 356). Ribera (1915: 134) reported eight encomiendas in Jujuy in 1607, the largest having 200 Indians, and 20 years later Albornoz (1939) reported six or seven encomiendas of 80 to 100 Indians. If there were eight encomiendas, each having ten groups of 500 Indians, as with the Villanueva grant, we can calculate 40,000 adult males for the area. If the encomiendas averaged only about 300 Indians, which is the largest number reported by Sotelo Narváez, the total adult male population might be closer to 2,400, which I accept as more reasonable than 40,000. For the total adult male population of Jujuy, I increase this amount somewhat (see Table 6.2) to take into consideration part of the Mataguayo population. Lozano (1941: 81) reported 50 towns of Mataguayo near Jujuy, and Torres (1927: 35) reported 2,000 Ocloya between Salta and Peru.

Table 6.3
Estimates of Aboriginal Population, Northwest Argentina

Place	Number[a]	Enumeration Unit[b]	Year[c]	Source
Tucumán (colonial province)	54,000	indios varones	1586	Canelas Albarrán, cited by Rosenblat, 1945: 182
	270,000	indios de todas edades y sexos	1586	Canelas Albarrán, cited by Rosenblat, 1945: 78
	56,500[d]	yndios	1596	Ramírez de Velasco, 1914: 231
	200,000	ánimas	1596	Ramírez de Velasco, 1914: 227
	20,000[e]	yndios Xpiaños, almas	1609	Torres, 1927: 34
	80,000[e]	yndios ynfieles	1609	Torres, 1927: 34
	80,000	personas xpañas	1610	Torres, 1927: 41
	10,000	infieles	1610	Torres, 1927: 41
	10,000–12,000[f]	almas	1629–1630	Albornoz, cited by Larrouy, 1914: 26
Jujuy	500	yndios	1557	Obando, 1931: 356
	3,000	yndios	1596	Ramírez de Velasco, 1914: 231
	690[g]	yndios	1607	Ribera, 1915: 134
	2,000	personas, Ocloyas servidores	1609	Torres, 1927: 35
Salta (formerly Lerma)	4,000	hombres de guerra	(1550)	Díaz Caballero, 1915: 76
	1,500[h]	indios	1582	Sotelo Narváez, 1931: 329
	9,272[i]	infieles	1585–1587	Bárzana, cited by Furlong Cardiff, 1941: 10–11
	5,000	varones de encomienda	1586	Canelas Albarrán, cited by Rosenblat, 1945: 182
	5,000	yndios	1596	Ramírez de Velasco, 1914: 231
	1,800[j]	yndios de pas	1607	Ribera, 1915: 134

188

Location	Number	Category	Year	Source
Calchaquí Valley	1,500	indios	1581	Lerma, 1931: 276
	2,500	indios	1582	Sotelo Narváez, 1931: 328
	100,000	ánimas	1585	Bárzana, 1968: 87
	50,000	indios	1589	Ramírez de Velasco, cited by Jaimes Freyre, 1914: 187
	9,000 or 10,000	almas infieles	1610	Torres, 1927: 75
	5,000 or 6,000[k]	almas	1617	Oñate, 1929: 121
	14,000	almas	1618	Oñate, 1929: 179
	4,000	indios de guerra	1631	Albornoz, 1931: 418
	12,000	almas	1631	Albornoz, 1931: 418
San Miguel de Tucumán	3,000[l]	indios de servicio	1582	Sotelo Narváez, 1931: 328
	3,000	varones de encomienda	1586	Canelas Albarrán, cited by Rosenblat, 1945: 182
	2,000	yndios	1596	Ramírez de Velasco, 1914: 231
	1,100	yndios de pas	1607	Ribera, 1915: 133
	2,500	yndios	1609	Torres, 1927: 36
	6,000 or 7,000	almas	1609	Torres, 1927: 36
	12,000	yndios	1618	Oñate, 1929: 173
La Rioja	10,000 or 12,000	yndios	1591	Ramírez de Velasco, 1931: 337
	20,000 or 25,000	indios (repartidos)	1591	Ramírez de Velasco, cited by Jaimes Freyre, 1914: 177
	20,000–24,000[m]	indios	1591	Ramírez de Velasco, cited by Larrouy, 1914: 26
	20,000	yndios	1596	Ramírez de Velasco, 1914: 230
	6,000[n]	indios de pas	1607	Ribera, 1915: 133
	6,000	ynfieles, Diaguitas	1609	Torres, 1927: 36
	14,000	yndios	1618	Oñate, 1929: 175

(continued on following pages)

Table 6.3, *continued*

Place	Number[a]	Enumeration Unit[b]	Year[c]	Source
Nueva Madrid[o]	1,500	yndios	1596	Ramírez de Velasco, 1914: 231
	188	(indios)	1607	Ribera, 1915: 134
Talavera de Esteco	6,000 or 7,000	indios (de servicio)	1582	Sotelo Narváez, 1931: 329
	13,000	varones de encomienda	1586	Canelas Albarrán, cited by Rosenblat, 1945: 182
	5,000	yndios	1596	Ramírez de Velasco, 1914: 231
	2,000	indios	1605	Barraza, cited by Difrieri, 1961: 35
	1,636	yndios	1607	Ribera, 1915: 133
	30,000[p]	tributarios, Tonocotés	(1630)	Machoni de Cerdeña, 1878: 20
Santiago del Estero	800–1,000[q]	casas	1543	Fernández, 1913–14: 2:28
	86,000	indios repartidos	1553	Lozano, cited by Serrano, 1938: 26
	80,000[r]	(yndios)	1553	Albornoz, 1939: 609
	25,000	indios de tasa	(1553)	Bárzana, 1968: 85
	12,000	indios (de servicio)	1582	Sotelo Narváez, 1931: 324
	18,000	varones de encomienda	1586	Canelas Albarrán, cited by Rosenblat, 1945: 182
	80,000	guerreros	1586	Techo, cited by Jaimes Freyre, 1914: 106
	8,000	yndios	1596	Ramírez de Velasco, 1914: 230
	6,729	indios dedoctrina	1607	Ribera, 1915: 133
	20,000	almas de yndios	1618	Oñate, 1929: 172

190

Córdoba			
30,000	indios	1573	Cabrera, 1931: 318
40,000	indios guerreros	1573	Techo, cited by Rosenblat, 1945: 183
12,000[s]	indios de repartimiento	1582	Sotelo Narváez, 1931: 330
30,000	ánimas	1585	Bárzana, 1968: 87
15,000	varones de encomienda	1586	Canelas Albarrán, cited by Rosenblat, 1945: 182
12,000	yndios	1596	Ramírez de Velasco, 1914: 230
8,000	(indios)	1600	Techo, cited by Rosenblat, 1945: 183
6,103	indios	1607	Ribera, 1915: 133

[a]Estimates in original sources may or may not have included women and children, or men over 50. Usually the statement is clear, and if a source reported both types of estimates, both are included in the table. Italicized figures represent total population, including women and children.

[b]Spelling in source is maintained. See Glossary for translation. Parentheses denote enumeration unit assumed from context.

[c]Year is given where indicated in source. Parentheses denote an approximate date.

[d]Ramírez de Velasco (1914: 227) gave numbers for individual places following a statement that Tucumán had more than 50,000 Indians who gave no tribute, only personal service, from which I assume that his figures referred to adult males. Jaimes Freyre (1914: 42) reported "56,000 *indios empadronados*," citing Ramírez de Velasco.

[e]Torres added that "six or eight thousand leave their lands to serve three towns of Spaniards, but not always nor in an organized fashion."

[f]In letters of 6 December 1629, 16 April 1630, and 9 November 1630, Albornoz gave the cited figure, which included 3,000 to 4,000 *indios de tasa* (Larrouy, 1914: 26). In a letter of 28 December 1628 he listed tribute-paying Indians in general terms and indicated that the province would have had about 7,000 total (Larrouy, 1914: 25). In a letter of 2 December 1629, he mentioned "scarcely seven to eight thousand Indians" (Albornoz, 1939: 609).

(continued on following page)

Table 6.3, *continued*

gRibera listed the number of encomiendas for various places, indicating the number of Indians included in them. He showed 8 in Jujuy, 30 in Salta, 30 in San Miguel de Tucumán, 62 in La Rioja, 10 in Nueva Madrid, 33 in Talavera de Esteco, 33 in Santiago del Estero, and 70 in Córdoba.

h"The valley of Salta . . . has no Indians [in encomienda] because the 1,500 available are people of no fixed abode, although they sow and have livestock."

iThis is the sum of the Lule that were reported baptized in 1585, 1586, and 1587.

j"1,000 peaceful Indians and there are many warriors."

k"Five or six thousand, if not more."

l"It has more Indians assigned [repartidos], although they do not serve."

mIncludes Catamarca and Londres.

n"6,000 peaceful Indians, plus many others still at war."

oNeuva Madrid, at the junction of the road to Salta from San Miguel de Tucumán and Talavera de Esteco, was joined to Talavera in 1609 and the new place was called Talavera de Madrid.

pRosenblat (1945: 183) said Machoni de Cerdeña reported 30,000 tribute-paying Tonocoté near Esteco in the Chaco, and a suspiciously identical number was reported for the Mataguayo, who were also identified with the Chaco (Osorio, in Mastrillo Durán, 1929: 260). Machoni de Cerdeña (1878: 31) reported 60,000 Tonocoté near Concepción, and the 86,000 listed for Santiago del Estero were reported as Juri and Tonocoté (Lozano, in Serrano, 1938: 26). The Tonocoté are usually associated with San Miguel de Tucumán, but their placement is problematic because Tonocoté was also a language widely spoken in the general area and because many fled during the early years of conquest (Serrano, 1938: 26–27; Machoni de Cerdeña, 1878: 18). The Matará (see Table 6.6) may have been a subgroup of the Tonocoté (Métraux, 1946: 228; Machoni de Cerdeña, 1878: 19).

q". . . they discovered a large, much-populated province with towns half a league from each other, of from 800 to 1,000 houses placed along the streets."

rIn a letter to the king in 1629, Albornoz (1939) complained that Indians were so few that they scarcely amounted to 1,500, while the city had had 80,000 at the time of founding, according to the old books of the municipal government (*cabildo*).

sIn addition, he said that the city had 40 encomenderos served by more than 6,000 Indians.

The Diaguita occupied a large part of the present-day province of Salta, the mountainous parts of Tucumán, almost all of Catamarca and La Rioja, and the northern part of San Juan. They proved particularly difficult to subjugate, especially in the Calchaquí Valley. Continuing warfare contributed to low estimates, in the early years because eyewitness estimation was difficult and in later years because the number of Indians declined. Perhaps Ramírez de Velasco was only tempting Bárzana when he suggested that there were 100,000 unbaptized souls in the Calchaquí Valley (Bárzana, 1968: 87), for earlier he had estimated 50,000 (Jaimes Freyre, 1914: 187). Sotelo Narváez estimated 4,000 (males) for Salta and the Calchaquí Valley, whereas Torres (1927: 75) estimated 10,000 and Larrouy (1914: 26), generally conservative, estimated roughly 12,000 (total) for the Calchaquí Valley alone. My estimate for Salta and the Calchaquí Valley (Table 6.2) takes the more generous estimates, in view of the Diaguita's continuing ability to wage war successfully.

The present-day province of Tucumán is relatively small (22,524 km^2) and thus probably contained fewer people than its neighbors. The two earliest estimates of 3,000 for the town of San Miguel de Tucumán, by Sotelo Narváez and Canelas Albarrán, are in agreement, although considering Sotelo Narváez' statement of other Indians still unsubjugated, my estimate of 3,000 (Table 6.2) may be too low.

For Catamarca and La Rioja, my estimate of 7,000 adult males (Table 6.2) may also be low. Although Ramírez de Velasco estimated 20,000 to 24,000 Indians after a triumphal march through the territory, Larrouy (1914: 26) insisted that the total population could not have been larger than 5,000.

The totals estimated for the Diaguita (55,000 individuals according to Serrano, 1938: 135; and 50,000 cited by Larrouy, 1914: 26) cannot be used alone for the population of the Northwest, but must be augmented by estimates of Indian groups at lower elevations to give totals for the colonial province of Tucumán. Agriculturalists, as well as cultures transitional between agriculturalists of the highland valleys and the hunters and gatherers of the interior Chaco (e.g., the Tonocoté, Lule, Juri) are incorporated into the estimate of 25,000 adult males for Talavera de Esteco and Santiago del Estero (Table 6.2). This total represents a compromise between Sotelo Narváez and Canelas Albarrán. Later estimates are probably quite low to be used for contact population, as many of the more peaceful Indians were moved north into Bolivia and west to Chile.

The great bolson of Salinas Grande separated the Diaguita from the Comechingón, who inhabited the mountains of Córdoba and San Luis. For this area, Canelas Albarrán's figure of 15,000 is accepted rather than the lower 12,000 estimated by Sotelo Narváez and Ramírez de Velasco because of Fernández' (1913–14: 2:28) earlier report of a dense network of villages.

The grand total I suggest for the Northwest, 61,000 adult males (Table 6.2), is slightly above sixteenth- and early seventeenth-century estimates for the colonial province of Tucumán. A calculation based on the number of reported encomiendas, similar to that done above for Jujuy, gives a still larger estimate, about 80,000.

Cuyo

The Cuyo region is not distinguished from the Northwest by obvious physical barriers but was inhabited by the culturally distinct Huarpe. The impoverished territory of Mendoza, San Luis, and southern San Juan and the rudimentary technology of the semisedentary Huarpe suggest small numbers (Canals Frau, 1946: 169), but numerical estimates of population are scarce and none of these apparently include specifically the Indians living near Lake Guanacache (northeast of Mendoza). If the population decline reflected by the estimates made by López de Velasco in 1571 and Vázquez de Espinosa in 1618 (see Table 6.4) holds also for San Luis, the total male population of the Cuyo in 1571 would have been 5,700 (Table 6.2).

Pampa

To give credence to Schmidl's description of the Paraná-Paraguay is to demand greatly increased numbers for the Pampa and Chaco regions. By defending Schmidl's estimate of 23,000 warriors in a confederation of four tribes, adding his estimate of 12,000 Corondá, and including half the reported Quiloazá (see Table 6.5), who were said to be expanding into the Paraná Delta, I obtain a total of 55,000 adult males (Table 6.2). Only groups along the Paraná between Buenos Aires and Santa Fe were described by Schmidl in the Pampa, and they included groups technically outside the Pampa, in the Paraná Delta. Most native peoples were hunters and gatherers and probably were found close to the rivers, because water was not easily obtained elsewhere. No estimates were made for the drier parts of the Pampa until long after the horse had been adopted and migration of the Araucanians into western Argentina had taken place (Cooper, 1946c: 130, 138). Exaggeration by Schmidl, if any, can be accommodated by unknown groups of the western and southern Pampa.

Chaco

Regional delimitation of the Chaco is ill defined. The bulk of the population was certainly in the upper reaches of the Paraguay River and along the margins of the Andes, north of the upper Bermejo. Even on the lower reaches

Table 6.4

Estimates of Aboriginal Population, Cuyo

Place	Number[a]	Enumeration Unit[b]	Year[c]	Source
Cuyo (region)	20,000	indios (repartidos)	(1560)	Olivares, cited by Rosenblat, 1945: 182
	100,000	indios	(1560)	Olivares, cited by Rosenblat, 1945: 183
	12,000 or *15,000*	almas	1608	Torres, 1927: 21
Mendoza and San Juan	5,000	yndios	1596	Ramírez de Velasco, 1914: 231
Mendoza	2,500[d]	indios tributarios	(1560)	Olivares, cited by Rosenblat, 1945: 183
	2,500	tributarios	1571	López de Velasco, 1971: 266
	16,000	almas	1618	Oñate, 1929: 167, 194
	1,500	indios	(1618)	Vázquez de Espinosa, 1948: 679
San Juan	1,500[d]	indios tributarios	(1560)	Olivares, cited by Rosenblat, 1945: 183
	1,500	tributarios	1571	López de Velasco, 1971: 266
	800	indios, Guarpes	(1618)	Vázquez de Espinosa, 1948: 680
San Luis	1,000	indios, Guarpes	(1618)	Vázquez de Espinosa, 1948: 679

[a]Estimates in original sources may or may not have included women and children, or men over 50. Usually the statement is clear, and if a source reported both types of estimates, both are included in the table. Italicized figures represent total population, including women and children.

[b]Spelling in source is maintained. See Glossary for translation. Parentheses denote enumeration unit assumed from context.

[c]Year is given where indicated in source. Parentheses denote an approximate date.

[d]". . . besides many others who are not peaceful."

195

Table 6.5
Estimates of Aboriginal Population, Pampa

Place or Indians Named	Number[a]	Enumeration Unit[b]	Year[c]	Source
Pampa (region)	30,000–40,000	indios	—[d]	Fasulo, cited by Rosenblat, 1954: 1: 319
	2,716	habitantes indios	1620	Cited by Difrieri, 1961: 46; no source given
Buenos Aires	500	yanaconas	1609?	Memoria, 1907: 79
	500	ynfieles de servicio	1609?	Memoria, 1907: 79
	500	indios	1611	Marín Negrón, cited by Difrieri, 1961: 53
Santa Fe	25,000	indios (repartidos)	1573	Guevara, cited by Rosenblat, 1945: 183
	50,000[e]	varones	1609?	Memoria, 1907: 79
	1,500	yndios cristianos	1609?	Memoria, 1907: 79
	1,500	indios cristianos	1612	Cited by Difrieri, 1961: 53; no source given
	500	Chanás	1612	Cited by Difrieri, 1961: 53; no source given
	4,000	Charrúas	1612	Cited by Difrieri, 1961: 53; no source given

Querandí	3,000	hombres formados	(1535)	Schmidl, 1938: 44
	4,000	hombres	(1535)	Schmidl, 1938: 46
Querandí, Guaraní, Charrúa, Chaná-Timbú	23,000	hombres	(1535)	Schmidl, 1938: 53
Timbú	15,000	hombres	(1535)	Schmidl, 1938: 56
	6,400[f]	(hombres)	(1535)	Schmidl, 1938: 56
Corondá	12,000	gente adulta[g]	(1539)	Schmidl, 1938: 62
Quiloazá	40,000	hombres de pelea	(1539)	Schmidl, 1938: 63

[a]Estimates in original sources may or may not have included women and children, or men over 50. Usually the statement is clear, and if a source reported both types of estimates, both are included in the table. Italicized figures represent total population, including women and children.

[b]Spelling in source is maintained. See Glossary for translation. Parentheses denote enumeration unit assumed from context.

[c]Year is given where indicated in source. Parentheses denote an approximate date.

[d]Pre-Columbian ("época indígena").

[e]"In a nation of the unfaithful 45 leagues from Santa Fe." Rosenblat (1945: 182) reported this as 45,000. Torres (1927: 51) also reported 50,000 in a province called Luruay near Santa Fe.

[f]Calculated from Schmidl's estimated 400 canoes, each with a capacity for 16 men.

[g]"Adult people who are engaged in warfare."

197

Table 6.6
Estimates of Aboriginal Population, Chaco

Place or Indians Named	Number[a]	Enumeration Unit[b]	Year[c]	Source
Chaco (region)	*50,000*[d]	indios	1626	Osorio, in Mastrillo Durán, 1929: 260
	30,000	indios	1626	Mastrillo Durán, 1929: 252
Río de la Plata and Paraguay (region)[e]	60,000	indios	1586	Canelas Albarrán, cited by Rosenblat, 1945: 78, 182
	199,200	infieles	1609?	*Memoria*, 1907: 79
	8,050	yndios cristianos	1609?	*Memoria*, 1907: 79
	330,000	reducidos e infieles	(1600)	Cervera, 1907: 1:253 (several governors cited)
	200,000	indios infieles	1609	Torres, 1927: 41
	20,000	xpaños de paz	1609	Torres, 1927: 41
	300,000	naturales	1610	Marín Negrón, 1907: 74
	1,160,000[f]	ynfieles	1610	Torres, 1927: 85
	110,000[f]	fieles	1610	Torres, 1927: 85
	1,000,000[f]	almas ynfieles	1611	Torres, 1927: 482
	110,000[f]	fieles	1611	Torres, 1927: 482
Corrientes	1,000	ynfieles	1609?	*Memoria*, 1907: 79
	4,425	indios	1622	Góngora, 1907: 85
Mocoretá	18,000	hombres para pelear	(1539)	Schmidl, 1938: 64
Chaná-salvaje	2,000	hombres de gente de pelea	(1539)	Schmidl, 1938: 66

Group	Number	Category	Date	Source
Mapení	100,000	hombres	(1539)	Schmidl, 1938: 66
	10,000g	(hombres)	(1539)	Schmidl, 1938: 66
Guaicurúh	500[i]	indios	(1540)	Torres, 1927: 48
	4,000	warriors	1542	Núñez Cabeza de Vaca, 1891: 147
	6,000	Mbayá [Guaicurú]	1612	Cited by Difrieri, 1961: 39; no source given
	7,000–8,000	(none given)	n.d.	Sánchez Labrador, cited by Difrieri, 1961: 39
	1,000	Guaicurús y Payaguás	(1620)	Relación de los Indios, cited by Difrieri, 1961: 40
	1,500	Guaicurús del Pilcomayo	(1620)	Relación de los Indios, cited by Difrieri, 1961: 40
Mahoma	800	familias	n.d.	Cited by Métraux, 1946: 225; no source given
Abipón (Frentón)	8,000[j]	Abipones	(1600)	Lozano, 1941: 94
	100,000[j]	indios	(1600)	Lozano, 1941: 94
	6,000	yndios ynfieles, Frentones	1609	Torres, 1927: 16
	400[k]	yndios de tasa	1609	Torres, 1927: 16
	14,000[l]	Frentones	1609	Torres, 1927: 35
	6,000[m]	indios Frentones	1610	Torres, 1927: 81
	350	yanaconas	1612	Cited by Difrieri, 1961: 39; no source given
	389	indios	1622	Góngora, 1907: 85
Mat-aguayo	30,000[d]	indios	1628	Osorio, in Mastrillo Durán, 1929: 260
Toba and Mataguayo	6,000	habitantes	(1620)	Relación de los Indios, cited by Difrieri, 1961: 40
	4,000	indios	(1600)	Lozano, 1941: 60

(continued on following pages)

Table 6.6, *continued*

Place or Indians Named	Number[a]	Enumeration Unit[b]	Year[c]	Source
Toba	*12,000*[n]	indios	(1600)	Lozano, 1941: 60
	2,000	yndios de guerra	1609	Torres, 1927: 16
Matará	*20,000*	yndios	1585	Vera y Aragón, 1943: xxv
	7,000[o]	(none given)	(1591)	Cited by Métraux, 1946: 232; no source given
	600[p]	indios	(1600)	Lozano, 1941: 115
	7,000[j]	indios	(1600)	Lozano, 1941: 94
	60,000	(indios)	(1600)	Machoni de Cerdeña, 1878: 31
Mar Chiquita	2,097	confesiones	1603	Romero, cited by Serrano, 1938: 57

[a]Estimates in original sources may or may not have included women and children, or men over 50. Usually the statement is clear, and if a source reported both types of estimates, both are included in the table. Italicized figures represent total population, including women and children.

[b]Spelling in source is maintained. See Glossary for translation. Parentheses denote enumeration unit assumed from context.

[c]Year is given where indicated in source. Parentheses denote an approximate date.

[d]Osorio's letter states: "They tell me there are more than 50,000 Indians, although I can't say for sure until I see it. They are of the opinion that there are 30,000 just for the Mataguayo. When I told the governor that we believe there are only half that many, he laughed at me." Lozano (1941: 81) reported 50 towns of Mataguayo near Jujuy. The estimates may refer to groups transferred to the Chaco, to groups having fled from the Spanish, or simply to groups of lower elevations along the eastern margin of the Andes, which is similar in habitat to the Chaco.

[e]Includes many Indians in present-day Paraguay and Brazil.

[f] Includes the provinces of Chile and Tucumán.

[g] Calculated from a reported 500 canoes, each with a capacity for 20 men.

[h] Both Schmidl (1938) and Núñez Cabeza de Vaca (1891) referred to Agaces across the river from Asunción, who agreed with Núñez Cabeza de Vaca (1891: 132) to leave Asunción in peace "whenever they descended the Paraguay." Difrieri (1961: 26) referred to Schmidl's Agaces as Payaguá and to Núñez Cabeza de Vaca's as Mbayá (Guaicurú). The main bodies of both Mbayá and Payaguá lived farther upstream and cannot be considered as aboriginals of Argentina. The Agaces whom Difrieri attributes to Schmidl seem to be Schmidl's Cario or Guaraní (Schmidl, 1938: 69, 74) and also properly belong outside Argentina. Schmidl's (1938: 41) Mbayá, described as living much farther up the Paraguay, were numbered at 20,000; he gave no number for the Agaces.

[i] Torres (1927: 48) expressed amazement that a bellicose group of Guaicurú across the river from Asunción, who were not 500 strong when the Spaniards arrived, were "many more than double" that figure in 1609.

[j] "Abipón . . . used to be very numerous because P. Juan Fonte found more than 8,000 in one town . . . and Matará or Amulalá eight leagues from Concepción, one town with 7,000 . . . and it is certain there were more than 100,000 Indians in the vicinity of that city of the Río Bermejo."

[k] In a town near Concepción del Bermejo.

[l] In 40 to 50 towns near Concepción.

[m] In three towns.

[n] "Between the Bermejo and Pilcomayo are more than 12,000 Indians from the mountains to the Paraguay River. . . ." In another place, Lozano (1941: 82) listed 19 Toba towns.

[o] Métraux stated that Alonso de Vera, founder of Concepción, settled 7,000 in La Rioja.

[p] "The greater part of the Matará were baptized but . . . more than 600 Indians died in an epidemic a few days before the arrival of the fathers."

of the Paraguay, however, Schmidl reported groups living in large, fortified villages with cultivated fields of manioc, as well as groups subsisting largely on fish and meat. An estimate of 34,000 adult males for the riverine Chaco (Table 6.2) sums Schmidl's figures (Table 6.6), using 10,000 for the Mapení, based on a calculation of canoes and their capacities rather than on a vague "It is calculated that they are about one hundred thousand men." The estimate for interior groups (Table 6.2), concentrated in the former Concepción del Bermejo, combines an estimated 20,000 Abipón and 2,000 Toba (Table 6.6). I suggest that possible exaggeration in these figures is compensated for by unreported groups.

Mesopotamia and Patagonia

There are no good estimates for the regions of Mesopotamia and Patagonia; some of those available are given in Table 6.7. Considering the expansion of the Quiloazá reported by Schmidl and the later successes of the Jesuit missions, an estimate of 10,000 adult males for the Paraná Delta and a total population of 33,000 for the Guaraní (see Table 6.2) should not be too high.

Hunters and gatherers of Tierra del Fuego (mainly the Ona) were grouped in bands of perhaps 100 persons (Cooper, 1946b: 118). Similar groups probably extended along the rivers on the eastern margins of the Andes and along the coast, but no good descriptions are reported for the vast territory of Patagonia (765,720 square kilometers). The Patagonians were hunters of the guanaco and rhea, and it is assumed that as guanaco do not form numerous groups, neither did the hunters (Difrieri, 1961: 29).

CONCLUSION

Accepting, however tentatively, the reasoning and estimates of the preceding paragraphs, there remains the choice of a multiplier to represent average family size, in order to estimate the total population. Several of the contemporary missionary accounts reported in Tables 6.3 through 6.7 use 5.0 as an average family size, which Difrieri (1961: 22) reported to be an average for licenses in the national archives. He also said that the Jesuit missions recorded an average of 4.5 for the eighteenth century, and at least one report uses 6.0 as an average (Torres, 1927: 129). In calculating his totals, Difrieri seems to have used a multiplier of 4.0.

If family size were 4.0, and were applied to my estimate in Table 6.2 of 187,700 adult males, with 43,000 other men, women, and children, the total population would be approximately 793,800. If the family size were in-

Table 6.7

Estimates of Aboriginal Population, Mesopotamia and Patagonia

Region	Number[a]	Enumeration Unit[b]	Year[c]	Source
Mesopotamia	*40,000*	(almas)	1618	Oñate, 1929: 166
	20,000[d]	indios	(1625)	Mastrillo Durán, 1929: 248
	42,300	población total	(1630)	Berthod y Benavídez, cited by Difrieri, 1961: 43
	33,506	almas	_[e]	Furlong Cardiff, 1962: 146 ff.
	28,714[f]	almas	1647	Leonhardt, 1927: lxxix
Patagonia	*4,000*	almas	1780–1783	Viedma, 1837: 79
	4,000	hombres	1826	Muñiz, cited by Difrieri, 1961: 54
	8,000[g]	indios	1825	Núñez, cited by Difrieri, 1961: 54
	4,000–5,000[h]	indígenas	_[h]	Difrieri, 1961: 54
	2,000[i]	Ona population	(1875)[i]	Cooper, 1946a: 108

[a]Estimates in original sources may or may not have included women and children, or men over 50. Usually the statement is clear, and if a source reported both types of estimates, both are included in the table. Italicized figures represent total population, including women and children.

[b]Spelling in source is maintained. See Glossary for translation. Parentheses denote enumeration unit assumed from context.

[c]Year is given where indicated in source. Parentheses denote an approximate date.

[d]Referring to a report by Governor Francisco de Cespedes. Mastrillo Durán added that the Indians in Jesuit missions totaled more than 10,000 souls.

[e]The figure given is the total population reported for 15 missions in Argentina over a period of years extending from 1644 to 1711.

[f]Reported for 20 villages or reductions.

[g]Citation referred to Auca (Araucanian?), Pampa, Huiliche (Araucanian), Tehuelche, and Ranquele (Araucanian); thus, it included the dry Pampa as well as Patagonia.

[h]"According to the missionaries, in all Tierra del Fuego—Argentine and Chilean territory—there would have been in the second half of the nineteenth century a maximum oscillating between 7,000 and 8,000 Indians." Difrieri (1961: 54) stated, without giving his source, that the Yahgan [in Chile] numbered about 3,000, leaving 4,000 to 5,000 in Argentina.

[i]"Earlier estimates from the last quarter of the last century." Cooper (1946b: 118) also described Ona country as divided into 39 distinct territories, each held by a group of 40 to 120 persons.

creased to 4.5, the total rises to 887,650; and if to 5.0, the total becomes 981,500. The most conservative of these is well over double the currently accepted estimates.

Although considerable effort still needs to be applied to studying the aboriginal population of southern South America, I think that higher estimates than the standard ones are in order. The exaggeration assumed for the estimates of missionaries and soldiers needs careful attention, but even if present they may well be offset by other factors that lead to underestimation: omission of uncounted groups, notably the Huarpe east and south of reported populations, the interior cultures of the Chaco, Pampa groups south and west of the Río de la Plata, and cultures of the lake region; reduction in populations prior to dates of estimates, especially by disease, which is reported in the Jesuit letters but which has received little attention; and reduction by migration, both forced and voluntary. The Jesuit letters for the later dates repeatedly refer to Indians fleeing from the demands for personal service as well as to deportations of Indians for personal service in Chile. Examination of earlier letters and reports may reveal details of both disease and migration. Finally, more thorough examination of the cultural ecology of native peoples should suggest likely or optimum populations against which the original estimates can better be judged. The population question is still open.

CHAPTER 7 The Aboriginal Population of Amazonia

William M. Denevan

INTRODUCTION

Amazonia[1] is generally conceded to have had one of the lowest pre-Columbian aboriginal population densities of any major region of the New World. Steward and Faron (1959: 53), for example, gave a total population for the tropical forests of interior South America of only 2,188,970 people, plus 387,440 more in the savannas of eastern Brazil. Dobyns (1966: 415) gave a much larger, but only vaguely supported, estimate of 6,000,000 for all of tropical South America, apparently including the densely settled Caribbean coast.[2] I believe that Amazonia could potentially support and actually

---

Reprinted, with corrections and revisions, from "The Aboriginal Population of Western Amazonia in Relation to Habitat and Subsistence," *Revista Geográfica* (Rio de Janeiro), No. 72, 1970, pp. 61–86, with permission of the Instituto Panamericano de Geografía e História and the author. An earlier version was presented at the 37th International Congress of Americanists, Mar del Plata (Argentina), September 1966. Some new material and citations have been added. The riverine habitat density has been increased, with a resulting increase in the population estimates.

1. As used in this chapter, the terms Amazonia and Amazon Basin comprise the lowland and lower upland drainage area of the Amazon River and its tributaries, and greater Amazonia includes roughly the area of South America east and south of the Andes and north of the Tropic of Capricorn, except for the Gran Chaco region. Greater Amazonia thus incorporates all the tropical lowlands and plateaus of interior South America, an area substantially larger than the Amazon Basin proper.

2. Estimates representing low and high calculations for the Amazon Basin are 500,000 by Moran (1974: 137), which may be less than the current Indian population, and 10,000,000 by Joaquím Rondón (Comas, 1951: 256). Anthropologists Yolanda and Robert Murphy (1974: 23) accept 1,500,000 for Brazilian Amazonia, and Eduardo Galvão (1967: 181) believes that there were "almost two million Indians" in Brazil. For

205

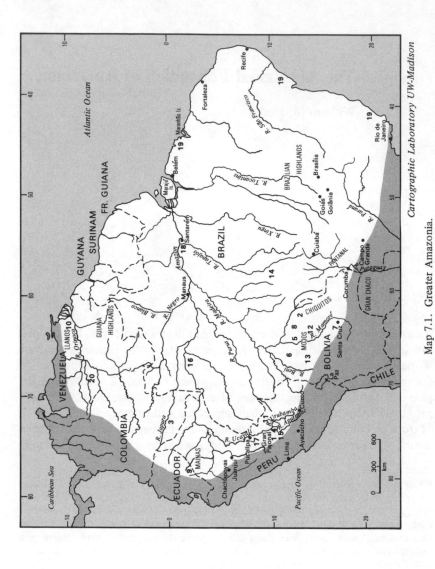

Map 7.1. Greater Amazonia.

Key to List of Tribes

1. Amuesha
2. Baure
3. Bora
4. Campa
5. Canichana
6. Cayubaba
7. Chiriguano
8. Itonama
9. Jívaro
10. Karinya
11. Machiguenga
12. Mojo
13. Movima
14. Nambicuara
15. Nomatsiguenga
16. Omagua
17. Shipibo
18. Tapajós
19. Tupinamba
20. Yaruro

did support a relatively large number of people, and that even Dobyns' estimate is too conservative.

Julian Steward (1949) made the only systematic estimates of early post-contact populations of all the native peoples of Amazonia. His calculations are unreasonably low for several reasons, some of them recognized by Steward himself. In the first place, Steward generally used relatively late historical data, mostly after 1650, so that the initial decline, which often was very considerable and very rapid, was not considered. Second, Steward had a general mistrust, not always justified, of many of the early estimates. Third, Steward often used too large an area for a given tribal population, so that the resulting density was much lower than it should have been. Fourth, Steward made a very incomplete search of the early literature for references to Indian populations, and this resulted in such extremely low figures as 6,000 for the province of Mojos in northeastern Bolivia in 1680, whereas there is actually good documentary evidence for 100,000 or more Indians there in the 1690s. Finally, the very low population densities given by Steward and later Steward and Faron to various parts of Amazonia are not adequate to account for the numerous large villages reported by early travelers, the elaborate ceramics known from a number of very large archacological sites, or the historically documented organizational, agricultural, and material accomplishments of the chiefdoms of eastern Bolivia. These developments all suggest the former existence in Amazonia of at least locally dense populations with sufficient economic surpluses to support social classes and specialists.

Historical evidence for sizes of aboriginal populations in Amazonia in the early sixteenth century is quite meager and does not permit the direct derivation of a total population for the region. There is, however, sufficient prehistorical, historical, and contemporary evidence, in combination with conservative depopulation ratios, to estimate population densities for representative tribes or areas of the major physical habitats of Amazonia, and these estimates can be projected over each habitat region. The distribution of aboriginal population in Amazonia was very uneven and was for the most part very sparse. This distribution, given the prevailing subsistence patterns, including technology, crops, and domesticated animals, was closely related to the nature of the natural habitat. I propose to examine the main habitats in Amazonia and the subsistence patterns of each in relation to resources, and to estimate the possible aboriginal population density of each. Most of my evidence is drawn from western Amazonia (eastern Peru and northeastern Bolivia), with which I am most familiar. The habitats, distinguished on the basis of differences in both soil and wildlife resources and in order of decreasing population density, are: (1) floodplain, (2) coastal, (3) lowland

---

further discussion and references, see Rosenblat (1954: 1:316), who allowed 1,000,000 for all of Brazil.

savanna, (4) upland forest, (5) upland savanna, (6) and lowland forest. This relative sequence of population densities coincides roughly with that mapped by Steward (1949: 659) and by Steward and Faron (1959: 52).

Subsistence Patterns and Resources

Tropical-forest agriculture in Amazonia—and very few tribes were not at least part-time farmers—was (and still is) characterized by a strong emphasis on starchy root crops, especially sweet or bitter manioc. Maize, a more nutritionally complete food than manioc, was invariably a secondary or minor crop, while protein-rich crops such as beans and peanuts were also minor or even absent. Thus, the food from cultivated plants was decidedly deficient in protein content, in contrast to the maize-beans-squash complex which dominated the diet of Mesoamerica and parts of the Caribbean and Andean areas. Furthermore, domesticated animals were of minimal importance for food, in contrast to their role in the Old World tropics, where starchy vegetable foods were also often the staples. In Amazonia the major sources of proteins and fats were fish, eggs, birds, insects, and wild game.

A valid argument can be made, I believe, for an ecological zonation of population density in Amazonia based on variations in the density and availability of wild game and especially fish. A population distribution could therefore be expected that was somewhat different from that of modern Amazonian settlement, where transportation, distance to markets, possession of livestock, advanced technology, finance, and soil fertility are often, although not always, more critical than wildlife resources. The concept of an ecological zonation of cultural levels and economic systems in Amazonia has been emphasized by Lathrap (1962: 549; 1968b; 1970: 128–29), Denevan (1966a; 1971), and Gross (1975). The most highly developed aboriginal societies in Amazonia were located along the Brazilian coast, on the large floodplains of the major rivers, and in seasonally flooded savannas such as on Marajó Island and the Llanos de Mojos of Bolivia. All these areas are rich in aquatic sources of protein. Less intensive agriculturalists were found on the smaller streams, and seminomadic part-time agriculturalists-hunter-gatherers were found in the interfluvial forests and upland savannas.[3] Where there is some relationship in this zonation to soil fertility and also to ease of mobility, the most important factor seems to have been the relative richness of the wildlife resource. The availability of meat protein lessens progressively

3. The longest archaeological sequences and largest sites in Amazonia are within the floodplains and wet savannas; shorter sequences and smaller sites occur along the smaller headwater streams; and the few known nonriverine sites are very small and indicative of small groups of nomadic or seminomadic people (Lathrap, 1962: 551–52).

upstream, away from the wide floodplains, and is even more unreliable in the forests between rivers. A floodplain agricultural tribe that moved, for whatever reason, upstream or into the forest would have had to rely less on fishing and more and more on hunting over large areas of forest, with a necessary deemphasis of agriculture, probable social deterioration, and a decrease in population density.

Of the major ecological zones, the best aboriginal agricultural opportunity was found on the alluvial river soils, then the forested upland slopes and terraces, the lowland interfluve and coastal forests, the lowland savannas, the upland savannas, and finally the areas of excessive slope, rainfall, rockiness, or flooding, which supported very little or no aboriginal population. For wildlife resources, the best areas were along the large rivers with extensive floodplains and in the seasonally flooded lowland savannas and along the coasts, then in the upland and lowland forests, and finally in the upland savannas. Where good soils and rich wildlife resources coincide, there can be expected the densest and most permanent native settlement, as along the Amazon and its major tributaries; where both soils and fish-game resources are poor, sparse and unstable human populations can be expected, as in the lowland interfluvial forests and in the upland savannas in the Guiana Highlands and the Brazilian Highlands.

The agricultural potential of all areas can be and often was improved by various techniques such as terracing steep slopes, as in the high *montaña,* and by ridging and mounding and composting (or mulching) seasonally flooded savanna soils, as in the Llanos de Mojos. However, relatively little was done to improve the wildlife resource in Amazonia, in contrast to the high level of animal domestication in the Old World. The ecological zonation of population that prevailed in Amazonia can be viewed, then, in terms of a lack of emphasis on domesticated animals or on cultivated plants with a high protein content. Those areas of the New World that did emphasize seed crops were much less dependent on fish and game resources; the tropical, lowland Maya civilization, for example, was by no means floodplain oriented. As Lathrap (1962: 552) and also Reichel-Dolmatoff (1965: 80–81) point out, only with intensified maize production—which in South America came historically later or, as in most of Amazonia, not at all—is this ecological zonation broken down by the movement of major settlements away from the semiaquatic environments.

THE LOWLAND SAVANNA HABITAT

Most of the lowland savannas in South America are seasonally inundated by overflowing rivers or standing rainwater, including the Llanos de Mojos, the lower Orinoco Llanos, the Pantanal of western Brazil, and eastern Marajó Island. These semiaquatic landscapes are rich in wildlife and are comparable in this respect to the floodplain habitat; however, soil resources are generally much poorer.

The Llanos de Mojos occupies about 180,000 square kilometers in the center of the department of the Beni in northeastern Bolivia. For from four to eight months of the year the savannas are under several inches to several feet of water as the Río Mamoré and its tributaries overflow. Large quantities of fish swarm onto the plains, and millions of migratory birds flock to the region to feed on the fish. The grasslands abound in wild game including a variety of rodents, deer, and the rhea, which are confined to the *islas* of high ground during flooding and are easily hunted. During the dry season the *llanos* are desiccated; however, there are thousands of permanent lakes and *curiches* where fish are abundant and where game and birds concentrate.

The alluvial soils of the forested natural levees crossing the Llanos de Mojos are comparable to those of the larger rivers of Amazonia but are not as extensive. The actual savannas, on the other hand, have mostly very poor claypan soils low in organic matter, and there is little attempt to cultivate them today. Nevertheless, pre-Spanish aboriginal people in Mojos did culti- vate these soils, as is evident from the remnants of tens of thousands of ridges, drainage ditches, and raised platforms which provided high ground for crops when the savannas were inundated during the growing season (Denevan, 1966b: 84–96). Some of the platforms are up to 25 meters wide and 300 meters long, while the smaller ridges occur in groups with several thousand in each. When these fields and associated causeways and habitation mounds were built is not known, and they may have been in use until the Conquest; however, they are certainly indicative of large, well-organized populations. Furthermore, since a greater effort was required to cultivate the poor savanna soils than the well-drained and richer gallery forest soils, the fact that the savannas were cultivated is probably indicative of a population size that could not be supported by the limited forest areas. The availability of unusually good game resources apparently encouraged large, localized populations which were ultimately forced laboriously to cultivate the poor savanna land, and this lends support to the concept that for aboriginal agriculturalists with starchy tubers for staples, the fish-game resource was more important in determining population density than was the quality of the soil. If the soils were poor, they could be improved, as in Mojos, or farm plots could be shifted frequently, but there was less flexibility in the fish-game resource. Seasonally flooded lowland savannas seem to have sustained relatively large populations elsewhere, compared with the lowland forest habitat, even with- out cultivation, as in eastern Marajó Island and parts of the Orinoco Llanos.

Mojos Population

See Denevan (1966b: 112–20) for a discussion of the Mojos population. There is good documentary evidence for a Mojos savanna population of at least 100,000 Indians in the 1690s (primarily the Mojo, Baure, Cayubaba, Itonama, Movima, and Canichana tribes). Incomplete Jesuit estimates between 1693 and 1700 total 112,259. Taking this figure at face value, allowing for uncounted people, and allowing for a prior decrease in the populations reported after 1693, a figure of at least 150,000 for the early 1690s would seem reasonable; however, in view of the possibility of exaggeration by the Jesuits for some of the tribes, a minimum figure of 100,000 is a fair estimate. Support is given to such a figure by Padre Eguiluz (1884: 63) who in 1696 reported that in addition to 19,759 mission Indians there were "70,000 other friendly Indians" who wished to be Christianized; this gives a total of nearly 90,000, and presumably there were additional unfriendly Indians. An earlier estimate in 1677 (Castillo, 1906: 302) gave only 50,000 for Mojos, but this was before any of the northern tribes in Mojos had been visited. A minimum estimate for the early 1690s of 100,000 could well be low, considering that there were still 35,250 counted mission Indians in 1737 (Argamosa, 1906: 113) and probably a total of at least 50,000, since the Jesuits were still very actively rounding up Indians in 1737. Thus, there was still a sizable Indian population after about 50 years of intense mission activity and numerous major epidemics.

The initial contact between Mojos tribes and Spanish explorers was in 1580, although epidemic disease may have preceded the first explorers. The Mojos Indians were thus subjected to at least 100 years of direct or indirect contact with explorers, slave raiders, missionaries, and from trade expeditions to Santa Cruz before the first settlement was founded, the Jesuit mission of Loreto in 1682. Constant Indian-European contact and probable rapid population decline from epidemic disease dated from 1667, when a slave-raiding expedition from Santa Cruz entered Mojos and left behind a group of Jesuit priests who traveled constantly among the various Indian groups until the mid-1690s, by which time all the tribes had been visited and the main missions established. Between 1667 and 1695 several epidemics were reported, including the first big smallpox epidemic in 1670, and disease was a constant menace throughout the Jesuit period.

How much did the population of Mojos decline between 1580 and the early 1690s? Two general rates of aboriginal population decline have recently been suggested for the New World. Borah (1964: 382) believes that there was at least a 90 percent (or 10 to 1) depopulation during the first 100 years after initial contact. Dobyns (1966: 414) proposes a 20 to 1 depopulation ratio from initial contact to the population nadir (date of recovery), which usually involved a period longer than 100 years. If Borah's rate of decline is applied to Mojos, using a conservative starting date of 1637, which is 20 years after the first major expedition entered Mojos, and a 100-year date of 1737, when the population numbered about 50,000, then a figure of 500,000 is obtained. Applying Dobyns' ratio of 20 to 1 and using a nadir population of 10,000 in 1900, an initial population of only 200,000 is obtained. Because of the considerable amount of disease reported in the latter part of the seventeenth century, I lean more toward 500,000 but will compromise with the average between the two figures of 350,000,[4] which converts to a 35 to 1 depopulation ratio from contact to nadir. Dobyns' 20 to 1 depopulation ratio is, I believe, too low for those tropical lowland areas of the Americas where contact was fairly continuous, as in Mojos, the Caribbean, the Amazon floodplains, and the Brazilian coast, where epidemic disease seems to have been much more devastating than in temperate latitudes and altitudes. Dobyns (1966: 413–14) has suggested some very high depopulation ratios for tropical America, and he believes that a ratio of 50 to 1 or more usually resulted in near or actual tribal extinction. A compromise of 35 to 1, midway between a hemisphere-wide depopulation ratio of 20 to 1 and the extinction ratio of 50 to 1, would seem to be a reasonable average for those tropical people, such as the Mojos tribes, who experienced fairly intense contact prior to the introduction of modern medicine and still did not become extinct.

For Mojos, a decline from 350,000 to 100,000 during the first century after initial contact provides a depopulation ratio of only 3.5 to 1, which is well below that suggested by Borah. However, as indicated above, for most of the first 100 years contact was sporadic, and the same was true in most of tropical South America. In western Amazonia, missionary activity, which was most responsible for the introduction of epidemic disease, did not become significant until between the end of the sixteenth century and the middle of the seventeenth century, and it is for this period that the first fairly reliable population estimates are available. I believe that the Mojos depopulation ratio of 3.5 to 1 for roughly the first 100 years after contact can be safely applied as a minimum ratio to most of tropical, interior South America where contact was sporadic for the first 100 years. Accordingly, population figures for the central and upper Amazon area for the mid-seventeenth century and for the Brazilian coast and lower Amazon for the early seventeenth century can be increased at least 3.5 times for the contact period 100 years earlier, recog-

4. The precontact total of 350,000 Indians in Mojos and the total of 100,000 in the 1690s contrast with Steward's (1949: 662) extremely conservative total of only 6,000 for the province of Mojos in 1680, which is based on a Jesuit estimate for just one tribe, and with Métraux's (1942: 55) figure of 19,789, for the end of the seventeenth century, which is a mission count only.

nizing that in many areas the initial 100-year depopulation ratio may have been much more. Thus, for example, the missionary estimate of 15,000 Omagua along the middle Amazon in 1641, cited by Steward (1949: 662), could be increased to 52,500 at the time of Orellana's voyage in 1542. (Sweet [1969: 103] estimates 20,000 to 25,000 for the Omagua in the year 1600.)

A contact population of 350,000 for the Llanos de Mojos, an area of nearly 180,000 square kilometers, gives an average population density of 2.0 persons per square kilometer. However, this was very unevenly distributed, with much sparser or no population in the vast, very poorly drained portions of Mojos, while around the lakes, along the rivers, and in the areas of earthworks, densities probably equaled or exceeded those of the Amazon floodplain and Brazilian coast.

Not all lowland savannas had an average aboriginal population density as high as that of Mojos, depending on whether or not the grasslands were cultivated, and, if not, on how much cultivable forest land existed within the savannas. Much of the lower, seasonally flooded Orinoco Llanos has extremely poor soil and no evidence of ever having been cultivated.[5] For one such area in Venezuela occupied by Yaruro Indians, Leeds (1961: 21) calculated that with the existing ecological conditions and aboriginal technology a stable population density of about 0.6 persons per square kilometer would be possible. Such a density is still above the densities given below for the lowland forest (0.2 per km^2) and upland savanna (0.5 per km^2) habitats. For an average density for lowland savannas other than Mojos, for which little is known about aboriginal populations, I suggest a density of 1.3 per square kilometer, which is the average of the densities of Mojos (2.0) and the poor-resource upland savannas (0.5).

THE FLOODPLAIN HABITAT

The riverine and coastal orientation of the densest populations in Amazonia is well known. Archaeology, early historical accounts, and present population distributions are all indicative of relatively dense aboriginal populations along the Amazon itself and the floodplains of the major tributaries. High densities

5. A few relic ridged fields have been described for one site in southeastern Barinas within the low savannas (Llanos Bajos) in Venezuela (Denevan and Zucchi, 1978). Much of the northern portion of the Orinoco Llanos are higher and well drained (Llanos Altos), and they are more comparable to the high savannas (campo cerrado) of central Brazil. The only known aboriginal agriculture in the Llanos Altos is that of ditched fields in moriche palm swamps in depressions and valleys by Karinya Indians (Denevan and Bergman, 1975).

generally continued at least as far upstream as the first rapids and the associated confinement of the floodplain and sometimes above the rapids if the floodplain again widened, as in the savannas of northeastern Bolivia.

The floodplains (*várzeas*) of recent alluvium, as well as the uplands (*terras firmes*) of Tertiary and Pleistocene sediments, well described and illustrated by Marbut and Manifold (1925, 1926) and Sternberg (1975), are complex landforms and thus diverse in soils, drainage, vegetation, and wildlife, although they are spoken of in generalized terms here. The floodplain habitat is a wide zone, mostly under 300 meters elevation, with rivers meandering between natural levees (*restingas*) backed by extensive overflow basins. The rivers are constantly changing course, leaving behind a complex network of oxbow lakes and swamps in the old meander scars, which alternate with the remnants of former levees. The full floodplain zone thus may be many kilometers across. Steward (1949: 662) estimated a zone of dense settlement 50 kilometers deep on each side of the main trunk of the Amazon; however, this is far too wide an average for all the floodplains. There are various estimates of the total extent of the floodplain zone in the Amazon lowlands; 10 percent of the total area is a figure often given, but more recent research suggests figures as low as only 1 percent. Sombroek (1966: 18) in his excellent book, *Amazon Soils,* states that the alluvial areas "comprise only about 1–2% of the total land surface of Amazonia," and this figure is used by Sternberg (1975: 17). The higher figure of 2 percent for the floodplain habitat would allow for a subtraction of land subject to long flooding and a substantial increase for high land directly marginal to the floodplains, which was also densely populated and ecologically oriented to the floodplains. This is the figure used by Meggers (1971: 14) in her recent study of Amazonia.[6]

River levels fluctuate considerably, up to 15 meters or more, and during the long high-water period the river banks overflow and the adjacent back-swamps and meander cutoffs are filled with water. During flooding, people withdraw to the high ground of terra firme or of the natural levees, where most villages and farmland are located anyway.[7] However, there is also

6. Camargo (1958: 17), in a region-by-region estimation, calculated an area of 64,400 square kilometers for the floodplain of the Brazilian Amazon, not including the tributaries, which equals about 1.6 percent of the forested area of about 4,000,000 square kilometers. If the tributary floodplains were added, the percentage would certainly rise to 2 percent or over. Lathrap (1970: 28) estimates 10 percent of 3,106,800 square kilometers of unconsolidated sediment in the entire Amazon Basin to be flood-plain, with about 5 percent—140,000 to 160,000 square kilometers—available to man. A higher floodplain percentage would, of course, greatly affect the population estimates arrived at here (presented in Tables 7.1, 7.2, and 7.3), which are based on 2 percent of all land being alluvial.

7. Many of the former village sites within the floodplains have been destroyed by river meandering (Lathrap, 1968a), but the várzea of the Amazon itself seems more permanent than those of the tributaries (Sternberg, 1975: 18).

intensive cultivation of the river banks, which are planted progressively as the river levels go down during the dry season; not only is the soil here improved by the annual deposition of silt, but it is unnecessary to clear the land of trees.

The main area of cultivation is the well-drained, forested high ground of the natural levees, where the soil consists of fertile, sandy river silt. The quality of the riverine soils varies with the amount of leaching, which is less where there is a marked dry season and lower annual rainfall, as along the central Ucayali, and with the type of silt deposited. The so-called "clear" or "blue" and "black water" streams coming out of the crystalline Brazilian and Guiana Highlands carry little silt and produce poorer soils and possibly less aquatic life than do the silt-laden "white water" rivers with sources in the Andes (Thornes, 1969; Sioli, 1968). Meggers (1971: 12–13) points out that the former are "notorious" as "starvation" rivers due to low subsistence potential. However, preliminary study has not demonstrated that this is clearly the case (Roberto Ibarra, pers. comm., 1972), so a major distinction is not made here between different types of rivers.

In general, the soils of the higher ground of the floodplains are superior to those of the old highly leached terrace soils of the interfluvial forests which do not receive annual deposits of new silt. Both the floodplain and inter-fluvial habitats will support shifting cultivation due to the initial residual fertility left when forest is cleared and burned, but the levee soils support crops for a longer period and fertility is renewed much faster after worn-out land is abandoned. Weed invasion is probably a more common reason for fallowing than loss of soil fertility.

It is probable, as already suggested, that ecologically more important than the superior soils of the floodplains are the superior wildlife resources which provide the vitally essential protein and fat supplements to a plant-foot diet based on starchy tubers. Land animals are most plentiful along the rivers and associated back swamps and oxbows; their abundance varies, however, de-pending on the extent of human activity and other factors. Important food species include peccary, capybara and other rodents, monkey, deer, and tapir. Birds are also very numerous, much more so in aquatic areas than in the forests, and they include many varieties of ducks, toucans, parrots, herons, and doves. Many birds are hunted for their plumage but are usually also eaten.

The most important source of animal protein for the majority of native people in Amazonia has been aquatic life, of which there is a tremendous variety and quantity. Important food fish include several kinds of catfish (*Pimelodidae*), the giant paiche (*Arapaima*), dorado (*Salminus*), bocachica (*Prochilodus*), paco (*Myletes*), and many others. River turtles are very impor-tant food sources; the caiman and the now nearly extinct manatee are also hunted; turtle, caiman, and bird eggs are gathered in large quantities. Generally, aquatic life is most numerous and easiest to catch with traps and fish poisons in the lakes, lagoons, and backswamps rather than in or along the main river courses. For this reason, the availability of aquatic resources decreases moving into the headwater and smaller river areas, where the streams are more confined to their banks and small, separate bodies of quiet water are less common. It was along these backwaters, connected by small channels to the large rivers, that the largest and greatest number of aboriginal settlements were located.

Thus, the smaller streams and foothill rivers with little or no floodplains have poorer wildlife resources than the main river courses as well as having only narrow or scattered strips of alluvial soils. For those streams originating in the sedimentary uplands of the Amazon Basin, even the alluvial soil is relatively poor owing to mineral deficiencies related to the poverty of the surrounding highly weathered soils (Sternberg, 1975: 14). As a result of the progressively more limited natural resources upstream, there tended to be a corresponding decrease in population density for riverine people with an Amazonian subsistence pattern.

There is also a seasonal component to resource availability in the várzea zone. During the high-water period, many croplands are inundated and aquatic resources are less available. The degree to which this period of food scarcity influences population potential would seem to vary with the ability of a given culture to store food, and the riverine tribes were capable of some storage (Meggers, 1971: 126–27). Seasonal variation in water level and the resulting ecological and cultural significance are described by Sternberg (1975: 18–26) and by Meggers (1971).

Early historical accounts claimed dense native populations along the Amazon floodplain, and archaeologists have recently used a variety of forms of evidence to reach the same conclusion. Meggers (1971: 124–25, 133–34, 142–46) states that the várzea population was "numerous" and had reached the maximum possible, given available resources. Lathrap (1968b; 1970; 1972) believes that large prehistoric migration waves in Amazonia can be explained as result of population pressure on the floodplains. Myers (1973: 247, 250) reports archaeological evidence for riverine villages in the lower and central Amazon with 4,000 inhabitants or more each. There is very little evidence, however, for estimating an average aboriginal population density for the floodplain habitat. Steward (1949: 662) allowed a density of only 0.2 to 0.6 per square kilometer along the main trunk of the Amazon, and this was increased slightly to between 0.39 and 0.77 per square kilometer (1 to 2 per mi^2) by Steward and Faron (1959: 52). These figures are far too low for the time of initial European contact, since probable drastic reductions in population from epidemic disease during the first 100 years or so of contact were not considered. Most of Steward's regional and tribal populations were based on missionary estimates from the mid-seventeenth century or later. Also, Steward applied too great an average depth for dense settlement along the Amazon (50 kilometers on each side). A reduced depth would greatly increase the population density.

The initial explorers, especially Carvajal (with Orellana) in 1540, were emphatic in their accounts of dense settlement along the Amazon, describing several long stretches of closely spaced villages (Medina, 1934: 198, 212, 216–17). The lands of the Omagua and Tapajós in particular seem to have been thickly populated (Meggers, 1971: 124, 131–34), and the Orinoco floodplain was also heavily populated (Morey and Marwitt, 1978). Aboriginal settlement must have been considerably reduced by 1640,[8] and without question by 1750, especially in the lower and middle Amazon where there was nearly continuous European activity (Sweet, 1974). Although the reduction during the first century may not have been nearly as great as elsewhere in the New World, the precontact total for the main Amazon floodplain surely exceeded the figure of 130,000 given by Steward (1949: 662).

In the original version of this essay (Denevan, 1970a), a very tenuous average density of 5.3 per square kilometer was used for the várzea; this figure represented an average of the densities for the Brazilian coast and the upland forest. The resulting population for the floodplains, except in Peru and Bolivia, was 536,678. This is clearly too low, considering the other habitat populations, historical and archaeological evidence, and Sweet's (1969: 105) estimate for just the Mainas region in the upper Amazon of 187,000 to 258,000 in 1600. It is especially out of proportion to the original lowland forest estimate of 992,388. This várzea density is one aspect of the original article that has particularly been singled out for criticism. A much higher density is now proposed here, based on a documented and fairly reliable local population for the Omagua.

In 1651 a Franciscan, Laureano de la Cruz (1942: 43–46), made a count of Omagua Indians on five Amazonian islands of comparable size. The area of only one of the islands was reported, so the total area involved is only approximate. The population data can be converted into accordingly approximate densities ranging from 5 to 21 per square kilometer for the five islands and averaging 8.0 per square kilometer (Sweet, 1969: 41–43). Other Omagua

---

8. However, in 1662 Heriarte reported 60,000 "bows" for the largest village of the Tapajós, which would convert into some 240,000 people (Sternberg, 1975: 32). This is probably an exaggeration, but Sternberg notes that he found 65 village sites in the Tapajós area of Santarém, and that the *terra preta de índio*, or Indian black earth from the organic material of former village sites, is reported to be nearly continuous along the bluffs in the area, with depths of up to 1.5 meters full of ceramics. These black earths are found both on floodplains and uplands and are often sought out by farmers because of their fertility.

areas were probably more densely settled, since the island settlements were distant from the main center of Omagua population. And this was after over 100 years of sporadic direct and indirect contact with Europeans.

The density of 8.0 per square kilometer can be taken as a potential density for the entire Amazon River várzea in 1651, with the assumption that while some areas were higher, as with the Omagua core, other areas were similar or possibly lower. For the time of original contact in 1540, the modest depopulation ratio of 3.5 to 1 for the first 100 years of contact, where contact was sporadic, as was derived for Mojos, can be applied. This gives a density of 28.0 per square kilometer for the large floodplains. Lower densities to as few as the 1.2 for the upland forest would be expected along some streams where soil and wildlife resources are poorer, along stretches of rivers where insect problems are especially bad, in the upper reaches with restricted floodplains, and in very poorly drained areas. For an average floodplain density, I suggest utilizing the 28.0 for the large floodplains and the 1.2 for the upland forest, which comes to 14.6 per square kilometer. This is conservative, considering that over half (64,400) of the 102,814 square kilometers of floodplain in Table 7.3 (see p. 230) are located along the main Amazon trunk in Brazil (Camargo, 1958: 17) and should be accorded the density of 28.0. The remaining 38,414 square kilometers are along the large rivers. The many additional small streams are thus given the densities of either the upland forest (1.2) or lowland forest (0.2), both of which are probably too low for the lesser rivers but which give additional support to at least those densities for those habitats in full.

A comparison with the 1970 total population density is instructive. For the six northern states of Brazil (Acre, Amapá, Amazonas, Pará, Roraima, and Rondônia), if a rough and modest 50 percent of the total 1970 population of 3,650,750 (Saunders, 1974: 179) is considered riverine and not supported by imported food (as for large cities such as Belém and Manaus), the riverine density (based on 2 percent of an area of 3,581,180 km^2) comes out to 25.0 per square kilometer, which is well above the aboriginal average of 14.6, even though large sections of várzea are today unsettled.

THE COASTAL HABITAT

Most of the tropical coastal areas of the New World, including the Caribbean islands, had relatively dense aboriginal populations, especially the sandy coasts along the Caribbean and along the Atlantic south of the Amazon, in contrast to the mangrove coasts on the Pacific and on the Atlantic north of the Amazon. This density was associated with an abundance of marine resources. The Tupinamba, who dominated the Brazilian coast from the Amazon to Rio de Janeiro, relied heavily on ocean fishing and lived almost exclusively on fish during some periods. For the coastal Tupinamba, one of the largest tribes in tropical America, Steward (1949: 662) gave a conservative total of 189,000 for the end of the sixteenth century.

Steward (1949: 662) arrived at an average density for the coastal Tupinamba of 0.6 per square kilometer, based on a late sixteenth-century average for three different areas totaling 27,000 Indians in 45,000 square kilometers. At the same time, however, there was a density of 9.06 per square kilometer on the island of Maranhão. Taking the average of the four areas as more representative of the coastal Tupinamba, a density of 2.7 per square kilometer is obtained. A much higher figure must be postulated for A.D. 1500, however, considering the numerous contacts with Europeans during the sixteenth century, although the contact was not nearly as intense as in Peru and Mexico, and consequently the mortality from disease was probably much less. The population decline during the first century of contact was at least equal to that of Mojos, if not greater, since early contact in Mojos was much more sporadic; however, the actual Mojos period considered is slightly longer. Applying the Mojos depopulation ratio of 3.5 to 1 for the first century of contact would raise the Tupinamba density from 2.7 to 9.5 per square kilometer. For a partial cross-check, Steward (1949: 664) gave very conservative densities, based on Rosenblat (1945), of 5.0 to 5.55 persons per square kilometer for Hispaniola, Puerto Rico, and the Lesser Antilles, where most of the population was concentrated in tropical, coastal habitats not too unlike coastal Brazil. Additional support has been given for large Tupinamba populations by recent discoveries of numerous Tupinamba archaeological sites along the Brazilian coast.

THE UPLAND FOREST HABITAT

For tropical Peru and Bolivia, geographers and ecologists usually place the boundary between upland and lowland forests at about 700 meters. Using an average annual temperature of 24°C. as the dividing point, Tosi (1960: 186, 196) gives a variable range between 500 and 800 meters, depending mainly on latitude. The upland forest (high *selva*) is characterized by progressively cooler temperatures, as well as by land which is sloping and rivers which are small and swift and lack floodplains. Alluvial soils are restricted to narrow strips along the rivers, and most cultivation is on hillside residual soils of only fair fertility. However, if rainfall is not too great or slopes too steep, successful shifting cultivation is possible, since after land abandonment fertility is fairly rapidly renewed due to natural erosion which exposes freshly weathered mineral material, in contrast to the deeply leached soils and nearly closed nutrient cycle of the flat to gently rolling lands of the lowland forest. Furthermore, at cooler elevations the rate of humus destruction is less rapid and nitrogen levels drop more slowly. Also, burning is easier and more complete on slopes than in the nearly flat lowland forest. Thus, in the upland forest the potential length of the cropping period increases and the necessary fallow period decreases. Nevertheless, aboriginal settlement in most of the upland forest of South America has been in small, unstable units because of the dispersal of the sources of meat protein.

The quantity of game in the upland forest varies considerably. In some areas it is plentiful, but may be rapidly depleted by hunting; elsewhere, especially where conditions are very wet or very dry, game other than birds is nearly impossible to find. Aquatic life is available in the numerous mountain rivers and streams but is difficult to catch in large quantities, especially during high water; rarely are there quiet backwaters and lagoons as along the big-river floodplains of the lowland forest. Fishing is best during the dry season when exposed river *playas* can be blocked off by weirs and *barbasco* and fish traps can be used; upland forest tribes generally make seasonal migrations down to the larger rivers. Lacking reliable sources of meat protein, many of the upland forest tribes rely heavily on insects, including ants, grubs, beetles, and snails, during part of the year. The upland forest tribes of Peru are seminomadic people who spend considerable time hunting and gathering, living in small family settlements which are moved frequently.

The upland forest habitat extends as high as 3,500 meters in some areas of the eastern Andes. The portion above about 2,500 meters, commonly referred to as cloud forest or *ceja de la montaña,* is almost constantly shrouded in moist clouds, although total rainfall generally does not exceed 2,000 millimeters annually. There are also zones of very high rainfall (over 3,800 millimeters annually and no dry season) at lower elevations where there are strong orographic influences (Tosi, 1960: 183, 211). The constant high humidity in the higher zone and the very heavy rainfall in parts of the lower zone make slash-and-burn agriculture extremely difficult. In addition, soils are very acid and game is sparse. Even today there is little settlement, and the aboriginal population density was mostly very small (probably 0.1 or less per km^2). Travelers entering remote portions of these wet zones today generally report no inhabitants at all; however, there is archaeological evidence of former settlement in some parts of the ceja.[9]

9. A National Geographic Society expedition across the Vilcabamba range between the Apurimac and Urubamba rivers in Peru encountered Indians (Machiguenga) only below 6,000 feet (Baekeland, 1964). Also, see Tosi (1960: 154, 214) on the lack of people in the superhumid upland forest. On the other hand, there is archaeological

Rainfall is still high in most of the rest of the upland forest of the eastern Andes, but where there is at least a short dry season, Indians were and still are present. Parts of the upland forest above 2,000 meters in Peru were occupied by Quechua-speaking *sierra* people in the early sixteenth century, as is true today, while the upper level of the tropical forest tribes was and remains between 1,000 and 2,000 meters.

Although ecological conditions would seem to be little better than those of the interfluvial forest of the lowland forest habitat, there nevertheless have been substantial numbers of aboriginal people in the upland forest, including two of the largest tribes still surviving in western Amazonia, the Jívaro and Campa. The reasons for greater aboriginal settlement in the upland forest than in the lowland forest are not entirely clear, but certainly include the soil factor mentioned above, milder temperatures and relief from insects, protective isolation, and also the greater ease of cross-country movement, despite rough terrain, than in much of the often poorly drained lowland forest habitat.

The rate of population decline of the relatively isolated upland forest tribes seems to have been far below that of the more vulnerable tribes of the floodplains and low savannas. This difference can be attributed to only sporadic contact with outsiders in the upland forest until well into the present century. The two most important groups are the Campa[10] (including the closely related Amuesha, Nomatsiguenga, and Machiguenga) now totaling about 38,000 in the central montaña of Peru, and the Jívaro (including the Shapra, Huambisa, Achual, and Aguaruna) now totaling about 20,000 in northern Peru, with more in Ecuador (Summer Institute of Linguistics, 1965).[11] It is very doubtful if these tribes now number any more than when first encountered, especially since large parts of their original territories are now occupied by colonists. There is no evidence that either group has ever numbered less than one-third of the present population, with the nadir probably reached toward the end of the rubber period, in the early twentieth century. Although the Campa and Jívaro did have periodic contact with

---

evidence of some highland-type settlement within the upper *ceja de la montaña* (3,500 to 3,600 meters elevation) north of Ayacucho (Bonavia and Guzmán, 1966). Also, extensive pre-Inca ruins have recently been discovered or rediscovered in the ceja of northern Peru south of Juanjui (Gran Pajatén) and east of Chachapoyas at elevations of 8,000 to 10,000 feet (Savoy, 1970; D. E. Thompson, 1973). Thus a density of only 0.1 per square kilometer may be far too low for some parts of the ceja.

10. For a discussion of Campa subsistence and ecology, see Denevan (1971).

11. Varese (1972: 413) in a more recent calculation estimates 45,000 for the Campa, 12,000 for the Machiguenga, and 5,000 for the Amuesha, for a total of 62,000 for the Campa groups, a figure this writer feels is somewhat high. Varese gives a total of 36,000 for the Jívaro groups in Peru.

explorers, missionaries, rubber gatherers, and traders, fairly frequent contact has only followed World War II, and has been accompanied by missionary medical care, which has greatly reduced deaths from epidemic diseases.

For the Campa, Lehnertz (1974: 359–62) found Franciscan mission head counts for the early eighteenth century suggesting a density of 1.2 per square kilometer in the Cerro de la Sal region and 1.7 to 2.0 in the southern Gran Pajonal; both areas were probably of higher than average density for the Campa. He believes that a depopulation ratio of 3.5 to 1 is reasonable for the period of the eighteenth century for the Campa, as well as for the central montaña of Peru in general. Lehnertz cites two Franciscan estimates of 10,000 Campa in portions of the Campa region in 1711 and 1723, but these are not reliable. Lehnertz (1969: 114) also estimates that from 40,000 to 50,000 Campa were baptized between 1709 and 1742, a period during which the Campa were being reduced considerably by epidemics.

Possibly more than any other tribe in eastern Peru, the Campa numbers are rapidly increasing, and the tribe is actually extending its territory northward and eastward from a center in the Gran Pajonal. The Campa proper were estimated to total from 24,000 to 26,000 Indians in 1970 (Denevan, 1971: 498), but they may have only numbered about 10,000 or even less in the 1920s (Navarro, 1924: 3). The Campa now occupy a territory of about 25,000 square kilometers. With an estimated population of about 25,000, the density thus equals 1.0 persons per square kilometer. The total contact population was undoubtedly higher. On the other hand, not all of the Campa territory is in the upland forest habitat. Due to outside influences, about 40 percent of the tribe is now located along the rivers that penetrate the east-central Peruvian Andes or on Peruvian *haciendas.* The density for the remaining 15,000 Campa is thus reduced to 0.6 per square kilometer. Recognizing a substantially greater Campa population at the time of contact, at least double, I would consider a density of 1.2 per square kilometer, or slightly higher than the present overall Campa density, a reasonable aboriginal average for the upland forest that is not superhumid. Steward (1949: 663) calculated a contact density of only 0.38 per square kilometer for the Campa, but his total population of 20,000 is too low, and his total Campa area of 51,000 square kilometers is too large.

A subdivision of the upland forest habitat is the higher portions of the Eastern (Guiana and Brazilian) Highlands (a fairly small area), where the population density was probably less than that of the Andean upland forest. In the Eastern Highlands, both residual and alluvial soils, derived mainly from crystalline rocks, tend to be very poor for agriculture. Also, there are very few rivers at upland forest elevations in these low mountains in contrast to the many rivers at over 500 meters elevation in the eastern Andes; the fish resource is therefore very poor. The Eastern Highlands may have had a density comparable to that suggested below for the upland savannas of Brazil of 0.5 per square kilometer, but even this figure may be too high. Steward's (1949: 659) conservative estimates for the Eastern Highland region range between about 0.10 and 0.15 per square kilometer but include areas of both upland savanna and lowland forest.

THE UPLAND SAVANNA HABITAT

Another major Amazonian habitat is that of the upland savannas, which cover extensive areas in central Brazil and the Guianas at elevations over 300 meters. These upland savannas are generally much better drained than the periodically flooded lowland savannas, except for localized waterlogging from rainwater. In contrast to the alluvial soils of much of the lowland savannas, the upland savannas contain some of the poorest soils in the world. The *campo cerrado* soils of Brazil are so deeply weathered and lacking in mineral nutrients that they can be successfully cultivated only with the aid of intensive applications of fertilizers (Denevan, 1965). Game and birds are sparse owing to poor forage and frequent scarcity of water. Rivers are usually small and well spaced. Most of the upland savannas have a long winter dry season lasting from three to seven months and an annual rainfall between 800 and 1,500 millimeters, or considerably less than the upland forest and lowland forest habitats.

For aboriginal man, soil and wildlife resources were poorer in the upland savannas than in any other major tropical South American habitat except for the very humid parts of the upland forest. Many of the tribes in the upland savannas have been classed as "marginal," although most have or had some agriculture. The upland savanna Indians were, as a rule, seminomadic and relied heavily on the gathering of wild fruits, seeds, roots, small game including insects, lizards, and rodents, and what larger game was available, such as deer and armadillo. Bitter manioc, peanuts, and other crops were planted during the wet season, usually in the gallery forests which penetrate the savannas; however, crops were often left while people went to hunt and gather, to return later with hopes of a harvest.

Thus, while resources are quite poor, they are adequate to have supported human settlement, and settlement was facilitated by the relative ease of overland movement compared with the lowland forest; however, population densities were undoubtedly quite low. In some areas, such as the Rupununi savannas of Guyana, there is little or no evidence of any aboriginal settlement until post-Conquest times (Evans, 1964: 433–34). Steward's (1949: 659) lowest densities in tropical South America are in the Eastern Highlands, which are mostly upland savannas, with 0.1 to 0.15 persons per square kilometer (except for a Nambicuara density of 0.2 per km^2), in contrast to Steward's densities of 0.15 to 0.25 per square kilometer for the Amazon forests. The present average density of population in the Brazilian savannas is only 1.8 persons per square kilometer, and this includes the populations of very large cities such as Brasília, Anápolis, Goiânia, Campo Grande, Goiás, and Cuiabá.

Steward's Nambicuara density of 0.2 per square kilometer is based on a 1907 figure. Although the tribe had had very little contact with whites previously, they had been known since the seventeenth century, and there must have been some reduction from disease before 1907. It seems reasonable to apply the 3.5 to 1 minimum ratio of population decline for the first 100 years of infrequent contact in tropical South America to the Nambicuara in 1907, which would give them an aboriginal population density of 0.7 per square kilometer. Since much of the central campo cerrado lands and the Guiana savannas are apparently poorer in resources than the Nambicuara region, I suggest a reduction to an average aboriginal density for the upland savannas of 0.5 per square kilometer. This figure is higher than that allotted to the lowland forests where the soils are better; however, the greater ease of movement in the savannas is a significant asset to seminomadic or nomadic people dependent mainly on hunting and gathering. A density of 0.5 per square kilometer would seem about right considering Steward's (1949: 661–62) conservative densities for similar seminomadic peoples in the Chaco of 0.6 (Chiriguano) and 0.29 (western Chaco) per square kilometer.

THE LOWLAND FOREST HABITAT

Of the habitats described here, by far the most extensive is that of the lowland, interfluvial forests (low selva). Two rough climatic subdivisions can be made: the drier forests where there is a distinct dry season lasting several months, and the wetter forests where there is little or no dry season. In the Holdridge classification and map of Peru (Tosi, 1960), the Bosque Húmedo Tropical has over 80 inches of rainfall and the Bosque Seco Tropical has 40 to 80 inches; elevations are below about 600 meters and mostly below 300 meters, and temperatures are high all year long with annual averages over 24°C. The soils of the low selva are generally highly leached, especially in the Bosque Húmedo, and are of low fertility; however, shifting cultivation is nevertheless possible. On the other hand, aquatic resources are absent except along small streams, where they are minimal. Birds and game are present but are dispersed, rather than concentrated and accessible as they are along the rivers. Thus, it is necessary for forest tribes to move about considerably—to the rivers for fish or through the forest in search of game, birds, and insects. Even though most forest tribes also did some cultivating, large stable villages were difficult to maintain in view of the dispersed sources of meat protein. The usual pattern, then, was one of small groups of seminomadic, part-time agriculturalists such as the Bora. Completely nomadic nonagriculturalists have been described for Amazonia, but there are indications that most represent pre- or post-Columbian deculturation (Lathrap, 1968b).

Population in the lowland forest was very sparse and still is, as one can verify by flying over the Amazon Basin and seldom seeing signs of human settlement off the rivers. Steward (1949: 661) gave a density of only about 0.2 per square kilometer for the "marginal" (nonagricultural) tribes of Amazonia. Some seminomadic agriculturalists must have had a density of at least double that, but vast areas seem to have been virtually uninhabited. I suggest using Steward's average density of only 0.2 persons per square kilometer, and I know of no evidence to indicate a greater overall density; however, even this density will add up to 1,260,000 Indians (including Peru and Bolivia) in the enormous lowland forest habitat of Amazonia. Undoubtedly, areas of very wet forest with little or no dry season, where soils are extremely leached and burning to prepare for shifting cultivation is difficult, had a significantly lower density than the regions with a dry season. There are also large permanently swampy areas which would have had a very low population density. Furthermore, regardless of the average density, the greatest concentrations of aboriginal people in the lowland forest habitat were still near minor waterways.

One area of the lowland forest that did have a population density substantially higher than 0.2 persons per square kilometer was the Santa Cruz region of eastern Bolivia. Here climatic conditions are intermediate between those of the wet lowlands of the Amazon Basin and the dry Gran Chaco, which was occupied mostly by nomadic tribes. As result of a long dry season, soils are not severely leached around Santa Cruz, and yet there is still enough rainfall to support shifting cultivation without irrigation. Part of this region of roughly 50,000 square kilometers was occupied by Chiquitos tribes and part by the Chiriguano. Numerous early reports by explorers and the first settlers spoke of large numbers of Indians in the area (see Vázquez-Machicado, 1957). Steward (1949: 662) gave a figure of 48,000 for the Chiriguano, for a density of 0.60 per square kilometer, on the basis of estimates made well after initial contact. The region must have had a density at least equal to that of the upland forest (1.2 per km²) and possibly equal to that of Mojos (2.0 per km²); applying the 3.5 to 1 depopulation ratio, derived earlier, to Steward's Chiriguano density gives a density of 2.1. I suggest using the average of the three figures of 1.8 per square kilometer.

SUMMARY OF HABITAT DENSITIES AT TIME OF CONTACT

1. Floodplain
   Large floodplains: 28.0 per square kilometer.
   Average: 14.6 per square kilometer.
   Upper courses of lowland forest rivers: between 1.2 and 14.6 per square
     kilometer.
2. Brazilian Coast
   Central coast (south of the Amazon): 9.5 per square kilometer.
   Mangrove coasts (north of the Amazon): probably considerably less than
     9.5 per square kilometer.
3. Lowland Savanna
   Llanos de Mojos: 2.0 per square kilometer.
   Other lowland savannas: 1.3 per square kilometer.
4. Upland Forest
   Drier upland forest of the eastern Andes: 1.2 per square kilometer.
   Superhumid upland forest of the eastern Andes: 0.1 or less per square
     kilometer.
   Upland forest of Guiana Highlands and Brazilian Highlands: 0.5 or possibly
     less per square kilometer.
5. Upland Savanna: 0.5 per square kilometer.
6. Lowland Forest
   Most of Amazon Basin: 0.2 per square kilometer.
   Santa Cruz region, Bolivia: 1.8 per square kilometer.
7. Uninhabitable: less than 0.1 per square kilometer.

The largest uninhabitable or very sparsely settled areas were in the super-humid portions of the upland forest. There are also scattered areas within the other habitats, which are excessively steep, or rocky, or poorly drained, and such areas have been taken into account in determining the average densities above.

I consider these densities to be conservative or minimum estimates of potential population. All are subject to considerable modification pending the availability of more precise representative densities for different habitats, such as the density carefully derived for the Yaruro by Leeds (1961) and that which I established for the present Campa (Denevan, 1971).

ESTIMATED ABORIGINAL POPULATION OF EASTERN PERU AND NORTHEASTERN BOLIVIA BASED ON HABITAT DENSITIES

Using the average densities above, a rough aboriginal population can be derived for greater Amazonia if the areas of the different habitats are known. Reliable habitat measurements are not available except for Peru, which has been mapped according to the Holdridge Natural Life Zone Classification (Tosi, 1960). This study provides total areas and descriptions for some 30 life zones in Peru, over half occurring in the humid tropics. These zones can be combined to coincide with the habitats discussed above, of which four occur in Peru (upland forest, superhumid upland forest, lowland forest, and floodplain). The floodplain is not a specific life zone, and no reliable area figures are available, so the Amazonian average of 2 percent will be used here. There are also some scattered areas of both upland and lowland savanna in eastern Peru, but they are so small that they are best combined with other habitats.

For eastern Peru, the aboriginal population of 477,940 and density of 0.61 per square kilometer (Table 7.1) compares with a 1965 Indian population of 126,000 (based on Summer Institute of Linguistics and other estimates), [12] and a 1960 total population of 1,487,632 and density of 1.8 per square kilometer (Peru, 1962). The present distribution pattern is roughly similar to the aboriginal one; however, a much higher percentage of the total is now located in the lower upland forest, which has had considerable colonization since World War II. This zone has relatively good soils compared with the lowland forest, but equally or more important are road connections to the sierra and a consequent semicommercial rather than subsistence basis of settlement. Furthermore, the population is not dependent on game and fish for meat protein, as is still much of the lowland forest and riverine population. Thus, the aboriginal ecological zonation patterns have been partly broken down by changes in food availability and technology.

For Bolivia, reliable area statistics for different habitats are not yet available; the rough estimates in Table 7.2 are based on topographic maps, air photo mosaics, and my own field work. The area covered is that north of the Gran Chaco, using the Santa Cruz-Corumbá Railroad as the southern limit. The greater average density for northeastern Bolivia (1.06 per km^2) compared with eastern Peru (0.61 per km^2) is the result of the large lowland forest which dominates eastern Peru. The present Indian population of northeastern Bolivia north of the Chaco is about 40,000 (Key, 1967: 127–28), and the total population of that area is only about 600,000 (Bolivia, 1964), for a density of 0.87 per square kilometer, both less than the figures suggested for

12. Varese (1972: 413) gives a much larger total of 226,400.

Table 7.1
Habitat Areas and Aboriginal Population Estimates
for Eastern Peru

Habitat	Area in km²	Density per km²	Population
Floodplain	11,700	14.6	170,820
Upland forest	157,000	1.2	188,400
Lowland forest	573,100	0.2	114,620
Superhumid upland forest	41,000	0.1	4,100
Totals	782,800	0.61	477,940

aboriginal times. Furthermore, the distribution pattern is significantly different from that of pre-Columbian times, even more so than in Peru. First, a much greater proportion of the population is now in the upland forest (*yungas*), as is also true in Peru. Second, an even greater percentage of the total population is now situated in the Santa Cruz region owing to good surface transportation outlets and modern agricultural technology. And third, there is a much smaller population today in the Llanos de Mojos, about 100,000 compared to an estimated 350,000 contact population, the difference being partly due to a shift from intensive aboriginal agricultural settlement to extensive ranching with little agriculture.

The total estimated aboriginal population for eastern Peru and northeastern Bolivia is 1,211,000 persons in an area of 1,472,800 square kilometers for an average density of 0.81 per square kilometer. The 1960 population was about 2,100,000 and has been increasing steadily; however, in some areas

Table 7.2
Habitat Areas and Aboriginal Population Estimates
for Northeastern Bolivia

Habitat	Area in km²	Density per km²	Population
Floodplain	7,400	14.6	108,040
Lowland savanna (mainly Mojos)	195,000	2.0	390,000
Santa Cruz area	50,000	1.8	90,000
Upland forest	59,000	1.2	70,800
Lowland forest	363,600	0.2	72,720
Superhumid upland forest	15,000	0.1	1,500
Totals	690,000	1.06	733,060

such as Mojos the aboriginal population was much greater than the present population. Steward's (1949: 662–63) aboriginal total for the same area was only 377,500 persons for a density of 0.26 per square kilometer.

ESTIMATED ABORIGINAL POPULATION FOR GREATER AMAZONIA

I have thus far concentrated on arriving at an aboriginal population for the upper Amazon region of eastern Peru and northeastern Bolivia, for which I have reliable area data on the various habitats as well as confidence in the estimated habitat densities. Table 7.3 is an attempt to utilize the same method and habitat densities in order to derive a total potential aboriginal population for greater Amazonia (see note 1). The area figures are only rough approximations, and the habitat densities are subject to greater error than in Peru-Bolivia because of greater variation in both habitat and subsistence patterns. Consequently, the populations derived are very tentative, but they will serve as a starting point for critical discussion until better information is available. The principal area measurements and 1960 populations and densities are derived from Cole's (1965: 49) figures, which, being based on vegetation types, are practical for the purposes of Table 7.3. Cole related population to vegetation in South America by comparing vegetation maps and population statistics for civil divisions.

The total estimated aboriginal, or initial contact, population for greater Amazonia in Table 7.3 is 6,800,000, an increase of 1,050,000 over my original total (Denevan, 1970a) of 5,750,000, a result mainly of increasing the average density for the floodplains from 5.3 to 14.6 per square kilometer. The total for the Amazon Basin alone is almost 5,000,000. The total for the Amazon River floodplain alone is 901,600, using Camargo's (1958: 17) area of 64,400 square kilometers and considering only half of it inhabitable, with a density of 28.0 per square kilometer.

The totals for greater Amazonia and for the Amazon Basin are larger than most previous estimates for Amazonia, and both even exceed the very conservative total for all of South America given by Kroeber (1939: 166) of 4,000,000. Granted that this early estimate for South America was far too low (Dobyns, 1966: 415, suggests 48,750,000), the total of 6,800,000 for greater Amazonia may still seem unreasonably large; however, one should keep in mind that the total area involved is enormous, nearly 10,000,000 square kilometers, over half the entire area of South America. Also, the total is far below the present steadily growing but still very sparse population of greater Amazonia. The overall density of 0.7 per square kilometer (1.81 per mi^2) is well above Steward and Faron's (1959: 53) density of 0.6 per square

Table 7.3
Habitat Areas and Aboriginal Population Estimates for Greater Amazonia

Habitat or Region	Area in km²	1960 Population and Density per km²	Estimated Aboriginal Density per km²	Aboriginal Population
Amazonia	(6,641,000[a])	9,200,000[b] (1.4)		
Eastern Peru and northeastern Bolivia	1,472,800[c]		0.8	1,211,000
Interior Amazonia	(5,140,700[d])			
Interior Floodplains	102,814[e]		14.6	1,501,084
Interior lowland forest	5,037,886[f]		0.2	1,007,577
Central Brazilian coast	105,000[g]		9.5	997,500
Dry northeast Brazil including coast	(500,000)	6,500,000 (13.0)		
Dry northeast Brazil minus coast	477,500[h]		0.5[i]	238,750
Brazilian central savannas	2,178,000	3,900,000 (1.8)	0.5	1,089,000
Colombian and Venezuelan (Orinoco) Llanos	395,000	1,300,000 (3.3)	1.3	513,500
Increment for unmeasured areas with higher densities than credited above				241,589[j]
Totals	9,769,000[k]	20,900,000[l] (2.14)	0.7	6,800,000

Sources: Areas and 1960 population and density figures are from Cole (1965: 49), unless otherwise indicated. Estimates of aboriginal density are from this chapter.

[a]Includes the north coast of Brazil (Amazon to the dry northeast). The total area for Amazonia is from Cole (1965: 49) and is somewhat higher than other figures for the Amazon Basin: 5,916,000 square kilometers given by Sternberg (1975: 15), 6,133,000 square kilometers by Oltman et al. (1964: 1); 6,288,000 square kilometers by Batista (1963); and 6,430,000 square kilometers by Leandro Tocantins (1974: 22). The *Encyclopaedia Britannica* (1974: 1:653), however, gives 7,050,000 square kilometers. The Cole figure does not include the central Brazilian savannas that fall within the Amazon drainage basin, but does include areas within the southern Orinoco drainage.

Table 7.3, *continued*

[b]The six states of northern Brazil (Acre, Amapá, Amazonas, Pará, Rondônia, Roraima) contained 2,601,519 people in 1960; there were less than 3,000,000 in the upper Amazon; and the remainder were in the humid portions of the northeast plus the states of Goiás, Minas Gerais, and Mato Grosso. Population distribution by vegetation categories is not available for 1970, but some idea of population change for Amazonia from 1960 to 1970 is indicated by the fact that the six northern states of Brazil increased in numbers by 40.3 percent, to 3,650,750 (Saunders, 1974: 163, 179).

[c]See Tables 7.1 and 7.2.

[d]Cole's Amazonia minus eastern Peru, northeastern Bolivia, and an estimated 27,500 square kilometers of coast between the Amazon and the dry northeast. The area includes the Guianas and the lowlands of Colombia and Venezuela south of the Orinoco Llanos.

[e]Two percent of interior Amazonia.

[f]Ninety-eight percent of interior Amazonia. Includes some small savannas.

[g]The coastal region dominated by the Tupinamba, from the Amazon nearly to Rio de Janeiro. The size of the area is based on that given by Steward (1949: 662) of 315,000 square kilometers; however, for applying the density of 9.5 per square kilometer, the depth inland has been reduced from Steward's 75 kilometers to only 25 kilometers for a total area of only 105,000 square kilometers.

[h]The coastal portion that has been subtracted from northeast Brazil is about 900 kilometers long and 25 kilometers deep for a total of 22,500 square kilometers.

[i]The *caatinga* zone which dominates dry northeast Brazil possibly had a higher aboriginal density than the upland savannas; however, for lack of reliable population data the upland savanna density of 0.5 persons per square kilometer is used. The subsistence patterns in the two habitats were similar.

[j]Owing to the lack of either good area or population information, the data in Table 7.3 do not take into consideration the probably higher than indicated population densities for the lowland savannas of Brazil, the Atlantic coast north of the Amazon, the eastern and southern Andean upland forest from Ecuador to Venezuela, the upland forest of the Guiana Highlands and the eastern Brazilian Highlands, the floodplain areas within both the upland and lowland savannas (except Bolivia), and the possibly higher than indicated densities of the dry northeast of Brazil and the Venezuelan-Colombian Llanos. The lowland savannas of Brazil, mainly in the Pantanal of western Mato Grosso and on Marajó Island, total about 130,000 square kilometers, which would result in 104,000 more people if based on a 1.3 per square kilometer density rather than on a density of 0.5. The upland forest of the northern Andes totals at least 100,000 square kilometers, which would result in another 100,000 people if based on a density of 1.2 per square kilometer rather than 0.2. I have added 37,589 more persons to round off the overall total.

[k]This total does not include the regional totals in parentheses.

[l]Does not include the southern half of the central Brazilian coast.

mile (0.23 per km^2) for the tropical forests of interior South America; however, 0.7 per square kilometer does not seem extreme when compared with better substantiated densities of other difficult habitats in the New World with extensive, rather than intensive, aboriginal economies, such as the deserts of Baja California. Dobyns (1966: 400, 404–5) examines previously estimated densities by Aschmann, Meigs, and Cook for all or part of Baja California, which range from 1.12 per square mile (0.43 per km^2) to 1.87 (1.56 plus or minus 0.31) per square mile (0.72 per km^2), and concludes that all are conservative since they are based on documentary historical evidence dating from the period after population decline began. If Dobyns is correct for Baja California, then an average density of 0.7 per square kilometer for greater Amazonia is not unreasonable, considering the nature of the aboriginal cultural ecology of Amazonia.

An independent check on the results obtained by the densities used here is provided by Sweet (1969: 156–59), who carefully examined the documentary evidence for Indian populations in the Jesuit mission province of Mainas in western Amazonia (Ecuador-Peru), mainly in the seventeenth century. For an area of about 500,000 square kilometers, he estimated an aboriginal population of between 187,000 and 258,000. By using the methods of this chapter, a total of 244,000 is obtained for the same area.

Finally, for those who would argue for only 1,000,000 to 2,000,000 Indians in either greater Amazonia or the Amazon Basin, it should be pointed out that there are close to 500,000 Indians still alive in greater Amazonia today, despite drastic reductions in numbers for *many* tribes and complete extinction for *most* tribes. The total of 500,000 is the author's estimate of current Indians based mainly on the country and tribal totals in Dostal (1972: 385), who gives a range of 704,050 to 960,650 for the lowland Indian population of South America. This includes areas outside greater Amazonia and some totals for the upper Amazon that are probably too high. For the Brazilian Amazon, Ribeiro (1967: 115) estimated 68,100 to 99,700 in 1959, and recent new discoveries of Indian groups suggest that 100,000 may be reasonable.

CONCLUSIONS

On the basis of the average densities derived for the different ecological or habitat regions, a total aboriginal population of 1,211,000 is obtained for eastern Peru and northeastern Bolivia, and a more tentative total of 6,800,000 is obtained for greater Amazonia. This total approximates Dobyns' (1966: 415) figure of 6,000,000 for all of tropical South America—a larger area. I believe that most of my estimates of aboriginal habitat densities are either reasonable or conservative. The densities here are not indicative of carrying capacity, the number of people who can be supported in a given environment under a given system of technology, but rather are usually well below carrying capacity.

I have suggested a habitat-density method for estimating the aboriginal populations, or at least potential populations, for large areas with diverse habitats for which there are few documentary data. Actually, the same or similar principle has been used by others: a known density for a group in a physical or cultural region is extended to the entire region for which there are not significant differences in resource or subsistence patterns. Very often, however, there are significant differences, and, as result, the habitat density system will not work too well. The method is especially applicable to Amazonia because of the emphasis by tropical forest cultures on starchy tubers and the consequent importance of protein obtained from unevenly distributed game and fish. Subsistence patterns and population densities do seem to have been more uniform within the major habitats of Amazonia than in other large regions of the New World. The factors responsible are not entirely clear, but they were probably as much cultural as environmental.

There are very few "hard" data for determining the aboriginal population of Amazonia, and consequently any figure arrived at by whatever method is only an educated guess. The habitat density method used in this chapter does, at least, provide a systematic and consistent way of estimating aboriginal populations. The average densities are only tentative figures, based on a few sample densities, but I do believe that the relative sequence of habitat densities is correct and that the proportional differences are about right. The accuracy of the densities and populations derived are dependent on the accuracy of the measurement of the habitat areas, on the definition of habitats that are significantly different ecologically, on the availability and reliability of representative aboriginal population density data, and on the reliability of the depopulation ratios used for projecting known population densities back to contact times. Although the habitat density method of estimating aboriginal populations has its limitations, the degree of error can be minimized by careful interpretation of what relevant information does exist.

ADDENDUM

An important consideration for estimating Amazonian populations has come to my attention from a recent statement by Thomas P. Myers ("Defended Territories and No-man's-lands," *American Anthropologist*, 78:354–55 [June

1976]). This is what might be termed the "buffer effect." Myers finds evidence that because of hostility many Amazon tribes were separated from one another by a no-man's-land of unoccupied territory that in some instances was almost as large as the territory occupied. Of course, not all neighboring tribes were hostile, and for low-density, seminomadic interflueve tribes moving about in large territories, buffer zones may have been relatively small or even utilized periodically for hunting. This is a topic badly in need of further research, both historical and ethnographic. If an overall rough reduction of 25 percent is made in the total of 6,800,000 obtained in Table 7.3, the result would be 5,100,000 which I believe is a reasonable buffer adjustment until the situation is better understood.

PART V North America

"The number of savages generally does not increase in North America.
Those living near the Europeans steadily diminish in numbers and strength"
(Benjamin Franklin, in Labaree, 1969: 13:351).

INTRODUCTION

With the major exception of California, North America has not been a focus of research and debate on the size of aboriginal populations, in contrast to Mexico and other regions in Latin America. The more frequently cited totals for North America are comparatively low and have infrequently been challenged. One assumption has been that the resource base in North America was very "limiting" in terms of native subsistence technology. This argument is not justified in view of known dense populations in even more marginal habitats in Latin America. Certainly a major problem is that most of the interior of North America was not explored, occupied, and adequately described until long after the first contacts on the East Coast and in the Southeast and Southwest. Generally well over a century passed, during which time unknown population declines occurred due to introduced disease which must have spread far beyond the few points of European activity, as well as due to other indirect effects such as migration of tribes away from the same points. The dates taken in the various studies for "aboriginal times" are usually much too late. For the Mississippi Basin, for example, we have archaeological evidence for substantial Indian populations at various times in prehistory but virtually no documentary evidence of the demographic situation in the sixteenth century.

Ironically, some scholars have maintained that the density of nonfarming Indians of the Pacific Coast was greater than for most of the farming areas in the Southeast, Midwest, and East. This is dramatically shown in the maps of Kroeber (1939) and more recently Driver (1969: Map 6). Driver (1969: 64) believes that where there was agriculture in the East and Midwest, it generally provided no more than half the total diet, and Kroeber (1939: 150) said we

235

must "think of the East as agricultural indeed, but as inhabited by agricultural hunters, not by farmers." These claims seem questionable, especially considering that some of the tribes in tropical America, while spending a large portion of their subsistence time hunting and/or fishing, still get most of their food from agriculture.

Mooney (1928) was the first modern scholar[1] to attempt a tribe-by-tribe estimate for North America, arriving at a total of 1,152,950 (including Greenland). Most other estimates have used Mooney as a point of departure. Kroeber (1939: 143, 166) reduced the total to 1,000,880 and, on the basis of his own lower figure for California, assumed that 900,000 was a more likely figure; Willcox (1931) reduced the total to 1,002,000; Rosenblat (1954: 1:102) to 1,000,000. A total of 1,000,000 for the United States and Canada would give a density of only about one person per 18 square kilometers. Sapper (1924) gave 2,500,000 to 3,500,000, W. C. MacLeod (1928: 16) 3,000,000; and Driver (1969: 63) in his comprehensive study of North American Indians is willing to raise the total to 3,500,000.[2] There isn't much to judge by, and the result has been conservatism. Dobyns (1966: 415) is one of the few to suggest a high total: 9,800,000. This figure receives support from historian Wilbur Jacobs (1972: 136, 1974: 128).

Kroeber (1939) reviewed Mooney's tribal estimates, adjusted them slightly on the basis of his own research, added new material particularly on California, and then calculated and mapped cultural-area densities. The result is essentially Mooney's total, reduced mainly for California. In addition, Kroeber suggested 3,000,000 for high-culture Mexico based on densities north of the Rio Grande, plus another 3,000,000 thrown in for the Andes on the assumption of a similarity with Mexico, thus arriving at most of his hemispheric total of 8,400,000. In other words, his total for the entire hemisphere is an extension of Mooney and little more. The dates for Mooney's various tribal and regional figures are long after initial White contacts (1650 for Gulf states, 1780 for Northern Plains, etc.). However, Kroeber's area densities, if considered relative rather than absolute, are useful for comparative purposes

1. Earlier, Morse (1822: 361–75) provided an incomplete tribe-by-tribe listing of populations, totaling 471,136; and Schoolcraft (1851–57: 3:553–72) reported government agents in contact with 313,264 Indians in 1857. A listing of populations for many tribes in the eighteenth century appears in Greene and Harrington (1932: 194–206).

2. Driver obtains a figure of 2,500,000 for the United States except for Alaska and Hawaii by following Dobyns' (1966) depopulation method but using a nadir of 250,000 for 1890 (Dobyns uses 332,000 for 1930) and a zenith-to-nadir depopulation factor of 10 to 1 (Dobyns uses 20 or 25 to 1; also see Driver, 1968). For Canada, Alaska, and Greenland, Driver uses a factor of only 5 to get an aboriginal population of 1,000,000. The total of 3,500,000 north of Mexico is a substantial increase from the estimate of 2,000,000 in the original edition of Driver's book (1961: 35).

and for pointing up apparent inconsistencies that require reconciliation. For example, his assumption of consistently higher shoreline densities[3] than in the interior, on the basis of rich and stable marine resources, needs further testing. For further discussion of Kroeber, see especially Dobyns (1966), Jennings (1975: 15–31), and Borah in this volume.

Mooney's tribal estimates were published only as a summary compiled after his death by Swanton (Mooney, 1928). The sources and reasons for his estimates were for the most part never published, and his research notes on file at the Smithsonian Institution were seldom examined by scholars. Kroeber, Rosenblat, and others accepted Mooney's figures on the basis of his reputation as a conscientious scholar who had researched the subject over many years: "It is because Mooney was experienced in balancing and comparing, within his area, that most anthropologists will feel him a safer authority . . ." (Kroeber, 1939: 181).[4]

In Chapter 8, Douglas Ubelaker goes to Mooney's notes at the Smithsonian and reconstructs, as well as possible, Mooney's derivation of populations, tribe-by-tribe, for 100 tribes or groups of tribes (plus 58 more in the Columbia region, listed in Table 8.1). This documentation should be a basic research aid for scholars working on North American Indian populations. A major result of Ubelaker's work is the indication that the totals in Mooney's notes are higher for many tribes than are those in his published list.[5] Also, the notes confirm the late dates of many of the tribal estimates and the fact that Mooney was well aware that original contact populations were probably substantially larger.

Elsewhere, Ubelaker (1976) examines recent recalculations of Indian populations in available manuscripts for the forthcoming *Handbook of North American Indians.*[6] For 45 tribes covered by Mooney, the magnitude of increase in the new studies is 88 percent, which if projected for Mooney's 311 tribes would give a total of 2,171,125 (compared to Mooney's 1,152,950).

We know more about the Indian population of California than of the rest

---

3. Since marine-oriented coastal tribes exploit large, difficult-to-measure areas of ocean for most or much of their food, the number of people per mile or kilometer of shoreline is a more useful way of measuring maritime densities than persons per square mile or per square kilometer. Kroeber therefore determined shoreline densities. Obviously, it is difficult to compare such linear densities with area densities.

4. But Kroeber (1939: 131) did believe that "the best of Mooney's estimates can hardly pretend to be nearer than by 10 per cent to the probable truth, and some may be 50 per cent or more from it."

5. Both Swanton and Kroeber thought that "Mooney's figures are probably mostly too high rather than too low, so far as they are in error. . . . Mooney himself was apparently reducing estimates as his work progressed" (Kroeber, 1939: 132).

6. In preparation, Smithsonian Institution, William C. Sturtevant, editor.

of North America, thanks to considerable field and archival research by Berkeley scholars. Interpretations of the data vary considerably, however, ranging from 133,000 by Kroeber (1925: 883) to 310,000 by S. F. Cook (1976a: 43), whereas Baumhoff (1963: 226) believes the total for the state could not have been less than 350,000. The initial study was by Merriam (1905), who obtained 260,000 mainly by projecting the densities of small, documented regions to larger, comparable regions.

Cook originally (1943) varied little from Kroeber on the California population. He subsequently researched the San Joaquin Valley (1955b), the North Coast (1956), and Alameda and Contra Costa counties (1957), making use of various head counts, the number of houses in an area, baptismal records, and the extension of the average density for a count of part of an area to the full area. In 1964 he suggested a total of 275,000. More recent research on the mission areas and the Sacramento Valley, with additional data from Brown (1967) on the Santa Barbara Channel, led Cook (1976a: 43) to a new total of 310,000 for the state. In his 1964 article Cook provides a summary of the evidence and of his own work, his methodology, and the results. Baumhoff (1963) gives a more detailed review of previous estimates and a favorable evaluation of Cook's estimates in comparison with Kroeber's.

Baumhoff's 1963 monograph, *Ecological Determinants of Aboriginal California Populations*, is particularly interesting because of its ecological methodology (also see his 1958 Athabascan paper). Focusing on a nonagricultural group, the hunting-fishing-gathering Indians of California, he attempted to relate tribal differences in population densities to regional variations in the amounts of the major wild food resources—the staples of acorns, large game animals, and fish. The tribal densities are based on estimates by Cook and by Baumhoff, which were derived from documentary sources. Indices are determined for each of the three resources for each of 28 tribes, and these indices are then plotted against the tribal populations to determine relationships.

For the Lower Kalamath culture region, population density usually shows a relationship only with the fish resource. For poor tribes, however, there is a relationship with the acorn and game resources. Also, there is a population level beyond which a greater fish resource does not result in a greater population, due to unclear factors. For the North Coast Range, in contrast, the population densities show a close relationship to the acorn, especially, and to game resources, but little to fish. Actual population size seems to have been held in check by resource availability. For the San Joaquin Valley, the original resource valuation showed no relation to population. The data were revalued, as were Cook's population figures, and the results suggested that the population density did vary with the fish resource.

In working out the resource indices, some arbitrary decisions were made, the quantity ratings of resources are rough, and other important wild resources such as waterfowl are not considered. Nevertheless, the technique does demonstrate a relationship between population and availability of wild food resources and might profitably be attempted for other aboriginal cultural areas in the New World.[7]

Using the tribal densities in his Summary Table, which are mainly based on data from the early to mid-nineteenth century, Baumhoff determined overall regional densities, adjusted them on the basis of what is known about the tribes without documented populations, and then obtained regional average densities, to arrive at a total of 248,300 for the Lower Kalamath, North Coast Range, and San Joaquin Valley regions. Roughly estimating for the rest of California, his total comes to 350,000. As Baumhoff points out, if this total is fairly correct, then of the 1,000,000 or so North American Indians estimated by Mooney, Willcox, Kroeber, and Rosenblat, over one-third were in California, and the California densities were well above those of the more socially complex and agriculturally sophisticated tribes of the Southwest and Southeast. An unusually high density for California could be attributed to rich wildlife resources, but an extreme disparity from most of the other regions of the United States is not likely. Baumhoff (1963: 227) also suggests that an agricultural economy failed to diffuse from the Southwest to California because it "would have been less productive than the native economy in the initial stages of introduction."

For the Southwest, discussion has concentrated on the Pueblo and related irrigation farmers, and the reader should refer to Kroeber (1939: 151–53) and Dobyns (1966: 402) for differing interpretations; also see Spicer (1962). Dobyns (1963a) also examined one small region in Arizona, the Santa Cruz River Valley, to determine the causes and extent of the extinction there of Northern Pima Indians. Apache raiding was a factor, but far more important were diseases. To estimate the Northern Pima population, Dobyns applied an infrequently used technique. He determined the number of villages (12) and their average size (200), where known from documentary evidence, to get a total of 2,400 for the year 1700. By 1800 there were less than 100 survivors, all in one mission village, giving a 100-year depopulation ratio of 24 to 1. In most New World regions, however, the number of settlements and average size are not known for a specific date in aboriginal times. For Texas, Ewers (1973) has raised Mooney's total from 42,000 to 50,000.

Jennings (1975: 15–31) recently examined the evidence for northeastern North America and is severely critical of the estimates of Mooney and Kroeber. Jennings, for his part, reviews some of the evidence for larger populations in the East, with particular attention to the lower New England

7. For an ecological approach making use of shell middens in California see Ascher (1959) and Glassow (1967).

tribes. He suggests a decline of the Narraganset from between 72,000 and 90,000 in 1600 to between 8,600 and 10,750 in 1674, whereas Mooney allowed for only 25,000 in all of New England in 1600. S. F. Cook (1973a), returning to research on North American. aboriginal demography, reviewed the history of disease in New England in the seventeenth century, especially the plague (probably bubonic or pneumonic) of 1616–1619 and the smallpox epidemic of 1633–1634. Using Mooney's (1928) tribal population estimates (which he believed to be too low), Cook found evidence for an 80 percent reduction in Indian populations by the end of the first century of European settlement. In another study, Cook (1973b) showed that of the Indian depopulation of New England from 36,000 in 1620 to virtually none in 1750, about 28.5 percent can be attributed to warfare.[8] For the Virginia Algonquians, Feest (1973) raised Mooney's total of 9,000 to 14,600 for the early seventeenth century (also see R. Turner, 1973; and Mook, 1944).

While the tendency of recent work is to raise tribal estimates for North America, one scholar, Heidenreich (1973: 91–106), has called for a reduction in the generally accepted figure for the Huron of 30,000 (based mainly on Champlain) in the early 1600s (although Mooney gave only 10,000). Heidenreich, using three different methods of estimation, obtained a range from 14,000 to 33,000 with an average of 20,200. For all the tribes of the Upper Great Lakes region Quimby (1960: 108–9) estimated 100,000 for about the year 1600.

For Canada and the Arctic regions of North America there is little information. Kroeber estimated very low densities for immense areas, with the largest populations located on the coasts. The situation is not unlike that for Amazonia, and resource evaluation may be the best means of estimating such Indian populations. H. P. Thompson (1966) applied a resource-potential method to the Chipewyan of central Canada. He estimated the "equilibrium population" (essentially the carrying capacity under a given technology, area, and resource base) by determining the equilibrium number of caribou, the dominant food resource, under aboriginal conditions. The result is a mean population of 6,426 persons for about 1770, which is well over Mooney's (1928: 26) estimate, based on fragmentary documentary evidence, of 3,500 (Chipewyan plus Caribou-eaters) for the year 1670, although Thompson claims "fair agreement" between the two. Thompson's figure would be modified upward somewhat if other resources were also considered. And, of course, it is speculation to assume that an equilibrium population had been

8. In a posthumously published survey of New England, Cook gave a total Indian population of 72,000: S. F. Cook, *The Indian Population of New England in the Seventeenth Century,* University of California Publications in Anthropology, Vol. 12 (University of California Press: Berkeley, 1976), p. 84.

reached. Other criticisms, some serious, are raised in the comments following the article, with claims that Thompson's figure is both too high and too low. Nevertheless, the method is a potentially useful one, but it is only as accurate as the precision of the numerical variables used in the calculation.

The Eskimo population of the coasts of Labrador and Ungava Bay in 1773 has recently been estimated from documentary material by Taylor (1968, 1975). Taylor's total of 2,630 is expressed in varying shoreline densities between two and ten per mile, the differences reflecting differences in resource adaptation.

For other regions and tribes of North America one should consult Mooney (1928) and Ubelaker (Chapter 8, below), Kroeber (1934, 1939), the discussions by Dobyns (1966; also 1976), and the forthcoming *Handbook of North American Indians*. There are surprisingly few serious studies. Since 1934 the "authority" of Kroeber has impeded serious consideration of North American aboriginal populations. Clearly it is time for a reconsideration, and the opportunities for such research would appear to be great.

CHAPTER 8 **The Sources and Methodology**

for Mooney's Estimates

of North American Indian Populations

Douglas H. Ubelaker

In 1910, James Mooney of the Bureau of American Ethnology, Smithsonian Institution, published the first, carefully calculated estimate of the aboriginal population in America north of Mexico at the time of initial European contact. This short article, published in the *Handbook of American Indians North of Mexico* (Mooney, 1910a), presented Mooney's estimate of 1,150,000 along with a brief discussion of the decline in the population after European contact and some of the factors involved in that decline. Following this article, Mooney continued his research on aboriginal population, not only refining his original estimates for the time of European contact, but also gathering information on population numbers for various periods after contact. This latter effort was designed to trace in detail the rate of population decline (or increase in some groups) and to identify the influencing factors. His reports to the Bureau of American Ethnology (on file in the National Anthropological Archives, Smithsonian Institution) indicate that he planned

My gratitude goes to the following Smithsonian colleagues: John C. Ewers, Adrian Heidenreich, William Sturtevant, and Waldo and Mildred Wedel of the Department of Anthropology for their encouragement and helpful suggestions; Herman Viola and his staff of the National Anthropological Archives for making the Mooney notes available and for providing a congenial atmosphere for their examination; and Jack Marquardt, Janette Saquet, and B. J. Swartz of the Smithsonian Institution libraries for their efficient assistance in locating primary sources.

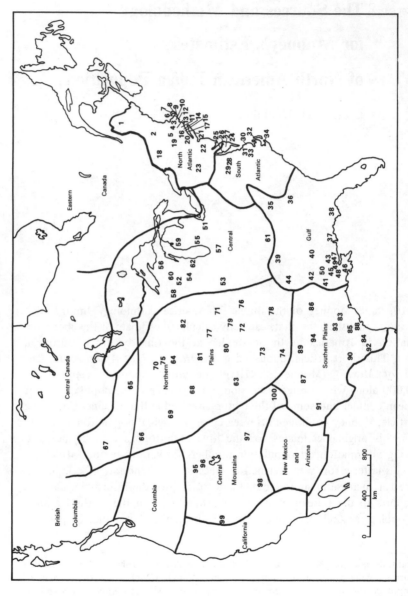

Map 8.1. Indian Tribes of North America. Approximate locations of tribal areas at about the time of initial European settlement.

Cartographic Laboratory UW-Madison

244

Map 8.1. Key to List of Tribes

Abnaki, including Passamaquoddy (North Atlantic) **1**
Acolapissa, including Tangipahoa (Gulf) **47**
Akokisa (Southern Plains) **83**
Apalachee (Gulf) **38**
Aranama (Southern Plains) **84**
Arapaho (Northern Plains) **63**
Arikara (Northern Plains) **64**
Arkansa or Quapaw (Gulf) **44**
Assiniboin (Northern Plains) **65**
Atsina (Northern Plains) **66**
Bannock (Central Mountains) **95**
Bayogoula, Mugulasha, and Quinipissa (Gulf) **48**
Bear River and Pamptico (South Atlantic) **33**
Bidai (Southern Plains) **85**
Biloxi, Pascagoula, and Moctobi (Gulf) **43**
Blackfoot (Northern Plains) **67**
Caddo, including Hasinai (Southern Plains) **86**
Canarsee and Montauk (North Atlantic) **21**
Chawasha, Washa, and Opelousa (Gulf) **49**
Cherokee (Gulf) **35**
Cheyenne (Northern Plains) **68**
Chickasaw (Gulf) **39**
Chitimacha (Gulf) **46**
Choctaw (Gulf) **40**
Chowanoc (South Atlantic) **31**
Coahuiltecan Tribes (Southern Plains) **92**

Comanche (Southern Plains) **87**
Conestoga (North Atlantic) **23**
Conoy or Piscataway, and Patuxent (South Atlantic) **24**
Coree and Neus (South Atlantic) **34**
Creek Confederacy, Seminole (Gulf) **36**
Crow (Northern Plains) **69**
Delaware and Munsee (North Atlantic) **22**
Erie (Central) **51**
Fox (Central) **52**
Gosiute, Pahvant, and Ute (Central Mountains) **97**
Hasinai and Caddo (Southern Plains) **86**
Hidatsa (Northern Plains) **70**
Houma (Gulf) **45**
Illinois Confederates (Central) **53**
Iowa (Northern Plains) **71**
Iroquois Confederacy (North Atlantic) **18**
Jicarilla (Central Mountains) **100**
Kansa (Northern Plains) **72**
Karankawa (Southern Plains) **88**
Kichai (Southern Plains) **89**
Kickapoo (Central) **54**
Kiowa (Northern Plains) **73**
Kiowa-Apache (Northern Plains) **74**
Koroa, Tunica, Yazoo, and Ofogoula (Gulf) **42**
Lipan (Southern Plains) **90**
Machapunga (South Atlantic) **32**
Mahican (North Atlantic) **19**

Manahoac Confederacy, Monacan Confederacy, Nottoway, Occaneechi, and Meherrin (South Atlantic) **29**
Mandan (Northern Plains) **75**
Marthas Vineyard (North Atlantic) **9**
Mascouten (Central) **55**
Massachuset (North Atlantic) **3**
Meherrin, Nottoway, Occaneechi, Monacan Confederacy, and Manahoac Confederacy (South Atlantic) **29**
Menomini (Central) **56**
Mescalero (Southern Plains) **91**
Miami, including Wea and Piankashaw (Central) **57**
Missouri (Northern Plains) **76**
Mobile and Tohome (Gulf) **37**
Moctobi, Biloxi, and Pascagoula (Gulf) **43**
Mohegan and Pequot (North Atlantic) **11**
Monacan Confederacy, Manahoac Confederacy, Nottoway, Occaneechi, and Meherrin (South Atlantic) **29**
Montauk and Canarsee (North Atlantic) **21**
Mugulasha, Bayogoula, and Quinipissa (Gulf) **48**
Munsee and Delaware (North Atlantic) **22**
Nanticoke (South Atlantic) **26**
Nantucket (North Atlantic) **8**
Narraganset and Eastern Niantic (North Atlantic) **10**

(continued on following page)

Map 8.1. Key to List of Tribes, *continued*

Natchez (Gulf) 41
Nauset (North Atlantic) 7
Neus and Coree (South Atlantic) 34
Niantic, Eastern, and Narraganset (North Atlantic) 10
Niantic, Western (North Atlantic) 12
Nipmuc (North Atlantic) 4
Nottoway, Occaneechi, Meherrin, Monacan Confederacy, and Manahoac Confederacy (South Atlantic) 29
Occaneechi, Meherrin, Nottoway, Monacan Confederacy, and Manahoac Confederacy (South Atlantic) 29
Ofogoula, Tunica, Yazoo, and Koroa (Gulf) 42
Ojibwa (Central) 58
Omaha (Northern Plains) 77
Opelousa, Chawasha, and Washa (Gulf) 49
Osage (Northern Plains) 78
Oto (Northern Plains) 79
Ozinies and Tocwogh (South Atlantic) 25
Pahvant, Gosiute, and Ute (Central Mountains) 97
Paiute, including Paviotso and Snake Oregon (Central Mountains) 98
Pamptico and Bear River (South Atlantic) 33
Pascagoula, Biloxi, and Moctobi (Gulf) 43
Pasquotank and Yeopim (South Atlantic) 30

Passamaquoddy and Abnaki (North Atlantic) 1
Patuxent and Conoy or Piscataway (South Atlantic) 24
Paugusset and Wepawaug (North Atlantic) 15
Paviotso, Snake Oregon, and Paiute (Central Mountains) 98
Pawnee (Northern Plains) 80
Pennacook (North Atlantic) 2
Pequot and Mohegan (North Atlantic) 11
Piankashaw, Wea, and Miami (Central) 57
Piscataway or Conoy, and Patuxent (South Atlantic) 24
Pocomtuc (North Atlantic) 5
Podunk (North Atlantic) 13
Ponca (Northern Plains) 81
Potawatomi (Central) 59
Powhatan Confederacy (South Atlantic) 28
Quapaw or Arkansa (Gulf) 44
Quinnipiac (North Atlantic) 14
Quinipissa, Bayogoula, and Mugulasha (Gulf) 48
Sauk (Central) 60
Seminole, Creek Confederacy (Gulf) 36
Shawnee (Central) 61
Sheepeater and Shoshoni (Central Mountains) 96
Shoshoni and Sheepeater (Central Mountains) 96

Sioux (Northern Plains) 82
Snake Oregon, Paviotso, and Paiute (Central Mountains) 98
Taensa (Gulf) 50
Tangipahoa and Acolapissa (Gulf) 47
Tocwogh and Ozinies (South Atlantic) 25
Tohome and Mobile (Gulf) 37
Tonkawa (Southern Plains) 93
Tunica, Yazoo, Koroa, and Ofogoula (Gulf) 42
Tunxis (North Atlantic) 16
Ute, Gosiute, and Pahvant (Central Mountains) 97
Wampanoag (North Atlantic) 6
Wappinger Tribes (North Atlantic) 20
Washa, Chawasha, and Opelousa (Gulf) 49
Washo (Central Mountains) 99
Wea, Piankashaw, and Miami (Central) 57
Wepawaug and Paugusset (North Atlantic) 15
Wicomoco (South Atlantic) 27
Wichita (Southern Plains) 94
Winnebago (Central) 62
Wongunk (North Atlantic) 17
Yazoo, Tunica, Koroa, and Ofogoula (Gulf) 42
Yeopim and Pasquotank (South Atlantic) 30

to publish his work as a book-length monograph in the bureau's Bulletin series. His letters further indicate that by 1913 he had compiled most of the necessary information, had completed detailed population estimates for most of the tribes, and had even prepared manuscripts for some of the eastern areas. However, at that point his work was interrupted, apparently by his increased field work with the Cherokee, his publication of other articles, and his declining health. He died in 1921 before completing the project.

Following Mooney's death, John R. Swanton, also of the Bureau of American Ethnology, examined Mooney's notes and found that he had completed aboriginal estimates for all tribal groups and had prepared a brief summary discussion for each of the 15 tribal areas that he had considered. In 1928, Swanton published these data, adding in the preface that although Mooney's exact sources were not documented, the estimates were the best available and could be trusted, since "It is known that, in some cases, he carried his investigations back to the original census rolls" (Swanton; in Mooney, 1928: 2).

In 1939, Alfred Kroeber used Mooney's population estimates as the basis for his well-known monograph, *Cultural and Natural Areas of Native North America*. In calculating population densities for his analysis, Kroeber utilized all of Mooney's figures except those for California, where he substituted his own data. Although he questioned some of the figures, he felt, "All in all, however, Mooney's estimates and computations have clearly been made on the basis of wide reading, conscientiousness, and experienced judgment. Until some new, equally systematic, and detailed survey is made, it seems best to accept his figures in toto rather than to patch them here and there" (Kroeber, 1939: 134). Through Kroeber's monograph or directly from the Swanton publication, Mooney's population estimates have been quoted frequently and still are recognized by many as the most accurate available, in spite of the fact that no one has determined the exact sources of the estimates or the methodology employed. According to Swanton, all of Mooney's actual calculations were "contained in loose notes, with which practically nothing can be done" (Swanton; in Mooney, 1928: 1).

In 1971, I calculated a prehistoric population estimate for part of southwestern Maryland through an analysis of human skeletal material recovered archaeologically from Late Woodland prehistoric ossuaries (Ubelaker, 1974). My analysis indicated that the area of southwestern Maryland occupied historically by the Conoy was probably once occupied by an aboriginal population of over 7,000 persons. In contrast, Mooney had estimated only 2,000 for the same area. Wondering how Mooney derived such contrasting figures, I examined his unpublished notes mentioned by Swanton (now on file in the National Anthropological Archives, Smithsonian Institution) and discovered his actual calculations for that area. The notes revealed that

Mooney had relied exclusively upon John Smith's warrior counts for villages located along the Maryland side of the Potomac River (Arber, 1884: 348). Apparently Mooney had not considered the population of the inland villages, partially listed on Smith's 1612 map (Arber, 1884: facing p. 384), but not included in Smith's discussion of warriors. The inclusion of these villages produces a population figure comparable to the one produced from the skeletal data, thus explaining the discrepancy.

At the time of the research described above, I noticed that Mooney's notes contained the sources and calculations for most of his other population estimates as well. Due to the historical importance of Mooney's population figures and the current need for even more accurate estimates, I reexamined Mooney's notes in an effort to document his sources. This essay is the result of that effort and is intended primarily to document wherever possible the ethnohistorical sources of Mooney's estimates and the logic he employed in their derivation. Once documented, Mooney's estimates may then be evaluated by individual scholars with more thorough knowledge of each specific tribe or area.

TRIBAL POPULATIONS: SOURCES AND CALCULATIONS

For the most part, Mooney's notes consist of notecards and strips of brown paper containing isolated notes, references, and calculations. For some tribal areas, the notes and population figures had been collected partially and summarized, usually with a list of population numbers through time for individual tribes. Preliminary manuscripts had been compiled by Mooney for New England and the Upper Plains. For most areas, however, the calculations are recorded on isolated notes with no compilation figures available. All of the notes are stored by the National Anthropological Archives in folders organized under the same general tribal area headings that are used in Mooney's 1928 publication. For example, all notes and calculations for the Southern Plains are stored together in a folder with that name. I examined all of the notes within these folders to discover either Mooney's actual calculation of his published tribal estimate, or the earliest sources that he cited. I then examined the quoted source to determine as exactly as possible how Mooney interpreted it to produce his published estimate. Since both Mooney and I utilized sources within the library of the Department of Anthropology of the Smithsonian, which was formerly the library of the Bureau of American Ethnology, I frequently found his notes and calculations in margins and endpapers of the volumes, which provided additional data concerning his methodology.

Mooney's notes for some tribes and areas are more complete (and more legible) than for others. Thus while his sources for the North Atlantic states and other areas are relatively well documented, his exact sources for Canadian tribes remain unknown and are not treated here. The following presents Mooney's sources and methodology for the population of each tribe in the order the tribes are presented in his 1928 publication.[1] In the discussion of the tribes, the italicized headings include the names and parenthetical information as given by Mooney (1928). Only the lengthy tribal names from the Columbia region are abbreviated, to conserve space in Table 8.1. Some related tribal groups are discussed collectively. The figure following each tribal name in the headings represents Mooney's published estimate for that tribe or the combined total for several groups. Individual tribes are omitted if my examination of Mooney's notes failed to reveal additional information concerning his logic or sources.[2]

North Atlantic States in 1600

1. *Abnaki tribes (including Passamaquoddy)–3,000.* According to Mooney's notes: "the best estimate of the original population is probably of the Jesuit Biard who, from observation in 1611–3 estimates 3000 Indians from the Penobscot to the Saco (Relations, I)." The reference is to Pierre Biard, in Thwaites (1896–1901: Vol. 1); the exact citation, however, could not bc located.

2. *Pennacook–2,000.* Mooney's manuscript reads: "The Pennacook were originally one of the most powerful Indian confederacies of New England. Gookin, with his usual exaggeration, makes them originally about 3000 warriors or equal to the Massachuset or Wampanoag (Mass. 1st. I) [Gookin, 1806: 149]. They probably numbered at least 2500 souls .... In 1631, they were estimated at 400 to 500 warriors (Schoolcraft V), or between 1600 and 2000 souls." Mooney discounted the estimate of Gookin (1806) and relied upon the comments of Schoolcraft (1851–57: 5:230): "The Pennacooks must have numbered at this time from twelve hundred to fifteen hundred souls, as Dudley [Farmer, 1838: 6] mentioned, in 1631, that Passaconnaway had 'under his command four or five hundred men,' plainly meaning warriors . . . two thousand would doubtless be a fair estimate for the tribe." Thus, Mooney's estimate is ultimately based on the following com-

1. Tribes are located by number on Map 8.1, and are listed alphabetically in the map key.
2. References in brackets within quotations identify Mooney's sources as listed in the Bibliography here. Within quotations, spelling and punctuation appear exactly as in Mooney's notes and the cited publications, with these exceptions: long *s* has been modernized and *v* has been changed to *u* where appropriate.

ment by Dudley: "Uppon the river Merrimack is seated Sagamore Passaconnaway haveing under his comand 4 or 500 men" (Farmer, 1838: 6).

3. *Massachuset—3,000.* According to Mooney's manuscript: "They were originally one of the most important tribes of New England. Smith in 1614 [Arber, 1884: 205] found their coast 'all along large corn fields' with 'great troops' of people, and estimated those along the coast at near 3000 people according to report. He names eleven towns, most of which were depopulated three years later. Johnson in 1654 [Jameson, 1910: 41], as already quoted, says that they were originally 'most populous' with three kingdoms or sagamoreships and having under them seven dukedoms or petty sagamores. Hubbard also, 1682, says that the country, before the epidemic, was 'of all the Indians thereabouts the most populous' (Mass. 2d VI 95) [Hubbard, 1815: 195]. Gookin says that they were a 'numerous and great people', and credits them, with his usual exaggeration, with 3,000 men (Mass, 1st, I) [Gookin, 1806: 148]. They were probably about 3000 souls."

Thus Mooney's estimate is based on John Smith's comments written in June 1616: "The Sea Coast as you passe, shewes you all along large corne fields, and great troupes of well proportioned people . . . if there be neer three thousand people upon these Iles" (Arber, 1884: 205).

4. *Nipmuc, independent—500.* Mooney originally felt the Nipmuc population was closer to 1,000 and later reduced it to 500. The estimate is apparently a guess since Mooney wrote: "Those acknowledging no outside jurisdiction, may have numbered originally 1000 souls, but had probably been reduced by disease and the Mohawk wars to not over 800 before the outbreak of King Philip's war in 1675."

5. *Pocomtuc, etc. (central Mass.)—1,200.* Originally Mooney estimated their population at 2,000 and later reduced it to the published figure of 1,200. According to his notes: "The Pocomtuc seem to have been of considerable importance before their war with the Mohawk, about 1660 but as, by reason of their remote position, they were not well known to the English, and as they abandoned their country soon after the outbreak of King Philip's war, we have no estimate of their population. They were allies of the Narraganset, and dreaded enemies of Uncas and the Mohegan, who several times invoked the aid of Connecticut against them, notably in 1648, when they were reported to have assembled at Pocomtuc 1000 warriors, 300 of them with guns, to invade the Mohegan territory (DeForest 234) [DeForest, 1851: 234]. Mason states that in 1638, on occasion of great scarcity in Connecticut, the Indians of Pocomtuc town sold and brought down to the English 'fifty canoes laden with corn at one time. Never was the like known

to this day!' (Mason, about 1670, Mass. 2d, VIII, 153) [Mason, 1819: 153].
It would probably be within limit to assume that their various bands numbered originally at least 2000 souls."

6. *Wampanoag, etc.–2,400.* Again Mooney originally estimated a higher
figure (3,500) and then reduced it to the published figure for unknown
reasons. He wrote that "it is sometimes difficult to know whether the earlier
statements are intended to apply only to the tribe proper or to the tribe with
its dependencies . . . Gookin's [1806: 148] estimate of an original 3000 men
is undoubtedly exaggerated. As they seem to have been second only to the
Narraganset, whom he puts at 1000 men in 1674, after heavy losses by
smallpox and other causes, we may assume that the Wampanoag, before their
losses by epidemics, may have numbered at least 3500 souls and perhaps
more."

7. *Nauset–1,200.* Mooney's notes show he originally estimated 2,000
for this group and then later reduced it to the published figure of 1,200. He
wrote: "They probably numbered originally at least 2000 souls, but owing to
their isolated position and the fact that they took no part in the Indian wars,
they are not as prominent in history as their numbers would warrant." Other
notes indicate the source of the 2,000 estimate was Gookin (1802: 171): "In
1685, when an account of the praying Indians in the colony of Plymouth was
transmitted to England by Governour Hinkley, it was found that they
amounted to five hundred men and women, within the limits of Mr. Treat's
parish, beside boys and girls, who were supposed to be more than three times
that number."

8. *Nantucket–1,500.* Mooney's manuscript reads: "The Indians of Nantucket Island, Mass. seem to have constituted two distinct bodies, an eastern
and a western, whose tribal names are unknown, and probably numbered
originally at least 1500 souls. . . . In 1674, according to the missionary
Thomas Mayhew, they numbered about 300 families, which may still have
been near their original strength (Mayhew, in Mass. 1st I, 205) [Mayhew,
1806: 205]." The reference is to a letter of Thomas Mayhew: "Upon that
Island are many praying Indians. Also the families of that island are about
three hundred. I have often-times accounted the families of both islands; and
have very often, these thirty-two years, been at Nantucket."

9. *Marthas Vineyard–1,500.* Mooney wrote: "According to the missionary, Thomas Mayhew, they numbered about 1500 souls at the first settlement
of the island in 1642." Mooney must refer to Mayhew's statement: "the
families here are three hundred at least" (Mayhew, 1806: 205).

10. *Narraganset, etc., and E. Niantic–4,000.* Mooney wrote: "Most of the early estimates evidently include the Niantic, who alone in later times retained the Narraganset name . . . Johnson's estimate of a former 30,000 warriors! (Wonder-Working Providence 1654, Mass. 2d. IV, 42) [Jameson, 1910: 162] . . . or even Gookin's [1806: 148] claim of a former 5,000 warriors . . . need not be seriously considered. Gookin's [1806: 148] estimate of about 1000 warriors in 1674 seems nearly correct for the two tribes at that time and agrees closely with Bradford's contemporary statement that their chief led 900 or 1000 warriors against the Mohegan in 1643 (Bradford, 505) [1898: 505]." Thus Mooney discounted Daniel Gookin's comments in 1674 that "The Narragansitts were reckoned, in former times, able to arm for war more than five thousand men as ancient Indians say" (Gookin, 1806: 148), and also Johnson's statement that "They were able to set forth, as was then supposed, 30000. fighting men" (Jameson, 1910: 162). He relied upon Bradford's statement concerning the Narraganset chief Myantinomo: "He came suddenly upon him [Uncas, chief of the Mohegan] with 900. or 1000. men (never denouncing any warr before)" (Bradford, 1898: 505), and upon Gookin's comment in 1674 that "these Indians are now but few comparatively: all that people cannot make above one thousand able men" (Gookin, 1806: 148). Mooney then must have multiplied the figure of 1,000 by 4 to allow for nonwarriors in the population.

11. *Pequot–2,200; Mohegan–600.* According to Mooney's notes: "Gookin's estimate of an original 4000 warriors, (Mass. 1st. I, 147) [Gookin, 1806: 147] like his other estimates based upon Indian report, is greatly exaggerated. Palfrey's [1866] estimate of 'not fewer than a thousand' hostile Pequot warriors at the beginning of the war is also much too high. Judging from the best estimates of the number destroyed, and from the statements of the number of Pequot and Mohegan gathered into villages after the war and making allowance for those who escaped by flight or were held in slavery, it is probable that the combined strength of both tribes before the English occupation was not more than 2700 souls, of whom the Mohegan proper constituted not more than 200." Thus Mooney guessed at the number rather than rely upon Gookin's statement: "These Pequots, as old Indians relate, could in former times raise four thousand men, fit for war" (Gookin, 1806: 147).

12. *Niantic, Western–250.* Mooney's notes refer to DeForest's statement about the Niantic: "They seem to have been not inconsiderable in numbers, by their still retaining an existence; yet they never furnished any noted characters, never performed any remarkable exploit, and will fill but a small space in the subsequent narrative" (DeForest, 1851: 57). Mooney adds:

"DeForest thinks that the fact that they maintained their existence in 1850 argues that they were 'not inconsiderable in numbers' in the beginning. They may have been originally 250 souls."

13. *Podunk (E. Windsor, E. Hartford)–300.* Mooney's notes show an original calculation of 400 for the Podunk, which later was reduced to the published estimate of 300. Specifically, Mooney wrote: "Stiles, about 1783, says the tribe 'in King Philip's war contained between two and three hundred men, who went off in the war, and never returned' (Mass. 1st X, 105) [Stiles, 1809: 105]. De Forest mentions a story that they had helped King Philip with 200 warriors, but says that they could probably not muster at the time more than 60 warriors (De Forest 280) [1851: 280]. This estimate is probably much too low. The facts that they had two chiefs; that they defied the power of Uncas, the principal Mohegan chief in 1656, and met his warriors with 'an equal number' compelling him to turn back; and the further fact that in 1657 they scornfully rejected Eliot's offer of missionary teaching, contrary to the attitude of the broken and dependent tribes, all indicate a considerable and conscious tribal strength. They probably numbered at least 100 warriors or perhaps 400 souls." The Stiles account rejected by Mooney is as follows: "*Podunk* tribe, at the dividing line between Windsor and Hartford east side [of Connecticut river], in king Philip's war contained between two and three hundred men, who went off in that war, and never returned" (Stiles, 1809: 105). The DeForest account that Mooney considered too conservative reads: "The other tribes of Connecticut mostly remained neutral, except that a few of the Nipmucks of Windham County joined Philip, and also the Podunks of East Windsor and East Hartford. The latter, it is said, assisted him with two hundred men; but this estimate rests entirely upon tradition, and is altogether too large to be worthy of the slightest credit. Probably the Podunks at this time could not have mustered more than sixty warriors" (DeForest, 1851: 280).

14. *Quinnipiac (New Haven)–250.* According to Mooney: "They sold most of their lands in 1638 and 1639 at which time the main body, about New Haven, had only 47 warriors, while those further east had apparently not over 25 more. Their whole strength may have been 75 warriors or perhaps 300 souls." His notes do not reveal why he later reduced the figure to 250; they indicate, however, that he based the estimate on these comments of DeForest: "This last author was told, in 1785, by one of the old citizens of Branford, that, fifty years before, that town was inhabited by fifty Indian men; and a Mr. Pardee of East Haven assured him that, in 1730, there were as many as three hundred Indians in East Haven, and that he could himself remember when their grown men outnumbered the town militia. I must

confess that I look upon these estimates and comparisons as sheer exaggerations. If they were correct, then the aboriginal population of Branford and East Haven in 1730, must have been five hundred souls. Yet in 1638, nearly a century before, the Quinnipiacs only counted forty-seven men, while the Indians of Guilford, if they were a separate tribe at all, (which I do not believe) must have been considerably less numerous" (DeForest, 1851: 361).

15. *Paugusset and Wepawaug (Milford, Bridgeport)–400.* Mooney's notes do not reveal the original sources he consulted, but this statement reveals the logic he employed to produce the estimate: "We have no statement or estimate of the original population, but from the facts that they had at least two stockaded forts, that they were at times a source of serious alarm to the first settlers, and that on one occasion they defeated an invasion of the dreaded Mohawk, we may assume that they were of some importance, possibly 100 warriors and 400 souls."

16. *Tunxis (Farmington)–400.* According to Mooney: "From the extent of their claim, the importance in which Sequassen was held by Dutch and English, from their aggressive war with the powerful Pequot and Mohegan, and their alliance with the powerful Pocomtuc and Narraganset, it is evident that they were a large tribe. We get a standard for comparison from the statement that when, in 1658, the Tunxis, Pocomtuc and Narraganset, under the leadership of the Pocomtuc . . . fined the Tunxis ten fathoms of *wampum*, and the other two tribes fifteen each. . . . Stiles about 1780 says that the Farmington band was 'the largest tribe' on Connecticut river (Mass. 1st X 104) [Stiles, 1809: 104]. DeForest roughly estimates the same band at 80 to 100 warriors. It is probable that the whole tribe represented originally at least 250 warriors or about 1200 souls." Mooney later reduced his estimate to the published 400, apparently relying on DeForest's statement: "If it was worth while to make estimates based upon nothing, we might perhaps assign to this tribe a population of eighty to one hundred warriors, or about four hundred individuals" (DeForest, 1851: 52).

17. *Wongunk (Wethersfield, Middleton)–400.* According to Mooney: "We have no figures for their early population. Stiles, writing about 1780, says the band at Middletown had been 'once a great tribe' (Mass. 1st X, 105) [Stiles, 1809: 105]. From comparison with principal villages of the same general region, and from other data for calculation it is probable that their two chief towns averaged nearly 50 warriors each and that, including those about Haddam, they had at least 125 warriors or perhaps 500 souls originally." For unknown reasons, Mooney later reduced the figure to the published 400.

18. *Iroquois confederacy (excluding Tuscarora)—5,500.* Mooney apparently based this estimate on two passages from the *Jesuit Relations,* both of which imply populations of 2,000 warriors. The first is from a letter of Reverend Jacques Bruyas, from the mission of St. Francis Xavier among the Iroquois, January 21, 1668: "tous les Iroquois Ensemble ne sont pas plus de 2000 hommes portans les armes" (Thwaites, 1896–1901: 51:138). Mooney also refers to a letter from "a Frenchman in Captivity Among the Agnierounous, to a Friend of His at Three Rivers 1660–1661." It reads: "La premiere: Que de deux mille Iroquois ou environ, qu'il y a, en voila quinze ou seize cent qui mettent les armes bas" (Thwaites, 1896–1901: 47:104). Mooney multiplied the 2,000 warriors by 4 to allow for the rest of the population. He then reduced the figure to 5,500, apparently reasoning that the population was increasing at the time of the Jesuit observations.

19. *Mahican—3,000.* Mooney wrote: "Ruttenber, who thinks they outnumbered the Wappinger and Long Island tribes, enumerates 11 'castles' or stockaded villages, and says that local research would probably discover 40 villages within their territory. They probably numbered at least 3000, and have been estimated by Indian authority at 4000. As the early authorities usually include them, in whole or part, with the neighboring and closely cognate Munsee, Delaware and Wappinger, under the collective name of Loups or 'Wolves', it is impossible to give any satisfactory separate figures."

The quotation from Ruttenber is as follows: "That their villages and chieftaincies were even more numerous than those of the *Montauks* and *Wappingers* there is every reason to suppose ... Local research would, it is believed, develop forty villages in the territory of the Mahicans" (Ruttenber, 1872: 86).

20. *Wappinger tribes (excluding Conn.)—3,000.* According to Mooney's notes: "Ruttenber [1872], in fact, includes under this name the bands along the coast as far east as Connecticut river. Those commonly included under the designation were divided into some half dozen bands or subtribes with about 30 recorded villages and probably at least 3000 souls." Mooney's estimate of 3,000 souls must be his own guess since Ruttenber did not offer an estimate and Mooney mentioned no other sources.

21. *Montauk, Canarsee, etc., of Long Island—6,000.* Mooney's only statement is: "The whole population was probably something over 6000." Mooney lists no sources for this estimate. It may be a guess based on Ruttenber's comment: "Montauks ... they were considerable in numbers" (Ruttenber, 1872: 75).

22. *Delaware and Munsee—8,000.* The Mooney manuscript provides a detailed discussion of these estimates: "From the number of the subtribes and fortified 'castles' in the early Dutch period, from their strength shown in the Esopus wars, and from their historic persistence as a people, it is probable that the Munsee numbered originally at least 1200 souls, most of whom were concentrated about the lower Hudson. The great body of the other two divisions, when first known, was within the limits of New Jersey, those formerly on the west side of Delaware river having mostly crossed over to the east side before 1634 to escape the Susquehanna. We get some idea of the destruction caused by the Susquehanna from the statement of De Vries [Vries, 1857: 30] that while ascending the Delaware in 1633 he was told by fugitives that this tribe had just massacred 90 men of one Delaware band and had burnt the town of another, killing several and driving the rest into the woods. While the number reported killed was probably exaggerated, the statement corroborates the testimony from other early sources as to the exterminating warfare carried on of the Susquehanna against their eastern and southern neighbors. Of these two subdivisions, Evelin, our first authority writing about 1640 with several years' knowledge of the country, names 8 subtribes on the east side of Delaware river below Trenton Falls, with a total of about 940 warriors, besides another of which no estimate is given, but which we may assume would bring the total up to about 1,000 warriors or 7,000 souls for this section. Another author of 1648, after noting Evelin's statement, says that 'besides' those named by him, there were at least 1200 (warriors) subject to the Raritan in east New Jersey, with two other small bands along the east shore of about 40 men each, and a third 'reduced' (probably by smallpox) to 14 men. (Evelin and anonymous author, Description of the Province of New Albion, 1648; quoted in Smith, New Jersey 29—31, 1765, reprint 1890) [Smith, 1765: 28—31]. This would give the Delaware bands within New Jersey at that date, including perhaps a part of the Munsee, from about 2100 to 2300 warriors. As there were other small bands on the west side of the river between Philadelphia and Wilmington (see Brinton, Walan Olum, 37—38) [Brinton, 1885: 37—38] we may probably add at least a hundred warriors to this total. Adding to these the Munsee, and allowing for considerable exaggeration in the Raritan estimate, we shall have a total about the year 1640 of at least 2500 warriors or about 10,000 souls. As one great smallpox epidemic visitation, if not two, had already swept the Delaware country, while liquor and dissipation had also been at work for a generation, we can hardly escape the conclusion that the Delaware confederacy in 1600 numbered close to 12000 souls. This would accord with the extent of their territory, the number of the clans and subdivisions and their dominant position among the Algonquian tribes."

Mooney later reduced the figure to his published estimate of 8,000, but his notes do not indicate why.

23. *Conestoga—5,000.* The origin of this estimate is not clear. Mooney's notes show one reference to 1,300 warriors in 1647, attributed to the *Jesuit Relations,* 1647–1648 (Thwaites, 1896–1901). This figure multiplied by Mooney's usual factor of 4 would give a population estimate of 5,200, only 200 more than his published figure of 5,000.

South Atlantic States in 1600

Mooney's notes for the South Atlantic states are only partially complete. All of the material consists of unorganized notes, but even these are lacking for many of the tribes in this area. Notes were found relating to only the following tribes.

24. *Conoy or Piscataway, Patuxent, etc.—2,000.* Mooney definitely based this estimate on the following two passages from John Smith: "On the north of this river is *Secowocomoco* with 40 men. Somewhat further *Potapaco* with 20. In the East part of the bought [branch] of the river is *Pamacacack* with 60 men. After, *Moyowances* with 100. And lastly, *Nacotchtanke* with 80 able men" (Arber, 1884: 52). "The fifth river is called *Pawtuxunt* ... Upon this river dwell the people called *Acquintanacksuak, Pawtuxunt,* and *Mattapanient.* 200 men was the greatest strength that could bee there perceived" (Arber, 1884: 53). Mooney's notes reveal that he added all of the above estimates by Smith for a total of 500 warriors. He then multiplied by a factor of 4, apparently to include all of the nonwarrior population, to produce a total of 2,000. His notes then show an additional calculation labeled "add several small villages on map—28 on map," from which he added 400 to produce a new total of 2,400. This addition must have been made to allow for all of the villages listed on Smith's map of 1612 that were not included in his discussion of warrior counts in the text. He later dropped this estimate altogether since his published estimate is only 2,000.

Through my demographic analysis of human skeletons from ossuaries, I demonstrated that Mooney's ratio of warriors to nonwarriors in the Maryland population was approximately correct (Ubelaker, 1974). However, Mooney's estimate of 2,000 is still much too conservative, due to his failure to include the population of villages shown on Smith's map but not mentioned in Smith's discussion of warriors. Assuming that those inland villages not given warrior estimates were of approximately the same size as those mentioned by Smith, I calculated that the Conoy population must have been at least 7,000. The figure could be even higher, if additional inland villages existed that were not known by Smith.

25. *Tocwogh and Ozinies—700.* Mooney's notes indicate he consulted the following statement by John Smith: "On the East side the *Bay* is the river

of *Tockwhogh*, and upon it a people that can make 100 men, seated some 7 miles within the river . . . Next to them is *Ozinies* with 60 men" (Arber, 1884: 55). Mooney must have multiplied this total of 160 warriors by his factor of 4 for a total of 640, which he then altered to the published figure of 700.

26. *Nanticoke, etc.—1,600.* Mooney based this calculation on the following passage from John Smith: "neere unto which is the river of *Kuskara-waock*, upon which is seated a people with 200 men" (Arber, 1884: 55). Using Mooney's factor of 4, this would imply a population of 800. Mooney apparently added an additional 800 people to allow for "2 other small villages" listed on Smith's map of 1612 but not mentioned in his text. Again this estimate would have to be regarded as conservative, due to John Smith's unfamiliarity with that part of Maryland and thus the possible existence of villages or larger populations that were undetected by Smith.

27. *Wicomoco—400.* This estimate is based directly upon John Smith's statement: "After that is the river of *Tants Wighcocomoco* and on it a people with 100 men" (Arber, 1884: 55). Mooney thus multiplied the "100 men" by 4 to produce his estimate of 400 for the total population.

28. *Powhatan confederacy—9,000.* The Mooney notes do not reveal his calculations for the Virginia tribes, but Mooney's publication on the Powhatan Confederacy does include a discussion of population. There he wrote: "The twenty-eight Powhatan tribes enumerated in detail by Smith [Arber, 1884: 51–54] as existing in 1607, numbered, according to his estimate, about 2,385 fighting men; but as he omits from this count the people of Warraskoyac and of several other 'king's houses' or tribal capitals indicated on his map, we are probably justified in making it a round 2,500. Strachey [1849: 56–62], writing about 1616, makes it 3,320, but some of his figures are plainly too high. Taking the lower estimate we should have, on a reasonable calculation, a total population for the confederacy of about 8,500, or about one inhabitant to the square mile" (Mooney, 1907b: 130). Mooney later must have raised this estimate to his published figure in 1928 of 9,000.

29. *Monacan confederacy; Manahoac confederacy; Nottoway (Mangoac of 1585); Occaneechi; Meherrin—6,100.* Mooney's notes do not reveal his calculations for these groups, but his 1907 publication does have relevant discussion: "As it was nearly a century after the founding of Jamestown before the white settlements extended beyond tidewater, we hear but little of these inland tribes until they were already far advanced toward ultimate extinction through wars, disease, and invasion by the dispossessed tribes. It is

therefore impossible to form any definite calculation of their original population ... Making due allowance for the difference between mountain and lowland, and between hunting and agricultural or fishing habit, it seems reasonable to assume for these inland tribal groups—Mannahoac, Monacan, Nottoway, Meherrin, Occaneechi, and Mohetan—holding altogether four-fifths of the area of Virginia, a total original population at least equal to that of the single tribal group concentrated in the remaining one-fifth or tidewater section. This would give some 17,000 Indians as a conservative estimate for the whole state" (Mooney, 1907b: 131–32). This estimate of 8,500 (half of the total for the state) for these groups was reduced later to the published estimate of 6,100. Of course he also reduced his total estimate for Virginia from 17,000 to 15,100. The conservative nature of these figures is emphasized by a recent estimate of the Virginia Algonquian population alone of 14,300 to 22,300 (Feest, 1973: 74).

30. *Yeopim, Pasquotank, etc. (Weapemeoc of 1585)–800.* Mooney apparently began by estimating their number in 1700. He interpreted Lawson's estimates: "Paspatank Indians, town, 1; Paspatank River, fighting men, 10; Poteskeit, town, 1; North River, fighting men, 30" (Lawson, 1860: 383), and "Jaupin Indians, six people" (Lawson, 1860: 384), to imply an estimated population of 165. He then must have guessed that in 1600 the population was about 800.

31. *Chowanoc–1,500.* Mooney referred to John Smith's statement: "and there is a towne called *Ohanock*, where is a great corne field, it is subject to *Chawonock*, which is the greatest Province upon the river, and the Towne it selfe can put seven hundred men into the field, besides the forces of the rest" (Arber, 1884: 312). By his usual factor of 4 this would produce a total estimate of 2,800. Mooney must have felt Smith's count was exaggerated and thus reduced the estimate to 1,500.

32. *Machapunga, etc. (Wingandacoa of 1585)–1,200.* Mooney's notes refer to Lawson's comments from 1700: "Machapunga town, 1, Maramiskeet, fighting men, 30" (Lawson, 1860: 383), to which Mooney added 16 warriors for "Mathena" for a total warrior count of 46 and a total population in 1700 of 184. He then guessed that the population in 1600 was about 1,000. Later, he apparently raised the estimate to the published figure of 1,200.

33. *Pamptico and Bear River (Pomouik of 1855 [1585])–1,000.* Again Mooney quotes Lawson's comments: "Bear River town 1, Raudauqua-quank, fighting men 50" (Lawson, 1860: 383) and "Pampticough Indians, town 1; Island, fighting men, 15" (Lawson, 1860: 384), for a total of 65 warriors and 260 souls. He then guessed that the figure in 1600 would have been about 1,000.

34. *Neus and Coree (Nusiok and Cawruuock of 1585)—1,000.* Mooney first estimated a total of 40 warriors and 160 souls in 1700 from Lawson's account: "Connamox Indians, towns 2; Coranine, Raruta, fighting men, 25; Neus Indians, towns, 2; Chattooka, Rouconk, fighting men, 15" (Lawson, 1860: 383–84). He then guessed that the population in 1600 must have been five times that in 1700, or 800 souls. Later, he increased the figure to the published estimate of 1,000.

The sources for Mooney's estimates of the remainder of the tribes in North Carolina and South Carolina are not revealed by his notes.

Gulf States in 1650

35. *Cherokee—22,000.* The source of this estimate is not clear. In his article on the Cherokee in the *Handbook of American Indians*, Mooney (1907a: 247) commented: "With the exception of an estimate in 1730, which placed them at about 20,000, most of those up to a recent period gave them 12,000 or 14,000, and in 1758 they were computed at only 7,500. The majority of the earlier estimates are probably too low, as the Cherokee occupied so extensive a territory that only a part of them came in contact with the whites."

His notes refer to estimates of 500 men in 1708 by Nathaniel Johnson, 4,000 warriors and 11,210 souls in 1715 by a trade commission report, 10,000 souls in 1720 (also attributed to Johnson), and 20,000 in 1730 (no source given). The estimates for 1715 and 1720 are reproduced in W. J. Rivers (1874: 93, 94, 103). The Johnson 1708 reference is: "The Cherokee Indians . . . are settled in 60 towns, and are at least 500 men" (Johnson, Broughton, Gibbs, Smith, and Beresford letter of September 17, 1708, in Rivers, 1856: 238). The source of the 1730 estimate of 20,000 is not given, but probably is the following passage from Stevens (1847: 1:48–49) referred to by Mooney (1907a): "On the purchase of Carolina from the proprietary grantees by Parliament, in 1729, . . . it was deemed essential, by the government, to secure the alliance of this large and warlike tribe, computed at this time to number twenty thousand, distributed in sixty-four towns and villages, affording at least six thousand warriors." Mooney's comments in the *Handbook* indicate he considered all of these estimates too conservative and guessed that the original figure must have been about 22,000.

36. *Creek confederacy; Seminole (later offshoot from Creeks)— 18,000.* Mooney's notes do not show his actual calculation of the published estimate, but they do refer to three sources: Bartram, 1775; Hawkins, 1785; and Knox, 1789. The original statements are as follows: "Siminoles . . . In all fifty-five towns, besides many villages not enumerated; and reckoning two

hundred inhabitants to each town on an average, which is a moderate computation, would give eleven thousand inhabitants" (Bartram, 1792: 462–63). Earlier Bartram wrote: "The Siminoles are but a weak people with respect to numbers. All of them, I suppose, would not be sufficient to people one of the towns in the Muscogulge . . . which alone contains near two thousand inhabitants" (Bartram, 1792: 209). According to Hawkins: "The Upper and Lower Creek nation, from an agent who resided seven years in their towns, and employed by John Stewart, for the purpose,—5400 [gun-men]" (Hawkins et al., 1832: 39). Knox in 1789 wrote: "The gun-men, or warriors of the whole nation, are estimated at six thousand" (Knox, 1832: 15). The Hawkins and Knox estimates imply a population of 20,000 to 24,000, which Mooney must have felt was a slight exaggeration.

37. *Mobile; Tohome–2,000.* Mooney's notes suggest he consulted two primary sources in making this estimate: D'Iberville and Bénard de La Harpe. D'Iberville presented four references to the population of these tribes: "Les Mobiliens et Tohomes . . . 350 familles" (Margry, 1876–86: 4:602); "Les Mobiliens et Tohomés sont près du fort; ils sont trois cent cinquante familles" (Margry, 1876–86: 4:594); "Ils sont dans ces deux nations 350 hommes" (Margry, 1876–86: 4:514); and finally, "Le village de la Mobile est à trois jours d'icy, au nord-est; il y a, dans ce village, trois cents hommes. Les Tohomés en sont à une journée, sur la mesme rivière de la Mobile, et sont trois cents hommes" (Margry, 1876–86: 4:427). The first three references date from 1702 and all suggest a "warrior" count of 350 and a total population of about 1,400. The last reference, dated April 1700, suggests a "warrior" count of 600 and thus a population of about 2,400. This higher estimate is supported by Bénard de La Harpe in 1699: "Le 8 août il arriva au fort des sauvages Mobiliens et Thomés, nations composant ensemble plus de sept cents hommes" (Bénard de La Harpe, 1831: 17). This suggests 700 warriors and thus 2,800 souls. Mooney guessed between the estimates at 2,000.

38. *Apalachee, etc.–7,000.* Mooney's estimate of 7,000 is based on an apparent conservative interpretation of the following estimate of 2,000 men by D'Iberville: "Il le pourroit bien faire, car les Apalaches sont deux mille, desquels il peut lever mille, qui ne sont armés que de flesches" (1702; in Margry, 1876–86: 4:595). This estimate represents the number of men fighting with the governor of Florida against the Apalachicola (Apalachee).

39. *Chickasaw–8,000.* This estimate is definitely based upon D'Iberville's estimate of 2,000 families and warriors in 1700–1702. Mooney's notes refer to the following statements by D'Iberville: "Les Chicachas sont cinq

cent quatre-vingts cabanes, à trois et quatre hommes par cabane, qui font au moins deux mille hommes" (Margry, 1876–86: 4:519); "Les Chicachas . . . en deux villages, où ils ont environ cent vingt hommes" (Margry, 1876–86: 4:519); "sont les Chicachas, par 35 degrés 20 minutes, qui sont deux mille familles au moins" (Margry, 1876–86: 4: 594); and "Les Chicachas . . . 2,000 familles" (Margry, 1876–86: 4:602). Mooney's notes cite the corroborative evidence of Sieur de Tonty's statement in 1681: "Chikasas savages . . . They have 2,000 warriors, the greatest number of whom have flat heads" (French, 1846: 60).

40. *Choctaw—15,000.* Mooney's notes refer to the following early population estimates for the Choctaw: 6,000 men (D'Iberville, 1700); 4,000 families, 3,800 to 4,000 families, 3,800 to 4,000 men (D'Iberville, 1702); 3,000 to 4,000 men (*Jesuit Relations,* 1730); 5,000 warriors (Bénard de La Harpe, 1721–1722); 7,000 to 8,000 souls (Roulieaux de La Vente, 1704). Specifically, the passages cited by Mooney are as follows: "J'ay beaucoup raisonné avec eux du pays des Chaquitas et de cette nation, qui a plus de cinquante villages. De la manière qu'ils en parlent, il faut qu'il y ait plus de six mille hommes" (D'Iberville, 1700; in Margry, 1876–86: 4:427); "Les Chactas . . . 4,000 familles" (D'Iberville, 1702; in Margry, 1876–86: 4:602); "sont les Chactas . . . qui sont trois mille huit cents à quatre mille familles" (D'Iberville, 1702; in Margry, 1876–86: 4:593); "Les Chactas sont, dans trois villages différens, mille quatre-vingt-dix cabanes, à trois et quatre hommes par chaque, qui font environ trois mille huit cents à quatre mille hommes" (D'Iberville, 1702; in Margry, 1876–86: 4:519); "Tchactas . . . qui est maintenant réduite à trois ou quatre guerriers" (letter from Père le Petit to Père d'Avaugour, July 12, 1730; in Thwaites, 1896–1901: 68:194); "Cette nation Chacta était pour lors de quarante villages renfermant cinq mille guerriers" (Bénard de La Harpe, 1831: 36); and "Je lui pouvois mander il est constant que les chatta est est [*sic*] la plus belle et la plus nombreuse de toutes les nations qu'on connoit ci bas [;] on croit que cette nation est de 90 cabanes mais il est certain qu'elle est de plus de 7 a 5 cents et que cela compose sept a huit mille ames mais qui a ving [*sic*] lieues en Etendue." This last passage has been translated into English as follows: "I am able to report that it is established that the Chatta is the most handsome and the most numerous of all the nations that they [the French] know down here; they [the French] think that this nation has 90 dwellings, but it is certain that it has more than 500 to 700 constituting 7,000 to 8,000 souls who are, however, spread over 20 leagues."[3]

3. Letter from Henri Roulieaux de La Vente, September 20, 1704, from Fort Louis, Louisiana, Seminary of Quebec Archives, Lettres R: 77:16. This transcription of the

Although Mooney consulted all of the above references, he apparently relied chiefly upon D'Iberville's estimate of 3,800 to 4,000 men and thus a total population of about 15,000.

41. *Natchez—4,500.* Mooney's notes refer to three estimates for the Natchez: 1,200 men by Bénard de La Harpe in 1700; 1,500 warriors by D'Iberville in 1702; and 1,500 men by Henri de Tonty in 1686–1689. Specifically, the quoted references are as follows: "Les Nadechès [*sic*] . . . 1,500 familles" (D'Iberville; in Margry, 1876–86: 4:602); "nous arrivasmes au village des Nachés, où le chef m'attendoit sur le rivage avec le calumet. C'est une nation qui peut fournir quinze cents combattants" (Henri de Tonty, 1686; in Margry, 1876–86: 3:556); and "Le 11 ils arrivèrent aux Natchès, nation de douze cents hommes" (Bénard de La Harpe, 1831: 28). Mooney's published estimate of 4,500 suggests a conservative interpretation of these statements.

42. *Tunica; Yazoo; Koroa; Ofogoula—2,000.* For the Tunicas, Mooney's notes cite two sources: (1) an estimate of 2,000 souls from a letter by M. de Montigny, dated January 2, 1699: "Tonicas . . . they make about 2000 souls" (De Montigny; in Shea, 1861: 76); and (2) D'Iberville's estimate of 300 families: "Les Tonicas et voisins . . . 300 familles" (D'Iberville, 1702; in Margry, 1876–86: 4:602).

For the Koroa, Mooney cited the reference to 1,000 men by Henri de Tonty in Quebec, November 14, 1684: "le village des Coroas . . . nous fusmes surpris de nous voir entourez par plus de mille homme" (Henri de Tonty; in Margry, 1876–86: 1:608).

Mooney's notes suggest that at that time he allowed 2,000 souls for the Tunicas and another 2,000 for the Yazoo and Koroa, apparently relying upon the estimate of De Montigny for the Tunicas, and upon a conservative interpretation of De Tonty's statement for the others. Later, he reduced the estimate to only 2,000 for all of the groups.

43. *Biloxi; Pascagoula; Moctobi—1,000.* Mooney's notes refer to the following statements by D'Iberville and Bénard de La Harpe: "Les Bilocchy, Capinans, Pascoboulas . . . 100 familles" (D'Iberville, 1702; in Margry, 1876–86: 4:602); "les villages des Pascoboulas, Biloxi et Moctobi, qui ne sont pas vingt cabanes en tout" (D'Iberville, 1699; in Margry, 1876–86: 4:451); "Pascaboula . . . au village, dans lequel il y a environ vingt familles" (D'Iber-

original French manuscript and the English translation were provided by Mildred Mott Wedel, Research Associate, Department of Anthropology, Smithsonian Institution (pers. comm.).

ville, 1700; in Margry, 1876–86: 4:427); "au village des Biloxys . . . ce village plus de trente à quarante cabanes" (D'Iberville, 1700; in Margry, 1876–86: 4:425); and "les villages Pascagoula, Biloxi et Moctoby, dont les habitans faisaient ensemble cent trente guerriers" (Bénard de La Harpe, 1831: 16).

The above statements indicate a population of 100 families (D'Iberville) or 130 warriors (Bénard de La Harpe) for the three groups. Mooney's published estimate of 1,000 implies he felt the statements were too conservative.

44. *Quapaw or Arkansa–2,500.* Mooney's notes refer to D'Iberville's statement in 1702: "Les Acansa, Aesetooue, Tongenga–200 familles" (Margry, 1876–86: 4:601); but also to D'Iberville's comment in 1702: "Cette nation des Akansas est destruite" (Margry, 1876–86: 4:599). Thus he interpreted D'Iberville's estimate of 200 families (800 souls) as applying to the population after they already had decreased greatly in numbers and guessed that the original figure in 1650 was about 2,500.

45. *Houma–1,000.* This estimate was based upon the following two statements by D'Iberville: "Les Oumas . . . 150 familles" (D'Iberville, 1702; in Margry, 1876–86: 4:602); and "Ommas . . . Ce village est composé de six à sept cent personnes" (D'Iberville, 1699; in Margry, 1876–86: 4:270). Mooney apparently guessed that while D'Iberville's statements indicate a population of 600 to 700 in 1699, the population must have been about 1,000 in 1650.

46. *Chitimacha–3,000.* Mooney based his estimate on the following estimate of 700 to 800 men by Bénard de La Harpe: "de la nation Ouacha, située dans cette branche auprès de celle des Thoutimachas et Yaguenet-chitou, qui composaient ensemble sept à huit cents hommes" (Bénard de La Harpe, 1831: 9).

47. *Acolapissa (including Tangipahoa)–1,500.* Mooney's notes refer to the following statements by D'Iberville (250 families, 150 men) and Bénard de La Harpe (300 men): "Les Colapissas . . . 250 familles" (D'Iberville, 1702; in Margry, 1876–86: 4:602); "Colapissas . . . Ils ne sont pas plus de cent cinquante hommes, mais très bien faits" (D'Iberville, 1699; in Margry, 1876–86: 4:449); and "au village de Colapissa: ils trouvèrent cette nation composée de plus de trois cents guerriers" (Bénard de La Harpe, 1831: 14). Mooney apparently felt Bénard de La Harpe's estimate was more reliable and guessed that the population in 1650 was 1,500, or 300 more than that implied by Bénard in 1699.

48. *Bayogoula; Mugulasha; Quinipissa–1,500.* Mooney's notes refer to the following statements by D'Iberville in 1699 and 1702 and Bénard de La

Harpe in 1699: "Les Bayagoulas . . . 100 familles" (D'Iberville, 1702; in Margry, 1876–86: 4:602); "il pouvoit y avoir environ deux cents à deux cent cinquante hommes, peu de femmes, la picote" (D'Iberville, 1699; in Margry, 1876–86: 4:171); "les Bayogoulas et Mougoulachas, qui sont deux nations jointes ensemble" (D'Iberville, 1699; in Margry, 1876–86: 4:167); and "Le 14 ils arrivèrent au Bayagoula et au Mongoulacha, nations faisant ensemble cent guerriers" (Bénard de La Harpe, 1831: 9). Bénard's and D'Iberville's statements imply populations of 400 and 1,000 persons respectively, which Mooney apparently felt suggested a population of 1,500 in 1650.

49. *("Les Gens de la Fourche"): Chawasha; Washa; Opelousa– 1,400.* Mooney's notes refer to the statement by D'Iberville in 1702; "Les gens de la Fourche . . . 200 familles" (Margry, 1876–86: 4:602); and by Bénard de La Harpe in 1699: "Ces Ouachas étaient alliés aux Chaouchas et aux Onquilouzas, peuples errans du côté de la mer, formant ensemble deux cents hommes" (Bénard de La Harpe, 1831: 18). Mooney's estimate of 1,400 must be a guess based upon the above estimates of 200 families and 200 men.

50. *Taensa, etc.–800.* Mooney's notes refer to the following statements: "Les Taensas . . . 150 familles" (D'Iberville, 1702; in Margry, 1876–86: 4: 602); "Taensas . . . Il peut y avoir dans cette nation cent vingt cabanes dans l'espace . . . Cette nation a été autrefois nombreuse, mais à présent ils ne sont pas plus de trois cents hommes" (D'Iberville, 1700; in Margry, 1876–86: 4:413–14); "The Taensas are only about 700 souls" (De Montigny, 1699; in Shea, 1861: 76); and "ils arrivèrent aux Temas le 14. Cette nation était de deux cent cinquante hommes" (Bénard de La Harpe, 1831: 29). Mooney's estimate of 800 is more than the 600 implied by D'Iberville's estimate of 150 families but substantially less than the 1,000 to 1,200 persons suggested by D'Iberville in 1702 and Bénard de La Harpe in 1700.

Central States in 1650

51. *Erie–4,000.* Mooney's notes show two references relative to this estimate, both from the *Jesuit Relations:* (1) 2,000 to 3,000 warriors, in the letter of Jean de Quens, Quebec, September 7, 1656: "Ils estoient deux à trois mille combatans, sans les femmes & les enfants" (Thwaites, 1896–1901: 42:178); (2) 2,000 men, in the letter of François le Mercier, Quebec, September 21, 1654: "Cette Nation du Chat est grandement peuplée . . . On fait estat de deux mille hômes bien agueris" (Thwaites, 1896–1901: 41:82). Mooney's notes also refer to an estimate from "Lewis and Clark, 1806, page 55," of 300 warriors and 1,000 souls, which I was not able to locate.

In spite of the fact that the Jesuit accounts describe the Erie as having 2,000 to 3,000 warriors, and thus a total population of 8,000 to 12,000,

Mooney estimated only 4,000. The conservative nature of this estimate is emphasized by the following remarks by Hewitt in his article on the Erie in the *Handbook of American Indians:* "it is possible to make a rough estimate of the population of the Erie at the period of this final war. At the taking of the Erie town of Riqué in 1654 it is claimed that the defenders numbered between 3,000 and 4,000 combatants, exclusive of women and children; but as it is not likely that all the warriors of the tribe were present, 14,500 would probably be a conservative estimate of the population of the Erie at this time" (Hewitt, 1907: 431).

52. *Fox (now represented by a band in Iowa)—3,000.* Mooney's notes refer to the following three passages from the *Jesuit Relations:* (1) 1,000 warriors, "Outagami . . . ce sont peuples nombreux d'environ mil hommes portans armes" (letter of François le Mercier, Quebec, November 10, 1667; in Thwaites, 1896–1901: 51:42); (2) 400 warriors, "Cette Nation est renommée pour être nombreuse, ils sont plus de quatre cens hommes portans les armes: le nombre des femmes & enfans y est plus grand, à cause de la polygamie qui regne parmy eux, chaque homme ayant communément quatre femmes, quelques-uns six, & d'autres jusques à dix" (letter of Claude Allouez, Ste. Marie du Sault, June 1670; in Thwaites, 1896–1901: 54:218); and (3) 1,000 to 4,000 families, "Ces peuples sont superbes, parce qu'ils sont nombreux, on y compte plus de deux cens Cabanes, dans chacune desquelles, il y a cinq à six, & mesme jusques à dix familles" (letter of Claude Dablon, Quebec, 1671; in Thwaites, 1896–1901: 55:218). Mooney apparently relied upon the most conservative of the above statements, that of François le Mercier, suggesting a population of 1,000 men and thus 4,000 souls.

53. *Illinois confederates (now about 1/6 of Peoria, etc., in Oklahoma)— 8,000.* Mooney's notes refer to a variety of estimates for the Illinois, ranging from 1,500 warriors by Jean Cavelier in 1690 (Margry, 1876–86: 3:589), to an undocumented estimate of 100,000 in 1697. His published estimate of 8,000 is apparently based on the following passage by Claude Dablon, from Quebec in 1674: "quelques-unes de 300, comme celle des Ilinois qui a plus de 8,000 âmes" (Thwaites, 1896–1901: 58:96).

54. *Kickapoo (including perhaps 350 or more in Mexico in 1907)—2,000.* Mooney's notes refer to estimates of 80 warriors in 1836, 180 warriors in 1763, 300 warriors in 1764, 3,000 souls in 1759, 2,000 in 1817, 2,200 in 1820, 2,200 in 1822, and 55 in 1855. He apparently placed particular importance upon the estimates for 1759 and 1822. These two original statements are as follows: "18. Kekopos, about 80 miles beyond Fort

Detroit, 600 [fighting men] . . . fighting men be computed at one in five of all the inhabitants" (Croghan, 1759; in Rupp, 1846: 146), which would mean a total of 3,000; and Morse's estimate of 2,200 Kickapoo in both Indiana and Illinois (Morse, 1822: 363). Mooney's estimate of 2,000 in 1650 must be a conservative guess based upon these two accounts.

55. *Mascouten–1,500.* The only estimate referred to in Mooney's notes is the estimate of 400 men by Claude Dablon from Quebec, 1671: "la Nation du Feu [Mascouten] . . . Elle est jointe . . . à un autre peuple, nommé Oumami [Miami] . . . Ils sont ensemble plus de trois mille ames, pouvant fournir chacune quatre cens hommes" (Thwaites, 1896–1901: 55:200), which implies a population of 1,600 souls.

56. *Menomini–3,000.* Mooney's notes show estimates of 350 souls in 1764, 2,000 warriors in 1778, 300 warriors and 1,350 souls in 1806, 4,170 souls in 1820, 3,900 souls in 1825, and 4,200 souls in 1829. Mooney also notes "closest estimate = 600 w (total 3900!) = say 3000," apparently referring to data presented by Morse (1822: 375) listing 600 warriors in a total population of 3,900. Mooney apparently felt the ratio was closer to 1 to 5, and thus used a total population figure of 3,000. However, Morse's estimate of 3,900 applied only to those Menomini in Wisconsin along three rivers. Actually, he listed an additional 270 living along a fourth (Illinois) river for a total of 4,170 (Morse, 1822: 362–63), making Mooney's estimate even more conservative. The questionable nature of this estimate is verified by Mooney himself: "The earliest statements of Menominee population are unreliable. Most of the estimates in the nineteenth century vary from 1300 to 2500, but those probably most conservative range from 1600 to 1900" (Mooney and Thomas, 1907b: 843).

57. *Miami (including Wea and Piankashaw)–4,500.* Mooney's notes cite the following estimates: 24,000 souls in 1657–1658, 3,000 souls in 1671, 1,200 to 1,500 warriors and 4,800 to 6,000 souls in 1680, 1,500 warriors in 1690, 500 families in 1702, 200 warriors in 1736, 350 warriors in 1812, and 1,400 souls in 1822. These estimates are located in the following original sources: "La sixiéme Nation, dont les peuples s'appellent les Oumamik, est distante de soixante lieuës, ou environ, de S. Michel. Elle a bien huit mille hommes, ce sont plus de vingt quatre mille ames" (Jacques Renault, 1657–58; in Thwaites 1896–1901: 44:246); "La Nation du Feu [Mascouten] . . . Elle est jointe . . . à un autre peuple, nommé Oumami [Miami] . . . Ils sont en- semble plus de trois mille ames, pouvant fournir chacune quatre cens hommes" (Claude Dablon, 1671; in Thwaites, 1896–1901: 55:200); "Les

Iroquois de tous les villages ne font au plus que quinze cents combat-
tans ... les Miamis de mesme" (Jean Cavelier, 1690; in Margry, 1876–86:
3:589); "les Miamis de 1,200 à 1,500 [guerriers]" (Cavelier de La Salle,
1679–1681; in Margry, 1876–86: 1:505); "Les Miamis ... 500 familles"
(D'Iberville, 1702; in Margry, 1876–86: 4:602); "200 warriors" (Chauvignerie, 1736; in Schoolcraft, 1851–57: 3:555); "350 fighting men"
(Hutchins, 1764; in Schoolcraft, 1851–57: 3:555); "300 fighting men" (an
Army officer, 1812; in Schoolcraft, 1851–57: 3:555); and "Miamies, Weas &
Eel river Indians 1400 [souls]" (Morse, 1822: 363).

Mooney apparently ignored the early estimate of 24,000 and relied upon a
conservative interpretation of the Jesuit estimates. The difficulties in making
early estimates are emphasized by Mooney and Thomas (1907c: 854): "It is
impossible to give a satisfactory estimate of the numbers of the Miami at any
one time, on account of confusion with the Wea and Piankashaw, who
probably never exceeded 1,500. An estimate in 1764 gives them 1,750;
another the following year places their number at 1,250."

58. *Ojibwa (United States and Canada)–35,000.* Mooney's notes cite
the following references on the Ojibwa (or Chippewa): "Chippeways of Lake
Superior and Lake Michigan ... 5,000 [fighting men]" (Hutchins, 1764; in
Schoolcraft, 1851–57: 3:556); "Chipwas ... 5000 [warriors]" (Bouquet,
1764; in Schoolcraft, 1851–57: 3:559); "Chippawas ... 8,335 ... Col. Dick-
son, long a resident among the Chippawas, states their number residing about
the Great Lake, at 10,000. Others make the whole number of the tribe,
30,000" (Morse, 1822: 362). Mooney estimated their number in 1650 at
35,000 mainly to allow for bands that may have been unknown by the early
observers: "The principal estimates are as follow: In 1764, about 25,000;
1783 and 1794, about 15,000; 1843, about 30,000; 1851, about 28,000. It is
probable that most of these estimates take no account of more remote
bands" (Mooney and Thomas, 1907a: 279–80).

59. *Potawatomi (including 180 in Canada)–4,000.* Mooney's notes indicate he consulted the following statements on Potawatomi population: (1)
300 warriors, "Nous les avons tous veus icy, au nombre de trois cents
hommes, portans armes" (Claude Jean Allouez, 1667; in Thwaites,
1896–1901: 51:26); (2) 700 men, 3,000 souls, "Le Pere Gabriel
Dreuillettes ... à fait porter le nom de Saint Michel au premier Bourg, dont il
fait mention. Ceux qui l'habitent, se nomment en Algonquin, les Oupou-
teouatamik. On compte dans ce Bourg environ sept cent hommes, c'est à dire
trois mille ames, dautant que pour un homme, il se trouve pour le moins trois
ou quatre autres personnes, sçavoir est, les femmes & les enfans" (Paul

Ragueneau, 1657; in Thwaites, 1896–1901: 44:244). Schoolcraft (1851–57: 3:556) listed three estimates: (1) 310 warriors, attributed to Chauvignerie in 1736; (2) 350 fighting men, attributed to Hutchins in 1764; and (3) 500 fighting men, attributed to an Army officer in 1812. Mooney's estimate is 1,000 more than he and Hewitt guessed in 1910: "The tribe probably never greatly exceeded 3,000 souls, and most estimates place them far below that number" (Mooney and Hewitt, 1910: 291).

60. *Sauk–3,500.* Mooney's notes cite estimates of 150 warriors by Chauvignerie in 1736 (Schoolcraft, 1851–57: 3:554); 400 fighting men by Hutchins and Bouquet in 1764 (Schoolcraft, 1851–57: 3:554); 700 warriors and 2,850 souls by Pike in 1806 (Coues, 1895: 346); 500 warriors and 2,000 souls by Lewis and Clark in 1804 (Thwaites, 1904–5: 6:92); and 4,500 souls in 1820 (Morse, 1822: 363). Although the exact source of Mooney's 3,500 estimate is not available, the estimate does agree with Hewitt's statement: "the close relations of the Sauk with the Foxes in historical times make it difficult to form more than an approximate estimate of their numbers in the past, but it is probable that the population of the tribe never exceeded 3,500 souls" (Hewitt, 1910: 479).

61. *Shawnee–3,000.* Mooney's notes refer to the 1736 estimate of 200 warriors by Chauvignerie, 500 fighting men by Hutchins in 1764, 300 fighting men by an Army officer in 1812 (Schoolcraft, 1851–57: 3:555), and 2,183 souls by Morse in 1820 (Morse, 1822: 362, 366). His 3,000 figure must have been a guess above these estimates, since he commented that "the early estimates of the numbers of the Shawnee are only partial, owing to the fact that the tribe was not united. The highest estimate given is that of 1817 [undocumented], which places them at 2,000 souls" (Mooney, 1910b: 536).

62. *Winnebago–3,800.* The earliest estimate noted by Mooney is 3,000 men by Jean de Quens in Quebec, September 7, 1656: "Un François m'a dit autrefois, qu'il avoit veu trois mille hommes dans une assemblée, qu se fit pour traiter de paix, au Païs des gens de Mer" (Thwaites, 1896–1901: 42:222). Other estimates cited by Mooney are 80 warriors by Chauvignerie in 1736, 700 fighting men by Hutchins in 1764; 300 fighting men by an Army officer in 1812 (Schoolcraft, 1851–57: 3:556); 450 warriors by Pike in 1806 (Coues, 1895: 346); and the estimates "5,800 [souls] . . . Major O'Fallon states the number of Winnebagoes at about 4,000" (Morse, 1822: 362). Mooney apparently felt the 1656 estimate was too high and most of the others too low, guessing the population in 1650 at 3,800.

Northern Plains in 1780

63. *Arapaho—3,000.* First of all, whereas Swanton's edited, published version of Mooney's estimate is 3,000 for the year 1780, Mooney's manuscript indicates the estimate should be 3,100. Mooney noted Lewis and Clark's estimate of 300 warriors and 1,400 souls in 1805 (Thwaites, 1904–5: 6:87), but apparently based his estimate on his interpretation of Alexander Mackenzie's earlier comments: "The Fall, or Big-bellied Indians, are from the South-Eastward also, and of a people who inhabit the plains from the North bend of the last mentioned river, latitude 47.32. North, longitude 101.25. West, to the South bend of the Assiniboin River, to the number of seven hundred men" (Mackenzie, 1801: lxxi). A note in Mooney's handwriting located in the back of an edition of the Mackenzie volume in what was formerly the library of the Bureau of American Ethnology (and is now the library of the Department of Anthropology, Smithsonian Institution) indicates Mooney interpreted the above estimate to apply to the Arapaho. He apparently multiplied the 700 warrior count by 4 for a total count of 2,800. He then apparently guessed that the actual figure ten years earlier, in 1780, must have been 300 greater.

64. *Arikara—3,000.* Mooney's notes indicate that the 3,000 estimate for 1780 is a conservative projection of Lewis and Clark's estimate in 1804 of 500 warriors and 2,000 souls (Thwaites, 1904–5: 6:88). Mooney noted that by 1804 the Arikara population had already been greatly reduced by the smallpox epidemics of 1781 and 1802; he thus guessed that in 1780 the population may have numbered 3,000.

65. *Assiniboin—10,000.* Mooney's notes show that he consulted the following estimates: 150 warriors in 1736 by Chauvignerie, 1,500 warriors in 1764 by Hutchins (Schoolcraft, 1851–57: 3:556), 900 warriors and 3,200 souls in 1804 by Lewis and Clark (Thwaites, 1904–5: 6:104), 2,000 warriors in 1825 by Atkinson (1826: 12), 8,000 souls in 1829 by Porter (Schoolcraft, 1851–57: 3:594), 8,000 in 1835 by Catlin (Donaldson, 1887: 118), 3,500 warriors in 1837 by Atkinson (1837: 20), and 8,000 souls in 1839 by Farnham (Thwaites, 1906: 156). Mooney's estimate of 10,000 appears to be a conservative guess, based largely on the 8,000 estimate by Catlin in 1835: "A tribe of 8,000 . . . Four thousand of these people [later] destroyed by the smallpox in 1838, since I was amongst them" (Donaldson, 1887: 118). The conservative nature of Mooney's estimate is emphasized by these comments from his notes: "It is possible that the earlier estimates here given for the Assiniboin may be entirely too low as the trader Benville in 1823 says that they had always been considered to number nearly as many as the Sioux, and

Maximilian in 1833 seems to agree. The Assiniboin were among the principal sufferers of the great smallpox of 1781 and perhaps suffered again in 1802. They lost heavily also of the same disease in 1837, one camp of over 1000 persons being reduced to 150 (Hayden) and again in 1870 when it is said one half the 'Stoney' band of Canada died. The Canadian figures cannot always be separated from those for other tribes, but those in Montana have decreased from 2365 in 1880 to 1248 in 1906."

66. *Atsina–3,000.* The earliest population estimates referred to in Mooney's notes are 600 warriors in about 1790 by Mackenzie (1801: lxx) and 500 warriors and 2,500 souls by Lewis and Clark in 1804 (Thwaites, 1904–5: 6:91). The Mackenzie estimate implies a population of 2,400 in 1790. Mooney must have guessed that ten years earlier (1780) the population was about 3,000. The estimate must be considered conservative, since according to Mooney's notes "the Atsina were directly in the path of the great smallpox epidemic of 1781. They were heavy losers also about 1820 and 1837, while in the summer of 1870 they lost 741 by the same disease."

67. *Blackfoot–15,000.* An unpublished manuscript in Mooney's notes shows the following estimates and discussion: "1780–15000, 1790–10,000 (2250 to 2550 warriors Mackenzie), 1833–18000, 1842–13000, 1850–9600, 1854–6720 (Stevens), 1906–4549. The Blackfeet were principal sufferers of the smallpox of 1781, Mackenzie estimates that they lost one-half, altho it is hardly possible that they were reduced to 8 or 9000, as the lowest estimates 40 years later (1825–1833) give them 5000 warriors. They suffered heavily of the same disease in 1837–8, 1845, 1857–8, and in 1869, when it was officially estimated that those of the U.S. alone lost 1400 souls. In 1845 an entire band was exterminated by the crows. In 1864 measles destroyed many. In 1870 Colonel Baker killed 173 in the 'Piegan Massacre.' In 1883–4 some 700 starved to death in Montana. Those in Canada have decreased by 248 in the last 4 years. They are still decreasing on both sides of the line."

Thus Mooney based his 1790 estimate on Mackenzie's comments: "Opposite to those Eastward, on the head-waters of the South Branch, are the Picaneaux, to the number of from twelve to fifteen hundred men. Next to them, on the same water, are the Blood-Indians, of the same nation as the last, to the number of about fifty tents, or two hundred and fifty men. From them downwards extend the Black-Feet Indians, of the Same nation as the two last tribes: their number may be eight hundred men" (Mackenzie, 1801: lxx). He felt that the above estimates for the three groups implied a population of 10,000 in 1790 and probably 5,000 more in 1780, before the 1781 epidemic.

68. *Cheyenne, etc.—3,500.* An unpublished manuscript in Mooney's notes shows the source of this estimate: "1780—3500?, 1822—3460 (Morse), 1875—3782, 1890—3674, 1900—3446, 1906—3334. Owing to the remoteness of the Cheyenne from traders and trade communications in the early period it is difficult to make any reliable estimate of their number. In the middle period we find the same difficulty, due to the facts that they were in two widely separated bands and were almost constantly at war with the whites. From 1875 they have been under constant government supervision. Morse's estimate in 1822 is probably nearly right and they may have numbered more before the smallpox of 1781. They seem not to have been much affected by the smallpox of 1837, but lost heavily in the cholera of 1849. Not withstanding these often heavy war losses between 1864 and 1879 they seem actually to have increased until finally restricted to a reservation, since which they have steadily decreast."

Mooney's notes indicate he consulted Lewis and Clark's estimate in 1804 of 300 warriors and 1,200 souls (Thwaites, 1904—5: 6:100), but relied upon Morse's comments in 1822: "Chayennes, or Chiens 3,260 [souls] on Chayenne river, above Great Bend. 200 [souls] Head of the above river" (Morse, 1822: 366).

69. *Crow—4,000.* Mooney's notes list the following population figures: 1780—4,000, 1804—3,500, 1833—4,500, 1842—4,000, 1866—3,900, 1880—3,470, 1890—2,456, 1900—1,941, 1906—1,804. His notes refer to a variety of estimates, mostly in the early nineteenth century, but he apparently relied upon the 1804 estimate of Lewis and Clark of 900 warriors and 3,500 souls (Thwaites, 1904—5; 6:103). Apparently he noted but discounted the 1876 statement by Bradley: "Here they suffered from the visitation of the small-pox, already described, by which their numbers were reduced from about one thousand lodges, or ten thousand souls, to six hundred lodges with six thousand souls" (Bradley, 1896: 179).

70. *Hidatsa, etc.—2,500.* Mooney's estimate for the Hidatsa is based on a conservative interpretation of Lewis and Clark's estimate of 550 warriors and 2,700 souls in 1804 (Thwaites, 1904—5: 6:90—91). His notes cite estimates as high as 15,000 in 1835, but he apparently considered them unreliable.

71. *Iowa—1,200.* Mooney's unpublished manuscript presents the following estimates and discussion: "1780—1200; 1804—800 (L.C.); 1806—1200 (300 w. 1400 souls—Pike); 1829—1000 (Porter); 1822—1000 (Morse); 1847—706 (Special census). According to Alcedo, the Iowa about 1766 had 700 warriors, but this seems doubtful. Chauvignerie in 1736 gives them 1100

souls, which Bouquet in 1764 makes *warriors,* a great exaggeration. Pike in 1806 gave them 1400 souls and an estimate of 1836 gave them 1500. Their swift decline has been due chiefly to dissipation, particularly after the establishment of the California emigrant trail thru their county about 1850. Of late they seem to be increasing, but the difference may be due to the intermarriage of whites."

Thus Mooney apparently based his 1,200 estimate on what he thought was an estimate of 1,100 souls by Chauvignerie in 1736. Actually, the estimate attributed to Chauvignerie by Schoolcraft is "80 warriors" and not 1,100 souls as indicated by Mooney. Mooney apparently misread the estimates in Schoolcraft (1851–57: 3:557), which on the same line as the Chauvignerie estimate lists Hutchins' 1764 estimate of 1,100 warriors. Mooney's reference to Bouquet's estimate of 1,100 warriors is correct (Schoolcraft, 1851–57: 3:559).

There is also some question whether Chauvignerie even authored the report in 1736, attributed to him by Schoolcraft. Schoolcraft took this estimate from an anonymous manuscript in 1736 that stated: "The Ayowois are settled at the south of the River de Missouris, at the other side of the Mississippi. They are no more than eighty" (O'Callaghan, 1855: 1055). The editor of this volume, E. B. O'Callaghan, attributes authorship to Joncaire (O'Callaghan, 1855: 1058). Schoolcraft attributed it to Chauvignerie and felt it meant warriors and not souls. The original document is a manuscript in the French Canadian Archives (No. C11, 66:247).

72. *Kansa–3,000.* Mooney's notes contain the following estimates and discussion: "1702–6000 (1500 families) (Iberville), 1804–1300 (Lewis and Clark), 1820–1500 (Long), 1836–1471 (Porter), 1843–1588, 1850–1300, 1866–670 . . . The Kansa were at one time one of the most important tribes on Missouri r. being rated by Iberville at 1500 families, possibly 7000 souls, and as his estimates for other tribes seem good, this also is probably not far wrong.

Thus Mooney's estimate of 3,000 for the Kansa is based on a conservative interpretation of D'Iberville's statements: "Les Cansés . . . 1,500 familles" (D'Iberville; in Margry, 1876–86: 4:601) and "On y peut faire venir pour l'habiter les Kansés, que l'on estime quinze cents familles" (D'Iberville; in Margry, 1876–86: 4:599).

73. *Kiowa–2,000.* Mooney's notes contain the following estimates and discussion: "1780–2000, 1836–1800 (Schoolcraft III est.), 1846–2000 (Bent), 1854–1500 est., 1867–1680, 1873–1600 (Battey) . . . The earlier estimates for the Kiowa are entirely unreliable, owing to the remote position & wandering habit of the tribe, and the confusion of synonyms, resulting in

the listing of the tribe under different names 2 or 3 times by the same writer. Thus Lewis and Clark in 1805 give them 200 warriors while Pike in 1810 gives them 1000 warriors. The Indian Report for 1867 gives them and the Comanche together 4,000 souls, while the Peace Commission in the same year estimates these two tribes at 14800. Bent, their trader and Battey, their camp teacher, were in best position to know the facts. They suffered heavily from the smallpox of 1801 and the cholera of 1849, but not so much from the smallpox of 1837–8."

Thus Mooney referred to both the accounts of Lewis and Clark: "70 [tents or lodges]; 200 [warriors]; 700 [souls]" (Thwaites, 1904–5: 6:100), and of Pike: "The Kyaways [Kiowas] wander on the sources of La Platte and are supposed to be 1,000 men strong" (Coues, 1895: 2:743–44). Mooney's estimate of 2,000 in 1780 represents a conservative average between the two accounts.

74. *Kiowa-Apache–300.* Mooney's notes contain the following: "1780–300?, 1805–300, 1850–320?, 1878–344 ... The earliest estimate for the Kiowa Apache is by Lewis and Clark, who call them Cataka. They were probably then about as numerous as at any earlier period, having probably not suffered much, if any, from the smallpox of 1781 or 1801. Later estimates are frequently unreliable, from the fact that until very recently they had usually living with them a number of the closely cognate Lijan and Mescalero. They suffered from the cholera of 1849 and again from measles in 1892 and have steadily declined since."

Thus Mooney based the estimate on Lewis and Clark's estimate of 25 tents, 75 warriors, and 300 souls (Thwaites, 1904–5: 6:101).

75. *Mandan–3,600.* Mooney lists the following: "1780–3600, 1804–1250, 1833–1000, 1842–300, 1878–273, 1890–244, 1900–250, 1906–264. This tribe when first visited, may have exceeded 4000 souls. In 1738 (Verendrye) & until about 1780 or later (Lewis and Clark) the Mandan had 6 villages, which were said to be the remains of 9 earlier villages. According to Verendrye the smallest of these in his time had 130 houses. In 1804 Lewis and Clark give them 2 villages with about 1250 souls or 625 each. In 1833 Maximilian gives these 2 villages about 100 houses, averaging about 10 persons each, with total of 900 or 1000 souls. They were principal sufferers by the smallpox of 1781, which seems to have started in their tribe and from which probably dates their decline. In their weakened condition they were further wasted by the Sioux. The great smallpox of 1837–8 also started in their villages—June 15, 1837—and within a few months destroyed so many that for some time it was believed that the tribe had been exterminated. DeSmet says only 10 families were left. By intermarriage with alien Indians,

who then took the name of Mandan, they gradually built up a small tribe,
apparently keeping about at the same point for the last 65 years."

The earliest reference cited by Mooney is that by Vérendrye (1738): "He
begged me to stay at his fort, which was the nearest, a smaller one than the
others . . . There were six forts, he said, belonging to the same tribe" (Burpee,
1927: 320), and "I gave orders to count the cabins and we found that there
were about one hundred and thirty" (Burpee, 1927: 339). These statements
imply that the smallest of six villages had 130 houses, and thus all of the
villages had at least 780 houses. At about ten persons per house, this implies a
minimum population of 7,800, assuming that Vérendrye was given the
correct information by the Mandan and that his count of "cabins" referred
only to dwelling units and not to all structures.

Mooney also referred to estimates by Lewis and Clark in 1804 of two
villages containing 350 warriors and 1250 souls (Thwaites, 1904–5: 6:89) and
by Maximilian in 1833 of two villages containing 233 to 240 warriors and
900 to 1,000 souls (Bodmer, 1841: 372). Mooney's notes show calculations
of six villages with 50 houses each for a total of 300 houses, each house with
ten souls for a total of 3,000 souls. This appears to be Mooney's conservative
synthesis, which he increased slightly to his published figure of 3,600 in 1780
and unpublished figure of 4,000 in 1738.

76. *Missouri—1,000.* Mooney's notes reveal the following: "1702–800
(200 families—Iberville), 1804–300 (Lewis and Clark), 1829–100 (Porter)
and 1885–40. The Missouri when first known (1673—Marquette) were a
leading tribe. Their importance is shown by the fact that Hutchins and
Bouquet in 1764 even estimate them at 3000 warriors! Iberville, however,
probably an authority, puts them at 200 families in 1702, altho in an
accompaning table he gives them, in figures, 1500 families. As the first
estimate—200 families—is spelled out, we give it preference. They were
probably weakened later by epidemic visitations of which we have no record,
but which gave opportunity to the Sauk and Foxes to accomplish their
practical destruction, driving them from their village and making a final
massacre (noted by Maximilian 117, 1843) which compelled the Missouri to
take refuge with the Oto about 1798. They suffered heavily from the
smallpox of 1802. In 1804 Lewis and Clark described them as having been
'the most numerous nation inhabiting the Missouri, when first known to the
French,' but reduced to a dependent remnant by 'repeated attacks of the
smallpox' and by wars with the Sauk and Foxes."

Thus Mooney's estimate is based on D'Iberville's account in 1702: "les
Missouris, qui sont deux cents familles" (Margry, 1876–86: 4:599). Mooney
called attention to the estimate by Hutchins and Bouquet in 1764 of 3,000

warriors and the estimate of 1,500 families in D'Iberville's chart (Margry, 1876–86: 4:601), but considered the D'Iberville lower estimate to be more accurate.

77. *Omaha–2,800.* Mooney's notes list estimates of 4,800 for 1702, 2,800 for 1780, 600? for 1804, 1,500 for 1820, 1,600 for 1836, and 1,301 for 1843. He wrote: "The Omaha present the rare exception of an Indian tribe steadily increasing under modern conditions of civilization, after having lost heavily, like the others, by repeated epidemic visitation and other misfortunes. This exceptional record is due to several causes—first, the fact that they have never been removed from their own country; second, a constant abundant food supply from their own agriculture; third, government protection for a long period from their former merciless enemies, the Sioux; and fourth, comparative absence of dissipation and consequent disease, owing to the continuous effort of resident missionaries and teachers. Iberville's estimate may be too high, altho his figures generally seem reasonable, but there may easily have been some epidemic between then and the later period. They were nearly exterminated in the great smallpox of 1802. Lewis and Clark state that 10 years before they had had 700 warriors and were 'the terror of their neighbors,' but had been reduced by it to 'less than 300' (souls?). They give them in the 'Statistical View' 150 warriors and 600 souls. Both of these estimates are probably too low. They suffered again from smallpox in 1837, and lost heavily by the cholera in 1849. The estimate ostensibly for 1850 must have been made before this visitation since then there has been a constant and marked increase."

Thus Mooney's notes show two early estimates for the Omaha: (1) the 1780 estimate of 2,800, which was the one used by Swanton, and (2) an earlier estimate of 4,800 for 1702. The estimate for 1702 is based on D'Iberville's comments: "les Mahas, qui sont plus de douze cents familles" (Margry, 1876–86: 4:598) and "Les Maha . . . 1,200 familles" (Margry, 1876–86: 4:601). Mooney's published estimate of 2,800 for 1780 is based on Lewis and Clark's comment: "about ten years since, they boasted 700 warriors" (Thwaites, 1904–5: 6:88).

78. *Osage–6,200.* Mooney's notes show estimates of 6,200? in 1780 (no source), 6,000 in 1804 (Lewis and Clark), and 5,200 in 1820 (no source). He commented: "The Osage are estimated at 1600 warriors in 1764 by Bouquet, and at 1500 warriors and 6300 souls by Lewis and Clark in 1804. As they had probably suffered from the smallpox of 1802, if not from earlier consequences of white contact, they were probably then already on the decrease."

Actually, Bouquet's estimate is only 600 warriors in both the original (W. Smith, 1868: 154) and in Schoolcraft (1851–57: 3:559). Mooney apparently confused the Osage estimate with the 1,600 Kansa estimate, located immediately below it in the Schoolcraft volume.

79. *Oto—900.* Mooney's notes show the following estimates and discussion: "1780—800?, 1804—500 (Lewis and Clark), 1822—1500 (Morse), 1825—1400 (Atkinson). The Oto probably numbered 800 or 1000 before the incorporation of the remnant of the Missouri, about 1798 and the great smallpox epidemic of 1802. In 1804 Lewis and Clark estimate the Oto at 120 warriors and 500 souls, and the Missouri at 80 warriors and 300 souls."

Mooney refers to the following four sources: (1) Lewis and Clark, 120 warriors and 500 souls in 1804 (Thwaites, 1904—5: 6:85); (2) D'Iberville, 1702: "Les Toctata, les Ayooués—300 [familles]" (Margry, 1876—86: 4:601), and "Les Ayooués et les Octoctatas, leurs voisins, sont environ trois cents bons hommes" (Margry, 1876—86: 4:598); (3) 1,500 in 1822 by Morse (1822: 366)—the actual reference is "Ottoes, Missouries, & Ioways . . . 1,800 [souls]"; and (4) "The Ottoes reside on the Platte, 25 miles south of the Missouri, in a dirt village, consist of about 1400 souls, of whom 275 are warriors" (Atkinson, 1826: 7).

80. *Pawnee—10,000.* Mooney's notes contain the following: "1780—10,000, 1804—4,000 (3 bands only—L.C.), 1820—6500 (3 bands only—Long), 1825—8200 (2050 warriors; 10250 souls—Atkinson), 1835—10,000 (Dunbar and Allis) . . . Of all the tribes of the Plains the Pawnee afford the most striking instance of rapid decline within a brief historic period. Omitting a French estimate of 25000 in 1719, the estimates in the 18th century—Iberville in 1702 and Bouquet in 1764 give them 2000 warriors, or about 8000 souls. In 1802 they were ravaged by the smallpox, which seems to have destroyed more than half the Indian population of the middle and lower Plains. Lewis and Clark probably found them at their lowest point, but increasing."

Specifically, the accounts are as follows: "Les Panis, proches des Akansa 2,000 familles" (D'Iberville, 1702; in Margry, 1876—86: 4:601) and "Les Panis, qui sont deux mille hommes" (D'Iberville, 1702; in Margry, 1876—86: 4:599); "Panis blancs, south of Missouri—2000 [warriors] (Bouquet, 1764: in W. Smith, 1868: 154); "The Grand Paunees consist of about 5,500 souls, of which 1,100 are warriors, and the Paunee Republics at 1,250 souls, of whom 275 are warriors" (Atkinson, 1826: 7); "Pania proper . . . 400 [warriors]; 1,600 [souls]"; "Pania Loup . . . 280 [warriors]; 1000 [souls]"; "Pania Republicans . . . 300 [warriors] 1,400 [souls]" (Lewis and Clark, 1804: in Thwaites, 1904—5: 6:86—87).

Mooney's estimate of 10,000 and the 25,000 estimate of 1719 that he rejected both were taken apparently from the following statement by Dunbar: "Population. This is a matter of the greatest uncertainty till 1834. I find an estimate of them in 1719 (attributed to Mr. Dutisné already mentioned), at about 25,000 of no special value . . . In 1834 Major Dougherty, the Pawnee agent, and well versed in the affairs of the tribe, estimated them at 12,500. Messrs. Dunbar and Allis, while traveling with the tribe during the three years following, thought this too high, and placed them at 10,000" (Dunbar, 1880: 254).

81. *Ponca–800*. According to Mooney's notes: "The Ponca were always a small tribe, and seem to have varied little in number in a century. When met by Lewis and Clark in 1804 they had been greatly wasted by the smallpox of 1802, but it is evident that the figures given by these explorers are too low." Thus Mooney's estimate of 800 is a guess, well above the estimates of 50 warriors and 200 souls by Lewis and Clark in 1804 (Thwaites, 1904–5: 6:88).

82. *Sioux–25,000*. Mooney's notes contain the following estimates and discussion: "1702–16000 (4000 families–Iberville), 1780–20000, 1806–21675 (Pike), 1823–28100 (Long) . . . Of all the Plains tribes, the Sioux alone seem actually to have increased in the last century. Altho they suffered heavily from the smallpox epidemics of 1781 and 1801, it is evident from a comparison of authorities and known facts that Lewis and Clark's estimate of 2520 warriors and 8410 souls in 1804 is entirely too low. Pike shortly afterward, gives them nearly three times as many, and they seem to have kept on a steady increase despite epidemics and frequent wars with the whites. This is due to their own original superior number, by which they were able to control a large hunting territory and to incorporate many captives of successful war upon their neighbors."

Thus Mooney ruled out estimates of 2,520 warriors and 8,410 souls by Lewis and Clark in 1804 as "too low." He accepted D'Iberville's estimate of 4,000 families (and warriors) in 1702 (Margry, 1876–86: 4:587, 601) and its implied estimate of 16,000 souls in 1702. However, he apparently based his 1780 estimate of 20,000 on Pike's estimate of 21,675 in 1806 and later raised the figure to the published 25,000.

Southern Plains In 1690

83. *Akokisa–500*. This estimate appears to be based directly upon population statistics sent by Herbert Bolton to Mooney in about 1906. According to the Bolton manuscript: "The earliest clue to the size of the Arkokesa tribe that I find is the statement made in 1748 that they had four rancheriás or villages (The viceroy to Orobio y Basterra, Jan. 29, 1748, Bexar Archives). Later I find this statement frequently verified by men writing from the

Arkokesa country (Domingo del Rio, 1756, in Nacogdoches Archives, Doc. No. 488). The ranchería of the head chief contained in 1756 'more than 20 Indios de fusil' (Miranda, in ibid.) If this was a representative village, there were 100 or more men in the tribe, or 400 or 500 persons."[4]

84. *Aranama–200.* The Aranama are not mentioned in the Bolton manuscript. Mooney's only note on the population refers to the 1820 comments by Morse: "Arrenamuses 120" (souls) (Morse, 1822: 374).

85. *Bidai–500.* Mooney apparently guessed at this figure, based on the following comments from Bolton: "We know that in the early eighteenth century there were several villages of this tribe southwest of the Nabedache, but figures are scarce. We frequently get figures for special bands but general ones rarely. The Bidai composed the larger number of the neophytes of Mission San Ildefonso, on the San Gabriel r, March 18, 1748; Juan Galvan reported that, when he was writing, a squadron of Bidai arrived at the mission and said that more than 400 Gentiles were on the way to it. They were presumably mainly Bidai, particularly as he mentioned the Arlokesa separately (Letter of Francisco Ganzabal after March 18, 1848). Some Bidai were already at San Xavier. In the epidemic at the San Xavier missions c. 1749 or 1759, about 400 died, and the Bidai, of San Ildefonso, were the heaviest sufferers (Arricivita, Cronica, Pt. II, 328) [Arricivita, 1792]. In March, 1778, Mezieres wrote from Bucareli near the Bidai settlement, that the latter contained about 100 men, an equal number having died in the recent epidemic (Mem. 28: 271) [Bolton, 1914: 2:189]. Croix wrote in Sept. of the same year that they had been reduced by the epidemic to 60 men (Relación Particular, Archivo General, P.I., 182) [Croix, 1778: 182]. The junta held at San Antonio Jan. 1778, estimated 70 men. Sibley (1805) [1806: 51] gives them 100 men, an overestimate, perhaps. Davenport (c. 1809) reported about 60 men (Noticia) [Davenport, 1809]. It is evident that within little more than a quarter of a century the Bidai were twice terribly reduced by smallpox, and that between 1776 and 1809 their numbers fell by more than 50%."

86. *Caddo (incl. Hasinai), etc.–8,500.* Mooney's personal notes do not list an early estimate above 2,000 souls for this group. Apparently he relied again on Bolton's unpublished comments: "Almost at the outset of the Spanish period these tribes suffered a severe loss through an epidemic. Jesus María [María Casañas, 1691], the author already quoted, tells us that during

---

4. This manuscript and other notes and letters by Bolton cited in the following discussions are on file in the National Anthropological Archives, National Museum of Natural History, Washington, D.C.

this plague as many as three hundred died within a month among the Hasinai, and among all the friendly tribes called 'Texias', some three thousand died during the year 1690–1691. This testimony is trustworthy, for he was on the ground, and was an intelligent witness . . . The earliest possible estimate of the numerical strength of this group that I have seen was made by Ramón in 1716. In that year he had assisted the Spanish fathers in establishing four missions at the four principal Hasinai villages . . . Ramón [1716] tells us that the four missions 'would comprise from four thousand to five thousand persons of all ages and (both) sexes.' Espinosa [1716], the president of the newly founded missions, corroborates this estimate by recording in his diary of 1716 the opinion that the Indians grouped round the three first of these missions (not including that among the Nacogdoches) would number 3000: and after a residence of a number of years among them he estimated that in his day there had been about four thousand persons within range of the four missions. This estimate must have had a good foundation for as Espinosa tells us, the padres kept visiting lists of all the 'ranchos', with the number of adults and children in each house-hold."

Mooney's figure of 8,500 in 1690 must be based on Bolton's comments that Jesús María suggested that 3,000 persons died in 1690 and 1691, and Ramón found 4,000 to 5,000 persons in 1716.

87. *Comanche–7,000.* The exact source of this estimate is not given; however, Mooney's earliest reference is from Lewis and Clark: "In the year 1724, they resided in several villages on the heads of the Kansas river, and could, at that time, bring upwards of two thousand men into the field (see Monsr. Dupratz history of Louisiana, page 71, and the map attached to that work)" (Thwaites, 1904–5: 6:108). This would imply a population of about 8,000, using Mooney's usual factor of 4 as the ratio between men and total population.

Mooney also relied upon estimates in 1835–1836 of 7,000 by Porter (1836), of 7,000 by the Indian agent Gibson (1835: 297), and the same by Agent Harris (1836: 403). However, he discounted an estimate of 19,200 made in 1837 by the Office of Indian Affairs; the comment by Farnham that "The Cumanches are supposed to be twenty thousand strong" (Thwaites, 1906: 149–50); and an estimate of 30,000 souls by Morse (1822: 374).

88. *Karankawa, etc.–2,800.* Mooney's notes show an original estimate of 3,000 for the year 1690 based on Farnham's 1839 comments: "In 1817, they amounted to about three thousand, of which six hundred were warriors" (Thwaites, 1906: 149). Mooney also noted an estimate from a 1791 report of about 2,500 souls. The source of the report is not clear, but it is probably taken from Mooney's communication from Herbert Bolton.

89. *Kichai—500.* This estimate is apparently a guess, based on the information provided by Bolton that by 1772 the population was already quite reduced to 80 warriors and 30 houses. Bolton's 1772 source was Athanacio de Mézières (Bolton, 1914: 1:285).

90. *Lipan—500.* Mooney's notes indicate he noted but discounted Morse's (1822: 374) estimate of 3,500 souls and relied upon estimates of 200 warriors by Burnett in 1847 and of 500 souls by Neighbors in 1849, both quoted by Schoolcraft (1851—57: 1:518).

91. *Mescalero—700.* This estimate apparently represents a very conservative interpretation of Burnett's calculation in 1847 of 1,000 to 1,500 warriors (Schoolcraft, 1851—57: 1:518).

92. *Coahuiltecan Tribes—15,000.* This estimate is taken directly from a letter by Herbert Bolton to Mooney, dated April 2, 1908, in which Bolton responded to an earlier Mooney request for population data with a detailed discussion of the early population estimates for each of the Coahuiltecan tribes. The estimates are taken from seventeenth- and early eighteenth-century Spanish accounts. In his letter, Bolton commented: "Herewith you have my guess. Before examining my notes I was inclined to say 10,000, simply because I was afraid to say more without study, notwithstanding the fact that I felt that the figure should be higher. I think my results are conservative, for I have clipped all the corners."

93. *Tonkawa, etc.—1,600.* Mooney's notes list 12 different estimates; the published figure of 1,600, however, must represent a guess based on an estimate of 300 warriors in 1778 that Mooney received from Bolton.

94. *Wichita, etc.—3,200.* Mooney based this estimate directly upon Bolton's comments: "The Taovayas-Wichita group, before it was joined by the Panis-Mahas, in 1778 numbered 800 men." According to Bolton's notes: "In March and April of 1778, Mézières visited the Tawakana and Taovayas. Apparently the Towakana village on the Trinity had settled on the Brazos above the village already there in 1772, and the small Wichita tribe had joined the Taovayas. Of neither of these suppositions am I certain, but the subsequent evidence seems to bear them out. There were now two 'Taovayas' villages on the Red River opposite each other. That north of the river had 123 houses and that south of it 37 houses. Each house had 10 or 12 beds, and Mézières gave a 'prudent' estimate of 'men, including youths' of more than 800, or 5 youths and men to a house, which seems reasonable (Letter of Apr.

18, 1778, Mem. de Nueva Espana, XXVIII, 277)" [see Mézières, 1778: 277;
also Bolton, 1914: 2:201–2].

The Columbia Region in 1780

As Mooney stated in his published introduction to this section, he relied
heavily upon the estimates of Lewis and Clark (Thwaites, 1904–5:
6:114–19): "Their estimates for the principal groups at that period seem very
nearly correct as compared with later statements of the Hudson Bay Com-
pany officer, Hale and others" (Mooney, 1928: 14). Table 8.1 compares
tribal population estimates from the Mooney article edited by Swanton,
estimates from the original Mooney notes, and those estimates by Lewis and
Clark that Mooney utilized. The table shows that Mooney frequently used the
Lewis and Clark estimates unchanged, while at times he altered the figures,
probably to allow for the difference in time between the date of Lewis and
Clark's journal (1804–1806) and the theoretical date of the estimate (1780).
The table also shows that the published estimates are slightly greater (730
individuals) than the original estimates (Mooney's notes) for those tribes for
which both estimates are available.

California in 1769

For this state, Mooney did not attempt a tribe-by-tribe inventory, but
relied on Merriam's (1905: 598) published estimate of 260,000. This estimate
is based upon Merriam's careful analysis of mission records within the
"mission strip" area of California and upon Merriam's following assumptions:
(1) that baptized Indians comprised three-fourths of the total population
within the "mission strip"; (2) the "mission strip" comprised one-fifth of the
total fertile land area of the state; (3) population was distributed evenly
within the fertile areas of the state; (4) the population of the desert areas was
about 10,000; and (5) the population of the fertile areas had decreased by
about 50,000 by the close of the Mission period in 1834.

On March 28, 1911, Kroeber wrote to Mooney[5] arguing that the true
figure for California was 150,000, on the basis that (1) "the area tributary to
the missions comprises not a fifth of the fertile part of the state, but a fifth of
the entire state, which would be equivalent to nearly a third of the non-desert
portions"; (2) that a larger percentage of Indians was baptized than Merriam
estimated; and (3) that his own data and assumptions regarding the Yurok
supported this figure. In spite of Kroeber's arguments, Mooney relied upon

5. Letter on file in the National Anthropological Archives, National Museum of
Natural History, Washington, D.C.

Table 8.1
Comparison of Population Estimates for Individual Tribes in the Columbia Region

Tribe	Published Estimate (Mooney, 1928)	Original Estimate (Mooney notes)	Estimate by Lewis and Clark (Thwaites, 1904–5: 6:114–19)
Washington, West			
Makah	2,000	2,000	2,000
Chimakum	400	–	–
Quileute, etc.	500	350	–
Clallam	2,000	–	–
Quinaielt, etc.	1,500	1,250	–
Chehalis, etc.	1,000	1,360	700
Lummi, etc.	1,000	–	–
Skagit, etc.	1,200	–	–
Snohomish, etc.	1,200	–	–
Suquamish, etc.	1,200	–	–
Nisqually, etc.	1,200	–	–
Skokomish, etc.	1,000	–	–
Echeloot	1,500	1,300	1,000
Chiluktkwa, etc.	3,000	2,700	2,200
Shoto	600	600	460
Quathlapotle	1,300	1,200	900
Callamaks	250	250	200
Wahkiakum	300	250	200
Chinook	600	600	400
Killaxthokle	200	200	100
Kwalhioqua	200	–	–
Klikitat, etc.	600	–	–
Washington, East			
Lake	500	–	–
Colville	1,000	2,500	2,500
Sanpoil, etc.	800	1,300	1,300
Spokan	1,400	600	600
Okinagan, etc.	1,000	2,000	2,000
Methow, etc.	800	–	–
Piskwau, etc.	1,400	820	820
Palus	1,800	1,600	1,600
Wanapum	1,800	2,400	2,400
Chamnapum	1,800	1,860	1,860
Yakima proper	3,000	3,800	3,800
Tapanash, etc.	2,200	1,900	1,900

(continued on following page)

Table 8.1, *continued*

Tribe	Published Estimate (Mooney, 1928)	Original Estimate (Mooney notes)	Estimate by Lewis and Clark (Thwaites, 1904–5: 6:114–19)
	Montana, West; and Idaho, North		
Salish	600	350	350
Kalispel	1,200	1,600	1,600
Skitswish	1,000	2,000	2,000
Nez Percé	4,000	–	2,000
	Oregon, West		
Skilloot	3,000	2,500–3,000	2,500
Clatsop	300	200	200
Cathlamet	450	300	300
Wappatoo	3,600	2,730	2,730
Clackamas	2,500	1,800	1,800
Charcowah	300	200	200
Cushook	900	650	650
Shahala, etc.	3,200	3,100–3,700	3,100–3,700
Salishan	1,500	1,000	1,000
Tlatskanai	1,600	1,200	1,200
Yakonan	6,000	5,700	–
Kusan	2,000	1,900	1,500
Takelma	500	–	–
Athapascan:		–	–
Chocreleatan, etc.	5,600	–	–
Athapascan:			
Umpqua, etc.	3,200	–	–
Kalapooian	3,000	–	–
Shahaptian	2,900	–	–
Cayuse	500	250	250
Klamath	800	–	–
Modoc	400	–	–

Merriam's estimate of 260,000, commenting: "In view of Merriam's opportunities and detailed investigation we may take his figures (beginning with 1800) as the best approximation for the whole region, although the known decrease among the Mission Indians, almost from the start, would seem to make even his figures conservative" (Mooney, 1928: 19).

In 1925, Kroeber still preferred his own figures over those of Merriam (Kroeber, 1925: 880–83), producing an even more conservative estimate of 133,000. Then, in his 1939 study, *Cultural and Natural Areas of Native North America,* Kroeber utilized all of Mooney's figures, except those for California, where he substituted his own estimate of 133,000 over that of Merriam, commenting: "I have made this substitution not because I wish to give my figure precedence over Merriam's but because my total is arrived at through a tribe-by-tribe addition or 'dead reckoning' method, like all Mooney's other figures; whereas Merriam uses a mission to nonmission area multiplication ratio for the state as a whole . . . Mooney apparently had not himself worked at the data for California, and therefore took over Merriam's result in block, with the result that this is his one area without figures for separate tribes or groups. My computation appeared after his work was done" (Kroeber, 1939: 131). Actually, Kroeber's calculations also are based upon mission to nonmission ratios and, as documented above, he communicated his estimates to Mooney in 1911 and earlier, but they were rejected.

Central Mountain Region in 1845

95. *Bannock–1,000.* This estimate is apparently derived from a chart provided by A. P. Dennison, Indian agent for the Eastern District of Oregon, in his letter of July 14, 1859, to the Office of Indian Affairs. The chart reads: "Bannacks . . . 700" [whole number of tribes] (Dennison, 1860: 435). Mooney's notes suggest he guessed that 14 years earlier, in 1845, the figure must have been 1,000.

96. *Shoshoni and Sheepeater–4,500.* Mooney based this estimate directly upon the following account by the Indian agent Jacob Forney: "I have had intercourse with every tribe and band of Sho-sho-nes in the Territory, and have endeavored to learn from them their number. And in my opinion, they number about forty-five hundred" (Forney, 1860: 364).

97. *Ute (including Gosiute and Pahvant)–4,500.* Mooney discounted estimates by the Indian agent E. A. Graves (1853: 436) of 500 to 600 warriors in 1853 and 6,000 to 7,000 souls in 1854 (Graves, 1854: 386) and relied upon the 1859 estimate of 4,600 souls by Agent Jacob Forney (1860: 365).

98. *Paiute (including Paviotso and "Snake" Oregon)–7,500.* Mooney's notes refer to an estimate of 7,900 in an 1859 report, pages 362–77, apparently Forney's 1859 chart (Forney, 1860: 365). The chart actually shows 2,200 for "Pey-utes (South)" and 6,000 for "Pey-utes (West)" for a total of 8,200. In addition, Forney commented: "these Indians have evidently degenerated very rapidly during the last twelve years, or since white men have got among them" (Forney, 1860: 367).

99. *Washo–1,000.* Mooney consulted the following estimate: "The Washo nation numbers about 900 souls" (Dodge, 1860: 374). Dodge's actual count of individual bands suggests a total count of 982.

100. *Jicarilla—800.* This estimate is based largely on the following comments by two agents: "There are about two hundred and fifty Jicarilla
Apaches, of all classes, in the vicinity of their farm on the Rio Puerco . . .
They have greatly diminished, however, within a few years . . . They can
bring from one hundred to one hundred and fifty warriors into the field"
(Graves, 1853: 434–35); and "they are supposed to number about one
hundred and fifty warriors, and probably five hundred souls" (Merriwether,
1854: 378).

Mooney's notes for the remaining tribal areas (New Mexico and Arizona,
Greenland, Canada, and Alaska) are not complete and specific enough to
disclose the actual sources of his published estimates, although most of his
Canadian estimates appear to have been taken from the *Jesuit Relations,* his
southwestern estimates from early census data, particularly that of Garcés
(Coues, 1900), and his Alaskan estimates from Dall (1877, 1885) and Krause
(1885). Mooney's published estimates for these tribal areas are included in
Table 8.2.

CONCLUSIONS

The above discussion documents both the depth and variability of the
research that led to Mooney's published population estimates. For most tribal
areas, he evaluated original census data from many primary ethnohistorical
sources. For others, he relied upon secondary sources that he considered to
be reliable (Ruttenber, Schoolcraft, etc.), and for tribes in the Southern
Plains and California he relied upon estimates made by his colleagues (Bolton
and Merriam) whose expertise he respected.

His notes not only confirm Kroeber's (1939: 134) comments that Mooney's estimates clearly were "made on the basis of wide reading, conscientiousness, and experienced judgment," but also Swanton's impression that at least
for New England, Mooney reduced his figures through time (Mooney, 1928:
2). For example, Mooney's earlier estimate for the North Atlantic states is
63,750, 15 percent greater than his published estimate of 55,600. Similarly,
his earlier unpublished estimate for the South Atlantic states is 56,100, a
figure 7 percent greater than his published estimate of 52,200. The few early
unpublished estimates available for other areas tend to corroborate the above
data for the East.

The data do not support Swanton's opinion that "his figures, though
conservative as compared with most earlier undertakings of the kind, are still
somewhat high" (Mooney, 1928: 2), or Kroeber's (1939: 134) that "Moo-

Table 8.2
Mooney's Published Population Estimates for
Tribal Areas North of Mexico

Tribal Area	Date	Estimate
North Atlantic States	1600	55,600
South Atlantic States	1600	52,200
Gulf States	1650	114,400
Central States	1650	75,300
Northern Plains	1780	100,800
Southern Plains	1690	41,000
Columbia Region	1780	88,800
California	1769	260,000
Central Mountain Region	1845	19,300
New Mexico and Arizona	1680	72,000
Greenland	1721	10,000
Eastern Canada	1600	54,200
Central Canada	1670	50,950
British Columbia	1780	85,800
Alaska	1740	72,600
Total		1,152,950

Source: Mooney, 1928: 33.

ney's total of about 1,150,000, reduced to 1,025,000 by the California substitution will ultimately shrink to around 900,000, possibly somewhat farther." My impression from examining Mooney's notes is that he was attempting a minimal estimate for the date described. His notes continually use language such as "at least" and "no less than." When confronted with conflicting ethnohistorical estimates, Mooney usually chose the most conservative. Thus while the actual aboriginal number probably is no less than indicated by Mooney, it could be considerably higher.

A problem in utilizing Mooney's estimates rests with his use of different dates for different tribal areas. For example, some of his aboriginal estimates (North and South Atlantic, Eastern Canada) are for the year 1600, while his estimates for the Central Mountain Region are for the year 1845. These different dates represent what Mooney felt was the beginning of population decline due to European contact as revealed by existing historical records. However, as Ewers (1973: 106) has suggested, the numbers represent neither the aboriginal number immediately prior to European contact nor the maximum aboriginal number prior to the population decline. Since Mooney utilized ethnohistorical sources, he limited his estimates to the beginning of the ethnohistorical period, or the earliest point at which he could obtain reliable European estimates of aboriginal numbers. Of course, in most areas the aboriginal population could have been reduced considerably by the time of the earliest estimates. Accordingly, in some groups Mooney appeared to adjust his calculations when the date of the earliest ethnohistorical estimate differed from the date he utilized as the beginning of decline for that tribal area. Frequently he would offer his estimate, commenting that the "original" number must have been much higher. Thus, his estimates actually were designed to serve as a beginning point from which to trace the population effects of European contact, not as a definitive estimate of maximum population numbers prior to European contact. In the latter sense, if used at all, his figures should be regarded as highly conservative, minimal estimates to be corrected with further study, using new data from archaeology and physical anthropology and improved interpretations of the available ethnohistorical sources.

Epilogue

"What is involved here is truly one of the most fascinating numbers games in history, one that may well have a determining influence upon interpretive themes . . . of the history of all the Americas" (Jacobs, 1974: 123).

From the preceding discussions and essays the basic problems of reconstructing aboriginal populations become clear. The best documentary data occur well after initial European-aboriginal contact; they are seldom complete; and even censuses are of selected groups and are of uncertain reliability. Projection back in time is necessary, but the degrees and rates of depopulation are variable not only from region to region but within the same region. However, populations derived from adjusted documentary data and uncertain curves of population change can be corroborated in part by applying different types of statistical projection and extrapolation and by using archaeological, social, and ecological evidence. Given this situation, there is general agreement that what is now needed is (1) a cross-checking of results from a variety of methods, (2) a focus on detailed regional studies, (3) a continued effort to obtain populations from later dates in order to better establish curves of change, and (4) an application of more rigorous statistical techniques. It has been argued that more attention needs to be given to methods of analysis used in the social sciences and by demographers, especially European historical demographers. The literature presented and cited in this collection is dominated by New World historians, geographers, and anthropologists. The work is very much interdisciplinary and is often innovative, but nevertheless there is a degree of isolation from the scholarship and methodology on similar problems elsewhere in the world.[1] This criticism does not apply, however, to much of the research by Borah and Cook, who have used European historical

1. See the review by Dickler (1971) of the papers on "The Historical Demography of Latin America," from the Fourth Congress of the International Economic History Association (Deprez, 1970), and the essay by Petersen, "A Demographer's View of Prehistoric Demography" (1975).

demographic techniques where applicable, but such techniques often do not work for New World data.[2]

In reviewing the modern history of population calculation for the Americas, a pattern emerges. From the conservative figures of the 1930s and 1940s, we have moved into a period utilizing more detailed documentary evidence and more sophisticated analytical techniques. The resulting figures have often been high, and critics such as Rosenblat have been quick to point out that statistical analysis, no matter how elaborate, can result in great distortions if such analysis is based on invalid or unreasonable assumptions. Nevertheless, considerable and varied new evidence over the past 25 years has rather consistently pointed to larger populations than were admitted to previously. And these studies are coming not just from the Berkeley School, but from a large group of scholars and disciplines. Even some critics of very high figures, such as Sanders, arrive at populations well above those of Kroeber, Steward, and Rosenblat.

There is no single method appropriate for calculating a hemispheric total. And it is hazardous to attempt a total from the estimates in the various studies contained here and discussed here. Nevertheless an aboriginal population for 1492 can be postulated, relying mainly on those studies that give serious treatment to evidence. In calculating the total, some consideration, but not direct use, is given to low regional figures that have been challenged as unacceptable, as well as to the high figures of Dobyns based on average depopulation ratios. Admittedly, the selection of regional estimates is to some extent arbitrary, but it reflects the editor's familiarity with the massive literature on aboriginal populations, as well as the ethnographic literature, plus considerable field work on ecology and native subsistence in various parts of Latin America.

The resulting total for the Americas of 57,300,000 and the regional totals (Table 00.1) should be compared with the totals of other scholars shown in Table 0.1 (see p. 3). Errors in some subregional totals may amount to as much as 100 percent, but the high errors and the low errors will to a certain degree cancel one another out. Some regional totals are almost certainly too low because they don't take into account population decline between initial contact and the date of documentary evidence (as is true for northwest Mexico, Argentina, and Yucatán), or because they don't consider the full region. Other regional totals may be too high because they are based on

2. See Borah, this volume. A basic treatment of the methodology and use of evidence in historical demography is that by Hollingsworth, who approves of the methods and results of Borah and Cook (Hollingsworth, 1969: esp. 135). European scholars have had to use the same methods when confronted with periods and areas of fragmentary evidence (Borah, pers. comm.).

Table 00.1
A New Estimate of Aboriginal American
Population, ca. 1492

North America[a]	4,400,000
Mexico[b]	21,400,000
Central America[c]	5,650,000
Caribbean[d]	5,850,000
Andes[e]	11,500,000
Lowland South America[f]	8,500,000
Total	57,300,000

[a]*United States, Canada, Alaska,* and *Greenland:* 4,400,000 based on an arbitrary doubling of Ubelaker's 2,200,000 in order to take into account declines before available documentation and to give consideration to Driver's figure of 3,500,000 and the careful calculations by S. F. Cook and by Baumhoff of over 300,000 in California alone.

[b]*Central Mexico:* 18,300,000 based on the average of 25,200,000 by Borah and Cook and 11,400,000 derived proportionally from Sanders; *northern Mexico:* 700,000, including 540,000 from Sauer for the northwest, 100,000 from Kroeber for the northeast, and 60,000 for Baja California (based on Aschmann's density); *Yucatán, Chiapas,* and *Tabasco:* 2,400,000, based on 800,000 for Yucatán by Cook and Borah and comparable amounts for the other two regions.

[c]*Panama:* 1,000,000 (Bennett); *Nicaragua:* 1,000,000 (Radell); *El Salvador:* 500,000 (Daugherty); *Honduras* and *Belize:* 750,000 (comparative*); *Costa Rica:* 400,000 (comparative); *Guatemala:* 2,000,000 (comparative).

[d]*Hispaniola:* 1,950,000, based on the average of Cook and Borah's calculation of 3,800,000 for 1496 (assuming that the degree of decline from 1492 to 1496 is indeterminable) and Rosenblat's total of 100,000; *other islands:* 3,900,000 based on Rosenblat's belief that the other islands combined had double the population of Hispaniola.

[e]*Central Andes:* 7,500,000, from an average of 12,100,000 by C. T. Smith (based on a high early decline) and 2,900,000 by Shea (based on a low early decline); *Colombia:* 3,000,000 (Colmenares); *Venezuela:* 1,000,000 (comparative).

[f]*Greater Amazonia:* 5,100,000 (Denevan); *southern Brazil:* 500,000 (comparative); *Argentina:* 900,000 (Pyle); *central Chile:* 1,000,000 (Cooper); *remainder* (Uruguay, Paraguay, Guianas, other): 1,000,000 (comparative).

*Comparative: an estimate based on incomplete documentary figures, on other forms of evidence, and on comparisons with comparable regions with better information.

exaggerated reports, or poor estimates, or nonrepresentative or inaccurate samples. A reasonable degree of overall possible error for the hemisphere would be about 25 percent, which would give a range of 43,000,000 to 72,000,000.

If claims of high populations continue to be substantiated, then other basic questions about aboriginal society and cultural ecology will have to be pursued more vigorously than heretofore. What were the land-use systems that supported large populations? Had human carrying capacities, for given technology-environment systems, already been reached or even exceeded in some regions, resulting in environmental deterioration and population declines? Was the upset of a delicate man-land equilibrium a major reason for the demographic collapse in the face of a few Spaniards in the high-culture areas of Mexico and the Andes? Were levels of social organization actually higher than recognized in peripheral areas such as the Amazon floodplains where it is now believed there were significant populations? Did the lack of major epidemic diseases in the Americas prior to European arrival permit a more rapid rate of population growth than elsewhere in the world? Did the unimportance of domesticated animals in most of the New World contribute to greater sanitation, less disease, and less erosion and hence a potential for greater human population than in the Old World? What was the nature of both the hemispheric and regional population curves at the time of our inquiry? Had they flattened, reaching some degree of balance, or were they rising, falling, or fluctuating? How do past population densities compare with those of today? We do know that they are now less in some regions. What, then, are the technological and ecological lessons to be learned?

Obviously, if we come to accept high aboriginal populations, much of our interpretation of both prehistory and colonial history will have to be reconsidered. Certainly we must now acknowledge that the European occupation of the Western Hemisphere was seldom a quiet expansion into relatively unsettled lands, but was instead an invasion and destruction of native societies whose populations were substantial (Jacobs, 1974; Jennings, 1975).

The pursuit of man as a quantity in America in 1492 will surely continue to be lively, and along the way valuable insights will be attained quite beyond the calculation of original numbers.

Glossary

Bibliography

Index

Glossary

Aje. Unidentified cultigen; probably a variety of sweet potato or yam; not to be confused with *aji* (chili pepper).

Aldea. Village; dependent settlement.

Almas. Souls; the equivalent of persons in statements of population.

Al tubo. Technique of sowing in Mexico using a plow with an attached cylinder through which the inserted seed rolls down to the humid subsoil level.

Ánimas. Souls; the equivalent of persons in statements of population.

Arroba. Spanish measure of about 25 pounds (11.5 kilograms).

Arzobispado. Archbishopric.

Asistente. Assistant.

Audiencia. A high court of appeal and the territory of its jurisdiction in colonial Spanish America.

Barbasco. *Lonchocarpus* spp.; source of rotenone; root used by South American tropical tribes as a fish poison (stupefier).

Barrio. District or suburb of a city; dependent settlement.

Caatinga. Thorn woodland vegetation in northeast Brazil.

Caballero. Gentleman; nobleman; horseman.

Cabecera. Head town; seat of administration for a *municipio*.

Cabildo. Municipal council or government.

Cacique. Indian chief.

Cajete (or *a todo costo*). Technique of sowing in Mexico whereby small pits for planting seed are dug down to humid subsoil.

Calmil. Intensive house garden in Mexico.

Calpullec. Plural of *calpulli;* also the title of a calpulli chief.

Calpulli. A group of families owning land in common in Mexico; a territorial or social unit.

Campamento. Small, dependent settlement.

Campo cerrado. Scrub savanna in Brazil.

Casados. Married men; the term is also applied to all married people.

Casas. Houses.

Cédula (or *cédula real*). A royal order from the king of Spain.

Ceja (or *ceja de la montaña*). The cloud forest zone of the eastern Andes of Peru.

Chinampas. Platform gardens constructed in the lakes of central Mexico.

Colonia. Colony; dependent settlement.

Confesiones. Confessees.

Congregación. The settling of dispersed Indian populations in larger towns for administrative purposes.

Conuco. An Indian farm in the Caribbean region; varies from shifting cultivation to permanent cultivation of mounds (on Hispaniola).

Corregidor. Spanish official in charge of a district.

Corregimiento. Office or jurisdiction of a *corregidor*.

Cristianos. Christians.

Curaca. Indian chief.

Curiche. River meander cutoff filled with water.

Delegación. District; delegation.

Diezmo. Tribute of 10 percent; one tenth.

Ejido. Community land; dependent settlement; land owned by the government and allotted to a rural community.

Encomendero. A person holding an *encomienda*.

Encomienda. A grant of Indians for their tribute and/or labor.

Estación. Dependent settlement; season.

Estancia. Small Indian village; cattle ranch; dependent settlement.

Familias. Families.

Fanega. Spanish unit of dry measure of about 1.5 bushels, or about 46 kilograms, in colonial Mexico.

Fieles. Christians; the faithful.

Fuegos. Fires; army campfires.

Gente adulta. Adults; probably men only, as used by Schmidl.

Gente de confesión. Confessors; people above the age of confession (usually males over 14 years and females over 12 years).

Granja. Farm or farmhouse; small, dependent settlement.

Guácimo. *Guazuma ulmifolia;* a tropical fruit eaten mainly by livestock.

Guama (guamo). *Inga* spp.; tropical tree used for shade and for its edible fruit.

Guanajo. Turkey (Caribbean).

Guayaba (guava). *Psidium guajava;* edible tropical fruit.

Guerreros. Warriors.

Habitantes. Inhabitants.

Hacienda. Large landed estate; dependent settlement.

Hidalgo. Noble; illustrious person.

Hombre. Man.

Hombres formados. Adult men.

Hombres de guerra. Warriors.

Hombres para pelear (de pelea; de gente de pelea). Fighting men; warriors.

Hutía. *Capromys oedium;* a tropical rodent.

Iglezuela. A small church, usually in an outlying, dependent rural settlement.

Indígenas. Natives.

Indigenismo. The ideal of Indian-ness.

Indios (yndios). Indians.

Indios de doctrina. Converted Indians.

Indios de fusil. Indians armed with rifles.

Indios de guerra (guerro). Warlike Indians; unsubjugated natives.

Indios de paz (pas). Peaceful or conquered Indians.

Indios de servicio. Indian servants; also Indians giving labor or paying tribute.

Indios de tasa. Tribute-paying Indians.

Indios de todas edades y sexos. Indians of all ages and sexes.

Indios empadronados. Registered taxpaying Indians.

Isla. Island.

Jicaco (hicaco). *Chrysobalanus icaco;* tropical tree with edible fruit.

Legajo. File; bundle of documents.

Leyenda blanca. White legend; the belief that Spanish behavior in the conquest of the New World was not excessively brutal.

Leyenda negra. Black legend; the belief that Spanish behavior in the conquest of the New World was excessively brutal.

Lirén. Cultivated Caribbean tuber; probably *Calathea allouia.*

Llano. A plain, usually with savanna (grassy) vegetation.

Mapucy (yampee). *Dioscorea trifida;* cultivated New World tuber.

Mayeque. Indian serf in Aztec Mexico.

Montaña. Tropical forest region of eastern Peru.

Montones. Small cultivated mounds; especially manioc mounds in Hispaniola.

Mozo. Young man.

Muchachos, muchachas. Boys, girls.

Mujeres. Women.

Municipio. Township.

Naturales. Natives.

Niños. Young children.

Nueva ola. New wave; new trend.

Obispado. Bishopric.

Oidor. Judge of an *audiencia.*

Padrón. A list of people in a district or region; a count of population.

Parroquia. Parish.

Personas. Persons.

Peso. Variable monetary unit.

Pierna de manta. Strip of cotton cloth of a specified size.

Pitahaya (pitaya). *Cereus* spp.; cactus with edible fruit.

Playa. Beach; sand bar.

Población. Population.

Pochteca. Traveling Indian merchant (Aztec).

Presas. Small reservoirs; check dams to trap soil.

Pueblo. Village; dependent settlement.

Quinoa. *Chenopodium quinoa;* a major seed crop in the Andes.

Quipu. Knotted string recording device (Inca).

Ranchería. Small rural village; dependent settlement; dispersed settlement.

Rancho. Hamlet; dependent settlement; ranch.

Real. Spanish coin; royal; camp or encampment.

Reducción. The resettlement of Indians converted to Christianity.

Reducidos. Resettled Indians converted to Christianity.

Repartidos. Distributed Indians in a *repartimiento.*

Repartimiento. A levy of Indian labor to the Crown, to private individuals, or to institutions.

Restinga. The high ground of a natural river levee in Amazonia.

Revisitas. Revisits, or census recounts.

Regidor. Council member of a *cabildo.*

Selva. Tropical forest.

Servidores. Servants.

Sierra. Mountain range; the Andes in Peru.

Soltero. Unmarried male; unmarried person.

Sujeto. Subject town.

Tepetate. Limy hardpan exposed by erosion in central Mexico.

Terra firme (tierra firme). The high ground between rivers in Amazonia; continent; mainland.

Tomín. Spanish weight of one-third of a drachma; a silver coin.

Tributario. Tribute-paying Indian.

Tributo. Tribute; tax.

Varones. Young men.

Várzea. Floodplain zone in Amazonia.

Vasallo. Vassal; subject; tributary.

Vecino. Citizen or resident; householder.

Viejos. Old men; old people.

Visita. A formal tour of inspection by an official; small church visited by nonresident clergy.

Viuda, viudo. Widow, widower.

Wampum. Small beads made of shells and used by North American Indians as money and also for ornament.

Xpiaños (xpaños). Christians.

Yanacona. Indians giving service; Inca servant class.

Yautía. *Xanthosoma* spp.; a cultivated tropical tuber.

Yndios (indios). Indians.

Ynfieles (infieles). Unfaithful; infidels.

Ynfieles de servicio. Unconverted Indian servants.

Yuca (manioc, cassava). *Manihot esculenta;* a cultivated tuber; the staple food in Amazonia.

Yungas. The eastern Andean valleys in Bolivia.

Bibliography

Cross references are indicated by SMALL CAPITALS

Acsádi, György, and J. Nemeskéri. 1970. *History of Human Life Span and Mortality*. Akadémiai Kiadó: Budapest.

Albornoz, Felipe de. 1931 [1631]. "Carta del Gobernador de Tucumán, Don Felipe de Albornoz, á S. M. informando de los nuevas muertes y robo causados por los indios de Calchaquí . . . ," in LEVILLIER, ed., *Nueva Crónica*, 3:418–22.

———. 1939 [1629]. "Carta á S. M., del Gobernador de Tucumán, don Felipe de Albornoz, informando de los grandes inconvenientes que se siguen al Real Patronato . . . ," *Revisat de la Biblioteca Nacional* (Buenos Aires), 3:607–12.

Alburquerque, Rodrigo de. 1864 [1514]. "Repartimiento de la Isla Española," in CDI, 1:50–236.

Allan, William. 1965. *The African Husbandman*. Barnes and Noble: New York.

Al'perovich, Moisey Samoĭlovich. 1965. *Voĭna za nezavisimost' Meksiki, 1810–1824* [The War for the Independence of Mexico, 1810–1824]. Moscow.

Anonymous Conqueror (Alonso de Ulloa?). 1917. *Narrative of Some Things of New Spain and of the Great City of Temestitán, Mexico, Written by the Anonymous Conqueror, a Companion of Hernán Cortés,* edited and translated by M. H. Saville. Cortés Society: New York.

———. 1941. *Relación de algunas cosas de la Nueva España y de la gran ciudad de Temestitán, México,* edited by León Díaz Cárdenas. Editorial América: Mexico City.

———. 1961. *Relación de algunas cosas de la Nueva España y de la gran ciudad de Temestitán México, hecha por un gentilhombre del señor Fernando Cortés.* Mexico City.

Arber, Edward, ed. 1884. *Captain John Smith, Works 1608–1631*, The English Scholar's Library, No. 16. Birmingham.

Argamosa, Manuel Antonio de. 1906. "Informe de Don Manuel Antonio de Argamosa, Governador de Santa Cruz de la Sierra, sobre el estado de las misiones de Mojos y Chiquitos, 6 de febrero de 1737," in *Juicio de límites entre el Perú y Bolivia*, edited by Víctor M. Maurtua, 10:49–56. Hijos de M. G. Hernández: Madrid.

Armillas, Pedro. 1971. "Gardens on Swamps," *Science*, 174:653–61.

Arricivita, Juan Domingo. 1792. *Crónica seráfica y apostólica del Colegio de Propaganda Fide de la Santa Cruz de Querétaro en la Nueva España, Segunda parte*. Mexico City.

Ascher, Robert. 1959. "A Prehistoric Population Estimate Using Midden Analysis and Two Population Models," *Southwestern Journal of Anthropology*, 15:168–78.

Aschmann, Homer. 1959. *The Central Desert of Baja California: Demography and Ecology*, Ibero-Americana, No. 42. Univ. California Press: Berkeley.

Ashburn, Percy M. 1947. *The Ranks of Death: A Medical History of the Conquest of America*. Coward-McCann: New York.

Atkinson, H. 1826. "Expedition up the Missouri," Letter to James Barbour, Secretary of War, from Louisville, Kentucky, November 23, 1825, Document 117, 19th Congress, 1st Session, U.S. House of Representatives. Washington, D.C.

———. 1837. Report to L. F. Linn and A. G. Harrison, August 22, 1837, in *Western Frontier Correspondence*, pp. 19–21, Document No. 276, 25th Congress, 2nd Session, U.S. House of Representatives. Washington, D.C.

Baekeland, G. Brooks. 1964. "By Parachute into Peru's Lost World," *National Geographic*, 126:268–96.

Bandelier, A. F. 1879. "On the Social Organization and Mode of Government of the Ancient Mexicans," *Annual Report*, Peabody Museum, Harvard University, 13:557–699.

Barlow, Robert H. 1949. *The Extent of the Empire of the Culhua Mexica*, Ibero-Americana, No. 28, Univ. California Press: Berkeley.

Barón Castro, Rodolfo. 1942. *La población de El Salvador*. Instituto Gonzalo Fernández de Oviedo: Madrid.

———. 1959. "El desarrollo de la población hispanoamericana (1492–1950)," *Cahiers d'Histoire Mondiale*, 5:325–43.

Barrow, Mark V., Jerry D. Niswander, and Robert Fortuine. 1972. *Health and Disease of American Indians North of Mexico: A Bibliography, 1800–1969*. Univ. Florida Press: Gainesville.

Bartram, William. 1792. *Travels through North and South Carolina, Georgia, East and West Florida* . . . . J. Johnson: London.

Bárzana, Alonso [Alonzo]. 1968. "Carta de [Alonso] Bárzana al P. Juan Sebastián, Asunción, 8 de septiembre de 1594," in FURLONG CARDIFF, *Alonzo Bárzana*, pp. 81–94.

Batista, Djalma. 1963. *Da habitabilidade da Amazônia*. Instituto Nacional de Pesquisas da Amazônia: Manaus.

Baumhoff, Martin A. 1958. *California Athabascan Groups*, Univ. California
Publications: Anthropological Records, 16:157–237.
———. 1963. *Ecological Determinants of Aboriginal California Populations*,
Univ. California Publications in American Archaeology and Ethnology,
49(2):155–236.
Bénard de La Harpe, Jean-Baptiste. 1831. *Journal historique de l'établisse-
ment des Français à la Louisiane* . . . . A. L. Boimare: New Orleans.
Bennett, Charles F. 1968. *Human Influences on the Zoogeography of Pana-
ma*, Ibero-Americana, No. 51. Univ. California Press: Berkeley.
Benzoni, Girolamo. 1967 [1565]. *La historia del Mundo Nuevo*, Vol. 86.
Biblioteca de la Academia Nacional de la Historia: Caracas.
Bernheim, Ernst. 1903. *Lehrbuch der historischen Methode und der Ge-
schichtsphilosophie*, 4th ed. Leipzig.
Blasi, Olemar. 1966. Comment on "Estimating Aboriginal American Popula-
tion: An Appraisal of Techniques with a New Hemispheric Estimate," by
H. F. Dobyns, *Current Anthropology*, 7:426–27.
Bodmer, M. Charles, ed. 1841. *Voyage dans l'intérieur de l'Amérique du Nord
par le Prince Maximilien de Wied-Neuwied*, Vol. 2. Librairie de la Société
de Géographie de Paris: Paris.
Boletín Indigenista (Mexico City). 1961. "Guide to the Indian Population of
America" (special issue), Vol. 21.
Bolivia, Dirección General de Estadística y Censos. 1964. *Boletín Estadístico*
(La Paz), No. 89.
Bolton, Herbert E. 1908. "The Native Tribes about the East Texas Missions,"
Quarterly of the Texas State Historical Association, 11:249–76.
———. ed. 1914. *Athanase de Mézières and the Louisiana-Texas Frontier
1768–1780*, 2 vols. Arthur H. Clark: Cleveland.
Bonavía, Duccio, and Louis E. Guzmán. 1966. "Ceja de Selva Explorations in
Central Peru," *Current Anthropology*, 7:96–97.
Borah, Woodrow. 1951. *New Spain's Century of Depression*, Ibero-
Americana, No. 35. Univ. California Press: Berkeley.
———. 1954. *Early Colonial Trade and Navigation between Mexico and Peru*,
Ibero-Americana, No. 38. Univ. California Press: Berkeley.
———. 1962a. "Population Decline and the Social and Institutional Changes of
New Spain in the Middle Decades of the Sixteenth Century," *Akten des
34. Internationalen Amerikanistenkongresses* (Vienna, 1960), pp. 172–78.
———. 1962b. "¿América como modelo? El impacto demográfico de la expan-
sión europea sobre el mundo no europeo," *Cuadernos Americanos*,
6:176–85.
———. 1964. "America as Model: The Demographic Impact of European
Expansion upon the Non-European World," *Actas y Memorias, XXXV
Congreso Internacional de Americanistas* (Mexico City, 1962), 3:379–87.
———. 1968. Review of *La población de América en 1492: Viejos y nuevos
cálculos*, by Ángel Rosenblat, *Hispanic American Historical Review*, 48:
475–77.
———. 1970. "The Historical Demography of Latin America: Sources, Tech-

niques, Controversies, Yields," in DEPREZ, ed., *Population and Economics*, pp. 173–205.

―――. 1976. "Renaissance Europe and the Population of America," *Revista de História* (São Paulo), 105:47–61.

Borah, Woodrow, and Sherburne F. Cook. 1958. *Price Trends of Some Basic Commodities in Central Mexico, 1531–1570*, Ibero-Americana, No. 40. Univ. California Press: Berkeley.

―――. 1960. *The Population of Central Mexico in 1548*, Ibero-Americana, No. 43. Univ. California Press: Berkeley.

―――. 1962. "La despoblación del México central en el siglo XVI," *Historia Mexicana,* 12:1–12.

―――. 1963. *The Aboriginal Population of Central Mexico on the Eve of the Spanish Conquest*, Ibero-Americana, No. 45. Univ. California Press: Berkeley.

―――. 1967. "New Demographic Research on the Sixteenth Century in Mexico," in *Latin American History: Essays on Its Study and Teachings, 1898–1965*, edited by Howard F. Cline, 2:717–22. Univ. Texas Press: Austin.

―――. 1969. "Conquest and Population: A Demographic Approach to Mexican History," *Proceedings of the American Philosophical Society*, 113: 177–83.

―――. 1972. "La demografía histórica de América Latina: Necesidades y perspectivas," in *La historia económica en América Latina, II: Desarrollo, perspectivas y bibliografía*, pp. 82–99. Secretaría de Educación Pública: Mexico City.

Boserup, Ester. 1966. *The Conditions of Agricultural Growth*. Aldine: Chicago.

Boyd-Bowman, Peter. 1964. *Indice geobiográfico de cuarenta mil pobladores españoles de América en el siglo XVI*, Vol. 1: *1493–1519*. Instituto Caro y Cuervo: Bogotá.

Bradford, William. 1898. *Bradford's History of Plimoth Plantation*. Wright and Potter: Boston.

Bradley, James H. 1896. "Journal of the Campaign against the Hostile Sioux in 1876 under the Command of General John Gibbon," in *Contributions to the Historical Society of Montana*, 2:140–229. State Publishing Co.: Helena.

Bray, Warwick. 1972–73. "The City State in Central Mexico at the Time of the Spanish Conquest," *Journal of Latin American Studies*, 4:161–85.

Brinton, Daniel G. 1885. *The Lenâpé and Their Legends*, Brinton's Library of Aboriginal American Literature, No. 5. Philadelphia.

Brown, Alan K. 1967. *The Aboriginal Population of the Santa Barbara Channel*, Reports of the University of California Archaeological Survey, No. 69. Univ. California Archaeological Research Facility: Berkeley.

Buck, Alfred A., Tom T. Sasaki, and Robert I. Anderson. 1968. *Health and Disease in Four Peruvian Villages*. Johns Hopkins Press: Baltimore.

Burgos-Guevara, Hugo. 1974. "La población del Ecuador en la encrucijada de los siglos XVI y XVII," *Atti del XL Congresso Internazionale degli Americanisti* (Rome-Genoa, 1972), 2:483–87.

Burpee, Lawrence J., ed. 1927. *Journals and Letters of Pierre Gaultier de Varennes de la Vérendrye and His Sons.* Champlain Society: Toronto.

Cabeza de Vaca. *See* Núñez Cabeza de Vaca.

Cabrera, Gerónimo Luis de. 1931 [1573]. "Relación en suma y de la tierra y poblaciones . . . ," in LEVILLIER, ed., *Nueva Crónica,* 2:318–24.

Calnek, Edward E. 1973. "The Localization of the Sixteenth Century Map Called 'The Maguey Plan,' " *American Antiquity,* 38:190–95.

Calvo, Thomas. 1973. *Acatzingo, demografía de una parroquia mexicana.* Instituto Nacional de Antropología e Historia: Mexico City.

Camargo, Felisberto C. 1958. "Report on the Amazon Region," in *Problems of Humid Tropical Regions,* pp. 11–24. UNESCO: Paris.

Camavitto, Dino. 1935. *La decadenza delle popolazioni messicane al tempo della conquista.* Rome.

Canals Frau, Salvador. 1946. "The Huarpe," in STEWARD, ed., *Handbook of South American Indians,* 1:169–75.

Canelas Albarrán, Juan. 1586. "Descripción de todos los reinos del Perú, Chille y Tierra Firme . . . ," Ms. 3178, Biblioteca Nacional de Madrid, 15 fols. [Cited by Rosenblat, 1945: 77–78.]

Carbia, Rómulo D. 1943. *Historia de la leyenda negra hispano-americana.* Ediciones Orientación Española: Buenos Aires.

Carneiro, Robert L. 1960. "Slash-and-Burn Agriculture: A Closer Look at Its Implications for Settlement Patterns," in *Men and Cultures: Selected Papers of the Fifth International Congress of Anthropological and Ethnological Sciences,* edited by A. F. C. Wallace, pp. 229–34. Univ. Pennsylvania Press: Philadelphia.

———. 1967. "On the Relationship between Size of Population and Complexity of Social Organization," *Southwestern Journal of Anthropology,* 23:234–43.

Carrasco, Pedro. 1964. "Family Structure of Sixteenth-Century Tepoztlan," in *Process and Pattern in Culture,* edited by Robert A. Manners, pp. 185–210. Aldine: Chicago.

Carr-Saunders, A. M. 1936. *World Population: Past Growth and Present Trends.* Clarendon Press: Oxford.

Casas, Bartolomé de Las. *See* Las Casas.

Caso, Alfonso. 1964. "¿Existió un imperio olmeca?," *Memoria, El Colegio Nacional* (Mexico City), 5(3):5–60.

Castillo, Joseph de. 1906. "Relación de la provincia de Mojos," in *Documentos para la historia geográfica de la República de Bolivia, serie primera: Epoca colonial,* edited by M. V. Ballivián, Vol. 1: *Las provincias de Mojos y Chiquitos,* pp. 294–395. J. M. Gamarra: La Paz.

CDI. 1864–84. *Colección de documentos inéditos, relativos al descubrimiento, conquista y organización de las antiguas posesiones españolas de*

América y Oceanía . . ., 42 vols. Imprenta de Manuel B. de Quirós: Madrid.

CDN. 1921. *Colección de documentos referentes a la historia colonial de Nicaragua: Recuerdo del centenario de la independencia nacional, 1821–1921.* Tipografía y Encuadernación Nacional: Managua.

Cervera, Manuel M. 1907. *Historia de la ciudad y provincia de Santa Fe, 1573–1853*, 2 vols. La Unión: Santa Fe, Argentina.

Charlton, Thomas. 1970. "Contemporary Agriculture of the Valley," in SANDERS et al., *The Teotihuacán Valley Project*, 1:253–83.

Chaunu, Pierre. 1960. "Une histoire hispano-americaniste pilote: En marge de l'oeuvre de l'École de Berkeley," *Revue Historique*, 224:339–68.

———. 1963. "Las Casas et la première crise structurale de la colonisation espagnole (1515–1523)," *Revue Historique*, 229:59–102.

———. 1964. "La population de l'Amérique indienne (nouvelles recherches)," *Revue Historique*, 232:111–18.

———. 1969. *Conquête et exploitation des Nouveaux Mondes (XVIe siècle)*, Nouvelle Clio, L'histoire et ses problèmes. Presses Universitaires de France: Paris.

Chaunu, Pierre and Huguette. 1955–60. *Séville et l'Atlantique (1504–1650)*, 8 vols. École Pratique des Hautes Études: Paris.

Clavijero [Clavigero], Francisco Javier. 1964 [1780]. *Historia antigua de México.* Editorial Porrúa: Mexico City.

Cline, Howard F. 1962. *Mexico: Revolution to Evolution, 1940–1960.* Oxford Univ. Press: London.

Codex Kingsborough. 1912. *Memorial de los indios de Tepetlaoztoc al monarca español contra los encomenderos del pueblo*, edited by Francisco del Paso y Troncoso. Hauser y Menet: Madrid.

Codex Mendoza. 1938. *The Mexican Manuscript Known as the Collection of Mendoza and Preserved in the Bodleian Library, Oxford*, edited by James C. Clark, 3 vols. Waterlow and Sons: London.

Códice Franciscano. 1941. *Códice Franciscano, siglo XVI*, Nueva colección de documentos para la historia de México, edited by J. García Icazbalceta, Vol. 2. Chávez Hayhoe: Mexico City.

Coe, Michael D. 1961. "Social Typology and the Tropical Forest Civilizations," *Comparative Studies in Society and History*, 4:65–85.

Cole, J. P. 1965. *Latin America: An Economic and Social Geography.* Butterworths: Washington, D.C.

Collver, O. Andrew. 1965. *Birth Rates in Latin America: New Estimates of Historical Trend and Fluctuations.* Univ. California Institute of International Studies, Research Series, No. 7. Berkeley.

Colmenares, Germán. 1969. *Encomienda y población en la provincia de Pamplona (1549–1650).* Univ. de los Andes, Departamento de Historia: Bogotá.

———. 1970. *La provincia de Tunja en el Nuevo Reino de Granada: Ensayo de historia social (1539–1800).* Univ. de los Andes: Bogotá.

_____. 1973. *Historia económica y social de Colombia, 1537–1719.* Univ. del Valle: Bogotá.

Columbus, Christopher (Cristoforo Colombo). 1892–94. *Scritti di Cristoforo Colombo, pubblicati ed illustrati da Cesare de Lollis,* Raccolta di documenti e studi pubblicati dalla R. Commissione colombiana pel quarto centenario dalla scoperta dell'America, Pt. 1, 2 vols. Ministero della Pubblica Istruzione: Rome.

Comadrán Ruiz, Jorge. 1969. *Evolución demográfica argentina durante el período hispano (1535–1810).* Editorial Universitaria: Buenos Aires.

Comas, Juan. 1951. "La realidad del trato dado a los indígenas de América entre los siglos XV y XX," *América Indígena,* 11:323–70.

Cook, N. David. 1965. "La población indígena en el Perú colonial," *Anuario del Instituto de Investigaciones Históricas* (Rosario), 8:73–110.

_____. 1973. "The Indian Population of Peru, 1570–1620," Ph.D. dissertation. Univ. Texas, Austin.

Cook, Sherburne F. 1937. *The Extent and Significance of Disease among the Indians of Baja California, 1697–1773,* Ibero-Americana, No. 12. Univ. California Press: Berkeley.

_____. 1939. "Smallpox in Spanish and Mexican California, 1770–1845," *Bulletin of the History of Medicine,* 7:153–91.

_____. 1940. *Population Trends among the California Mission Indians,* Ibero-Americana, No. 17. Univ. California Press: Berkeley.

_____. 1943. *The Conflict between the California Indian and White Civilization: I. The Indian Versus the Spanish Mission,* Ibero-Americana, No. 21. Univ. California Press: Berkeley.

_____. 1946a. "Human Sacrifice and Warfare as Factors in the Demography of Pre-Colonial Mexico," *Human Biology,* 18:81–102.

_____. 1946b. "The Incidence and Significance of Disease among the Aztecs and Related Tribes," *Hispanic American Historical Review,* 26:320–35.

_____. 1947. "The Interrelation of Population, Food Supply, and Building in Pre-Conquest Central Mexico," *American Antiquity,* 13:45–52.

_____. 1949a. *The Historical Demography and Ecology of the Teotlalpan,* Ibero-Americana, No. 33. Univ. California Press: Berkeley.

_____. 1949b. *Soil Erosion and Population in Central Mexico,* Ibero-Americana, No. 34. Univ. California Press: Berkeley.

_____. 1955a. *The Epidemic of 1830–1833 in California and Oregon,* Univ. California Publications in American Archaeology and Ethnology, 43: 303–25. Univ. California Press: Berkeley.

_____. 1955b. *The Aboriginal Population of the San Joaquin Valley, California,* Anthropological Records, 16:31–78. Univ. California Press: Berkeley.

_____. 1956. *The Aboriginal Population of the North Coast of California,* Anthropological Records, 16:81–129. Univ. California Press: Berkeley.

_____. 1957. *The Aboriginal Population of Alameda and Contra Costa Counties, California,* Anthropological Records, 16:131–54. Univ. California Press: Berkeley.

_____. 1958. *Santa María Ixcatlán: Habitat, Population, Subsistence*, Ibero-Americana, No. 41. Univ. California Press: Berkeley.

_____. 1963. *Erosion Morphology and Occupation History in Western Mexico*, Anthropological Records, 17:281–334. Univ. California Press: Berkeley.

_____. 1964. "The Aboriginal Population of Upper California," *Actas y memorias, XXXV Congreso Internacional de Americanistas* (Mexico City, 1962), 3:397–403.

_____. 1968. "The Destruction of the California Indian," *California Monthly*, 79 (3):14–19.

_____. 1970. "The California Indian and Anglo-American Culture," in *Ethnic Conflict in California History*, edited by Charles Wollenberg, pp. 25–42. Tinnon-Brown: Los Angeles.

_____. 1972a. *Prehistoric Demography*, Addison-Wesley Modular Publications, No. 16. Reading, Penn.

_____. 1972b. "Can Pottery Residues Be Used as an Index to Population?," *Contributions of the Univ. California Archaeological Research Facility*, 14:17–39. Department of Anthropology, Univ. California: Berkeley.

_____. 1973a. "The Significance of Disease in the Extinction of the New England Indians," *Human Biology*, 45:485–508.

_____. 1973b. "Interracial Warfare and Population Decline among the New England Indians," *Ethnohistory*, 20:1–24.

_____. 1976a. "The Aboriginal Population of California," in S. F. Cook, *The Population of the California Indians, 1769–1970*, pp. 1–43. Univ. California Press: Berkeley.

Cook, Sherburne F., and Woodrow Borah, 1957. "The Rate of Population Change in Central Mexico, 1550–1570," *Hispanic American Historical Review*, 37:463–70.

_____. 1960. *The Indian Population of Central Mexico, 1531–1610*, Ibero-Americana, No. 44. Univ. California Press: Berkeley.

_____. 1963. "Quelle fut la stratification sociale au Centre du Mexique durant la première moitié du XVIe siècle?," *Annales: Économies, Sociétés, Civilisations*, 18:226–58.

_____. 1966. "On the Credibility of Contemporary Testimony on the Population of Mexico in the Sixteenth Century," in *Summa antropológica en homenaje a Roberto J. Weitlaner*, pp. 229–39. Instituto Nacional de Antropología e Historia: Mexico City.

_____. 1968. *The Population of the Mixteca Alta*, Ibero-Americana, No. 50. Univ. California Press: Berkeley.

_____. 1971–79. *Essays in Population History*, 3 vols. Univ. California Press: Berkeley.

Cook, Sherburne F., and Robert F. Heizer. 1965a. *The Quantitative Approach to the Relation between Population and Settlement Size*, Reports Univ. California Archaeological Survey, No. 64. Department of Anthropology, Univ. California: Berkeley.

_____. 1965b. *Studies on the Chemical Analysis of Archaeological Sites*, Univ. California Publications in Anthropology, Vol. 2. Univ. California Press: Berkeley.

_____. 1968. "Relationships among Houses, Settlement Areas, and Population in Aboriginal California," in *Settlement Archaeology*, edited by K. C. Chang, pp. 79–116. National Press Books: Palo Alto.

Cook, Sherburne F., and Lesley Byrd Simpson. 1948. *The Population of Central Mexico in the Sixteenth Century*, Ibero-Americana, No. 31. Univ. California Press: Berkeley.

Cook, Sherburne F., and A. E. Treganza. 1950. *The Quantitative Investigation of Indian Mounds*, Univ. California Publications in American Archaeology and Ethnology, 40:223–62. Univ. California Press: Berkeley.

Cooper, John M. 1946a. "The Araucanians," in STEWARD, ed., *Handbook of South American Indians*, 2:687–760.

_____. 1946b. "The Ona," in STEWARD, ed., *Handbook of South American Indians*, 1:107–25.

_____. 1946c. "The Patagonian and Pampean Hunters," in STEWARD, ed., *Handbook of South American Indians*, 1:127–68.

_____. 1946d. "The Southern Hunters: An Introduction," in STEWARD, ed., *Handbook of South American Indians*, 1:13–15.

Cortés, Hernán. 1945. "Cartas de Cortés," in *Cartas de relación de la conquista de América*, edited by Julio Le Riverend, 1:93–591. Editorial Nueva España: Mexico City.

_____. 1946. *Nuevos documentos relativos a los bienes de Hernán Cortés, 1547–1947*. Univ. Nacional Autónoma de México: Mexico City.

_____. 1971. *Hernán Cortés: Letters from Mexico*, edited and translated by A. R. Pagden. Orion Press: New York.

Coues, Elliot, ed. 1893. *History of the Expedition under the Command of Lewis and Clark*, 4 vols. Francis P. Harper: New York.

_____. 1895. *The Expeditions of Zebulon Montgomery Pike . . .* , 3 vols. Francis P. Harper: New York.

_____. 1900. *On the Trail of a Spanish Pioneer: The Diary and Itinerary of Francisco Garcés, 1775–76*, 2 vols. New York.

Croix, Caballero de. 1778. "Relation Particular of each Jurisdiction and of the Principal Indian Tribes of Texas, transmitted to the Viceroy, Chihuahua Sept. 23, 1778." Manuscript, Vol. 182, No. 2, in Provincias, Internas, Archivo General de la Nación, Mexico City.

Crosby, Alfred W., Jr. 1967. "Conquistador y Pestilencia: The First New World Pandemic and the Fall of the Great Indian Empires," *Hispanic American Historical Review*, 47:321–37.

_____. 1972. *The Columbian Exchange: Biological and Cultural Consequences of 1492*. Greenwood: Westport, Conn.

CS. 1954–57. *Colección Somoza: Documentos para la historia de Nicaragua* [for the period 1503–50], edited by Andrés Vega Bolaños, 17 vols. Imprenta Viuda de Gala Sáez: Madrid.

Cuevas, Mariano. 1946–47. *Historia de la iglesia en México*, 5th ed., 5 vols. Editorial Patria: Mexico City.

Dall, W. H. 1877. "Tribes of the Extreme Northwest," *Contributions to North American Ethnology*, 1:1–91. G.P.O.: Washington, D.C.

_____. 1885. "The Native Tribes of Alaska," *Proceedings of the American Association for the Advancement of Science,* 34:363–79.

Daugherty, Howard E. 1969. "Man-Induced Ecologic Change in El Salvador," Ph.D. dissertation. Univ. California, Los Angeles.

Davenport, Samuel. 1809. "Noticia de las naciones de indios de la Provincia de Texas." Manuscript, Vol. 201, Archivo General de la Nación, Mexico City. Also in Béxar Archives, Univ. Texas, Austin.

DeForest, John W. 1851. *History of the Indians of Connecticut from the Earliest Known Period to 1850.* W. J. Hamersley: Hartford.

Delbrück, Hans. 1900–1902. *Geschichte der Kriegskunst im Rahmen der politischen Geschichte,* 4 vols. Berlin.

Denevan, William M. 1961. *The Upland Pine Forests of Nicaragua,* Univ. California Publications in Geography, 12:251–320. Univ. California Press: Berkeley.

_____. 1965. "The Campo Cerrado Vegetation of Central Brazil," *Geographical Review,* 55:112–15.

_____. 1966a. "A Cultural-Ecological View of the Former Aboriginal Settlement in the Amazon Basin," *Professional Geographer,* 18:346–51.

_____. 1966b. *The Aboriginal Cultural Geography of the Llanos de Mojos of Bolivia.* Ibero-Americana, No. 48. Univ. California Press: Berkeley.

_____. 1966c. Comment on "Estimating Aboriginal American Population: An Appraisal of Techniques with a New Hemispheric Estimate," by Henry F. Dobyns, *Current Anthropology,* 7:429.

_____. 1970a. "The Aboriginal Population of Western Amazonia in Relation to Habitat and Subsistence," *Revista Geográfica* (Rio de Janeiro), 72:61–86.

_____. 1970b. "Aboriginal Drained-Field Cultivation in the Americas," *Science,* 169:647–54.

_____. 1970c. "The Aboriginal Population of Tropical America: Problems and Methods of Estimation," in DEPREZ, ed., *Population and Economics,* pp. 251–69.

_____. 1971. "Campa Subsistence in the Gran Pajonal, Eastern Peru," *Geographical Review,* 61:496–518.

_____. 1973. Review of Vol. 1 of *Essays in Population History: Mexico and the Caribbean,* by S. F. Cook and W. Borah, *Journal of Latin American Studies,* 5:289–90.

Denevan, William M., and Roland W. Bergman. 1975. "Karinya Indian Swamp Cultivation in the Venezuelan Llanos," *Yearbook of the Association of Pacific Coast Geographers,* 37:23–26.

Denevan, William M., and Alberta Zucchi. 1978. "Ridged-Field Excavations in the Central Orinoco Llanos, Venezuela," in *Advances in Andean Archaeology,* edited by D. L. Browman, pp. 235–45. World Anthropology, Sol Tax, general editor. Mouton: The Hague.

Dennison, A. P. 1860. Report No. 195, July 14, 1859, *Report of the Commissioner of Indian Affairs . . . 1859,* pp. 432–35, Senate Document No. 1, Serial No. 1078. U.S. Department of the Interior: Washington, D.C.

Deprez, Paul, ed. 1970. *Population and Economics: Proceedings of Section V of the Fourth Congress of the International Economic History Association* (Bloomington, Ind., 1968). Univ. Manitoba Press: Winnipeg.

DHA. 1927–29. *Documentos para la historia Argentina,* Vols. 19, 20: *Cartas anuas de la provincia del Paraguay, Chile y Tucumán, de la Compañía de Jesús, 1609–1614, 1615–1637,* Instituto de Investigaciones Históricas: Buenos Aires.

Díaz Caballero, Alonso. 1915. "Carta del capitán Alonso Díaz Caballero al rey de España" (1564), in JAIMES FREYRE, *El Tucumán colonial,* 1:34–40.

Díaz del Castillo, Bernal. 1927. *The True History of the Conquest of Mexico,* translated by Maurice Keatinge. McBride: New York. [Completed in 1568.]

_____. 1956. *The Discovery and Conquest of Mexico, 1517–1521,* translated by A. P. Maudslay. Grove Press: New York.

_____. 1960. *Historia verdadera de la conquista de la Nueva España,* 2 vols. Porrúa: Mexico City.

Dickler, Robert A. 1971. Review of *Population and Economics,* edited by Paul Deprez, *Journal of Economic History,* 31:708–11.

Diehl, Richard A. 1970. "Contemporary Settlement Patterns: An Overview," in SANDERS et al., *The Teotihuacán Valley Project, 1:103–79.*

Diffie, Bailey W. 1945. *Latin-American Civilization: Colonial Period.* Stackpole Sons: Harrisburg.

Difrieri, Horacio A. 1961. Población indígena y colonial," in *La Argentina, suma de geografía,* by H. A. Difrieri, 7:3–88. Ediciones Peuser: Buenos Aires.

Dobyns, Henry F. 1962. *Pioneering Christians among the Perishing Indians of Tucson.* Editorial Estudios Andinos: Lima.

_____. 1963a. "Indian Extinction in the Middle Santa Cruz River Valley, Arizona," *New Mexico Historical Review,* 38:163–81.

_____. 1963b. "An Outline of Andean Epidemic History to 1720," *Bulletin of the History of Medicine,* 37:493–515.

_____. 1966. "Estimating Aboriginal American Population: An Appraisal of Techniques with a New Hemispheric Estimate," *Current Anthropology,* 7:395–416.

_____. 1973. Review of Vol. 1 of *Essays in Population History: Mexico and the Caribbean,* by S. F. Cook and W. Borah, *Ethnohistory,* 20:292–96.

_____. 1976. *Native American Historical Demography: A Critical Bibliography.* The Newberry Library Center for the History of the American Indian, Bibliographical Series, Indiana Univ. Press: Bloomington.

Dodge, F. 1860. Report No. 175, January 4, 1859, *Report of the Commissioner of Indian Affairs . . . 1859,* pp. 373–77, Senate Document No. 1, Serial No. 1078. U.S. Department of the Interior: Washington, D.C.

Donaldson, Thomas. 1887. *The George Catlin Indian Gallery in the U.S. National Museum, with Memoir and Statistics.* G.P.O.: Washington, D.C.

Dostal, Walter, ed. 1972. *The Situation of the Indian in South America,* Publications of the Department of Ethnology, Univ. Berne, No. 3. World Council of Churches: Geneva.

Driver, Harold E. 1961. Indians of North America. Univ. Chicago Press: Chicago.

_____. 1968. "On the Population Nadir of Indians in the United States," *Current Anthropology*, 9:330.

_____. 1969. *Indians of North America*, 2nd ed. Univ. Chicago Press: Chicago.

Driver, Harold E., John M. Cooper, Paul Kirchhoff, Dorothy Ranier Libby, William C. Massey, and Leslie Spier. 1953. *Indian Tribes of North America*, Indiana Univ. Publications in Anthropology and Linguistics, Memoir 9. Waverly Press: Baltimore.

Duffy, John. 1951. "Smallpox and the Indians in the American Colonies," *Bulletin of the History of Medicine*, 25:324–41.

Dunbar, John. 1880. "The Pawnee Indians: Their History and Ethnology," *Magazine of American History*, 4:241–81.

Dunn, Frederick L. 1965. "On the Antiquity of Malaria in the Western Hemisphere," *Human Biology*, 37:385–93.

Edwards, Clinton R. 1957. "Quintana Roo: Mexico's Empty Quarter," Master's thesis. Univ. California, Berkeley.

Eguiluz, Diego de. 1884 [1696]. *Historia de la misión de Mojos*. Imprenta del Universo: Lima.

Eidt, Robert C. 1959. "Aboriginal Chibcha Settlement in Colombia," *Annals of the Association of American Geographers*, 49:374–92.

_____. 1973. "A Rapid Chemical Field Test For Archaeological Site Surveying," *American Antiquity*, 38:206–10.

Eidt, Robert C., and William I. Woods. 1974. *Abandoned Settlement Analysis: Theory and Practice*. Field Test Associates: Shorewood, Wis.

Encyclopaedia Britannica. 1974. *The New Encyclopaedia Britannica: Macropaedia*, 19 vols. Encyclopaedia Britannica: Chicago.

ENE. 1939–42. *Epistolario de Nueva España, 1505–1818*, 16 vols., edited by Francisco del Paso y Troncoso. Antigua Librería: Mexico City.

Espinosa, Isidro Félix de. 1716. "Diary of the Expedition to Texas." Manuscript, Vol. 394, Nos. 7–9, Archivo General y Público, Mexico City.

Espinoza Soriano, Waldemar, ed. 1964. *Visita hecha a la provincia de Chucuito por Garci Diez de San Miguel en el año 1567*. Casa de la Cultura del Perú: Lima.

Evans, Clifford. 1964. "Lowland South America," in *Prehistoric Man in the New World*, edited by J. D. Jennings and E. Norbeck, pp. 419–50. Univ. Chicago Press: Chicago.

Ewers, John C. 1973. "The Influence of Epidemics on the Indian Populations and Cultures of Texas," *Plains Anthropologist* 18:104–15.

Ezell, Paul H. 1961. *The Hispanic Acculturation of the Gila River Pimas*, American Anthropological Association, Memoir 90.

Fajardo M., Darío. 1969. *El régimen de la encomienda en la provincia de Vélez (población indígena y economía)*. Univ. de los Andes: Bogotá.

Farmer, John, ed. 1838. "Gov. Thomas Dudley's Letter to the Countess of Lincoln, March, 1631," in *Tracts and Other Papers Relating Principally to the Origin, Settlement, and Progress of the Colonies in North America*, Vol. 2, No. 4. Peter Force: Washington, D.C.

Feest, Christian F. 1973. "Seventeenth Century Virginia Algonquian Population Estimates," *Quarterly Bulletin of the Archeological Society of Virginia,* 28:66–79.

Fernández, Diego. 1913–14 [1571]. *Historia del Perú,* edited by Lucas de Torre, 2 vols. Biblioteca Hispania: Madrid.

Forney, Jacob. 1860. Report No. 174, September 29, 1859, *Report of the Commissioner of Indian Affairs . . . 1859,* pp. 362–73, Senate Document No. 1, Serial No. 1078. U.S. Department of the Interior: Washington, D.C.

French, B. F., ed. 1846–50. *Historical Collections of Louisiana,* 2 pts. Wiley and Putnam: New York.

Friede, Juan. 1963. *Los Quimbayas bajo la dominación española: Estudio documental (1539–1810).* Banco de la República: Bogotá.

———. 1965. "Algunas consideraciones sobre la evolución demográfia de la provincia de Tunja," *Anuario Colombiano de Historia Social y de la Cultura,* 2 (3):5–19.

———. 1967. "Demographic Changes in the Mining Community of Muzo after the Plague of 1629," *Hispanic American Historical Review,* 47:338–43.

Furlong Cardiff, Guillermo. 1941. *Entre los Lules de Tucumán.* San Pablo: Buenos Aires.

———. 1962. *Misiones y sus pueblos de Guaraníes.* Ediciones Theoria: Buenos Aires.

———. 1968. *Alonzo Bárzana, S. J. y su carta a Juan Sebastián (1594).* Ediciones Theoria: Buenos Aires.

Galvão, Eduardo. 1967. "Indigenous Culture Areas of Brazil, 1900–1959," in *Indians of Brazil in the Twentieth Century,* edited by Janice H. Hopper, pp. 167–205. Institute for Cross-Cultural Research: Washington, D.C.

Gamio, Manuel. 1922. *La población del valle de Teotihuacán,* 3 vols. Secretaría de Agricultura y Fomento: Mexico City.

———. 1942. "Consideraciones sobre el problema indígena en América," *América Indígena,* 2 (2):17–23.

García Icazbalceta, Joaquín. 1881. *Don fray Juan de Zumárraga . . . , 4 vols, Mexico City.*

Gautier, Étienne, and Louis Henry. 1958. *La population de Crulai, paroisse normande.* Presses Universitaires de France: Paris.

Genicot, Léopold. 1966. "Crisis: From the Middle Ages to Modern Times," in *The Cambridge Economic History of Europe,* Vol. 1: *The Agrarian Life of the Middle Ages,* edited by M. M. Postan, pp. 660–741. Cambridge Univ. Press: Cambridge.

Gerhard, Peter. 1972. *A Guide to the Historical Geography of New Spain.* Cambridge Univ. Press: Cambridge.

———. 1975. "Continuity and Change in Morelos, Mexico," *Geographical Review,* 65:335–52.

Gibson, Charles. 1952. *Tlaxcala in the Sixteenth Century.* Yale Univ. Press: New Haven.

———. 1964. *The Aztecs under Spanish Rule.* Stanford Univ. Press: Stanford.

Gibson, George. 1835. Report No. 11, November 12, 1835, *Annual Report of the Commissioner of Indian Affairs . . . 1835*, pp. 287–300, House Document No. 2, Serial No. 286. U.S. Department of War: Washington, D.C.

Giménez Fernández, Manuel. 1953–60. *Bartolomé de Las Casas*, 2 vols. Publicaciones de la Escuela de Estudios Hispano-Americanos de Sevilla, No. 70. Seville.

Glass, D. V., and D. E. C. Eversley. 1965. *Population in History: Essays in Historical Demography*. Edward Arnold: London.

Glassow, Michael A. 1967. "Considerations in Estimating Prehistoric California Coastal Populations," *American Antiquity*, 32:354–59.

Goetz, Walter. 1932–36. *Historia universal*, 10 vols. Espasa-Calpe: Madrid.

Góngora, Diego de. 1907. "Dos informes del Gobernador Diego de Góngora al Rey en al año de 1622" (extracts), in CERVERA, *Historia de . . . Santa Fe*, Vol. 1, Appendices, pp. 83–90.

Gookin, Daniel. 1802. "A Description and History of Eastham, in the County of Barnstable. September. 1802," in *Collections of the Massachusetts Historical Society*, 1st ser., 8:154–86. Munroe and Francis: Boston.

––––––. 1806. "Historical Collections of the Indians in New England," in *Collections of the Massachusetts Historical Society for the Year 1792*, 1st ser., 1:141–229. Munroe and Francis: Boston.

Gordon, B. Le Roy. 1957. *Human Geography and Ecology in the Sinú Country of Colombia*, Ibero-Americana, No. 39. Univ. California Press: Berkeley.

Goubert, Pierre. 1960. *Beauvais et le Beauvaisis de 1600 à 1730*, 2 vols. École Pratique des Hautes Études: Paris.

Grauman, John V. 1959. "Population Estimates and Projections," in *The Study of Population: An Inventory and Appraisal*, edited by Philip M. Hauser and Otis D. Duncan, pp. 544–75. Univ. Chicago Press: Chicago.

Graves, E. A. 1853. Report No. 80, August 31, 1853, *Annual Report of the Commissioner of Indian Affairs . . . 1853*, pp. 434–41, House Document No. 1, Serial No. 710. U.S. Department of the Interior: Washington, D.C.

––––––. 1854. Report No. 85, June 8, 1854, *Annual Report of the Commissioner of Indian Affairs . . . 1854*, pp. 385–92, House Document No. 1, Serial No. 777. U.S. Department of the Interior: Washington, D.C.

Greene, Evarts B., and Virginia D. Harrington. 1932. *American Population before the Federal Census of 1790*. Columbia Univ. Press: New York.

Gross, Daniel. 1975. "Protein Capture and Cultural Development in the Amazon Basin," *American Anthropologist*, 77:526–49.

Gumerman, George J., ed. 1971. *The Distribution of Prehistoric Population Aggregates*, Prescott College Anthropological Reports, No. 1. Prescott, Ariz.

Halberstein, Robert A., Michael H. Crawford, and Hugo G. Nutini. 1973. "Historical-Demographic Analysis of Indian Populations in Tlaxcala, Mexico," *Social Biology*, 20:40–50.

Hallam, H. E. 1961. "Population Density in Medieval Fenland," *Economic History Review*, 2nd ser., 14:71–81.

Hamerly, Michael T. 1974. "La demografía histórica de Ecuador, Perú y

Bolivia: una bibliografía preliminar," *Revista del Archivo Histórico del Guayas* (Guayaquil), 3 (6):24–63.

Hanke, Lewis. 1964. "More Heat and Some Light on the Spanish Struggle for Justice in the Conquest of America," *Hispanic American Historical Review*, 44:293–340.

———. 1971. "A Modest Proposal for a Moratorium on Grand Generalizations: Some Thoughts on the Black Legend," *Hispanic American Historical Review*, 51:112–27.

Harner, Michael J. 1970. "Population Pressure and the Social Evolution of Agriculturalists," *Southwestern Journal of Anthropology*, 26:67–86.

Harris, C. A. 1836. "Statement Showing the Number of Indians Now East of the Mississippi . . . ," Statement D, *Annual Report of the Commissioner of Indian Affairs . . . 1836*, pp. 402–3, House Document No. 2, Serial No. 301. U.S. Department of War: Washington, D.C.

Harvey, Herbert R. 1967. "Population of the Cahuilla Indians: Decline and Its Causes," *Eugenics Quarterly*, 14:185–98.

Haviland, William A. 1969. "A New Population Estimate for Tikal, Guatemala," *American Antiquity*, 34:429–33.

Hawkins, Benjamin, Andrew Pickens, Joseph Martin, and Lach'n McIntosh. 1832. Letter to Richard Henry Lee, Esq., President of Congress, from Hopewell, December 2, 1785, in *American State Papers, Class II, Indian Affairs*, 1:38–39. Gales and Seaton: Washington, D.C.

Heidenreich, Conrad E. 1973. *Huronia: A History and Geography of the Huron Indians, 1600–1650*. McClelland and Stewart: Toronto.

Heizer, Robert F., and Sherburne F. Cook, eds. 1960. *The Application of Quantitative Methods in Archaeology*, Viking Fund Publications in Anthropology, No. 28. Quadrangle Books: Chicago.

Helleiner, K. F. 1965. "The Vital Revolution Reconsidered," in *Population in History: Essays in Historical Demography*, edited by D. V. Glass and D. E. C. Eversley, pp. 79–86. Edward Arnold: London.

Henry, Louis. 1965. "The Population of France in the Eighteenth Century," in *Population in History: Essays in Historical Demography*, edited by D. V. Glass and D. E. C. Eversley, pp. 434–56. Edward Arnold: London.

Hernández, Francisco. 1946. *Antigüedades de la Nueva España*, edited and translated by Joaquín García Pimentel. Editorial Pedro Robredo: Mexico City.

Herrera y Tordesillas, Antonio de. 1934–57 [1601–15]. *Historia general de los hechos de los castellanos en las islas y Tierra Firme del Mar Océano*, 17 vols. Academia Real de la Historia: Madrid.

———. 1944–47. *Historia general de los hechos de los castellanos en las islas y Tierra Firme del Mar Océano*, 10 vols. Editorial Guarania: Buenos Aires.

Hester, Joseph A., Jr. 1954. "Natural and Cultural Bases of Ancient Maya Subsistence Economy," Ph.D. dissertation. Univ. California, Los Angeles.

Hewitt, J. N. B. 1907. "Erie," in HODGE, ed., *Handbook of American Indians*, 1:430–32.

———. 1910. "Sauk," in HODGE, ed., *Handbook of American Indians*, 2:471–80.

Hodge, F. W., ed. 1907–10. *Handbook of American Indians North of Mexico*,

Smithsonian Institution, Bureau of American Ethnology Bulletin No. 30, 2 pts. [vols.]. G.P.O.: Washington, D.C.

Hollingsworth, T. H. 1969. *Historical Demography.* Cornell Univ. Press: Ithaca.

Howells, W. W. 1960. "Estimating Population Numbers through Archaeological and Skeletal Remains," in HEIZER and COOK, eds., *The Application of Quantitative Methods in Archaeology,* pp. 158–85.

Hubbard, William. 1815. "A General History of New England from the Discovery to MDCLXXX," in *Collections of the Massachusetts Historical Society,* 2nd ser., Vol. 5. Little and Brown: Boston.

Iglesia, Ramón. 1944. *El hombre Colón y otros ensayos.* El Colegio de México: Mexico City.

Ixtlilxochitl, Don Fernando de Alva. 1952. *Obras históricas,* 2 vols., edited by Alfredo Chavero. Editorial Nacional: Mexico City.

Jacobs, Wilbur R. 1971. "The Fatal Confrontation: Early Native-White Relations on the Frontiers of Australia, New Guinea, and America—A Comparative Study," *Pacific Historical Review,* 40:283–309.

———. 1972. *Dispossessing the American Indian: Indians and Whites on the Colonial Frontier.* Scribner's: New York.

———. 1973. "The Indian and the Frontier in American History: A Need for Revision," *Western Historical Quarterly,* 4:43–56.

———. 1974. "The Tip of an Iceburg: Pre-Columbian Indian Demography and Some Implications for Revisionism," *William and Mary Quarterly,* 3rd ser., 31:123–32.

Jaimes Freyre, Ricardo. 1914. *El Tucumán del siglo XVI.* Univ. Tucumán: Buenos Aires.

———. 1915. *El Tucumán colonial (documentos y mapas del archivo de Indias),* Vol. 1. Univ. Tucumán: Buenos Aires.

Jakeman, Max W. 1938. "The Maya States of Yucatan (1441–1545)," Ph.D. dissertation. Univ. California, Berkeley.

James, Preston E. 1959. *Latin America,* 3rd ed. Odyssey Press: New York.

Jameson, J. Franklin, ed. 1910. *Johnson's Wonder-Working Providence, 1628–1651,* Original Narratives of Early American History. Scribner's: New York.

Jaramillo Uribe, Jaime. 1964. "La población indígena de Colombia en el momento de la Conquista y sus transformaciones posteriores," *Anuario Colombiano de Historia Social y de la Cultura,* 1:239–93.

Jarcho, Saul. 1964. "Some Observations on Disease in Prehistoric North America," *Bulletin of the History of Medicine,* 38:1–19.

Jennings, Francis. 1975. *The Invasion of America: Indians, Colonialism, and the Cant of Conquest.* Univ. North Carolina Press: Chapel Hill.

Jennings, Jesse D., and Edward Norbeck, eds. 1964. *Prehistoric Man in the New World.* Univ. Chicago Press: Chicago.

Johannessen, Carl L. 1963. *Savannas of Interior Honduras,* Ibero-Americana, No. 46. Univ. California Press: Berkeley.

Juderías y Loyot, Julián. 1917. *La leyenda negra: estudios acerca del concepto de España en el extranjero*, 2nd ed. Barcelona.

Keen, Benjamin. 1969. "The Black Legend Revisited: Assumptions and Realities," *Hispanic American Historical Review*, 49:703–19.

———. 1971. "The White Legend Revisited: A Reply to Professor Hanke's 'Modest Proposal,' " *Hispanic American Historical Review*, 51:336–55.

Keesing, Felix M. 1941. *The South Seas in the Modern World*. John Day: New York.

Kelly, Isabel, and Ángel Palerm. 1952. *The Tajin Totonac, Part I: History, Subsistence, Shelter and Technology*, Smithsonian Institution, Institute of Social Anthropology, Publication 13. G.P.O.: Washington, D.C.

Key, Harold and Mary. 1967. *Bolivian Indian Tribes: Classification, Bibliography, and Map of Present Language Distribution*. Summer Institute of Linguistics: Norman, Okla.

Kniffen, Fred B. 1931. *The Primitive Cultural Landscape of the Colorado Delta*, Univ. California Publications in Geography, 5:43–66. Univ. California Press: Berkeley.

Knox, H. 1832. Report No. 2, "Relating to the Southern Indians," July 6, 1789, in *American State Papers, Class II, Indian Affairs*, 1:15–16. Gales and Seaton: Washington, D.C.

Konetzke, Richard. 1963. *Endecker und Eroberer Amerikas*. Fischer Bücherei: Frankfurt.

———. 1965. *Die Indianerkulturen Altamerikas und die spanisch-portugiesische Kolonialherrschaft*, Fischer Weltgeschichte, Vol. 22, Süd- und Mittelamerika, I. Frankfurt.

Krause, Aurel. 1885. *Die Tlinkit-Indianer, Ergebnisse einer Reise nach der Nordwestküste von Amerika und der Beringstrasse*. Auftrage der Bremer Geographichen Gesellschaft, 1880–81. Jena.

Kroeber, Alfred L. 1925. *Handbook of the Indians of California*, Smithsonian Institution, Bureau of American Ethnology Bulletin 78. G.P.O.: Washington, D.C.

———. 1934. "Native American Population," *American Anthropologist*, 36:1–25.

———. 1939. *Cultural and Natural Areas of Native North America*, Univ. California Publications in American Archaeology and Ethnology, Vol. 38. Univ. California Press: Berkeley.

———. 1946. "The Chibcha," in STEWARD, ed., *Handbook of South American Indians*, 2:887–909.

Kubler, George. 1942. "Population Movements in Mexico, 1520–1600," *Hispanic American Historical Review*, 22:606–43.

———. 1946. "The Quechua in the Colonial World," in STEWARD, ed., *Handbook of South American Indians*, 2:331–410.

Labaree, Leonard W., ed. 1969. *The Papers of Benjamin Franklin*, 18 vols. Yale Univ. Press: New Haven.

Laffont, Robert. 1965. *Histoire universelle des armées*. Éditions Robert Laffont: Paris.

Lange, Frederick W. 1971a. "Marine Resources: A Viable Subsistence Alternative for the Prehistoric Lowland Maya," *American Anthropologist*, 73:619–39.

———. 1971b. "Una reevaluación de la población del norte de Yucatán en el tiempo del contacto español: 1528," *América Indígena*, 31:117–39.

Langlois, Charles V., and Charles Seignobos. 1898. *Introduction to the Study of History*, translated by G. G. Berry. Henry Holt: New York.

Larrouy, P. A. 1914. *Los indios del valle de Catamarca, estudio histórico*, Publicaciones de la Sección Antropológica, No. 14. Univ. Buenos Aires: Buenos Aires.

Las Casas, Bartolomé de. 1598. *Narratio regionum Indicarum per Hispanos quosdam devastatorum verissima*. T. de Bry: Frankfurt. Copy in Edward E. Ayer Collection, The Newberry Library, Chicago.

———. 1957–58. *Obras escogidas de Fray Bartolomé de Las Casas*, edited by Juan Pérez de Tudela, 5 vols. (Biblioteca de Autores Españoles, Vols. 95, 96, 105, 106, 110). Ediciones Atlas: Madrid. (*Historia de las Indias*, Vols. 1, 2; *Apologética historia*, Vols. 3, 4; *Opúsculos, cartas y memoriales*, Vol. 5; "Brevísima relación de la destruición de la Indias," Vol. 5, Ch. 14, pp. 134–81.)

Lastres, Juan B. 1951. "La medicina en el virreinato," in *Historia de la medicina Peruana*, 2:73–300. Univ. Nacional Mayor de San Marcos: Lima.

Lathrap, Donald W. 1962. "Yarinacocha: Stratigraphic Excavations in the Peruvian Montaña," Ph.D. dissertation. Harvard Univ., Cambridge.

———. 1968a. "Aboriginal Occupation and Changes in River Channel on the Central Ucayali, Peru," *American Antiquity*, 33:62–79.

———. 1968b. "The 'Hunting Economies' of the Tropical Forest Zone of South America: An Attempt at Perspective," in *Man the Hunter*, edited by R. B. Lee and I. DeVore, pp. 23–29. Aldine: Chicago.

———. 1970. *The Upper Amazon*. Praeger: New York.

———. 1972. "Alternative Models of Population Movements in the Tropical Lowlands of South America," *Actas y memorias, XXXIX Congreso Internacional de Americanistas* (Lima, 1970), 4:13–23.

Laureano de la Cruz. 1942. *Nuevo descubrimiento del Río Marañón, llamado de las Amazonas, hecho por los misioneros de la Provincia de San Francisco de Quito el año de 1651*, Biblioteca Amazonas, No. 7. Quito.

Lawson, John. 1860. *The History of Carolina, Containing the Exact Description and Natural History of that Country*. Strother and Marcom: Raleigh.

Leeds, Anthony. 1961. "Yaruro Incipient Tropical Forest Horticulture: Possibilities and Limits," in *The Evolution of Horticultural Systems in Native South America, Causes and Consequences: A Symposium*, edited by Johannes Wilbert, pp. 13–46. Sociedad de Ciencias Naturales La Salle: Caracas.

Lehnertz, Jay F. 1969. "Cultural Struggle on the Peruvian Frontier: Campa-Franciscan Confrontations, 1595–1752, Master's thesis. Univ. Wisconsin, Madison.

_____. 1974. "Lands of the Infidels: The Franciscans in the Central Montaña of Peru, 1709–1824," Ph.D. dissertation. Univ. Wisconsin, Madison.

Leonhardt, Carlos. 1927. "Introducción," in DHA, 19:xvii–cxxviii.

León Pinelo, Antonio Rodríguez de. 1958. *Relación sobre la pacificación y población de las provincias del Manché i Lacandón*. J. P. Turanzas: Madrid.

Lerma, Hernando de. 1931. "Pregón del licenciado . . . hecho en Potosí, en abril de 1580 . . . ," in LEVILLIER, ed., *Nueva crónica*, 3:270–92.

Levillier, Roberto, ed. 1926–31. *Nueva crónica de la conquista del Tucumán*, 3 vols. Editorial Nosotros: Buenos Aires.

Lewis, Oscar, and Ernest E. Maes. 1945. "Base para una nueva definición práctica del indio," *América Indígena*, 5 (2):107–18.

Lipschutz, Alejandro. 1966. "La despoblación de las Indias después de la conquista," *América Indígena*, 26:229–47.

López de Gómara, Francisco. 1943 [1552]. *Historia de la conquista de México*, 2 vols., edited by Joaquín Ramírez Cabañas. Editorial Pedro Robredo: Mexico City.

_____. 1964. *Cortés, the Life of the Conqueror by His Secretary*, translated and edited by L. B. Simpson. Univ. California Press: Berkeley.

López de Velasco, Juan. 1971. *Geografía y descripción universal de las Indias*, Edición de Don Marcos Jiménez de la Espada, Biblioteca de Autores Españoles, Vol. 248. Ediciones Atlas: Madrid. [Completed in 1574.]

Lovén, Sven. 1924. *Über die Wurzeln der tainischen Kultur*, Vol. 1: *Materielle Kultur*. Elanders boktryckeri aktiebolag: Göteburg.

Lozano, Pedro. 1941 [1733]. *Descripción corográfica del Gran Chaco Gualamba*, Univ. Nacional de Tucumán, Publicación No. 288. Instituto de Antropología: Tucumán.

Machoni de Cerdeña, Antonio. 1878 [1732]. *Arte y vocabulario de la lengua lule y tonocoté*, edited by Juan M. Larsen. P. E. Coni: Buenos Aires.

McBryde, Felix W. 1940. "Influenza in America during the Sixteenth Century (Guatemala: 1523, 1559–1562, 1576)," *Bulletin of the History of Medicine*, 8 296–302.

Mackenzie, Alexander. 1801. *Voyages from Montreal, on the River St. Lawrence, through the Continent of North America, to the Frozen and Pacific Oceans: In the Years 1789 and 1793*. R. Noble, Old-Bailey: London.

MacLeod, Murdo J. 1973. *Spanish Central America: A Socioeconomic History, 1520–1720*. Univ. California Press: Berkeley.

MacLeod, William C. 1928. *The American Indian Frontier*. Knopf: New York.

MacNeish, Richard S. 1964. *El origen de la civilización mesoamericana visto desde Tehuacán*, Instituto Nacional de Antropología e Historia, Departamento de Prehistoria, Publicaciones 16. Mexico City.

_____. 1970. "Social Implications of Changes in Population and Settlement Pattern of the 12,000 Years of Prehistory in the Tehuacán Valley of Mexico," in DEPREZ, ed., *Population and Economics*, pp. 215–50.

MacNutt, Francis Augustus. 1909. *Bartholomew de las Casas: His Life, His Apostolate, and His Writings*. Putnam's: New York.

Madariaga, Salvador de. 1966. Review of *The Early Spanish Main*, by Carl O. Sauer, *The New York Review of Books*, Dec. 1, 1966, pp. 34–36.

Marbut, C. F., and C. B. Manifold. 1925. "The Topography of the Amazon Valley," *Geographical Review*, 15:617–42.

———. 1926. "The Soils of the Amazon Basin in Relation to Agricultural Possibilities," *Geographical Review*, 16:414–42.

Margry, Pierre, ed. 1876–86. *Découvertes et établissements des Français dans l'ouest et dans le sud de l'Amérique Septentrionale (1614–1754)*, 6 vols. Imprimerie D. Jouaust: Paris.

María Casañas, Jesús. 1691. "Relación," August 15, 1691. Manuscript in Talamantes Collection, Vol. 394, No. 1, Archivo General de la Nación, Mexico City.

Marín Negrón, Diego. 1907 [1610]. "Informe de Diego Marín Negrón al Rey" (extract), in CERVERA, *Historia de . . . Santa Fe*, 1:74.

Markuzon, F. D. 1957. "Naselenie mira ot nachal nashei ery do serediny XX veka" [The World Population from the Beginning of Our Era to the Middle of the Twentieth Century], in *Voprosy ekonomiki, planirovaniia i statistiki*, edited by V. S. Nemchinov, pp. 388–404. Moscow.

Martyr D'Anghiera, Peter. 1912 [1530]. *De Orbe Novo: The Eight Decades of Peter Martyr D'Anghera*, 2 vols., edited and translated by Francis A. MacNutt. Putnam's: New York.

———. 1944 [1530]. *Décadas del Nuevo Mundo*, translated by Joaquín Torres Asensio. Editorial Bajel: Buenos Aires.

Mason, John. 1819. "A Brief History of the Pequot War," in *Collections of the Massachusetts Historical Society*, 2nd ser., 8:120–53. Nathan Hale: Boston.

Mastrillo Durán, Nicolás. 1929. "Carta del P. Nicolás Mastrillo Durán," in DHA, 20:223–384.

Matrícula de Tributos. N.d. Manuscript, 15 fols. Museo Nacional de Antropología: Mexico City.

Mauro, Frédéric. 1961. "Marchands et marchands-banquiers portugais au XVIIème siècle," *Revista Portuguesa de História*, 9 (8):63–78.

Mayhew, Thomas. 1806. "Of the Progress of the Gospel among the Indians at Martha's Vineyard and Nantucket . . . ," in *Collections of the Massachusetts Historical Society for the Year 1792*, 1st ser., 1:201–5. Munroe and Francis: Boston.

Means, Philip A. 1931. *Ancient Civilizations of the Andes*. Scribner's: New York.

Medina, José Toribio. 1934. *The Discovery of the Amazon according to the Account of Friar Gaspar de Carvajal and Other Documents*, edited by D. C. Heaton, and translated by D. T. Lee. American Geographical Society, Special Publication, No. 17. New York.

Meggers, Betty J. 1971. *Amazonia: Man and Culture in a Counterfeit Paradise*. Aldine-Atherton: Chicago.

Meigs, Peveril. 1935. *The Dominican Mission Frontier of Lower California*, Univ. California Publications in Geography, Vol. 7. Univ. California Press: Berkeley.

Melchor de Navarra y Rocaful. 1859. "Relación del Estado de Perú," *Memorias de los Vireyes*, Vol. 2. Librería Central de Felipe Bailly; Lima.

Mellafe, Rolando R. 1965. "Problemas demográficos e historia colonial hispanoamericana," in *Temas de historia económica hispanoamericana*, Colección Nova Americana, No. 1, pp. 45–55. Paris.

———. 1970. "The Importance of Migration in the Viceroyalty of Peru," in DEPREZ, ed., *Population and Economics*, pp. 303–13.

Memoria. 1907 [1609?]. "Memoria de las poblaciones y provincias destas govuernaciones del Paraguay y Río de la Plata," in CERVERA, *Historia de . . . Santa Fe*, 1:77–80.

Mendieta, Jerónimo de. 1945. *Historia eclesiástica indiana*, edited by J. García Icazbalceta, 4 vols. Chávez Hayhoe: Mexico City. [Completed in 1596.]

Mendizábal, Miguel Othón de. 1946–47. "La demografía mexicana; Epoca colonial 1519–1810: Demografía colonial del siglo XVI, 1519–1599," in M. O. de Mendizábal, *Obras completas*, 3:307–35. Talleres Gráficos de la Nación: Mexico City.

Merriam, C. Hart. 1905. "The Indian Population of California," *American Anthropologist*, 7:594–606.

Merriwether, D. 1854. Report No. 84, September 1, 1854, *Annual Report of the Commissioner of Indian Affairs . . . 1854*, pp. 374–85, House Document No. 1, Serial No. 777. U.S. Department of the Interior: Washington, D.C.

Métraux, Alfred. 1942. *The Native Tribes of Eastern Bolivia and Western Matto Grosso*, Smithsonian Institution, Bureau of American Ethnology Bulletin 134. G.P.O.: Washington, D.C.

———. 1946. "Ethnography of the Chaco," in STEWARD, ed., *Handbook of South American Indians*, 1:197–370.

———. 1948. "The Tupinamba," in STEWARD, ed., *Handbook of South American Indians*, 3:95–133.

México, Dirección General de Estadística. 1901–7. *Censo general de la República Mexicana verificado el 28 de octubre de 1900*, 28 vols., Secretaría de Fomento. Mexico City.

———. 1918–20. *Tercer censo de población de los Estados Unidos Mexicanos verificado el 27 de octubre de 1910*, 3 vols., Secretaría de Agricultura y Fomento. Mexico City.

———. 1925–28. *Censo general de habitantes, 30 de noviembre de 1921*, 30 vols. Mexico City.

———. 1932–36. *Quinto censo de población, 15 de mayo de 1930*, 6 vols. Mexico City.

———. 1943–48. *6° censo de población, 1940*, 31 vols., Secretaría de la Economía Nacional. Mexico City.

———. 1952–53. *Séptimo censo general de población, 6 de junio de 1950*, 32 vols., Secretaría de Economía. Mexico City.

———. 1962–64. *VIII censo general de población, 8 de junio de 1960*, 35 vols., Secretaría de Industria y Comercio. Mexico City.

Mézières, Athanacio de. 1778. "Expedition." Manuscript in Memorias de Nueva España, Vol. 28, No. 37, pp. 269–89, Archivo General de la Nación, Mexico City.

Millon, René. 1964. "The Teotihuacán Mapping Project," *American Antiquity,* 29:345–52.

———. 1970. "Teotihuacán: Completion of Map of Giant City in the Valley of Mexico," *Science,* 170:1077–82.

Miranda, José. 1952. *El tributo indígena en la Nueva España durante el siglo XVI.* Colegio de México: Mexico City.

———, coordinator. 1964. "Simposio: Los cambios habidos en la cantidad y distribución de la población indígena durante la Época Colonial," *Actas y memorias, XXXV Congreso Internacional de Americanistas* (Mexico City, 1962), 3:371–406.

Mols, Roger. 1954–56. *Introduction à la démographie historique des villes d'Europe du XIVe au XVIIIe siècle,* 3 vols. J. Duculot: Gembloux.

Monsalve, Miguel de. 1604. *Redución universal de todo el Pirú.* Manuscript, British Museum, London. Photostatic copy in Memorial Library, Univ. Wisconsin, Madison.

Mook, Maurice A. 1944. "The Aboriginal Population of Tidewater Virginia," *American Anthropologist,* 46:193–208.

Mooney, James. 1907a. "Cherokee," in HODGE, ed., *Handbook of American Indians,* 1:245–49.

———. 1907b. "The Powhatan Confederacy, Past and Present," *American Anthropologist,* 9:129–52.

———. 1910a. "Population," in HODGE, ed., *Handbook of American Indians,* 2:286–87.

———. 1910b. "Shawnee," in HODGE, ed., *Handbook of American Indians,* 2:530–38.

———. 1928. *The Aboriginal Population of America North of Mexico,* edited by John R. Swanton, Smithsonian Miscellaneous Collections, Vol. 80, No. 7. Smithsonian Institution: Washington, D.C.

Mooney, James, and J. N. B. Hewitt. 1910. "Potawatomi," in HODGE, ed., *Handbook of American Indians,* 2:289–93.

Mooney, James, and Cyrus Thomas. 1907a. "Chippewa," in HODGE, ed., *Handbook of American Indians,* 1:277–81.

———. 1907b. "Menominee," in HODGE, ed., *Handbook of American Indians,* 1:842–44.

———. 1907c. "Miami," in HODGE, ed., *Handbook of American Indians,* 1:852–55.

Morales Figueroa, Luis de. 1866 [1591]. "Relación de los indios tributarios que hay al presente en estos reinos y provincias del Pirú . . . ," in CDI, 6:41–61.

Moran, Emilio F. 1974. "The Adaptive System of the Amazonian Caboclo," in WAGLEY, ed., *Man in the Amazon,* pp. 136–59.

Morey, Robert V., and John P. Marwitt. 1978. "Ecology, Economy, and Warfare in Lowland South America," in *Advances in Andean Archaeology,* edited by D. L. Browman, pp. 247–58. World Anthropology, Sol Tax, general editor. Mouton: The Hague.

Morgenstern, Oskar. 1963. *On the Accuracy of Economic Observations*, 2nd ed. Princeton Univ. Press: Princeton.

Morin, Claude. 1972. "Population et épidémies dans une paroisse mexicaine: Santa Inés Zacatelco, XVIIe–XIXe siècles," *Cahiers des Amériques Latines, Série Sciences de l'Homme*, 6:43–73.

———. 1974. *Santa Inés Zacatelco (1646–1812): Contribución a la demografía histórica del México colonial*. Mexico City.

Mörner, Magnus. 1967. *Race Mixture in the History of Latin America*. Little, Brown: Boston.

———. 1973. Review of Vol. 1 of *Essays in Population History: Mexico and the Caribbean*, by S. F. Cook and W. Borah, *Hispanic American Historical Review*, 53:109–12.

Morse, Jedidiah. 1822. *A Report to the Secretary of War of the United States, on Indian Affairs*. S. Converse: New Haven.

Motolinía (Toribio de Benavente). 1914. *Historia de los indios de la Nueva España*, edited by D. S. García. Barcelona. [Completed ca. 1540.]

Muñoz, Juan Bautista. 1793. *Historia del Nuevo Mundo*. Madrid.

Murphy, Yolanda, and Robert F. Murphy. 1974. *Women of the Forest*. Columbia Univ. Press: New York.

Murra, John V., ed. 1967–72. *Visita de la provincia de León de Huánuco en 1562, Iñigo Ortiz de Zúñiga, visitador*, 2 vols. Univ. Nacional Hermilio Valdizán: Huánuco, Peru.

Myers, Thomas P. 1973. "Toward the Reconstruction of Prehistoric Community Patterns in the Amazon Basin," in *Variation in Anthropology: Essays in Honor of John C. McGregor*, edited by D. W. Lathrap and J. Douglas, pp. 233–52. Illinois Archaeological Survey: Urbana.

Naroll, Raoul. 1962. "Floor Area and Settlement Population," *American Antiquity*, 27:587–89.

Navarrete, Martín Fernández de. 1954–55. *Colección de los viajes y descubrimientos que hicieron por mar los españoles desde fines del siglo XV*, in *Obras de D. Martín Fernández de Navarrete*, edited by Carlos Seco Serrano, 3 vols. (Biblioteca de Autores Españoles, Vols. 75, 76, 77). Ediciones Atlas: Madrid.

Navarro, Manuel. 1924. *La tribu Campa*. Colegio Huérfanos San Vicente: Lima.

Neel, James V. 1971. "Genetic Aspects of the Ecology of Disease in the American Indian," in *The Ongoing Evolution of Latin American Populations*, edited by F. M. Salzano, pp. 561–90. C. C. Thomas: Springfield, Ill.

Neve, Clemente Antonio. 1870. "Estadística de Anáhuac mandada formar después de la toma de México en 1519 por el conquistador Hernando Cortés," *Boletín de la Sociedad Mexicana de Geografía y Estadística*, 2:451–52.

Núñez Cabeza de Vaca, Alvar. 1891. *The Commentaries of Alvar Núñez Cabeza de Vaca*, Pt. 2 of *The Conquest of the River Plate (1535–1555)*, edited by Luis L. Domínguez. Hakluyt Society, Ser. 1, No. 81. London.

Nye, P. H., and D. J. Greenland. 1960. *The Soil under Shifting Cultivation*,

Commonwealth Bureau of Soils, Technical Communication, No. 51. Farnham Royal, England.

Obando, Gutierre Velázquez de. 1931. "Información inédita de méritos y servicios . . . hecho en 1581 acerca de una encomienda en Humahuaca . . . ," in LEVILLIER, ed., *Nueva crónica*, 3:350–64.

O'Callaghan, E. B., ed. 1855. *Documents Relative to the Colonial History of the State of New York, Procured by John Romeyn Brodhead*, Vol. 9. Weed, Parsons: Albany.

Office of Indian Affairs. 1837. "Statement Showing the Number of Indians Now East of the Mississippi . . . ," Statement No. 28, December 1, 1837, in *Annual Report of the Commissioner of Indian Affairs . . . 1837*, pp. 592–94, Senate Document No. 1, Serial No. 314. U.S. Department of War: Washington, D.C.

Oliver, Douglas. 1962. *The Pacific Islands*, rev. ed. Harvard Univ. Press: Cambridge.

Oltman, R. E., and H. O'R. Sternberg, F. C. Ames, and L. C. Davis, Jr. 1964. *Amazon River Investigations: Reconnaissance Measurements of July 1963*, U.S. Geological Survey Circular 486. G.P.O.: Washington, D.C.

Oñate, Pedro de. 1929. "Cartas escrita por el P. provincial Pedro de Oñate" [1616–1620], in DHA, 20:3–222.

Onody, O. 1970. "Quelques traits caractéristiques de l'évolution historique de la population du Brésil," in DEPREZ, ed., *Population and Economics*, pp. 335–63.

Oviedo y Valdés, Gonzalo Fernández de. 1943–45 [1535]. *Historia general y natural de las Indias, islas y Tierra Firme del Mar Océano*, 4 vols. Paragua.

――――. 1959. *Historia general y natural de las Indias*, edited by Juan Peréz de Tudela, 5 vols. (Biblioteca de Autores Españoles, Vols. 117–21). Ediciones Atlas: Madrid.

Pacific Science Association. 1958. "Special Symposium on Climate, Vegetation, and Rational Land Utilization in the Humid Tropics," *Proceedings of the Ninth Pacific Science Congress* (Bangkok, 1957), Vol. 20.

PAHO (Pan American Health Organization). 1968. *Biomedical Challenges Presented by the American Indian*, PAHO Scientific Publication, No. 165. World Health Organization: Washington, D.C.

Palerm, Ángel. 1973. *Obras hidráulicas prehispánicas en el sistema lacustre del Valle de México*. Instituto Nacional de Antropología e Historia: Mexico City.

Palfrey, John G. 1866. *The History of New England*. Hurd and Houghton: New York.

Parsons, James J. 1968. *Antioqueño Colonization in Western Colombia*, 2nd ed. Univ. California Press: Berkeley.

――――. 1969. "Ridged Fields in the Río Guayas Valley, Ecuador," *American Antiquity*, 34:76–80.

Parsons, James J., and William A. Bowen. 1966. "Ancient Ridged Fields of the San Jorge Floodplain, Colombia," *Geographical Review*, 56:317–43.

Parsons, Jeffrey R. 1971. *Prehistoric Settlement Patterns in the Texcoco*

Region, Mexico. Memoirs of the Museum of Anthropology, Univ. Michigan, No. 3. Ann Arbor.

Pavlovsky, Evgeny N. 1966. *Natural Nidality of Transmissible Diseases*. Univ. Illinois Press: Urbana.

Pedersen, Jean Jay. 1974. "The Antiquity of Sylvan Yellow Fever in the Americas," Ph.D. dissertation. Univ. California, Los Angeles.

Peralta, Manuel M. de, ed. 1883. *Costa Rica, Nicaragua y Panamá, en el siglo XVI*. M. Murillo: Madrid.

Peru, Banco Central de Reserva del Perú. 1962. *Memoria 1962*. Lima.

Peru, Instituto Nacional de Planificación. 1963. "Mapa del uso de la tierra," *Zona arida del Perú*. Lima.

Petersen, William. 1961. *Population*, 1st ed. Macmillan: New York.

———. 1975. "A Demographer's View of Prehistoric Demography," *Current Anthropology*, 16:227–45.

Phelan, John L. 1967. *The Kingdom of Quito in the Seventeenth Century*. Univ. Wisconsin Press: Madison.

Plog, Fred. 1975. "Demographic Studies in Southwestern Prehistory," *American Antiquity*, 40 (No. 2, Pt. 2):94–103.

PNE. 1905–48. *Papeles de Nueva España: Segunda serie, geografía y estadística*, edited by Francisco del Paso y Troncoso, 9 vols. Establecimiento Tipográfico: Madrid (1905–6), and Vargas Rea: Mexico City (1944–48).

Porter, Thomas J. 1836. "Letter to Editor from Nashville, Tennessee, August 1, 1836," in *Nashville National Banner*, Wednesday, August 3, 1836, p. 3.

Postan, Michael M. 1966. "England," in *The Cambridge Economic History of Europe*, Vol. I: *The Agrarian Life of the Middle Ages*, edited by M. M. Postan, pp. 548–659. Cambridge Univ. Press: Cambridge.

Prescott, William H. 1936 [1843, 1847]. *History of the Conquest of Mexico* and *History of the Conquest of Peru*. Random House: New York.

Pyle, Jane. 1972. "Indigenous and Colonial Population of Argentina," *Geographical Survey*, 1 (3):55–61.

Quimby, George I. 1960. *Indian Life in the Upper Great Lakes: 11,000 B.C. to A.D. 1800*. Univ. Chicago Press: Chicago.

Rabelais, François. 1944 [1567]. *The Complete Works of Rabelais: The Five Books of Gargantua and Pantagruel*, edited by Jacques Le Clercq. Random House: New York.

Radell, David R. 1969. "Historical Geography of Western Nicaragua: The Spheres of Influence of León, Granada, and Managua, 1519–1965," Ph.D. dissertation. Univ. Calif., Berkeley.

Radell, David R., and James J. Parsons. 1971. "Realejo: A Forgotten Colonial Port and Shipbuilding Center in Nicaragua," *Hispanic American Historical Review*, 51:295–312.

Ramírez de Velasco, Juan. 1914 [1596]. "Carta del gobernador Ramírez de Velasco al rey de España," in JAIMES FREYRE, *El Tucumán del siglo XVI*, pp. 226–39.

———. 1915 [1596]. "Carta del gobernador . . . al rey de España," in JAIMES FREYRE, *El Tucumán colonial*, pp. 102–23.

_____. 1931 [1591]. "Carta a S. M. de Juan Ramírez de Velasco, en la cual, entre otras noticias, da cuenta de la conquista y población de la villa de Londres y fundación de la Nueva Rioja," in LEVILLIER, ed., *Nueva crónica,* 3:339–42.

Ramón, Domingo. 1716. "*Derrotero* of his expedition to Texas." Manuscript, Documentos para la Historia Eclesiástica y Civil de la Provincia de Texas, Bk. 1, Vol. 27, No. 19, Archivo General de la Nación, Mexico City.

Ratliff, James L. 1973. "What Happened to the Kalapuya? A Study of the Depletion of Their Economic Base," *The Indian Historian,* 6 (3):27–33.

Rawlinson, George, ed. 1859–60. *The History of Herodotus,* 4 vols. D. Appleton: New York.

Razzell, P. E. 1965. "Population Change in Eighteenth Century England: A Reinterpretation," *Economic History Review,* 2nd ser., 18:312–32.

Reichel-Dolmatoff, Gerardo. 1965. *Colombia.* Praeger: New York.

Ribeiro, Darcy. 1967. "Indigenous Cultures and Languages of Brazil, 1900–1959," in *Indians of Brazil in the Twentieth Century,* edited by Janice H. Hopper, pp. 167–205. Institute for Cross-Cultural Research: Washington, D.C.

Ribera, Alonso de. 1915. "Cartas del gobernador de Tucumán, don Alonso de Ribera al rey de España" [1607, 1608], in JAIMES FREYRE, *El Tucumán colonial,* pp. 131–41.

Richards, P. W. 1952. *The Tropical Rain Forest: An Ecological Study.* Cambridge Univ. Press: Cambridge.

Rivers, W. H. R., ed. 1922. *Essays on the Depopulation of Melanesia.* Cambridge Univ. Press: Cambridge.

Rivers, William James. 1856. *A Sketch of the History of South Carolina.* McCarter: Charleston.

_____. 1874. *A Chapter in the Early History of South Carolina.* Walker, Evans, and Cogswell: Charleston.

Rivet, Paul, G. Stresser-Péan, and Č. Loukotka. 1924. "Langues américaines," in *Les langues du monde,* edited by A. Meillet and M. Cohen, 16:597–712. Société de Linguistique de Paris: Paris.

_____. 1952. "Langues de l'Amérique," in *Les langues du monde,* edited by A. Meillet and M. Cohen, 2:941–1160. Société de Linguistique de Paris: Paris.

Robertson, William. 1777. *The History of America,* 2 vols. London.

Rojas, Gabriel de. 1927. "Descripcion de Cholula," *Revista Mexicana de Estudios Históricos,* 1 (6):158–69.

Rojas Rabiela, Teresa, Rafael A. Strauss K., and José Lameiras. 1974. *Neuvas noticias sobre las obras hidráulicas prehispánicas y coloniales en el Valle de México.* Instituto Nacional de Antropología e Historia: Mexico City.

Rosenblat, Ángel. 1935. "El desarrollo de la población indígena de América," *Tierra Firme,* 1 (1):115–33, 1 (2):117–48, 1 (3):109–41.

_____. 1945. *La población indígena de América desde 1492 hasta la actualidad.* Institución Cultural Española: Buenos Aires.

_____. 1954. *La población indígena y el mestizaje en América,* 2 vols. Editorial Nova: Buenos Aires.

_____. 1967. *La población de América en 1492: Viejos y nuevos cálculos.* Colegio de México: Mexico City.

Rowe, John H. 1946. "Inca Culture at the Time of the Spanish Conquest," in STEWARD, ed., *Handbook of South American Indians,* 2:183–330.

Rupp, Israel D. 1846. *Early History of Western Pennsylvania, and of the West, and of Western Expeditions and Campaigns, from 1754 to 1833.* Daniel W. Kauffman: Pittsburg.

Russell, Josiah C. 1958. "Late Ancient and Medieval Population," *Transactions of the American Philosophical Society,* new ser., Vol. 48, Pt. 3.

_____. 1965. "Recent Advances in Mediaeval Demography," *Speculum,* 40:84–101.

Ruttenber, E. M. 1872. *History of the Indian Tribes of Hudson's River.* J. Munsell: Albany.

Saco, José Antonio. 1932. *Historia de la esclavitud de los indios en el Nuevo Mundo,* 2 vols. Havana.

Salzano, Francisco M. 1968. "Survey of the Unacculturated Indians of Central and South America," in PAHO, *Biomedical Challenges Presented by the American Indian,* pp. 59–67.

Samaran, Charles M. D. 1961. *L'histoire et ses méthodes.* Gallimard: Paris.

Sánchez-Albornoz, Nicolás. 1974. *The Population of Latin America: A History,* translated by W. A. R. Richardson. Univ. California Press: Berkeley.

Sanders, William T. 1956. "The Central Mexican Symbiotic Region," in WILLEY, ed., *Prehistoric Settlement Patterns in the New World,* pp. 115–27.

_____. 1962–63. "Cultural Ecology of the Maya Lowlands," *Estudios de Cultura Maya,* 2:79–121, 3:203–41.

_____. 1966. Review of *The Aboriginal Population of Central Mexico on the Eve of the Spanish Conquest,* by W. Borah and S. F. Cook, *American Anthropologist,* 68:1298–99.

_____ 1970. "The Population of the Teotihuacán Valley, the Basin of Mexico, and the Central Mexican Symbiotic Region in the Sixteenth Century," in SANDERS et al., *The Teotihuacán Valley Project,* 1:385–457.

_____. 1972. "Population, Agricultural History, and Societal Evolution in Mesoamerica," in *Population Growth: Anthropological Implications,* edited by Brian Spooner, pp. 101–53. MIT Press: Cambridge.

Sanders, William T., Anton Kovar, Thomas Charlton, and Richard A. Diehl. 1970. *The Teotihuacán Valley Project, Final Report,* Vol. 1: *The Natural Environment, Contemporary Occupation and 16th Century Population of the Valley,* Occasional Papers in Anthropology, No. 3. Department of Anthropology, Pennsylvania State Univ.: University Park.

Sanders, William T., and Barbara J. Price. 1968. *Mesoamerica: The Evolution of a Civilization.* Random House: New York.

Sapper, Karl. 1924. "Die Zahl und die Volksdichte der indianischen Bevölkerung in Amerika vor der Conquista und in der Gegenwart," *Proceedings of the 21st International Congress of Americanists* (The Hague, 1924), 1:95—104.

_____. 1948. "Beiträge zur Frage der Volkszahl und Volksdichte der vorkolumbischen Indianerbevölkerung," *Reseña y trabajos científicos del XXVI Congreso Internacional de Americanistas* (Seville, 1935), 1:456—78.

Sauer, Carl O. 1935. *Aboriginal Population of Northwestern Mexico*, Ibero-Americana, No. 10. Univ. California Press: Berkeley.

_____. 1948. *Colima of New Spain in the Sixteenth Century*, Ibero-Americana, No. 29. Univ. California Press: Berkeley.

_____. 1966. *The Early Spanish Main.* Univ. California Press: Berkeley.

Saunders, John. 1974. "The Population of the Brazilian Amazon Today," in WAGLEY, ed., *Man in the Amazon*, pp. 160—80.

Savoy, Gene. 1970. *Antisuyo: The Search for the Lost Cities of the Amazon.* Simon and Schuster: New York.

Schmidl, Ulrico. 1938 [1567]. *Derrotero y viaje a España y las Indias*, translated by Edmundo Wenicke. Instituto Social, Univ. Nacional del Litoral: Santa Fe, Argentina.

Schmitt, Robert C. 1972. "Garbled Population Estimates of Central Polynesia," in *Readings in Population*, edited by William Petersen, pp. 71—76. Macmillan: New York.

Scholes, France V., and Eleanor B. Adams, eds. 1957. "Información sobre los tributos que los indios pagaban a Moctezuma: Año de 1554," in *Documentos para la historia de México colonial*, edited by F. V. Scholes and E. B. Adams, Vol. 4. Mexico City.

Schoolcraft, Henry R. 1851—57. *Historical and Statistical Information Respecting the History, Condition and Prospects of the Indian Tribes of the United States*, 6 vols. Lippincott, Grambo: Philadelphia.

Secoy, Frank. 1953. *Changing Military Patterns on the Great Plains (17th Century through Early 19th Century)*, Monographs of the American Ethnological Society, No. 21. J. J. Augustin: Locust Valley, N.Y.

Serrano, Antonio. 1938. *La etnografía antigua de Santiago del Estero* . . . . Casa Predassi: Paraná.

_____. 1947. *Los aborígenes Argentinos.* Editorial Nova: Buenos Aires.

Serrano y Sanz, Manuel. 1918. *Orígenes de la dominación española en América*, Nueva Biblioteca de Autores Españoles, Vol. 25. Bailly-Bailliere: Madrid.

Shea, John Gilmary, ed. 1861. *Early Voyages Up and Down the Mississippi.* Joel Munsell: Albany.

Sherman, William L. 1979. *Forced Native Labor in Sixteenth-Century Central America.* Univ. of Nebraska Press: Lincoln.

Shimkin, Demitri B. 1973. "Models for the Downfall: Some Ecological and Culture-Historical Considerations," in *The Classic Maya Collapse*, edited by T. P. Culbert, pp. 269—99. Univ. New Mexico Press: Albuquerque.

Sibley, John. 1806. "A Statistical View of the Indian Nations Inhabiting the Territory of Louisiana and the Countries Adjacent to Its Northern and Western Boundaries," in *Message from the President of the United States, Read in Congress February 19, 1806*, pp. 9–81. Hopkins and Seymour: New York.

Simmons, Marc. 1966. "New Mexico's Smallpox Epidemic of 1780–1781," *New Mexico Historical Review*, 41:319–26.

Simpson, Lesley Byrd. 1952. *Exploitation of Land in Central Mexico in the Sixteenth Century*, Ibero-Americana, No. 36. Univ. California Press: Berkeley.

Sioli, Harod. 1968. "Zur Ökologie des Amazonas-Gebietes," in *Biogeography and Ecology in South America*, edited by E. J. Fittkau et al., 1:137–70. W. Junk N. V.: The Hague.

Slicher van Bath, Bernard. 1963. *The Agrarian History of Western Europe, A.D. 500–1850*, translated by Olive Ordish. St. Martin's: New York.

Smith, C. T. 1970. "Depopulation of the Central Andes in the 16th Century," *Current Anthropology*, 11:453–64.

Smith, C. T., W. M. Denevan, and P. Hamilton. 1968. "Ancient Ridged Fields in the Region of Lake Titicaca," *Geographical Journal*, 134:353–67.

Smith, Samuel. 1765. *The History of the Colony of Nova-Caesaria, or New Jersey*. Burlington: New Jersey.

Smith, William. 1868. *Historical Account of Bouquet's Expedition against the Ohio Indians in 1764*. Robert Clarke: Cincinnati.

Sombroek, W. G. 1966. *Amazon Soils*. Centre for Agricultural Publications and Documentation: Wageningen, Netherlands.

Sotelo Narváez, Pedro. 1931. "Relación de las provincias de Tucumán que dió Pedro Sotelo Narváez . . . ," [1582 or 1583], in LEVILLIER, ed., *Nueva crónica*, 3:324–32.

Spicer, Edward H. 1962. *Cycles of Conquest*. Univ. Arizona Press: Tucson.

Spinden, Herbert J. 1928. "The Population of Ancient America," *Geographical Review*, 18:641–60.

Spores, Ronald. 1964. "Cultural Continuity and Native Rule in the Mixteca Alta, 1500–1600," Ph.D. dissertation. Harvard Univ., Cambridge.

_____. 1965. "The Zapotec and Mixtec at Spanish Contact," *Handbook of Middle American Indians*, edited by Robert Wauchope, 3:962–87. Univ. Texas Press: Austin.

Stearn, E. Wagner, and Allan E. Stearn. 1945. *The Effect of Smallpox on the Destiny of the Amerindian*. Bruce Humphries: Boston.

Sternberg, Hilgard O'Reilly. 1975. *The Amazon River of Brazil*, Geographische Zeitschrift, Beihefte, Erdkundliches Wissen, No. 40. Wiesbaden.

Stevens, William Bacon. 1847. *A History of Georgia . . .* , 2 vols. D. Appleton: New York.

Steward, Julian H., ed. 1946–59. *The Handbook of South American Indians*, 7 vols., Smithsonian Institution, Bureau of American Ethnology Bulletin No. 143. G.P.O.: Washington, D.C.

_____. 1949. "The Native Population of South America," in STEWARD, ed., *Handbook of South American Indians*, 5:655–68.

Steward, Julian H., and Louis C. Faron. 1959. *Native Peoples of South America*. McGraw-Hill: New York.

Stewart, T. D. 1973. *The People of America*. Scribner's: New York.

Stiles, Ezra. 1809. "Indians on Connecticut River," in *Collections of the Massachusetts Historical Society*, 1st ser., 10:104–5. Munroe, Francis and Parker: Boston.

Strachey, William. 1849. *The Historie of Travaile into Virginia Britannia*, edited by R. H. Major, Hakluyt Society, Ser. 1, Vol. 6. London.

"Suma de visitas de pueblos por orden alfabético." 1905. In PNE, Vol. 1, [Compiled ca. 1547–1551.]

Summer Institute of Linguistics. 1965. Mimeographed data, including present populations, on the montaña tribes of Peru. Summer Institute of Linguistics Office: Lima.

Swanton, John R. 1952. *The Indian Tribes of North America*. Smithsonian Institution, Bureau of American Ethnology Bulletin No. 145. G.P.O.: Washington, D.C.

Sweet, David G. 1969. "The Population of the Upper Amazon Valley, 17th and 18th Centuries," Master's thesis. Univ. Wisconsin, Madison.

_____. 1974. "A Rich Realm of Nature Destroyed: The Middle Amazon Valley, 1640–1750," Ph.D. dissertation. Univ. Wisconsin, Madison.

Taylor, J. Garth. 1968. "An Analysis of the Size of Eskimo Settlements on the Coast of Labrador during the Early Contact Period," Ph.D. dissertation. Univ. Toronto, Toronto.

_____. 1975. "Demography and Adaptations of Eighteenth-Century Eskimo Groups in Northern Labrador and Ungava," in *Prehistoric Maritime Adaptations of the Circumpolar Zone*, edited by William Fitzhugh, pp. 269–78. World Anthropology, Sol Tax, general editor. Mouton: The Hague.

Thompson, Donald E. 1973. "Investigaciones arqueológicas en los Andes orientales del norte del Perú," *Revista del Museo Nacional* (Lima), 39:117–25.

Thompson, H. Paul. 1966. "Estimating Aboriginal American Population: A Technique Using Anthropological and Biological Data," *Current Anthropology*, 7:417–24.

Thompson, J. Eric S. 1970. "The Maya Central Area at the Spanish Conquest and Later: A Problem in Demography," in J. Eric S. Thompson, *Maya History and Religion*, pp. 48–83. Univ. Oklahoma Press: Norman.

Thornes, John. 1969. "Black and White Waters of Amazonas," *Geographical Magazine*, 41:367–71.

Thwaites, Reuben Gold, ed. 1896–1901. *The Jesuit Relations and Allied Documents: Travels and Explorations of the Jesuit Missionaries in New France, 1610–1791*, 73 vols. Burrows Brothers: Cleveland.

_____. 1904–5. *Original Journals of the Lewis and Clark Expedition, 1804–1806*, 8 vols. Dodd, Mead: New York.

_____. 1906. *Part I of Farnham's Travels in the Great Western Prairies, etc.,*
May 21–October 16, 1839, Vol. 28 of Early Western Travels, 1748–1846.
Arthur H. Clarke: Cleveland.

Titow, J. Z. 1961. "Some Evidence of the Thirteenth Century Population
Increase," *Economic History Review,* 2nd ser., 14:218–24.

Tocantins, Leandro. 1974. "The World of the Amazon Region," in WAG-
LEY, ed., *Man in the Amazon,* pp. 21–32.

Torquemada, Juan de. 1943–44 [1723]. *Monarquía indiana,* 3 vols. Chávez
Hayhoe: Mexico City.

Torres, Diego de. 1927. "Cartas de P. Diego de Torres" [1609–1615], in
DHA, 19:3–545.

Tosi, Joseph A., Jr. 1960. *Zonas de vida natural en el Perú,* Boletín Técnico,
No. 5, Proyecto 39, Programa de Cooperación Técnica, Instituto Inter-
americano de Ciencias Agrícolas de la OEA, Zona Andina. Lima.

Toussaint, Manuel, Federico Gómez de Orozco, and Justino Fernández. 1938.
"Planos de la ciudad de México, siglos XVI y XVII," in *Estudio histórico,*
urbanístico y bibliográfico. Instituto de Investigaciones Estéticas de la
Univ. Nacional Autónoma. Mexico City.

Turner II, B. L. 1974. "Prehistoric Intensive Agriculture in the Mayan
Lowlands," *Science,* 185:118–124.

_____. 1976. "Population Density in the Classic Maya Lowlands: New Evi-
dence for Old Approaches," *Geographical Review,* 66: 73–82.

Turner, Randolph. 1973. "A New Population Estimate for the Powhatan
Chiefdom of the Coastal Plain of Virginia," *Quarterly Bulletin, Archeologi-*
cal Society of Virginia, 28:57–65.

Ubelaker, Douglas H. 1974. *Reconstruction of Demographic Profiles from*
Ossuary Skeletal Samples: A Case Study from the Tidewater Potomac,
Smithsonian Contributions to Anthropology, No. 18. G.P.O.: Washington,
D.C.

_____. 1976. "Prehistoric New World Population Size: Historical Review and
Current Appraisal of North American Estimates," *American Journal of*
Physical Anthropology, 45: 661–66.

United Nations. 1963. *Production Yearbook, 1962.* United Nations Food and
Agricultural Organization: Rome.

United States, Bureau of the Census. 1972. *Census of Population 1970:*
General Population Characteristics. G.P.O.: Washington, D.C.

Unrau, William E. 1973. "The Depopulation of the Dheghia-Siouan Kansa
Prior to Removal," *New Mexico Historical Review,* 48:313–28.

Varese, Stefano. 1972. "Indian Groups of the Peruvian Selva," in *The*
Situation of the Indian in South America, edited by W. Dostal, pp.
412–13. World Council of Churches: Geneva.

Vázquez de Espinosa, Antonio. 1948. *Compendio y descripción de las Indias*
Occidentales, edited and translated by Charles Upson Clark, Smithsonian
Miscellaneous Collections, Vol. 108. Smithsonian Institution: Washing-
ton, D.C. [Completed ca. 1628].

Vázquez-Machicado, Humberto. 1957. "Die Lebensbedingungen des Indianers und die Arbeitsgesetzgebung in Santa Cruz de la Sierra (Ostbolivien) im 16. Jahrhundert," *Saeculum,* 8:382–91.

Veblen, Thomas T. 1974. "The Ecological, Cultural, and Historical Bases of Forest Preservation in Totonicapán, Guatemala," Ph.D. dissertation. Univ. California, Berkeley.

Vera y Aragón, Alonso de. 1943 [1585]. "Carta del fundador de la ciudad de la Concepción de Nuestra Señora . . . ," in José Torre Revello, *Esteco y Concepción del Bermejo, dos ciudades desaparecidas,* pp. xxv–xxvii, Publicaciones del Instituto de Investigaciones Históricas, No. 85. Peuser: Buenos Aires.

Verlinden, Charles. 1968. "Le 'repartimiento' de Rodrigo de Alburquerque à Española en 1514: Aux origines d'une importante institution économico-sociale de l'empire colonial espagnol," in *Mélanges offerts à G. Jacquemyns,* pp. 633–46. Éditions de l'Institut de Sociologie, Université Libre de Bruxelles: Brussels.

Viedma, Antonio de. 1837 [1783]. "Descripción de la costa meridional del sur, llamada vulgarmente Patagónica," in *Colección de obras y documentos relativos á la historia antigua y moderna de las provincias del Río de la Plata,* edited by Pedro de Angelis, Vol. 6, Item 67, pp. 63–81. Imprenta del Estado: Buenos Aires.

Vollmer, Günter. 1973. "La evolución cuantitativa de la población indígena en la región de Puebla (1570–1810)," *Historia Mexicana,* 23:43–51.

Vries, David Pieterszen de. 1857. "Voyages from Holland to America, A.D. 1632 to 1644," in *New York Historical Society Collections,* 2nd ser., Vol. 3 (Pt. 1), pp. 1–136. New York.

Wagemann, Ernesto. 1949. *La población en el destino de los pueblos,* translated by Carlos Keller R. Editorial Universitaria: Santiago.

Wagley, Charles. 1940. "The Effects of Depopulation upon Social Organization as Illustrated by the Tapirape Indians," *Transactions of the New York Academy of Science,* Ser. 2, Vol. 3, No. 1, pp. 12–16.

––––––. 1951. "Cultural Influences on Population: A Comparison of Two Tupí Tribes," *Revista do Museu Paulista,* new ser., 5:95–104.

––––––, ed. 1974. *Man in the Amazon.* Univ. Presses Florida: Gainesville.

Wagner, Helmuth O. 1968. "Die Besiedlungsdichte Zentral-amerikas vor 1492 und die Ursachen des Bevölkerungsschwundes in der frühen Kolonialzeit unter besonderer Berücksichtigung der Halbinsel Yucatáb," *Jahrbuch für Geschichte von Staat, Wirtschaft und Gesellschaft Lateinamerikas,* 5:63–102.

––––––. 1969. "Subsistence Potential and Population Density of the Maya on the Yucatán Peninsula and Causes for the Decline in Population in the Fifteenth Century," *Verhandlungen des XXXVIII Internationalen Amerikanistenkongresses* (Stuttgart-Munich, 1968), 1:179–96.

Wedin, Ake. 1965. *El sistema decimal en el imperio incaico,* Instituto Ibero-Americano, Göteborg, Sweden. Insula: Madrid.

West, Robert C., and John P. Augelli. 1966. *Middle America: Its Lands and Peoples.* Prentice-Hall: Englewood Cliffs, N.J.

Willcox, Walter F. 1931. "Increase in the Population of the Earth and of the Continents since 1650," in *International Migrations,* edited by W. F. Willcox, 2:33–82. National Bureau of Economic Research: New York.

Willey, Gordon R., ed. 1956. *Prehistoric Settlement Patterns in the New World,* Viking Fund Publications in Anthropology, No. 23, Johnson Reprint Corp.: New York.

Wood, Corine S. 1975. "New Evidence for a Late Introduction of Malaria into the New World," *Current Anthropology,* 16:93–104.

World Almanac. 1975. *The World Almanac and Book of Facts.* Newspaper Enterprise Association: New York.

Wrong, Denis H. 1961. *La población.* Editorial Paidós: Buenos Aires.

Zavala, Silvio A. 1973. *La encomienda indiana,* 2nd ed. Editorial Porrúa: Mexico City.

Zimmerman, Arthur F. 1938. *Francisco de Toledo.* Caxton: Caldwell, Idaho.

Zorita [Zurita], Alonso de. 1941. *Breve y sumaria relación.* Chávez Hayhoe: Mexico City. [Written ca. 1566–1585].

Zubrow, Ezra B. W. 1975. *Prehistoric Carrying Capacity: A Model.* Cummings: Menlo Park, Calif.

Index

333